FOR THE LOV

MW00769654

JOSEF PIEPER

For the Love of Wisdom

Essays on the Nature of Philosophy

Edited by Berthold Wald
Translated by Roger Wasserman

IGNATIUS PRESS   SAN FRANCISCO

Title of the German original:
Schriften zum Philosophiebegriff, Band 3 (2d ed.)
© 1995, 2004 by Felix Meiner Verlag, Hamburg

Cover art: Bernard Buffet (1928–1999)
The Holy Spirit (1961)
Collezione d'Arte Religiosa Moderna
Vatican Museums, Vatican State
Scala/Art Resource, New York

Cover design by Riz Boncan Marsella

© 2006 Ignatius Press, San Francisco
ISBN 978-1-58617-087-5
ISBN 1-58617-087-2
Library of Congress Control Number 2006922686
Printed in the United States of America ∞

CONTENTS

Translator's Note 7

Philosophical Education and Intellectual Labor 13

What Does It Mean to Philosophize? Four Lectures 27

A Plea for Philosophy 81

On the Platonic Idea of Philosophy 157

Creatureliness and Human Nature: Reflections on the
    Philosophical Method of Jean-Paul Sartre 173

Heidegger's Conception of Truth 185

Language and the Philosophizing Person: Aperçus of an
    Aquinas Reader 197

What Is Interpretation? 209

Tradition: Its Sense and Aspiration 233

On the Dilemma Posed by a Non-Christian Philosophy 295

Philosophy and the Sense for Mystery 303

A Possible Future for Philosophy 311

Editorial Postscript: Truth and Sense 319

Abbreviation Key to the Works of Thomas Aquinas 331

Index of Persons 333

TRANSLATOR'S NOTE

It is only fair and meet in a volume of this length, where ready access may be had to Pieper's own formulations and which already includes an extended postscript by one of Pieper's most distinguished exegetes, that the first-time reader of Pieper's works be granted, so far as possible, the opportunity to discover the author's meaning for himself, with all adulterating commentary held to a minimum. This notwithstanding, it may not be considered entirely inappropriate for the translator to insert himself briefly in that interpretational divide separating author and reader, if only to provide the orientation necessary for distinctly American sensibilities to wend their way unhindered through the text.

In particular, there are two fundamental assumptions, taken by Pieper as a matter of course, which threaten from the outset to alienate the sympathies of today's philosophically informed reader: the one derives directly from Saint Thomas Aquinas, to whose basic ontological tenets Pieper remains faithful; the other underlies Pieper's apocalyptic vision of a future where academic philosophy, now long since reduced to an "empty seriousness," is superseded by theology in accordance with biblical prophecy. Both assumptions bear directly on the issue of the feasibility of the traditional metaphysical quest for ultimate causes, and insofar as postmodern thought has rejected them as unlikely, their repudiation has encouraged talk of what Wittgenstein once dubbed "the heir to the subject that used to be called philosophy" and what Heidegger has called "the task of thinking" after "the end of philosophy."

Pieper's underlying realist (and in its provenance ultimately Platonic) assumption that there is a plan, a design to the world, "a complete fact," which corresponds to "the totality of the real," is on view intermittently throughout this work but particularly in those chapters on Sartre, on the defense of philosophy, and on the possible future of philosophy (the fifth, third, and twelfth chapters, respectively). There is no doubt that Pieper, to the extent that he identifies philosophy with the knowledge of ultimate causes—with the search for a final and comprehensive definition of reality, albeit knowable perhaps only

7

a limine—is committed to some kind of world-structure and to the possibility of epistemic access to that structure through causal theories based on law-like relations among theoretical entities. Still, it would be a mistake to believe that Pieper, who is here riding piggy-back on Aquinas' notion of cause, attributes to that structure—"reality"—the sort of determinateness which is typically associated with causality in the classical and non-probabilistic sense and which has since been rendered problematic by the discovery of the phenomenon of non-locality in quantum mechanics. The reader should bear in mind that when Pieper, following Aquinas, speaks of causality, he is referring not to a cause in the efficient or material sense but rather to "cause" in the sense of an explanatory scheme, a mode of explanation, such as might be embodied in a revolutionary, new physical theory. In this sense, as Kuhn has most recently observed, "one is tempted to say . . . that the term 'cause' functions primarily in the meta-scientific, not the scientific, vocabulary of physicists."[1]

And yet there is, in fact, a sense in which the reader would be correct to point to a difference between the strictly scientific notion of causality, which is roughly equivalent to that of physical law, and the peculiarly Thomist notion of final cause, which Pieper regards as the only proper object of philosophical inquiry. The difference is perhaps best brought out by Pieper's remark that "science comes to an end at the limits of knowledge whereas philosophy begins with those very limits." To buttress the conception of science he is here endorsing, Pieper goes on to cite a passage from one of Albert Einstein's letters, composed only a few weeks before his death: "If I have learned anything from the ruminations of a long lifetime," Einstein writes, "it is that we are much farther away from acquiring a deeper insight into the elementary processes than most of our contemporaries believe." This deeper insight, Pieper feels, can be achieved only by bringing a uniquely philosophical interest to bear on these selfsame elementary processes; insofar as elementary particle physicists continue to neglect final causes, which reflect the role these processes play in the totality of what is experienced, "even the exact sciences find them-

---

[1] Thomas Kuhn, "Concepts of Cause in the Development of Physics," *The Essential Tension: Selected Studies in Scientific Tradition and Change.* Chicago and London: University of Chicago Press, p. 22.

selves increasingly running up against their own limits." This prognosis has been startlingly corroborated by one of the leading physicists of our age, Richard Feynman, who foresees, as one of physics' ultimate prospects, an endless and tiresome repetition of the same, with scientific experimentation continually uncovering new layers of physical lawfulness or causality, limits continually giving way to new limits, without the scientific enterprise ever coming to an actual end:

> This thing cannot keep on going so that we are always going to discover more and more new laws. If we do, it will become boring that there are so many levels one underneath the other. It seems to me that what can happen in the future is either that all the laws become known . . . or it may happen that the experiments get harder and harder to make, more and more expensive, so you get 99.9 per cent of the phenomena, but there is always some phenomenon which has just been discovered, which is very hard to measure, and which disagrees; and as soon as you have the explanation of that one there is always another one, and it gets slower and slower and more and more uninteresting.[2]

In Hegelian terms, we stand here in the presence of the "bad" infinite, and before the concomitant ennui of a limit or barrier [Schranke] that, once overcome, is continually reasserting itself. What, by contrast, enables the philosopher's notion of an ultimate cause to escape these limitations and to lead scientific explanation to the "good" or true infinite is that it is not restricted to the notion of cause and effect per se but carries in itself a reference to the totality of Being to which the cause qua being belongs: What an agent does—how it acts, the peculiar mode of its causality—reflects what it is (omne agens agit sibi simile). Causes involve not simply a doing or bringing-about (poesis in the Aristotelian sense) but also a showing or reflecting. As Davies has Aquinas say in his revealing and suggestive paraphrase, "all of God's creatures show us what God is—somehow."[3] Philosophy (literally, philo + sophia, the love of wisdom), as the perhaps never-ending but infinitely variegated search for ultimate causes, is charged with the

---

[2] Richard Feynman, *The Character of Physical Law*. Cambridge, Mass., and London: The M.I.T. Press, 1989, p. 172.

[3] Brian Davies, "Aquinas on What God Is Not," *Thomas Aquinas: Contemporary Philosophical Perspectives* (ed. Brian Davies). New York and Oxford: Oxford University Press, 2002, p. 230.

task of investigating just this "somehow"—of discovering how individual causes fit into a unified design or plan, the world conceived
as a rich, differentiated totality. This is not to say, however, that the
final causes which form the object of the philosopher's search are essentially at variance with those causes identified by the elementary
particle physicist; on the contrary, these elementary processes, when
properly understood, gesture toward something beyond themselves,
opening up new and previously unanticipated vistas for the interpretation of nature. There are thus indications that the position which
Pieper here adopts is not so far removed from those views on the
philosophy of science which have come to be identified with the
name of the American philosopher, Willard V. Quine: For Pieper, as
for Quine, metaphysics—to the extent that it may be said to constitute a legitimate enterprise at all—must be coterminous with that
ongoing epistemological endeavor which we call "natural science."

At the same time, the identification of ultimate causes presupposes
an ability on our part as philosophizing persons or genuine lovers of
wisdom to recognize the divinity revealed in things, which brings us
to Pieper's second fundamental assumption. In his attempt to delin-
eate a possible future for philosophy, one in which it has become
virtually indistinguishable from theology, he is assuming, counter to
the prevailing (post-Cartesian) spirit of our times, the veridicality, or
evidential force, of the kind of religious experience which finds its
expression in the apocalyptic Book of Revelation and other eschatological texts. He is arguing, in short, that "religious experiences and
religious utterances can and ought to be treated as having cognitive
content."[4] By contrast, our current philosophical situation, powerfully
molded as it has been by Heidegger's contribution to postmodernity,
denies to religious consciousness the experience of any form of transcendence "beyond the subject's own psychological states,"[5] taking
for granted the Lutheran conception of what Sean J. McGrath has
called "the God-forsakenness of human existence."[6] As McGrath has

[4] Caroline Franks Davis, *The Evidential Force of Religious Experience*. New York and Oxford: Oxford University Press, 1999, p. 230.

[5] *Ibid.*

[6] Sean J. McGrath, "The Facticity of Being God-Forsaken: The Young Heidegger and Luther's Theology of the Cross," *American Catholic Philosophical Quarterly*, vol. 79, no. 2, Spring 2005, p. 283.

shown, Heidegger, whose analytic of existence (*Daseinsanalytik*) was profoundly influenced by his reading of Luther, accepted as a basic consequence of the post-lapsarian corruption of man's nature that "genuine religiosity is no longer one of our basic possibilities for being"; we can, as a result, have no direct knowledge of God.[7] The problem, however, with Heidegger's diagnosis of our spiritual plight, which purports to be a theologically neutral description of our factic experience of God's withdrawal, is that it is made from within a theology of revelation which Heidegger steadfastly fails to acknowledge explicitly. Presciently—presciently because Pieper's essay on Heidegger's quixotic equation of truth with freedom predates McGrath's analysis of the early Freiburg lectures—Pieper fixes on just this tension as the defining characteristic of Heidegger's philosophizing, namely, that "motivated by what is at bottom a theological impulse, questions are posed with a provocative radicalism that in themselves would require a theological answer and that, at the same time, such a response is just as radically rejected." In his essay on Heidegger's conception of truth, Pieper exposes a vacillation in Heidegger's determination of truth as freedom, where the disclosedness of *Dasein* is simultaneously understood as a "turn to the object," to ontic truth and the manifestness of existing things, and as the free standing-apart [*Gegenübersein*] of the subject, which holds itself out to the world. With transcendence now safely ensconced in "the basic structure of the subject," the self becomes a solipsistic, hermetically sealed prison which subsumes all forms of evidence to itself so that religious experience comes to be dismissed in our postmodern age as pathological, having no objective correlate. Thus, whereas Luther views revelation, or the uncovering of "the visible things of God," as coinciding with God's concealment of himself, that is, with his showing himself in and through his concealment, Heidegger's phenomenological approach takes God's showing of himself as hidden to be a form of genuine concealment or absence. Pieper, for his part, wants to see the notion of revelation, or religious transcendence, restored to a position of respectability within philosophical discourse so that the "things of God" can again be made visible through their ultimate causes. Pieper, I think, is prepared to accept that "like scientific systems, religious beliefs do not follow

---

[7] *Ibid.*, p. 287.

deductively from a set of 'raw' perceptual experiences," and that they must first be 'worked up' "before their full significance is realized"[8] but he firmly believes that a knowledge of ultimate causes is not to be had in the absence of religious experience.

In light of the above, one final remark, this time affecting a matter of translation, may not be out of order: Pieper draws a sharp distinction—which I have attempted to preserve in translation—between the "philosopher" (*der Philosoph*) as a professional designation and the "philosopher" (*der Philosophiernder*) as an expression for anyone engaged in a spiritual activity which, insofar as it touches upon questions concerning the totality of the real, affects him in the very core of that person's being. Insofar as the former entails mastery of a technique, it points to an essential completeness in the execution of the corresponding act of thought which is absent from an act of genuinely philosophizing reflection. To mark this difference, I distinguish in the text which follows between the philosopher *per se*, as an academic personality, and the philosophizing person, who can be anyone, and, accordingly, between a philosophical act and an act of (genuine) philosophizing. The term "person" is used here advisedly, in deliberate counterpoint to the Kierkegaardian "individual," who is related in passionate inwardness, but not rationality, to his God. While I certainly do not wish to exclude this connotation, if we take "person" with Aquinas to signify that which is most perfect in the whole of nature, i.e., "that which subsists in rational nature," then the philosophizing act relates the questioning being, as a person, to God—who contains within himself all perfections—as Person. In the act of philosophizing, man and God are thus joined by a common rationality or perfection in the contemplation of those ultimate causes which account for the totality of the real.

Roger Wasserman
Metropolitan College of New York
December 2006

---

[8] Caroline Franks Davis, *The Evidential Force of Religious Experience*, p. 240.

PHILOSOPHICAL EDUCATION
AND INTELLECTUAL LABOR

To an unassuming ear, the two neologisms "philosophical education" and "intellectual labor" may appear to interact quite harmoniously, even to the point of belonging together naturally. It is my intention in what follows to undermine this impression and to show that behind what today appears self-evident lies a previously unsuspected problematic. It can, however, form no part of the purpose of this short piece to provide a solution. As will soon become apparent, very profound issues are involved here whose ultimate resolution promises to be extremely difficult, if not perhaps entirely impossible.

Just a glance at the historical origin of the notion of a "philosophical faculty" suffices to make clear that the relationship that the concept of "work" bears to that of philosophical education was far from "always" possessing this kind of self-evident validity. In the Middle Ages, the philosophical faculty was called the "faculty of artists", after the *artes liberales*, the so-called "liberal" arts. The liberty of these arts consisted precisely in the fact that they were not "work"; they stood in marked contrast to the *artes mechanicae* or *artes serviles*, work in the genuine sense.

The concept of "intellectual labor" and the arguments that have been made in favor of its validity have several origins. Underlying this notion is, *first*, a certain conception of the nature of intellectual knowledge as such. In an essay published in 1796[1] and directed against the Romantic philosophy of Jacobi, Schlosser, and Stolberg, which was based on feeling and intuition, Kant, with polemical intent, characterizes philosophizing as "work". In philosophy, Kant writes, "the law of reason, of acquiring possessions through work", prevails.[2] And because it is not work, the Romantic philosophy is not genuine philosophy—an objection that is also leveled by Kant against Plato, the

---

[1] In the *Berliner Monatsschrift*.

[2] *Von einem neuerdings erhobenen vornehmen Ton in der Philosophie*, Akademie-Ausgabe, vol. 8, A 397.

"father of all rapturous fantasizing in philosophy",[3] while it is noted, with both approval and assent, that "the philosophy of Aristotle is, by contrast, work."[4] Out of the conviction of these philosophers that their Romantic philosophy stands above [*überhoben sein*] a philosophy of work arises "a newly raised [*erhobenen*] tone in philosophy"[5]—that of a pseudo-philosophy "in which one", as Kant writes, "is entitled, not to work, but only to heed and enjoy the oracle in oneself in order to take complete possession of that wisdom toward which philosophy aims".[6] Such pseudo-philosophy believes itself capable of politely prescinding from the work that is genuine philosophy.

We find this opposition more clearly, more objectively, and less polemically expressed in this same essay in terms of an opposition between the philosophy of "intuition" and that of discursive thought. And with this second opposition, the foundation has at once been laid bare in terms of which philosophizing must necessarily appear as "labor" and only "labor": For Kant, the sum of man's intellectual knowledge is exclusively discursive, that is, nonintuitive.[7] Thus, in Kant's view, human knowledge is essentially realized in the acts of researching, relating, comparing, differentiating, inferring, proving— in all manner and form of active intellectual exertion. By contrast, intuition is a receptive, accepting, and passive attitude of the soul. According to Kant, however, intuition is limited only to the realm of the senses.

Now it was the opinion of the ancient philosophers, both of the Greeks (and not just of Plato but of Aristotle as well!) and of the great medieval thinkers, that there is an element of purely receptive vision—or, as Heraclitus says, of "listening to things"[8]—not only in sense perception but also in man's intellectual knowing. Medieval philosophy distinguishes between reason as *ratio* and reason as *intellectus*, whereby *ratio* is understood in terms of the ability of discursive thought to search, investigate, abstract, specify, and infer, whereas *in-*

---

[3] Ibid., A 408.

[4] Ibid., A 437.

[5] This is also the title of essay cited here; ibid., A 389f.

[6] Ibid.

[7] In a recently published *Geschichte der Erkenntnislehre* (History of epistemology), by B. Jansen (Paderborn, 1940), p. 235, this thesis is described as one of the "most momentous presuppositions of Kant's theory of knowledge".

[8] Fragment 112 (Diels).

tellectus signifies the capacity for straightforward intuition, the *simplex intuitus*, to which the true offers itself up the way a landscape offers itself up to the eye. The ancients, then, understood man's faculty for knowing as a unity of *ratio* and *intellectus* and the act of knowledge itself as a simultaneous functioning of the two. Active discursive thought is accompanied by, and suffused with, the effortlessly perceiving gaze of the *intellectus*, which is a nonactive, that is, a passive or receptive —albeit an actively receptive—faculty of the soul.

Discursive thought is work; intuition is not. Consequently, it is only natural that someone who construes intellectual knowledge exclusively in terms of a functioning of the *ratio* and thus also—also, because knowledge not only has a claim on man, but man on knowledge —sees it as the hard-won fruit of subjective activity will be equally inclined to recognize in its labor-intensive character an essential attribute of knowing. By contrast, someone who assumes that intellectual knowledge includes, apart from rational discursive thought, a receptive gazing upon Being, an intellectual (perhaps even higher-order) seeing—someone who is able to recognize a contemplative strain especially in philosophical knowledge itself, which aims at the ground of Being and at Being as a whole—will have to conclude that the characterization of philosophy as labor is not exhaustive, indeed, that it fails to go to the heart of the matter. Of course, he need not then automatically be of the opinion that in philosophy it suffices to attend to and enjoy one's inner oracle.

In the *Quaestiones disputatae de veritate* of Thomas Aquinas it is asserted that, "although the act of knowing actually occurs in the human soul in the mode of *ratio*, it also has a share in that simple knowing, which is found in the higher beings, of whom it is therefore said that they have the power of spiritual vision."[9] This implies not only that an active exertion of discursive thought is involved in human knowledge but also that what is genuinely human in human knowledge is to be found in the discursive, in this discursive element. But at the same time it is also being asserted that in human knowledge there is a participation in the nondiscursive vision of the angels. For Aquinas as well, the activity of the *ratio* is associated with labor and exertion;[10] and thus he, too, would also find the distinctively human expressly

---

[9] *Ver.* 15, 1.
[10] 1, d. 33, 1 ad 3.

contained in the labor-intensive character of knowledge. And still he would maintain that, with such a characterization, something essential has been omitted. What has been omitted is just this participation in the faculty of knowledge of a purely spiritual entity, to whom it is given to perceive the spiritual the way our eyes perceive light and our ears sound. Aquinas does not yet intend this as a theological statement, which is in itself significant. Aquinas would say that man is more than man just as Goethe exclaims to those who "praise experience exclusively" that "experience is only half of experience."[11] It is on the basis of this view, that is, on the view that man's intellectual knowledge depends solely on the actively discursive operations of the *ratio*, that the concept of intellectual labor comes to acquire a special significance.

Discursive thought and intellectual intuition are related to one another, not simply as activity to passivity, as active tension to passive receptivity, but also as exertion and burden, on the one side, to effortlessness and sheer presence, on the other. And in this opposition can be found the origins of a *second*, more primordial reason for the special emphasis on the concept of "intellectual labor". In this context, we shall have to discuss a certain criterion to which Kant appeals in assessing the value or lack of value of human activity as such. It is not intended simply as description when Kant speaks of philosophizing as a "Herculean labor"; rather, he sees in its labor-intensive character a legitimation: Whether one allows it to make one's life miserable or not, that is how one recognizes genuine philosophy. The fact that it, as he contemptuously puts it, "costs nothing" is above all what makes him so suspicious of "intellectual intuition". Does this, not, however, bring Kant closer to asserting the view that it is the effort involved in knowing that provides the surety for epistemological truth? This is already not so far removed from the ethical view that recognizes in everything that man does out of natural inclination, that is, without effort, a violation of true moral rectitude. Indeed, on the Kantian view, it is implicit in the very nature of the moral law that "our natural urges contravene it."[12] The deliberate exertion involved in self-mastery is thus also a measure of what is morally right. From there, one need take only one additional step to be able to recognize

---

[11] *Maximen und Reflexionen*, no. 751, ed. G. Müller (Stuttgart, 1943).

[12] W. Windelband, *Geschichte der neueren Philosophie* (Leipzig, 1904), 2:138.

in the labor-intensive character of a philosophy a criterion for determining whether it constitutes true knowledge: What is not difficult
of achievement cannot really be virtue; knowledge that does not cost
anything cannot be real, genuine knowledge: The notion that "effort
is the good", can already be found in Antiphon, who also held up
Hercules as a role model for superhuman labor, a role model still recognized or perhaps rediscovered by Kant (but also by Carlyle, the pro-
mulgator of the religion of work). To this assertion Thomas Aquinas
opposes the counterthesis: "The essence of virtue lies more in the
good than in the difficult";[13] "not everything, then, that is difficult
must also be meritorious, but rather it must also be difficult in a way
that it is at the same time good in a higher sense."[14] The medievals
had said of virtue that it enables us to follow our natural inclinations
in the right way[15]—indeed, they argued, the best way to realize the
ethically good does not involve exertion at all; instead all difficulties
are overcome because the best way of realizing the good arises from
love.[16]

Similarly, the second position, that is, that the truth of a philosophy
shows itself in its labor-intensive character, might be attacked on the
grounds that the essence of knowledge does not lie in intellectual
exertion but in the fact that it reveals Being. Indeed, just as, in the
realm of the good, the highest form of virtue does not know anything
of the difficult, the highest form of knowing—the sudden stroke of
genius, the act of genuine contemplation—falls to man as a gift; it is
effortless and without toil the way games are.[17]

This is not to imply that the highest achievements of knowledge
are not preceded by an extreme exertion of thought; perhaps it is
in its nature to be prior (albeit as a condition, not a cause), just
as the sacred effortlessness of an act performed out of love presupposes a peremptory exertion of the moral will. But it is important to
note that although virtue presupposes moral exertion, it cannot be reduced to such exertion. Nor does knowledge exhaust itself in intellectual effort. Virtue is the actualization of the good; knowledge means
attaining to the Being of beings. Its work-intensive character is not,

---

[13] II, II, 1, 12 ad 2.
[14] II, II, 27, 8 ad 3.
[15] II, II, 108, 2.
[16] *Car.* 8 ad 17.
[17] 1, d. 2 (*expositio textus*).

then, a valid criterion for identifying true virtue and genuine philosophy.

These two theses, the claim that human knowing is an exclusively discursive activity and the view that the effort involved in knowing provides a measure of epistemological truth—these are the two streams whose waters are commingled in the concept of intellectual labor and, above all, in the usual ascription of validity to this concept.

(3) There is yet a *third* element to be discussed—perhaps the most crucial one, one that includes the other two: this is the social connotation that the notion of intellectual labor possesses—and, even more, the notion of an intellectual laborer. Labor, so construed, amounts to the performance of a social service. Intellectual labor constitutes an intellectual *occupation* insofar as it makes a contribution to the common good. But the notion of intellectual labor and, more importantly, that of the intellectual laborer imply more than that. These notions, in contemporary linguistic usage, include a reference to the working class. They imply the following: Not only a wage earner, not only a member of the proletariat, but even an educated person, the college graduate, is a laborer—an "intellectual" laborer, in fact. In this way, even the intellectual laborer is ensnared in the social system of the "working world"—as a "specialist".

With this, the problematic nature of the relationship between philosophical education and intellectual labor has taken on even sharper contours; it is a problematic that has begun to acquire a significance for many of our country's provinces—among them, Kant's homeland—that goes far beyond the purely theoretical.*

We do not intend to discuss the extent to which natural science, medicine, law, economics, and pedagogy have all been assigned a place and purpose within the functional division of labor typical of modern forms of social organization and hence the degree to which they may all be subsumed under the rubric of intellectual labor, understood in this social sense. Our question is instead: How does it stand with philosophy in this regard?—or, for that matter, with all the sciences just mentioned, insofar as there is still a drop of philosophical ferment in them, that is, insofar as they are still pursued in a philosophical

---

* [Pieper is referring here to the eastern provinces' submission to the Communist doctrine of work and society as a consequence of the initial division of Germany.—ED.]

manner, that is, in an "academic" manner, in the original sense of that word? Can philosophizing, or science conducted in the philosophical, that is, academic, manner, be considered "labor" in the sense that it performs a specific, well-defined, purposeful social function?

At this point, we need to revert to the ancient distinction between the *artes liberales* and the *artes serviles*, as it was understood at the time when philosophical education in the West underwent that process of institutionalization which has determined its form up to the present day. In his commentary on Aristotle's *Metaphysics*, Aquinas writes that "only those arts are free that are oriented toward knowledge; those arts, however, that are oriented toward a use realized in activity are called the mechanical or servile arts."[18] The great English humanist John Henry Newman also formally aligns himself with the same classical medieval tradition that emphasizes the liberty of a philosophical education. In a series of university addresses held one hundred years ago, he says: "I know well it may resolve itself into an art, and terminate in a mechanical process, and in tangible fruit; but it also may fall back upon that reason which informs it, and resolve itself into philosophy. In one case it is called useful knowledge, in the other liberal",[19] or "a gentleman's knowledge".[20] "Knowledge, I say, is then especially liberal, or sufficient for itself, apart from every external and ulterior object, when and so far as it is philosophical."[21]

The "liberty" of those "arts" for which *dialectica* or philosophy became the namesake—the liberty, then, of a philosophical education so called—consists in the fact that it does not derive its legitimation from its social function, that is, from its being work. This is not to say, however, that it is irrelevant for a people or for their common welfare whether this functionless form of knowledge and philosophical education as such are accorded rank and status in their society. On the contrary, as the medievals knew and stated, it is "necessary to the perfection of human society that there are human beings who have dedicated themselves to the essence of contemplation".[22]

---

[18] *In Met.* I, 3 (no. 59).

[19] John Henry Cardinal Newman, *The Idea of a University* (Garden City, N.Y.: Image Books, 1959), p. 137.

[20] Ibid.

[21] Ibid.

[22] 4, d. 26, 1, 2.

Whatever one might think of this distinction between free and useful knowledge—whether one thinks it correct or incorrect, productive or unproductive—it undoubtedly provides the soil from which the Western conception of the university has sprung. And undoubtedly the character of the university can be preserved and defended vis-à-vis that of the purely vocational institution or the advanced technical college only through this grounding in a nonfunctionalized, free philosophical education, that is, defended on the grounds that it is not exclusively (or even primarily) a question of training—only functionaries are trained—but one of educating human beings, who carry their purpose within themselves. And from this vantage point, it must, in turn, appear as counterproductive—if, however, symptomatic—that linguistic usage, including even academic usage, has accustomed itself to this talk of "intellectual laborers".

It is not, however, the point (of course!) to expose intellectual labor as something unphilosophical and to legitimate those who have found ingenious ways to make it easy for themselves; without difficult and painful intellectual labor, philosophical education is impossible. But there is something else involved in philosophical education—something essential—that is not work, not work in the sense of activity or of effort or of social function. The question here is not that of wanting to defend idleness but rather that of wanting to defend leisure. Even the defense of leisure, however, might appear today to be untimely insofar as the reconstruction of western Germany requires the exertion of all our energies. And still it is precisely for the sake of this new foundation that a defense of leisure is necessary. For one of the foundations of Western culture—one can already read about this in the first chapter of Aristotle's *Metaphysics*—is leisure, in Greek σχολή, in Latin *schola*. Thus our word for school originally meant, not "school", but leisure.

However, this concept of leisure has become completely unrecognizable in the programmatic leisurelessness of "work for work's sake": "One does not only work in order to live, but one lives for the sake of one's work."[23] We can understand this statement of Count Zinzen-

---

[23] Quotation from Max Weber, *Die Protestantische Ethik und der Geist des Kapitalismus* (Tübingen, 1934), p. 172, n. 2. [English trans.: Max Weber, *The Protestant Ethic and the Spirit of Capitalism*, trans. Talcott Parsons (New York, 1958), p. 264, n. 24.]

dorff's without further need of discussion; indeed, it expresses a common sentiment. We find it difficult to understand that it reverses the natural order of things; we would sooner be able to recognize evidence of an "inverted world" in Aristotle's statement to the effect that "we work in order to be at leisure." To the devotees of a total work culture such a statement must appear to be nothing short of immoral and a repudiation of the meaning and order of human society. From such a standpoint, leisure is either to be understood as a temporary break from work—in which case one writes it off as a necessary evil—or else leisure becomes another word for inertia and idleness. According to the teachings on life of the High Middle Ages, just the opposite, however, is true: it is leisurelessness that is related to inertia, and it is precisely from inertia that the restlessness associated with work for work's sake springs. Genuine leisure is not compatible with this kind of inertia, for leisure presupposes that man assents to his own nature. The ancient concept of inertia, or *acedia*, which is a metaphysical one,[24] suggests a man at variance with himself. And for this reason *acedia* is regarded as *vitium capitale*, which should be translated as "root" rather than "cardinal" sin.[25] Inertia gives rise above all—this is the medieval doctrine—to despair and the *evagatio mentis*, that rambling uneasiness of the spirit which manifests itself in the insatiability of curiosity, in inconstancy of residence and decision, and, more generally, in inner restlessness and leisurelessness.[26]

Now let us return to the concept of leisure. Leisure, considered as a state of the soul, is the counterpoint to the concept of "intellectual labor"—and that from all three of the perspectives previously discussed (labor as activity, labor as effort, and labor as social function). *First*, leisure, as an attitude of inner unpreoccupiedness, is that form of being silent which is a prerequisite for attending to reality:

---

[24] We can only hint at the interesting shift in meaning here from a metaphysical to an "industrial" sense.

[25] *Caput* also means "root" [*Quelle*].

[26] A brief aside may perhaps be permitted here. When one examines Heidegger's analysis of "everyday *Dasein*" and the fundamental concepts belonging to it more carefully— "*Dasein*'s flight before itself" [*Flucht des Daseins vor ihm selbst*], "idle talk" [*Gerede*], "curiosity" [*Neugierde*], "non-tarrying" [*Unverweilen*], "distraction" [*Zerstreuung*], and "sojournlessness" [*Aufenthaltslosigkeit*]—it becomes immediately evident that the ancient, derivative forms of the *evagatio mentis*, which are born of inertia, are here being enumerated.

only one who is silent can hear. Leisure is an attitude of receptive
listening, of intuitive, contemplative immersion in being. It stands,
as it were, perpendicular to the normal course of a business day: it
is not, like the work break, a part of that day; it stands in the same
relation to the workday as the simple gaze of the *intellectus* does to
the ongoing process of discursive thought.[27] *Secondly*, leisure involves
the adoption of an attitude of celebratory contemplation toward the
world; it is sustained by its relation to the origin of all real being,
by the consciousness of being in harmony with this origin and being
included within it. Leisure is, because of its affirmation of oneness
with the wellspring of all being, that disposition of soul in which
man can, as in sleep, without any laborious efforts, receive the gift of
perceiving "what holds the world together in its innermost being"—
a gift that is, in any event, unattainable by exertion—even if only for
a moment, a moment whose insights would then have to be rediscovered and reconstructed through strenuous labor. *Thirdly*, leisure,
as an attitude involving a contemplative and celebratory gazing at the
world, is not a working attitude in the sense that it is directed toward performing a social function. Its purpose is not through bodily
rest or mental relaxation to generate new energy for renewed labor
(although it also has this effect!). It derives its legitimation, not from
the fact that the functionary remains a human being, that he does not
fully identify himself with that cross-sectional milieu designated by
his narrowly circumscribed function, but rather from the fact that he
is able to view the world in its totality and to realize himself as a
being oriented toward that whole.

But does the genuinely philosophical not consist in precisely this,
that despite all exertion and effort—even at the intellectual level—
the posture of contemplative gazing, which is directed, acquiescingly,
at the world as a whole, remains alive? Indeed, is this not so much the
case that one might legitimately argue that its leisurely quality belongs
more essentially to philosophy, to philosophizing, and to philosophical education than its characterization as labor?

On the other hand, in Trübner's influential dictionary, *Deutsches
Wörterbuch*, the claim is made that, with the neologisms "intellectual
labor" and "intellectual worker", the "primeval and in modern times

---

[27] Boethius compared the *ratio* to time and the *intellectus* to the "always now" of eternity.

ever more intense" social conflict between manual laborers and the learned has finally been overcome.[28] If, then, we reject these terms, what are we to do? Should we reignite the old class conflict between an educated academic class, which can afford to pursue knowledge for its own sake, and the proletariat, which knows only the leisure of a work break that hardly suffices from day to day to replenish its expended energy? Plato speaks of the philosopher as someone

> whose breeding has been the antithesis of a slave's. Such are the two characters. . . . The one is nursed in freedom and leisure, the philosopher. . . . He may be excused if he looks foolish or useless when faced with some menial task, if he cannot tie up bedclothes into a neat bundle or flavor a dish with spices and a speech with flattery. The other is smart in the dispatch of all services, but has not learned to wear his cloak like a gentleman, or caught the accent of discourse that will rightly celebrate the true life of happiness for gods and men.[29]

Here a portrait of the philosopher is being opposed to that of the philistine. By the term *banausus* classical antiquity understood, not only the uneducated, the amusical, the man who has no intellectual relation to the world, but also, quite unmistakably, the man who lives by his hands, in contrast to the gentleman, who freely disposes over his time. To repeat: Should the concept of the philistine be revived with the social and educational connotations of the pre-Christian era? Of course not! Still, has this conclusion not already been forced upon us by our refusal to apply the epithet of "work"—an honorific title, we have always said—to the realm of philosophical education? No! Rather it is our firm conviction that one must do everything to eliminate this social conflict but that, in attempting to realize this goal, it is wrong, even nonsensical, to seek this consensus in, as it were, a *terminological* proletarianization of the educated class rather than in a *real* deproletarianization of the proletariat. In other words, the consensus should be sought in a loosening of the fetters that bind the proletariat —and, more generally, those forced to engage in the continuous reproduction of the wage-labor relationship—to the work process; this,

---

[28] Berlin, 1939, vol. 1, col. 118.

[29] *Theaetetus* 175d7–176a1. [Quoted after the translation by F. M. Cornford, in *Plato: The Collected Dialogues*, ed. Edith Hamilton and Huntington Cairns (Princeton, 1961), p. 880.]

in turn, will allow for the possibility of true leisure and, in conjunction with a program of popular education—itself a genuine form of
education—for the opportunity, in perceiving and reflecting on the
world, to celebrate it in its totality.

It is not enough, however, to multiply life's opportunities by eco-
nomic means and so enable leisure (although that already represents
a significant step forward). After all, leisure means more than simply
having time. More is required if the purpose of leisure is to be realized. If we were asked to define the actual purpose of leisure, this
would be the point at which leisure, including philosophical leisure,
receives its ultimate legitimation—indeed, whence it derives its inner
possibility. Leisure implies celebration. Leisure derives its sense from
the very same source that the festival and the holiday [holy-day] derive theirs: there is no festival that does not draw its lifeblood from
the cultic. And the ultimate legitimation for leisure as well lies in its
having a living relation to the cultic festival. The original meaning
behind all holidays—of all rest—is cultic. In the Bible, no less than
in antiquity, rest means this: giving over specific days and times "to
the exclusive ownership of God".[30] Rest creates room for the realization of that which may be regarded as the sense of the cultic festival:
that man becomes contemplative and in this state directly encounters
those higher realities on which his whole existence depends.[31]

It is the space of time for the festive, as it is cleared out from one's
workday schedule (just as space for the temple is cleared out from
the land occupied by field and settlements), that allows the essence of
leisure to unfold and be fulfilled. Leisure is a way of looking at the
world, born of an affirming oneness with the origin of all being and
an authentically free, gracelike experience of the meaning of reality as
a whole, in which one is festively raised beyond the instrumental con-
textuality of the workday. In the relation between leisure and cultic
festiveness can be found the explanation for that to which Aristotle
was referring when he wrote that man leads a life of leisure, "not as
a human being, but in virtue of something divine within him".[32]

---

[30] Cf. the article *Arbeitsruhe* in the *Reallexikon für Antike und Christentum*, vol. 1 (Stuttgart,
1950), cols. 590ff.

[31] This is the argument of the Hungarian historian of religion Karl Kerényi in his book
Die antike Religion (Amsterdam, 1940), p. 66.

[32] *Nichomachean Ethics* 10.7.1177b27f.—a thought that medieval Christianity formulated in

When leisure is deprived of its proximity to the cultic festival and its emanatory power, it cannot flourish any more than can the festival itself. Even in such cases, it is possible, of course, to enjoy a break from work, vacation, recreation—relaxation from work for the sake of more work. But here the place reserved for leisure remains empty. Instead, its space is taken up by the sheer killing of time and that boredom which stands in an immediate relation to the unleisurely. Under those circumstances philosophical leisure, in particular, runs the risk of descending to the "purely academic", which in ordinary linguistic usage carries connotations of the sterile, the unreal, and even the fantastic. As Goethe once said of the classicism of his time, the *inventa* of antiquity, all of which "had been articles of faith", were now being "imitated in a fantastic way, sheerly out of a love for the fantastic for its own sake".[33] One should not forget that the original academy, the Platonic one, was a genuine cultic association, which included the office of preparer of sacrifices; the real significance of this is constantly in danger of being supplanted by the imaginary world made familiar to us through its aesthetic/humanistic austerity of religious commitment and replete with such standard props as "the temple *qua* museum".

This, then, is our thesis: Philosophical education, if it is to unfold, must have room for leisure; leisure, in turn, draws its lifeblood from the cultic. Leisure [*Muße*], divorced from the cultic, is idle [*müßig*].

What, conversely, becomes of work if the corrective to work, leisure, is missing? One might just as well ask, since it amounts to the same thing: What becomes of work without the holiday ["holy-day"]? It becomes something other than just work without a pause. (Even if work is punctuated by pauses, a holiday is something different from, and more than just, a pause.) In such a situation, work itself assumes the character of the cultic. "To work is to pray", says Carlyle. Still, this spurious festiveness cannot disguise the fact that work, without leisure, becomes inhuman, becomes sheer unhoping exertion, whether it is borne apathetically or imperiously. And what becomes of intellectual labor—the Herculean labor of philosophy? It

---

this way: "Homo, inquantum est contemplativus, est aliquid supra hominem" (3, d. 35, 2, 1 ad 1), "the contemplative man is something beyond man."

[33] In a letter to Riemer dated March 26, 1814.

may, loaded down, in addition, with the unsustainable burden of having to draw from within itself the meaning of the world, push itself to ever greater—indeed, monstrous—exertions that in and of themselves would inspire awe. As long as it refuses to release itself from the heightened state of alertness characteristic of an exclusively work-oriented attitude into the contemplative detachment of a genuinely cultic leisure, it cannot flourish to the point where it might quiet man's needs by offering a vision of Being as a whole. Consequently, this Herculean effort must necessarily be in vain—not the work of a Hercules, but of a Sisyphus, the mythical archetype of a "laborer" fettered to his function, performed without pause or inner fruit.

WHAT DOES IT MEAN TO PHILOSOPHIZE?

Four Lectures

> *This is the reason why the philosopher may be likened to*
> *the poet: Both are concerned with the wondrous.*

Thomas Aquinas*

I. The world of work is transcended in the act of philosophizing
—Common utility and the *bonum commune*—The "totalitarian
world of work" has its foundation in the identification of common use with the *bonum commune*—Philosophy's station within
the world of work—The affinity between the philosophical act
and other acts: the artistic act, the religious act, and the shock
that *eros* and death cause to our relation to the world—Spurious
forms of these basic attitudes—The perennial disproportion between philosophy and the world of work: the Thracian maidservant, the figure of Apollodorus—The positive side of that incommensurability: the freedom (nonavailability) of philosophy
—The knowledge of the functionary and the knowledge of the
gentleman—The "nonfreedom" of the specialized sciences—
The freedom of philosophy and its "theoretical" character—
The presupposition of *theoria*—The belief that man's true wealth
lies neither in the satisfaction of his basic needs nor in the domination of nature.

II. Whither does the philosophical act penetrate in transcending the
world of work?—The world as a field of relations—The hierarchy of worlds—The concept of "environment" (von Uexküll)
—Spirit as the capacity for grasping the world—Spirit exists in
the midst of reality as a whole—Being as relatedness to spirit:
the truth of things—The levels of interiority: the relation to
totality and personality—The world of spirit: the totality of
things and the essence of things—Man not pure spirit—Man's

---

* [The epigraph comes from Aquinas' commentary on Aristotle's *Metaphysics* I, 3 (no. 55).]

field of relations: an intertwining of world and environment—
Philosophizing as a stepping beyond the environment *vis-à-vis
de l'univers*; the "superhuman" in this step—The crucial feature
of a philosophical question: that it stand within the horizon of
reality as a whole.

III. World and environment do not constitute separate realms—
The preservation of world *in* environment: wonder—The "nonbourgeois" character of philosophical wonder—The risk of being uprooted from the world of work—Wonder as "thought's
being confused by itself"—The inner directionality of wonder
culminates, not in doubt, but in a sense of mystery—Wonder as
a principle intrinsic to philosophizing—The structure of hope
underlying wonder and philosophizing—The distinctively human aspect of this—The special sciences move beyond wonder; philosophy does not—*Philosophia* as the loving search for
wisdom such as God possesses—The inherent impossibility of
a "closed" philosophical system—Philosophizing as the fulfillment of human existence.

IV. The received interpretation of the world that "always already"
precedes philosophy—The relation of Plato, Socrates, and the
Pre-Socratics to tradition—Plato: tradition as revelation—The
openness to theology: an essential feature of Platonic philosophizing—Christian theology as the only form of prephilosophical tradition to be found in the West—The vivacity of
philosophy depends on its relation to theology—How is a non-
Christian philosophy possible?—Christian philosophy distinguishes itself, not by its ability to offer more refined solutions,
but through its deeper grasp of the world's mysterious character
—Christian philosophy does not make things "easier" intellectually—The joy of incomprehensibility—Christianity not primarily doctrine but reality—The true foundation of Christian
philosophy: the living experience of "the Christian" as reality.

When the physicist poses the question, "What does it mean to en-gage in physics?" or "What is physical research?" then, to the ex-tent that he does so, the question he is raising is a provisional one. Clearly, in raising such questions and seeking an answer for them, he is not already engaged in doing physics—not already, or, if he was previously so engaged, then clearly no longer. Someone, on the other hand, who raises and attempts to answer the question, "What does it mean to philosophize?" is quite unmistakably engaged in doing philosophy. This question is not a provisional one but an imminently philosophical one; in raising it, one stands already at the very heart of philosophical questioning. To be more precise: I cannot say anything concerning the essence of philosophy and philosophizing without at the same time saying something about the essence of man—and, with this, we have entered one of philosophy's innermost provinces.

Our question, "What does it mean to philosophize?" falls, then, within this realm—the realm of philosophical anthropology.

Since it is, however, a philosophical question, it cannot, by the same token, be answered with absolute conclusiveness. For it belongs to the essence of a philosophical question that one cannot grab hold of the "well-rounded truth" (as Parmenides calls it) the way one can a freshly picked apple. (We shall have more to say later about the ele-ment of hope inherent in philosophy and philosophizing in general.) We should therefore not be expecting a handy definition, a formula-tion that completely comprehends its object, all the more so as four brief lectures will hardly suffice to illuminate the question to its full extent.

The following may be asserted in an attempt at a first approxima-tion: Philosophizing is an act in which the world of work is tran-scended. It must, then, first be determined what is understood here by the "world of work" and then what is meant by the "transcend-ing" of this world.

The world of work is the workday world, the world of use, of expediency, of performance, of functional adequacy; it is the world of needs and proceeds, the world of hunger and its satisfaction. The world of work is governed by one purpose: the realization of a "com-mon utility"; it is the world of work insofar as work is synonymous with gainful activity (which, as a result, belongs to the nature of both bustle and effort). The process of work is the process of realizing the "common utility"; this concept should not be identified with the concept of the *bonum commune*, or common good: the "common utility" is an essential component of the *bonum commune*, but the concept of the *bonum commune* is more inclusive. It is part of this concept (as Aquinas points out)[1] that there are men who devote themselves to the un-useful life of contemplation; it belongs to this concept of the *bonum commune* that philosophy is pursued at all—and this despite the fact that one can, with certainty, say that reflection, contemplation, and philosophy do *not* serve the "common utility".

Still, the *bonum commune* and common utility are today increasingly becoming identified with each other; at the same time it is true—and this amounts to saying much the same thing—that the world of work is coming to occupy our world more and more exclusively, that it is threatening to become exclusively our world: the claims of the world of work are becoming increasingly more absolute, more totalitarian; they are engulfing more and more of the totality of human existence.

If, then, it is true that philosophizing is an act that transcends, or goes beyond, the world of work, then our question, "What does it mean to philosophize?"—this very "theoretical" and "abstract" question—has suddenly and unexpectedly become an extremely topical question! We need only take one step—both intellectually and geographically—to find ourselves in a world in which the process of work, the process of serving the common utility, penetrates the entire spectrum of human existence; a boundary that has drawn ever closer, both inwardly and outwardly, need only be crossed in order to arrive at the totalitarian world of work, in which there would, accordingly, be no genuine philosophy and no genuine philosophizing. Let us assume, then, that the proposition that philosophizing involves transcending the world of work is correct and that it belongs, in turn, to the essence of the philosophical act, *not* to be of a piece with this world of expediencies and efficiencies, of needs and proceeds, with this world of the *bonum utile*, of "common utility", but rather to be essentially incommensurable with it. In fact, the more totalitarian the claims of the world of work, the more acutely this incommensurabil-

---

[1] 4, d. 26, 1, 2.

ity, this lack of affinity, must make itself felt. And one may perhaps say that it is this imperiling of philosophy through the world of total work that actually characterizes the situation of philosophy today, almost more so than the substance of its problematic. Philosophy is increasingly—and necessarily!—taking on the air of the curious—of sheer intellectual luxury—indeed, of the genuinely unacceptable and indefensible, the more exclusively the claims of the workday world of work come to monopolize man's existence.

First, however, more needs to be said concerning the incommensurability of the philosophical act, about that transcending of the world of work which occurs in the act of philosophizing. In what follows we shall now be discussing these matters more concretely.

Let us recall those things that today dominate man's workday, our workday; it requires no special feat of intellectual exertion to imagine them: we stand very much in the midst of the workday. There is, first of all, the daily running and chasing after the bare necessities of physical existence, after foodstuffs, clothing, shelter, warmth; then, transcending the cares of the individual (and at the same time conditioning them), come the demands of the new political order and of reconstruction, particularly in our own country, but in Europe and the world more generally. Power struggles in competition for the goods of this earth, conflicts of interest on a large and small scale. We find extreme tension and stress everywhere, only apparently mitigated by hastily enjoyed distractions and pauses: newspaper, cinema, cigarettes. I need not describe this in further detail; we all know from our life together what this world looks like. It is, however, not necessary that we consider only those crisis-like extremes that manifest themselves today; that to which I am referring corresponds simply to the everyday world of work, in which one must put one's back into what one is doing, in which extremely concrete objectives are carried through and realized—objectives that must be kept in view with a fixed eye toward what is next and nearest. And it is far from being our intention to deprecate this workday world from the putatively superior standpoint of philosophical festiveness. It would be superfluous to point out that even in this world of work the fundamentals of physical existence must first be secured, in the absence of which no man can philosophize. Nevertheless, let us imagine that among the voices that fill the workplace and the market (how is this or that thing relating to our daily needs to be acquired? how does one get this? where do you find that?) suddenly one voice grows loud with the question, "Why is there something at all rather than nothing?"—that is, with this primeval philosophical exclamation of wonder which Heidegger deemed the most fundamental question of all metaphysics?[2] Need we reiterate just how thoroughly incommensurable this question of the philosophers is with that workday world of usefulness and service-ability? If this question were uttered quite unexpectedly and without any form of explanation among achievement- and success-oriented people, would the questioner not be thought a madman? Through such extreme juxtapositions, however, the difference, which certainly exists, is made clear: it is clear that, with this question, a step has been taken that transcends the world of work and leads beyond it. The genuinely philosophical question pierces through the dome that encloses the world of the bourgeois workday.

The philosophical act is, however, not the only way to take this "step beyond". No less incommensurable with the world of work than the philosopher's question is the ring of genuine poetry: "The tree stands for always in the ends and midst, / Birds are singing and in God's loins / the circle of creation rests in bliss" (Immer steht der Baum in Mitt und Enden, / Vögel singen und in Gottes Lenden / ruht der Kreis der Schöpfung selig aus).[3] Within the realm of actively pursued ends, this poem likewise strikes us as something thoroughly peculiar. It is no different with the words of the praying individual: "We praise thee, we bless thee, we give thee thanks for thy great glory" (Wir loben Dich, wir preisen Dich, wir sagen Dir Dank ob Deiner grossen Herrlichkeit). How could that ever be understood solely in terms of the categories of rational utility and organizational expediency? And the lover stands out as well from the instrumental network of the workday world, as does anyone else who, by virtue of a profound existential shock, which is always accompanied at the same time by a shock in his relation to the world, comes up against

---

[2] M. Heidegger, *Was ist Metaphysik?* (Frankfurt, 1943), p. 22. The formulation is, inciden-tally, not new; it may already be found in Leibniz: "Pouquoy il y a plustôt quelque chose que rien?" (Leibniz, *Philosophische Schriften*, vol. 1, [Darmstadt, 1965], p. 426).

[3] Konrad Weiß, "In exitu (Anfangsverse)", which first appeared in the collection of po-ems *Die cumäische Sibylle* (Munich, 1921) and which has been made available again in Kösel's edition of his collected works (Konrad Weiß, *Gedichte, 1914 bis 1939* [Munich, 1961]).

the boundaries of human existence—for example, through the proximity to death. Through such shocks (the philosophical act, authentic poetry, experience of the fine arts in general, even prayer, are all based on a shock!), man experiences the in-conclusiveness of this world of everyday concerns: he transcends it; he takes a step beyond it.

And because of this common faculty of penetration and transcendence, these basic patterns in man's behavior have a natural commonality: the philosophical act, the religious act, the artistic act, and even the relation to world that is established through the existential shock caused by *eros* or the experience of death. It is well known how closely Plato associated philosophizing with *eros*. And as for the affinity between philosophy and poetry, there is a curious and little-known sentence concerning this topic in Aquinas' commentary on the *Metaphysics* of Aristotle: the philosopher is similar to the poet in that both are concerned with the *mirandum*, with the wondrous [*Erstaunliche*], with the wonder-ful, with that which evokes wonder.[4] This sentence, which is not easy to fathom, has all the more significance in that both thinkers, Aquinas as well as Aristotle, had completely sober minds, thoroughly disinclined to engage in a romantic blurring of subject boundaries. On the basis of this common orientation toward the *mirandum* (the *mirandum*, however, does not appear in the world of work!), that is, on the basis of this common faculty of transcendence, the philosophical act is considered related and adjacent to the poetic (act), more intimately and more closely related to it than to the exact specialized sciences. We shall be examining this in more detail shortly.

This affinity asserts itself to such a degree that wherever one member of the genus is effectively denied, none of the others can flourish, so that in a world of total work all these forms and means of transcending it must dry up (or, better said, *would have to* dry up, if it were possible to destroy man's nature completely): where religion is not allowed to bloom, where the artistic finds no home, where the twin shocks of death and *eros* are robbed of their depth and trivialized —there, as well, philosophy and philosophizing cannot flourish.

Worse still than their mere muting and extinction is their degeneration into sham and spurious forms; and there are such pseudo-realizations of these basic behaviors that only appear to pierce through

---

[4] *In Met.* I, 3 (no. 55).

the dome. There exists a form of prayer in which "this" world is not transcended, in which, rather, the attempt is made to incorporate the divine in the instrumental network of the workday as a functioning component. There is the degeneration of religion into magic—not devotion to the divine, but rather the attempt to overpower the divine and to make it available; there is the degeneration of prayer into a practice, precisely in order to continue making life under the dome bearable. Moreover, there is a degeneration of *eros* that involves making one's devotional energies subservient to the purposes of the constricted self and that arises from the fearful resistance to shocks from that larger and more profound world into which only those truly in love are able to enter. Pseudo-forms of the artistic exist; there is, in particular, a sham poetry, which, instead of penetrating the dome of the workday, paints, as it were, only deceptive ornaments on its inner wall and offers itself up as private or even "instrumental poetry" [*Gebrauchsdichtung*] more or less openly in the service of the world of work: such "poetry" does not transcend, even superficially (and it is clear that authentic philosophizing has more in common with the exact specialized sciences than with such *pseudo*-poetry!).

And, finally, there is also a kind of pseudo-philosophy whose distinguishing feature is precisely this: that in it the world of work is not transcended. In one of Plato's dialogues,[5] Socrates asks the sophist Protagoras, What exactly do you teach the young men who flock to you? And Protagoras responds, When they come to me, they learn to take proper care of their personal affairs, such as how best to manage their own households, as well as the state's affairs, how one can become a real power in the city, both as speaker and man of action. That is the classic program of philosophy that identifies philosophy with professional training, a pseudo-form of philosophy that is nontranscendent.

Worse still, it is common to all these sham-realizations that they not only fail to transcend the world but that they bring it ever more firmly and irrevocably under the one dome; that they serve to confine man ever more within the world of work. For this reason, all these spurious forms of behavior, but such pseudo-philosophy above all, constitute something far worse, something far more hopeless than the mundane

[5] *Protagoras* 318a6ff.

man's sealing himself off from the extraordinary. The person who is naïvely entangled in the workday world may yet be moved one day by the emotive force concealed in a genuine philosophical question; but a sophist, a pseudo-philosopher, cannot be moved! But let us return now to the path initiated by our original questioning. If one inquires after the true nature of philosophy, then one is already, in so doing, raising the kind of questions that go beyond the world of work. Hence it should be evident that such a question and a placing in question possesses a unique historical dimension that renders it acutely problematic, particularly in this day and age, when the world of work has emerged with a claim to totality hitherto unknown in the West. Nevertheless, more is involved here than simply a critique of contemporary society. What is at issue is at bottom a perennial incongruity.

The laughter of the Thracian maidservant, who saw Thales of Milet, the observer of the heavens, tumble down a well—that is for Plato the typical reaction of robust everyday common sense to philosophy. And this anecdote concerning the Thracian maiden stands at the origin of Western philosophy. "Time and again"—so Plato writes in the *Theaetetus*—the philosopher is the butt of ridicule, "the whole rabble will join the maidservants in laughing at him, as from inexperience he walks blindly and stumbles into every pitfall."[6]

Plato, however, does not express himself exclusively or even primarily in explicit language and in formal theses but speaks rather though persona. One such figure is, for example, Apollodorus, a secondary character (or so it would appear) in the *Phaedo* and *Symposium* dialogues. Apollodorus is one of those uncritically enthusiastic youths who surround Socrates and through whom Plato perhaps sought to represent himself. In the *Phaedo* it is reported that, as Socrates raised the cup of hemlock to his mouth in prison, Apollodorus was the only one among those present to break out in continuous sobbing and weeping: "You know what he is like, don't you?"[7] In the *Symposium*, Apollodorus says of himself that for years now he has made it his business to follow everything that Socrates says and does from

---

[6] *Theaetetus* 174b9ff. [Quoted after the translation by F. M. Cornford, in *Plato: The Collected Dialogues*, ed. Edith Hamilton and Huntington Cairns (Princeton, 1961), p. 879.]

[7] *Phaedo* 59b1. [Quoted after the translation by Hugh Tredennick, in *Plato: The Collected Dialogues*, p. 42.]

day to day; "before that I used to go dashing about all over the place, firmly convinced that I was leading a full and interesting life, when I was really as wretched as could be."[8] Now, however, he is effusively devoted to Socrates and to philosophy in an extravagant way. In the city he is known as "mad" Apollodorus; he is always raging at all the rest, with the sole exception of Socrates, and even at himself. With complete naïveté he announces to everyone how nothing gives him "greater pleasure" than when he himself is able to talk philosophy or when he can listen to others talk about it and that he is, on the other hand, unhappy that he has not yet achieved the ultimate purpose, to be like Socrates. Now one day this same Apollodorus encounters some friends from the past—precisely those who now think of him as the mad one, the wild one. They are, as Plato expressly notes, businessmen, moneyed people, who know quite well how to make something work and who "think they are really accomplishing something" in the world. These friends ask Apollodorus to relate something of the speeches about love that were delivered at a certain banquet in the house of the poet Agathon. It is clear that these rich and successful men in no way feel the need to be lectured to on the meaning of the world and human existence—and certainly not by Apollodorus! It is only an interest in the salacious or in the facetious, in the eloquence, the formal elegance, of the verbal disputation that motivates them. Apollodorus, in turn, has no illusions about any "philosophical interest" on the part of his interlocutors. On the contrary, he even tells them to their face how much he pities them because they "think they're being very busy when they're really doing absolutely nothing. Of course, I know your idea of me; you think I'm just a poor unfortunate, and I shouldn't wonder if you're right. But then, I don't *think* that *you're* unfortunate—I know you are." Nevertheless, he does not refuse to report on the speeches about love. Indeed he can hardly remain silent; ". . . if you want to hear it too I suppose I may as well begin", even if they consider him a madman! And then Apollodorus goes on to recount—the *Symposium* itself! Plato's *Symposium* has, in fact, the form of indirect speech, of a report—and that placed in the mouth of Apollodorus! One has, I think, given far too little thought

---

[8] *Symposium* 172c4ff. [Quoted after the translation by Michael Joyce, in *Plato: The Collected Dialogues*, p. 527.]

to the fact that Plato allows his most profound thoughts to be expressed by this gushing youth, reveling in uncritical enthusiasm—by this overzealous little student, Apollodorus—and that before a circle of listeners consisting of moneyed and self-made men who are neither capable of nor for that matter interested in pursuing these thoughts or even in taking them seriously in the first place! This situation has an element of hopelessness about it—against which (and this is, arguably, Plato's point here) only the youthfully steadfast search for truth, the genuine *philosophia*, is able to stand its ground. In any event, Plato could not have expressed with greater clarity the fundamental incommensurability between philosophizing and the self-sufficient workday world of work.

Still, this negative aspect constitutes only one side of the incommensurability; the other side we may call freedom. Philosophy is "of no use" as far as immediate implementation and application is concerned—that is the one side. The other side is that philosophy cannot be used; that it is not available for purposes that lie beyond it; that it is its own purpose. Philosophy is not functionary knowledge but rather, as John Henry Newman calls it, "gentleman" knowledge; not "useful" knowledge, but "liberal" knowledge.[9] This "liberality", however, implies that philosophical knowledge does not receive its legitimation from its usefulness and its applicability, from its social function, from its reducibility to a "common use". It is precisely in this sense that the freedom of the *artes liberales*—the "liberal" arts—is meant, as distinct from the *artes serviles*, the servile arts, which, as Aquinas writes, "can only be directed toward a use realized through activity".[10] Philosophy, however, has always been understood to be the "freest" of the free arts (the medieval "faculty of artists", which was named after the *artes liberales*, is identical with the philosophical faculty of today).

So, then, it is a matter of indifference whether I say that the philosophical act transcends the world of work or whether I say that philosophical knowledge is of no use or whether I say that philosophy is a "free art". This freedom may be attributed to the specialized sciences only to the extent that they are pursued in a philosophical manner.

---

[9] Discourse 5, 5, *The Idea of a University*.
[10] *In Met.* I, 3 (no. 59).

Herein lies the genuine sense of academic freedom (for "academic" is either synonymous with "philosophical"—or it means nothing at all!); a claim to academic freedom can exist, strictly speaking, only insofar as the "academic" is itself realized in the "philosophical" sense. And this is also true in a historically factual sense: academic freedom is lost in precisely the same measure in which the philosophical character of academic studies is lost, or, alternately expressed, to precisely the same degree in which the totalitarian claim of the world of work conquers the space of the university. This is the metaphysical root of the problem; the so-called "politicization" of the university is only a consequence and a symptom. It should, however, be noted that this is precisely the result of philosophy itself—of modern philosophy! We shall have a word to say about this shortly.

But first let us return to our topic, the "freedom" of philosophy vis-à-vis the specialized sciences, freedom construed as nonsuitability for specific ends. The special sciences are "free" in this sense only insofar as they are pursued in a philosophical manner, only insofar as they partake in the freedom of philosophy. "Knowledge, I say, is then especially liberal, or sufficient for itself, apart from every external and ulterior object," writes Newman, "when and so far as it is philosophical."[11] Considered for themselves, however, the specialized sciences are clearly—and in an essential way—"suitable for specific purposes"; they are in their essence applicable to "a use realized through activity" (as Aquinas says of the "servile arts").[12]

Let us try to be a bit more precise here! The government of a country might very well decide that it now needs, in order to implement its Five-Year Plan, physicists who can make up for the lead that the foreigners have in this or that field or that it needs physicians who through their scientific research can develop a more effective treatment for influenza. It is possible to speak of, and dispose over, things in this fashion, *without* contravening the essence of the specialized sciences. But if the same government were to say, "We now need philosophers to . . ."—well, what then? In that case, there is only one possibility: ". . . to develop, justify, and defend the following ideology"—but in

---

[11] *The Idea of a University*, discourse 5, 5. [Quoted from: John Henry Cardinal Newman, *The Idea of a University* (Garden City, N.Y., 1959), p. 137.]

[12] *In Met.* I, 3 (no. 59).

speaking this way, we simultaneously destroy the possibility of philosophy. Exactly the same would apply if the government were to say instead: "We now need poets to . . ." Here, too, there is only one possibility: ". . . [in the idiom of the current jargon] to use the word as a weapon in the struggle for certain ideals pursued with an eye to national needs . . ."—but in speaking this way, we simultaneously destroy the possibility of poetry. In the same moment, poetry would cease to be poetry; and philosophy would cease to be philosophy.

Now, it is not as if there were no relation between the realization of the public good and the kind of philosophy that is taught a people! This relation, however, cannot be organized and regulated by an administrator of the common good; what has its meaning and purpose in itself—what is in itself end—cannot be made the means to another end, just as one cannot love a person "so that" and "for the sake of"!

Now, this nonavailability, this freedom associated with the act of philosophizing, is intimately bound up with—and to notice this appears to me to be of the utmost relevance!—the theoretical character of philosophy, indeed, to the point of even appearing to be identical with it. Philosophizing is the purest form of *theoria*, of *speculari*, of a purely receptive gazing at reality, in which the things alone provide the measure and the soul only receives this measure. Whenever a being is regarded in a philosophical manner, questions are raised "in a purely theoretical way", that is, in a way that is unalloyed with anything practical, with any desire for change, and that hence is elevated beyond all considerations of expediency.

The realization of *theoria* in this sense is, in turn, tied to a certain presupposition. What is being presupposed is a certain relation to the world, a relation to the world that would seem to preexist all conscious positing and constituting. Man's gaze can be "theoretical" in this undiluted sense—that is, purely receptive in its beholding without any hint of a desire to change things but rather with a willingness to let the affirmation or denial of its will depend on that knowledge of essence through which the reality of being is brought to language— only if being and the world mean more to him than simply the arena, the stuff, the raw material of human activity. Only *someone* for whom the world is in some way venerable—creation in the strictest sense— will be able to view the world "theoretically" in the full acceptation of that term. The "purely theoretical", which belongs to the essence of philosophy, can prosper only on this basis. And thus it would have to be a connection of the ultimate and most profound kind that makes possible at the innermost level the freedom of philosophizing and, hence, philosophizing itself. And it would not be all too surprising if a lapse in that relation to the world, in that bond (by virtue of which the world is seen as creation and not merely as raw material), were to go hand in hand with a lapse in the genuinely theoretical character and in the freedom and nonfunctionality of philosophy, no less than in philosophy itself. A direct path leads from Francis Bacon, who wrote that knowledge and power coincide and that the purpose of all knowledge is to furnish human life with new inventions and technical aids,[13] to Descartes, who expresses himself in a more pointedly polemic manner in his *Discourse* and whose purpose it is to replace the old "theoretical" philosophy with a "practical" one through which we can "render ourselves the lords and possessors of nature"[14] —a path that culminates in the well-known formulation of Marx to the effect that philosophy had hitherto seen its task as interpreting the world, whereas its real task is to transform it.

This is the path along which the self-abnegation of philosophy has historically proceeded—that is, through the denial of its theoretical character, which, in turn, rests on the fact that the world is increasingly being regarded as providing the raw material for human activity. If the world is no longer seen as creation, then there can be no *theoria* in the full sense of that term. In the absence of *theoria*, the freedom associated with philosophizing *eo ipso* also expires—and its functionalization follows, along with the now exclusive emphasis on the "practical", the reliance on legitimation in terms of social function; in other words, the characterization of philosophy—which continues to be so called—as "work" now emerges. By contrast, our thesis, which has in the meantime assumed more distinct contours, states that it belongs to the very nature of the philosophical act that it transcend the world of work. This thesis, in which both the freedom and theoretical character of philosophy are by implication being asserted, does not deny the world of work (rather, it explicitly assumes it to be necessary), but it does assert that genuine philosophy rests on

---

[13] *Novum Organum* I, 3; I, 81.
[14] *Discours de la Méthode* 6.

faith, that man's real wealth lies, not in the satisfaction of his basic needs and not in our becoming "the lords and possessors of nature", but rather in his being able to perceive what there is—the totality of that which is. This is, in ancient philosophy, the highest perfection to which we may aspire, that is, that our soul become inscribed with the order of the totality of existing things[15]—a thought that the Christian tradition has taken up in the notion of the *visio beatifica*: "What do they not see who see him who sees all?"[16]

II *pp. 27-28*

Whoever philosophizes takes a step beyond the everyday world of work.

The significance of a step, however, is measured less in terms of the "whence" than of the "whither". Let us then ask the next question, namely, whither is the philosophizing person transported when transcending the world of work? Obviously he crosses a boundary: What kind of realm is this that lies beyond the boundary? And how is the realm into which the philosophical act penetrates related to the world that is surpassed and transcended through just this philosophical act? Does that realm, for example, represent the "authentic", as distinct from the "inauthentic", world of work? Is it, for example, the "whole" to which the world of work corresponds as part? Does it represent genuine reality as opposed to a shadow-world of mere appearance?

However these questions might be answered individually, *both* realms —the world of work and that other realm into which the philosophical act penetrates in transcending the world of work—belong, in any event, to man's world, which accordingly possesses a multi-layered structure.

This, then, is our question: What kind of world is the world of man?—a question that cannot be answered in abstraction from man himself.

In order to arrive at a somewhat precise answer, we must begin at the very outset and proceed from the bottom up.

---

[15] Cf. *Ver.* 2, 2.

[16] Gregory the Great, as cited by Thomas Aquinas, *Ver.* 2, 2.

It belongs to the nature of the living, of the living entity, that it is and lives in a world, in "its" world; that, in fact, it has a world. To be alive means to be "in" the world. But is the stone not also in the world? Is not absolutely everything that exists in any way at all "in" the world? Let us stick for a moment with that lifeless stone which is just lying around somewhere: Is it not with, and next to, other things "in" the world? "In", "with", "next to"—these are all prepositions; but the stone does not really have a relation to the world "in" which it is, nor does it have a relation to the surrounding things "next to" and "with" which it is "in" the world. Relations in the genuine sense are formed from inside out; relations are only possible where there is an interior, that, where that dynamic mean exists from which all agency derives and to which all receptivity and passivity is collectively related. The "interior" (one can speak of the "interior" of a stone in this qualitative sense only if one is referring to the spatial arrangement of its parts) is the power of a real thing to enter into a relation, to put itself in relation to an outside; the "interior" means the power to relate and to incorporate. And what about the world? The world is, in fact, equivalent to a field of relations. Only a being capable of entertaining relations, only a being with an interior—and that means only a living being—has a world; to him alone may be ascribed the property of existing in the midst of a field of relations. The pebbles that are assembled in a heap on the street and hence border on one another are subject to a fundamentally different kind of juxtaposition than obtains between a plant and the nutrients located within the reach of its roots in the soil. In the latter case, we are dealing, not with sheer spatial proximity as an objective fact, but with a genuine relation (in the original, active sense of incorporation): the nutrients are incorporated within the circuit of vegetative life by the genuine interior of the plant, by its power to relate and to incorporate. And all this, which is included in the power of the plant to incorporate, all this constitutes the field of relations   that is, the world of the plant. The plant has a world; the pebble does not.

This, then, is the first point to be noted: the world is a field of relations. To have a world means to be the core and carrier of a field of relations. The second point is this: The higher the status of the being with an interior, that is, the more expansive and comprehensive its power to enter into relations is, the broader and more multi-dimensioned is the field of relations associated with it; alternately expressed, the higher the being stands in the hierarchy of reality, the larger its world and the greater its status.

The most primitive world is that of plants, which, when measured simply in terms of its spatial extension, does not go beyond the proximity of contact. The in itself superior and spatially broader world of the animal reflects the animal's more developed ability to enter into relations. The ability of the animal to entertain relations with, and to incorporate, an outside is more powerful because the animal can perceive through its senses; this is a thoroughly unique mode of putting oneself in relation to an outside, completely distinct from what is to be found in the purely vegetative realm.

Still, it is by no means true that everything that an animal, conceived "in the abstract", as it were, is able to perceive (simply because it has eyes to see and ears to hear) already belongs, in fact, to that animal's world; it is not true that all the things that are visible to an animal endowed with sight are actually seen by it or even could be seen by it. A surrounding [*Umgebung*]—even a surrounding that is perceivable "in itself"—is not yet a world! This had been the general view until the environmental studies of the biologist Jakob von Uexküll; up until that point it had been, as Uexküll himself notes,[17] "generally assumed that all animals with eyes behold the same objects". Now it was Uexküll's discovery that this is not, in fact, true: "The environments of animals", Uexküll writes,[18] "are comparable in no way to open nature but rather to a cramped, ill-furnished apartment." One would, for example, think that a daw, insofar as it has eyes in its head, should be able to see a grasshopper, which is for it a particularly desirable object, whenever one enters its field of vision or—to be more precise—whenever it appears before its eyes. That is, however, not the case! On the contrary, the following is true (I am again citing Uexküll):

> The daw is completely incapable of seeing an unmoving grasshopper. . . .
> Here we would initially be tempted to assume that the shape of the resting
> grasshopper is well known to the daw, but as a result of the overlapping
> blades of grass the daw cannot recognize it as a coherent unity, just as
> we can only with difficulty abstract a familiar form from jigsaw puzzles.
> Only in leaping does the shape, on this way of conceiving things, resolve

---

[17] *Der unsterbliche Geist in der Natur* (Hamburg, 1938), p. 63.
[18] Ibid., p. 76.

itself from the distracting images that surround it. But after further experiments it is to be assumed that the daw does not recognize the form
of the resting grasshopper at all but is only attuned to the moving form.
This would explain the tendency of many insects to "play dead". If its
resting form is not present at all in the perceived world [*Merkwelt*] of the
pursuing enemy, then they will certainly drop out of its field of attention
[*Merkwelt*] and could not be found even after searching.[19]

On the one hand, the animal is fully attuned to this cross-sectional
milieu [*Ausschnittsmilieu*], but, on the other, it is completely enclosed
by it (so much so that it can in no way transcend its boundaries, as
is evidenced by the fact that it is unable to find an object that falls
outside the criterion of selection for this partial world, "[not] even
after searching" or with a search organ that is evidently extremely
well equipped for the task). Uexküll calls this cross section of reality, which is determined and delimited by the biological preservation
of either the individual or the species, the "environment" [*Umwelt*],
which he contrasts with the animal's "surroundings" [*Umgebung*] but
also—as emerged from our previous discussion—with the "world"
[*Welt*] as such. The animal's field of relations is not its surroundings,
and certainly not "the world"; it is rather that animal's "environment"
—environment in this specific sense, a world from which something
has been left out, a cross-sectional milieu to which its occupant is at
once accommodated and confined.

One might perhaps ask what all this has to do with our topic,
"what does it mean to philosophize?" Now, the connection is not
so remote and indirect as it might at first appear. The last question
we had raised concerned the world of man; and it is from this point
of view that Uexküll's concept of environment is of obvious interest, since in Uexküll's opinion our human world "can in no way lay
claim to being more real than the animal's perceived world";[20] since
man is in principle just as confined to his environment as the animal
is to its own, that is, to a cross-sectional milieu defined in terms of
its biological suitability; thus man, too, cannot perceive anything that
lies beyond his environment, "[not] even by searching" (just as little
as the daw with the unmoving grasshopper). One might, however, at

---

[19] Uexküll-Kriszat, *Streifzüge durch die Umwelten von Tieren und Menschen* (Berlin, 1934), p.
40.
    [20] *Die Lebenslehre* (Potsdam and Zurich, 1930), p. 131.

this point be tempted to ask: How does such a being, confined as it is, come to study the diverse environments?

We, however, do not intend to argue the point here; we shall set it aside for the time being and, focusing our attention now on man and the world associated with him, raise the question of how powerful man's ability is to enter into relations and in what it consists. We have maintained that the ability of the animal to perceive constitutes a new, more expansive means of entering into relations, when compared with that of vegetative beings. Now, does the ability to know, which is peculiar to man and which has always been identified with intellectual knowledge, not perhaps represent a mode of entering into relations fundamentally inaccessible to plant and animal life? Moreover: Is there not also a field of relations, that is, a world of fundamentally different dimensions, corresponding to this radically different ability to entertain relations? The answer to this question is that the Western philosophical tradition has, in fact, construed—even defined—the capacity for intellectual knowledge as the ability to enter into relations with the totality of existing things. As already noted, this is not intended as a mere description but as an essential attribute or definition. The spirit is, in its nature, constituted in the first instance, not so much by the property of immateriality, but primarily by the ability to enter into relations with Being as a totality. "Spirit" refers to an ability to enter into relations of such expansive and comprehensive power that the field of relations corresponding to it fundamentally transcends environmental boundaries. It belongs to the very nature of spirit that its field of relations is the world; the spirit does not have an environment, it has a world. It belongs to the very nature of a spiritual being to rise above the environment and so transcend both adaptation and confinement (this explains the at once liberating and imperiling character with which the nature of spirit is immediately associated).

In Aristotle's work *De anima*, there is a passage where he concludes: "Let us now summarize our results about soul, and repeat that the soul is in a way all existing things"[21]—a phrase that became practically a fixed expression in the anthropology of the High Middle

---

[21] *De anima* 3.8.431b21. [Quoted after Richard McKeon, *Introduction to Aristotle* (Chicago, 1973), p. 235.]

Ages: the soul is in a certain sense all, that is, everything ("anima est quodammodo omnia"). "In a certain sense" because the soul is all only insofar as it, in knowing, is able to put itself into relation with the totality of Being (and to know something means to become identical with the real being as known—this can, however, not be explored in more detail here). The spiritual soul, so writes Aquinas in his *De veritate* (*On Truth*), is essentially so constituted as to come together with all beings ("convenire cum omni ente"),[22] to enter into relation with the totality of that which has being. "Every other being has only a partial share in Being", whereas the ensouled creature "is able to grasp Being as a whole".[23] Insofar as there is spirit, "it is possible for the perfection of all that is to exist in a single being."[24] This, then, represents the judgment of Western tradition, that to have spirit, to be spirit, to be spiritual—all this means to exist amid reality as a whole, in the face of the totality of Being, *vis-à-vis de l'univers*. Spirit does not live in "a" world or in "its" world but in "the" world—world in the sense of *visibilia omnia et invisibilia*.

Spirit and the totality of the real—these are reciprocal concepts that correspond to one another. One cannot "have" the one without the other. An attempt (it is noted in passing) to ascribe to man superiority over his environment, that is, to assert that man has a world (not an environment) *without*, however, referring to his spirituality —even going so far as to assert that the one fact (that is, that man has a world and not simply an environment) has nothing to do with the other (that is, that man is an ensouled being)—such an attempt— was undertaken by Arnold Gehlen in his voluminous, much-discussed work *Der Mensch: Seine Nature und seine Stellung in der Welt* (*Man: His Nature and Place in the World*).[25] One cannot "have" the one without the other. Gehlen rightly objects to Uexküll's thesis by observing that man is not, like an animal, confined to an environment, that man is without environment and open to the world. Still, Gehlen continues, this distinction between the animal as a being with its own environ-

---

[22] *Ver.* 1, 1.

[23] *C.G.* 3, 112.

[24] *Ver.* 2, 2.

[25] Arnold Gehlen, *Der Mensch: Seine Natur und seine Stellung in der Welt* (Berlin, 1940). [English trans.: *Man, His Nature and Place in the World*, trans. Clare McMillan and Karl Pillemer (New York: Columbia Univ. Press, 1988).]

ment and man as a being open to the world is "not [based] on the property . . . of spirit".* But it is precisely this ability to have a world which *is* spirit!

For ancient philosophy—Plato, Aristotle, Augustine, Aquinas—the relation between the concepts of "spirit" and "world" (in the sense of reality as a whole) is itself so intimately and deeply rooted in both members of the relation that not only the one proposition, according to which "spirit is a state of relatedness to the totality of existing things" was deemed true; for the ancients, the corresponding proposition asserting the essential relatedness of all existing things to spirit was considered equally valid—and that in a very precise sense, which we are hardly able to put into words. Not only that it belongs to the nature of spirit that its field of relations is the totality of existing things but that it also belongs to the nature of existing things that they lie in the spirit's field of relations. Indeed, it is from the point of view of ancient philosophy a matter of indifference whether I say "the things have being" or whether I say "the things lie in the spirit's field of relations, they are related to spirit"—in saying this, of course, we are referring, not to a "free-floating" spirituality in some abstract sense, but to a personal spirit, an ability to entertain relations that is grounded in itself, and by this we mean, in turn, not only God but a created, nonabsolute human spirit! For ancient ontology it belongs to the nature of Being to lie within the reach of the intellectual soul, within its field of relations. "To have being" is synonymous with "lying within the spiritual soul's field of relations"; both expressions refer to one and the same state of affairs. This and only this corresponds to the meaning behind the old proposition whose understanding had completely eluded us—everything that exists is true ("omne ens est verum")—and behind that other proposition, which is identical in meaning with it—" 'being' and 'true' are interchangeable terms." What does truth in the sense of material truth, the truth of things, mean? "A thing is true" means that it is known and knowable—known by absolute spirit and knowable by nonabsolute spirit.

---

* [Ibid., p. 24. Gehlen, however, influenced by the criticism offered here, modified his position in later editions. Now, with a significant qualification, the concept of man's constitution is said to rest "*not* on the property of the understanding alone" (*Gesamtausgabe*, ed. K.-S. Rehberg [Frankfurt am Main, 1993]).—ED.]

(I must ask you simply to accept this; it is unfortunately not possible to defend this interpretation in detail here.)[26] The state of being known or knowable—what are these if not states of being related to knowing spirit? Thus, when in ancient philosophy it is asserted that it belongs to the nature of existing things that they be known and knowable, that there is absolutely no being that is not known or knowable (*every* being is true!), and when ancient philosophy even goes so far as to assert that the concepts "being" and "known/knowable" are interchangeable—the one can do proxy for the other so that it is a matter of indifference whether I say, "The things have being", or I say, "The things are known and knowable"—then ancient philosophy is expressing, with all that, precisely this thought, that is, that it lies in the nature of the things themselves to be related to spirit. (And this is the only element in the concept of a "truth of things" that is important for the consideration of our question.)

Let us then recapitulate: The world corresponding to spiritual being is the totality of existing things; this is true to such an extent that this correspondence belongs as much to the nature of spirit—spirit is the ability to grasp the totality of Being—as it does to the nature of existing things—to be means to be related to spirit.

A hierarchy of "worlds" has presented itself to us: at the bottom of that hierarchy was the world of plants, limited already spatially by proximity of contact; after that, the different environments corresponding to different animals; and finally, encompassing all these partial worlds, the world corresponding to spirit, the *real* world as the totality of Being. And this hierarchy of worlds, of fields of relations, corresponds, as we have seen, to a hierarchy of faculties for entering into relations: the more extensive the power to entertain relations, the more multi-dimensioned the accompanying field of relations, the corresponding "world". A third element has still to be added to this two-tiered hierarchy, namely, the fact that a more powerful ability to enter into relations corresponds to a higher degree of interiority; that the ability to entertain relations is more or less extensive, more or less inclusive, to the same degree that the bearer of relations is more or less "interiorized" [*innenhaft*]; that, for example, the most negligi-

---

[26] Cf. J. Pieper, *Wahrheit der Dinge: Eine Untersuchung zur Anthropologie des Hochmittelalters* (Munich, 1948).

ble ability to enter into relations corresponds not only to the most negligible form of world but also to the most negligible degree of being-in-itself just as the ultimate form of being-in-itself must correspond to spirit, as the ability to enter into relations with the totality of Being. The more comprehensive the ability to relate to the world of objective being, the more deeply rooted the support for such expansions is in the interior of the subject. And where an ultimate degree of "world breadth" has in principle been attained, that is, an orientation toward totality, then, theoretically, the highest stage of being-grounded-in-itself, which is peculiar to spirit, has also been reached. Thus the two, taken together, constitute the nature of spirit: not only the ability to enter into relations with the *totum* of world and reality, but also an utmost ability to reside within oneself, a faculty for being-in-oneself, a capacity for independence, for autonomy—precisely that which in the Western tradition has always been identified with being a person and with having a personality. To have a world, to be related to the totality of existing things, can be attributed only to a being that is grounded in itself, not a "what", but a "who", the self as "I", a person.

This is an appropriate time to cast a glance back at the questions from which we proceeded: There were two, one more immediate—How is man's world constituted?—the other farther off: What does it mean to philosophize?

Before we take these questions up again in a formal way, a note, first, on the structure of the world corresponding to spirit. Of course, it is not only the greater reach of its spatial expanse that distinguishes the world corresponding to the spiritual being from the environment of the nonspiritual being (in the controversy concerning the distinction between world and environment this is not always taken into account). It is not only the "totality of things" but the "essence of things" through which the world corresponding to spirit is constituted. *That is why* the animal is confined within a cross-sectional milieu, that is, because the essence of things remains closed to it. And only because spirit is able to attain to the essence of things has the ability been granted to it to grasp the *all*. This relationship was construed by the ancient theory of Being as suggesting that the cosmos as well as the essence of things is "universal". Aquinas writes, "Because it is capable of grasping the universal, the intellectual soul has the power of the infinite."[27] Whoever in knowing attains to the universal, unified essence of things gains, in so doing, a perspective from which the totality of being, all existing things, becomes accessible and perceivable; in the intellectual act of knowing, an outpost is reached or can be reached from which the terrain of the universe may be surveyed. A context has opened up here of which we can catch only a glimpse, but that glimpse leads right to the heart of a philosophical theory of being, of knowledge, and of spirit.

Now let us return, however, to those questions which we first set out to answer. First, let us take a step in the direction of the more immediate question: How is the world of man constituted? Is the world corresponding to spirit the world of man? One would have to reply: The world of man is coterminous with the totality of the real, man lives amid and in the face of the totality of existing things, *vis-à-vis de l'univers*—*insofar as* man is spirit! He is, however, not only not pure spirit; he is finite spirit—consequently, the essence of things and the totality of things are given to him, not with the finality of perfect comprehension, but "in hope". We will speak more extensively about this in our next lecture.

Prior to that, however, we must consider the following: Man is not pure spirit. One can utter this sentence with varying intonations. It is not uncommon to utter it in the form of a regret—an emphasis that is typically regarded by Christians and non-Christians alike as something specifically Christian. The sentence may be given such an intonation that it carries the following implication: Granted, man is not pure spirit, but the "real person" is identical with intellectual soul. These views, however, find no support in the classical dogmatic tradition of the Christian West. In Thomas Aquinas, there may be found in this connection a little-known but extremely pointed formulation; he raises the following objection: "Man's goal is, indeed, the perfect imitation of God. The soul, when separated from the body, is more similar to God, who is of course incorporeal, than the soul when combined with the body. And for this reason the souls are separated from the body in the state of final bliss." This is the substance of the objection in which the thesis that the genuine person is the intellectual soul is adorned with the seductive pomp of sublime theological

---

[27] I, 76, 5 ad 4.

argumentation. Aquinas responds to this objection as follows: "The soul, when united with the body, is more similar to God than the soul when separated from the body, because it possesses its own nature in a more perfect manner"[28]—a not easily comprehensible sentence that implies, not only that man is corporeal, but also that the soul itself is, in a certain sense, corporeal.

If, however, this is the case, if man is *by nature* "not only spirit"; if man is positively and most intrinsically a being in which the onto-logical realms of the vegetative, the animal, and the spiritual life are bound up into a unity and not on the basis of some inner failing or by virtue of his having fallen short of his genuine being—then man *by nature* does not live exclusively in the face of reality as a whole, the absolute world of essences. His field of relations consists, rather, of an intertwining of "world" and "environment"—and necessarily so, in keeping with the nature of man. Since man is not pure spirit, he cannot live only "under the stars", not only *vis-à-vis de l'univers*; he needs a roof over his head; he needs the trusted proximity to the environment of his day-to-day dwelling; he needs the sensuous near-ness of the concrete, he needs to accommodate himself within the fit of normal relations. In a word, the surrounding world [*Um-welt*], or environment—and in precisely that sense in which it is to be distin-guished from the world [*Welt*]—is just as much a part of a genuinely human life.

It is at the same time part of spiritual-corporeal man that the veg-etative and sensitive realms are informed by the intellectual soul—so much so that, for example, man's consumption of nutrients fun-damentally differs from that of animals (to say nothing of the fact that the human realm also has the "feast", something that is clearly spiritual). The remaining realms are so thoroughly informed by the intellectual soul that even when man "vegetates", this is possible only on the basis of spirit (the plant does not "vegetate", any more than animals do!). And even the in-human—the self-confinement of man within his environment (that is, within the cross-sectional world de-fined by the immediate necessities of life)—even this aberration is possible only on the basis of a *spiritual* aberration. By contrast, it is human to know of the stars above one's roof, to perceive the totality

---

[28] *Pot.* 5, 10 ad 5.

of existing things beyond the familiar housing of our habitual accommodation to the everyday, to perceive beyond the environment and,
encompassing it, the world.

With this, however, we have advanced, completely unawares, to our
actual question: What does it mean to philosophize? Philosophizing
means precisely this: to experience that the proximate environment
corresponding to the workday world of everyday life, which is governed by the immediate necessities of life, can be disrupted time and
again by the disquieting interjection of the "world", of reality as a
whole, as mirrored in the eternal archetypes of the things themselves.
The act of philosophizing consists in—remember, we had been asking: Whither does the philosophical act penetrate in transcending the
workday world?—taking the step from the cross-sectional milieu of
the workday world into the *vis-à-vis de l'univers*. It is a step that leads
to a state of "unhousedness"; the stars do not put a roof over one's
head. A step, then, that will always leave open the possibility of return,
for man cannot live indefinitely in this manner. Who would seriously
want to maintain that it is possible fully and irrevocably to desert the
workday world of the Thracian maiden—unless he abandons human
reality itself! Exactly the same point is being made here that Aquinas
made with reference to the *vita contemplativa*: the act of philosophizing
is actually something superhuman ("non proprie humana, sed super-
humana").[29] Still, man is himself something superhuman; man transcends himself, as Pascal says, to an infinite degree; the attempt to
formulate a polished definition does not measure up to man.

We have no intention here, however, of further developing these
thoughts, which seem to lead in the direction of fanaticism. We prefer
instead, on the basis of what has already been demonstrated, to pose
anew the question of what it means to philosophize, but this time in
a very concrete and, as it were, down-to-earth manner and to attempt,
in a first approximation, to answer it. How does a philosophical question differ from a nonphilosophical one? To philosophize means, as
we have already said, to direct one's glance at the totality of the world.
Is, then, *that* question—and only it—which expressly and formally
takes as its subject the totality of being, all existing things, a philosophical question? No! What is, however, peculiar to, and distinctive

---

[29] *Virt. card.* 1.

of, a philosophical question is that it cannot be posed, reflected on, or answered (insofar as an answer is possible at all) without at the same time invoking God and the world, that is, the totality of what is.

Let us speak, once again, very concretely. The question "what are we doing here and now?" can obviously mean different things; it *can* also be a philosophical question. Let us see! The question can be so formulated that a superficial answer relating to technical issues of organization is expected. "What is going on here?" "A lecture is being held here in connection with the week of higher learning in Bonn." This is a concise, informative statement, which belongs to a precisely demarcated, fully illuminated world (or rather, environment). This answer is given with a view to what is most immediately relevant. But the question may also have been intended differently; it may be that the questioner would be unsatisfied with such an answer. "What are we doing here and now?": one person speaks; the others listen to the words being spoken; and the listeners "understand" what is said. Roughly the same intellectual process takes place in the many listeners: what is spoken is interpreted, thought through, considered, acknowledged, rejected, accepted with reservations, incorporated within the individual's own conceptual framework. This question aims at eliciting the kind of answer given by the special sciences; it may mean that the physiology of the senses and psychology (the psychology of perception, the psychology of apprehension, the psychology of learning, the psychology of memory, and so on) are being called upon to answer it and would suffice for this purpose. Such an answer would in a broader, more multi-dimensional world correspond to the superficial answer, insofar as it responds to purely technical and organizational concerns. But the answer of the special sciences does not yet have as its horizon the totality of the real; this answer may be given *without* having at the same time to refer to God and the world. If, however, the question "what are we doing here and now?" is intended as a *philosophical* question, then that is not possible; if the question is intended in such a way that one is at the same time inquiring after the essence of knowledge, the essence of truth, or even simply after the essence of learning. What does it mean to teach, ultimately and in the final analysis? One person comes along and says a human being cannot really teach at all; it is just like when a person recovers from an illness: it is not the doctor who has cured him but nature, whose therapeutic powers the doctor has (perhaps) simply released. Another person happens along and says that it is God who provides inner instruction—on the occasion of mortal teaching. Now Socrates comes along and says that the teacher merely ensures that the learner, in recollecting, "recovers it [knowledge] for himself"; "there is no such thing as teaching, only recollection."[30] Still another comes along and says that we human beings all confront the same reality; the teacher gestures toward it; the learners, the listeners, then look for themselves.

What is it that are we doing here? Something that has been organized in connection with a series of lectures; something capable of being understood and investigated by physiology and psychology; something intermediate between God and the world.

This, then, is what is peculiar to and distinctive of a philosophical question, namely, that that which constitutes the nature of spirit, the *convenire cum omni ente* or the coming together with everything that is, appears in pure form. One cannot question and think philosophically without implicating the totality of being, all existing things, "God and the world".

III p. 28

We had established that both the need to adjust himself to his "environment" and his orientation toward the totality of Being, or world, are peculiar to man and that it is of the essence of the philosophical act to transcend the "environment" and to press forth into the "world".

Now, this should not, of course, be understood to mean that there exist two separate compartments, as it were, and that man can leave the one and enter the other; it is not as if there were some things that are characterized by their having a place in the "environment", and other things that are not to be encountered in the environment but only in this other realm, the "world". Clearly, environment and world (as we are employing these terms) do not stand for two separate realms of reality—as if the philosophical inquirer were letting himself out of the one realm and into the other! The philosophizing person

---

[30] *Meno* 85d4; 82a1f. [Quoted after the translation by W. K. C. Guthrie, in *Plato: The Collected Dialogues*, pp. 370, 364.]

does not turn his head the other way when he, in the act of philosophizing, transcends the workday environment; he does not avert
his gaze from the things belonging to the world of work, from the
concrete, useful, handy things of the work day; he does not look in
another direction in order to behold the universal world of essences.

On the contrary, it is the same visible, concrete world that lies
before all our eyes toward which philosophical contemplation is directed. This world, these things, these states of affairs are, however,
questioned in a special manner; they are questioned with regard to
their ultimate, universal, unified essence, whereby the interrogative
horizon becomes identical with the horizon of reality as a whole.
The philosophical question undoubtedly extends to "this" or "that",
to what lies before our eyes; it does not extend to something that
lies "outside the world" or "in another world", beyond the world of
everyday experience. But the philosophical question takes the form:
What is "this" *ultimately and in the final analysis*? Plato writes, "[T]he
philosopher drags the other upward to a height at which he may con-
sent to drop the question, 'What injustice have I done to you or you
to me?' and to think about justice and injustice in themselves . . . , or
to stop quoting poetry about the happiness of kings or of men with
gold in store and think about the meaning of kingship and the whole
question of human happiness and misery"[31]—that is, the meaning of
kingship, happiness, and misery, ultimately and in the final analysis.

Philosophical questioning is, then, clearly directed toward what lies
before our eyes every day. What lies before our eyes becomes, however, transparent to the questioner from one moment to the next; it
loses its compactness, its apparent finality, its matter-of-factness. The
things present an alien, an unknown, an unfamiliar, a more profound
physiognomy. The questioner, Socrates, who knows how to deprive
things abruptly of their matter-of-factness likens himself to a stingray
whose sting paralyzes. Every day we tell ourselves, this is "my" friend,
"my" wife, "my" house; that one "has" and "possesses" all this. All
of a sudden, we stop short: do we really have all these "possessions"?
Can they be "had" at all? What does it mean to possess something
ultimately and in the final analysis?

---

[31] *Theaetetus* 175c1ff. [Quoted after the translation by Cornford, in *Plato: The Collected
Dialogues*, p. 880.]

Philosophizing means distancing oneself, not from the things of everyday life, but from their common interpretations, from the prevailing valuations given these things. And this distancing takes place, not on the basis of any decision to stand out, to think "differently" from the many, but because, suddenly, the things have acquired a new physiognomy. It is just this state of affairs, that is, that the more profound physiognomy of the real becomes perceivable in the manipulated things of everyday life (and not in a realm of "essences", distinct from the "everyday" or whatever one chooses to call it); that is, that the extraordinary, that which is no longer self-evident concerning these things, opposes itself to our gaze, which is directed toward the things encountered in everyday experience—it is just this state of affairs that corresponds to that inner event in which one has always recognized, as constituting the origin of philosophy—wonder.

"Indeed, it is extraordinary how they set me wondering whatever they [these things] can mean. Sometime I can get quite dizzy with thinking of them", the young mathematician Theaetetus exclaims (paralyzed by wonder!), after Socrates, the affecting and paralyzing questioner, at once cunning and helpless, has made him recognize and concede his lack of knowledge. And this is followed in Plato's dialogue, the *Theaetetus*, by Socrates' reply: "This sense of wonder is the mark of the philosopher. Philosophy indeed has no other origin."[32] Here for the first time, in the serenity of an early morning, and without much fanfare, almost in passing, a thought is expressed that has practically become a commonplace in the history of philosophy: the origin of philosophy lies in wonder.

This fact, that philosophizing begins in wonder, points up the fundamentally nonbourgeois character of philosophy, for wonder is something nonbourgeois (if we may be allowed, not entirely in good conscience, to employ this all too common terminology for a moment). What, after all, does the process of becoming a bourgeois imply in the spiritual sense? Above all, the following: that one understand the proximate environment, which is governed by the immediate necessities of life, to be so compact that the things encountered are no longer capable of being made transparent. One no longer suspects the

---

[32] Ibid., 155d1ff. [Quoted after the translation by Cornford, in *Plato: The Collected Dialogues*, p. 860.]

existence of a larger, deeper, and more authentic—initially "invisible" —world of "essences"; the wondrous no longer shows itself [*vorkom-men*], is no longer brought forth [*hervorkommen*]; man is no longer capable of wondering.

The dulled sense of the philistine finds everything self-evident. What, then, is, in fact, self-evident? Is it self-evident that we exist? Is it self-evident that something like vision exists? Someone who is confined to the everyday, to the inner everyday, cannot ask such questions if only because he cannot succeed (at least not consciously in waking life but at best in a state of stupefaction) in completely forgetting the immediate necessities of life, while precisely this characterizes the wondering person, that is, that for him, for the person who has been struck by the deeper physiognomy of the world, the immediate necessities of life fall mute, if only for this one moment of impassioned gazing at the wonder-inspiring physiognomy of the world.

It is thus the wondering person who alone realizes that primordial relation to Being in pure form which, since Plato, has been called *theoria*, a strictly passive attending to reality, which is not troubled by any intercession of the will (we recall here what was said in the first lecture). *Theoria* only exists insofar as man has not become blind to the wondrous, which is wonder before the fact that something is. For it is not, in fact, what never was—the abnormal, the sensational —that incites philosophical wonder—something like that could be experienced as a substitute for authentic wonder only by a dulled intelligence. Whoever requires the unusual in order to fall into wonder shows himself by virtue of this very fact to be someone who has lost the ability to respond correctly to the *mirandum* of Being. The need for the sensational, even if it prefers to present itself under the guise of the bohemian, is an unmistakable sign of the absence of a genuine capacity for wonder and hence of a bourgeois mentality.

To preserve the genuinely unfamiliar and extraordinary, the *mirandum, in* the familiar and ordinary—that, then, is the origin of philosophizing. And in this the philosophical act, as Aristotle and Aquinas assert, is related to the poetic one: both the philosopher and the poet are concerned with the astounding [*Erstaunliche*], which calls forth and encourages wonder. As concerns the poet, specifically, the seventy-year-old Goethe concludes a short poem ("Parabase") with the verse, "I exist to be astounded [*zum Erstaunen*]", and the eighty-year-old says to Eckermann:[33] "The ultimate to which man can aspire is wonder [*das Erstaunen*]."

The "nonbourgeoisness" of the philosopher and the poet—that is, that they preserve the capacity for wonder in such pure and powerful form—also carries with it, however, the risk of their becoming uprooted from the workday world. A certain starry-eyedness with regard to life and the world is, in fact, an occupational hazard for the philosopher as well as the poet (of course there are no philosophers in the professional sense any more than there are professional poets; man *can*not live indefinitely in this state, as has already been noted). Wonder does not make one industrious, for wonder implies that one has been shaken. Whoever undertakes to live in accordance with that old exclamation of wonder "why is there something at all?" will have to prepare himself for the fact that he might some day lose his bearings in the workday world. The person for whom everything encountered has become a *mirandum* may sooner or later forget how to wield those very same things that he encounters on an everyday basis.

This notwithstanding, it remains true that the capacity for wonder belongs to the highest possibilities of man's nature. Aquinas finds precisely in this a proof of the fact that man can find satisfaction only in the vision of God, and, conversely, he recognizes in man's directedness toward knowledge of the absolute cause of the world the reason why man is capable of wonder. Aquinas believes that in the very first moment of wonder man sets his foot on the path at the end of which lies the *visio beatifica*, the blissful perception of the ultimate cause. That man's nature is geared toward nothing less than such an end is shown by the fact that man is capable of experiencing the *mirandum* of creation, of wonder.

The shock [*Erschütterung*] that the person in wonder experiences, the shaking-up [*Erschütterung*] of the hitherto self-evident, which now abruptly—in one moment—loses its compact matter-of-factness—this shaking-up can, as has been pointed out, uproot the wondering person. But not only in this way, that is, insofar as he loses the certainty of his everyday dealings (this is, at bottom, something innocuous), but also in the more pernicious sense that, as a *knower*, rather than simply as agent, the earth is removed from under his feet.

---

[33] Conversations with Eckermann, February 18, 1829.

Now it is something very curious to observe that modern philosophy has given almost exclusive attention to this aspect so that the
ancient maxim concerning wonder has been construed as meaning
that doubt stands at the beginning of philosophy.

Thus, when speaking of Socrates and of his method of engendering
wonder in his interlocutor in the face of the apparently self-evident,
Hegel claims in his lecture on the history of philosophy that his main
purpose in so doing is to create confusion: "It is confusion with
which philosophy must above all begin and that it calls forth from
itself; one must doubt everything, one must abandon all presuppositions in order to acquire them anew as something generated by the
Notion."[34] Windelband is thoroughly in keeping with this—in effect
—Cartesian approach when in his famous *Einleitung in die Philosophie*
(Introduction to Philosophy) he translates the Greek word θαυμάζειν
almost literally into German as "thought's being confused by itself".[35]
(Chesterton, let it be noted in passing here, made an apt remark on
such "presuppositionlessness" to the effect that there is a peculiar form
of madness that consists in losing everything but one's reason.)

Is, however, the true sense of wonder really supposed to lie in this
uprooting, in the raising of doubt? Or does it consist in allowing and
compelling thought to take new and deeper root? Certainly, in wonder (which, like disillusionment, is at bottom something positive: the
liberation from an illusion) and for the wondering person, the penultimate self-evident facts lose their hitherto unquestioned validity; it is
revealed that these "self-evident facts" are not definitively so. But the
meaning of wonder lies in the experience that the world is more profound, more commodious, more mysterious than it appears to our everyday understanding. The inner intentionality of wonder is fulfilled
in the development of a sense of mystery. This inner directionality
does not aim at raising doubt but at awakening the knowledge that
Being as Being is incomprehensible and mysterious—that Being is
itself a mystery, a mystery in the authentic sense, not sheer impass-
ability, not absurdity, not even genuine obscurity. Mystery implies,
rather, that a reality is *for this reason* incomprehensible, namely, that

[34] *Vorlesungen über die Geschichte der Philosophie II*, Sämtliche Werke, Jubiläums-Ausgabe, vol. 18, ed. H. Glockner (Stuttgart, 1927), p. 69.
[35] W. Windelband, *Einleitung in die Philosophie* (Tübingen, 1923), p. 6.

its light is unquenchable, unfathomable, inexhaustible. This is what the person in wonder actually experiences.

With this it has become evident that wonder and philosophizing are bound up with each other in a much more fundamental sense than the maxim "wonder is the origin of philosophy" would seem to suggest at first glance. Wonder is not simply the origin of philosophy in the sense of *initium*, beginning, first stage, preliminary step. Rather, wonder is the *principium*, the enduring wellspring inherent in philosophizing. It is not as if the philosophizing person, in philosophizing, "emerges from wonder"—he simply *fails* to emerge from wonder unless he ceases to philosophize in the genuine sense. The inner form of philosophizing is virtually identical with the inner form of wonder. Since we have posed ourselves the question, "what does it mean to philosophize?" we must therefore examine the inner form of wonder more carefully.

Wonder has two aspects: a negative and a positive one. The negative one is that the person in wonder does not know, does not comprehend; that he is not aware of "what is behind it all"; that, as Aquinas writes, "the cause of that which incites in us wonder is concealed from us."[36] Whoever wonders, then, does not know—or, more precisely, does not know completely—he does not comprehend. Whoever comprehends does not wonder. It cannot be said of God that he wonders—because God knows in the most complete manner. And what is more: the person in wonder not only does not know; he becomes conscious of the fact that he does not know; he identifies himself with his not knowing. Still this not-knowing is not the same as resignation. On the contrary, the wondering person is one who sets himself on a path; this is a part of wonder as well: that the person, once moved, not only falls mute but sets off on the search. In his *Summa theologica*,[37] Aquinas practically equates wonder with the *desiderium sciendi*, the yearning after knowledge, the active longing for knowledge.

Wonder, like not knowing, is not only not synonymous with resignation: from wonder stems joy, wrote Aristotle;[38] and the Middle

[36] *Pot.* 6, 2.
[37] I, II, 32, 8.
[38] *Rhetoric* 1.11.1371a30ff.

Ages followed him in arguing that what incites wonder and causes joy are the one and the same ("omnia admirabilia sunt delectabilia").[39] One might perhaps venture the hypothesis that wherever spiritual joy is to be found, there wonder may also be encountered; and wherever the capacity for joy exists, there is also the ability to wonder. The joy of the wondering person is the joy of the initiate, a spirit that is prepared for, and expectant of, the ever new, the still unheard.

In this combination of affirmation and negation is manifested that structure of hope—that blueprint for hope—which, while characteristic of wonder, is also peculiar to philosophizing and to human existence itself. We are essentially *viatores*, underway, "not yet" existing. Who among us would go so far as to claim that he already possesses the being that has been thought out for us? "We are not, we hope to be", as it is written in Pascal.[40] And in the fact that wonder has the structure of hope is revealed the extent to which wonder is a part of human existence. Ancient philosophy, in fact, understood wonder to be something distinctively human. Absolute spirit does not wonder because the negative aspect of wonder does not apply to it; because in God there is no not-knowing—only someone who does not comprehend wonders. But animals also do not wonder—because, as Aquinas points out, "it does not fall to the perceiving soul to trouble itself about the knowledge of causes";[41] because the positive aspect inherent in the structure of hope that underlies wonder does not apply to them—the intentionality of knowledge. Only those who do "not yet" know wonder. So convinced were the ancients that wonder is something distinctively human that there was even an "argument from wonder" that was proffered as an argument in favor of the genuine humanity of Christ in the controversies surrounding christological dogma. Arius had denied the divinity of Christ, to which Apollinaris opposed the thesis that in Christ the eternal *logos* had assumed the place of the intellectual soul and immediately fused itself to the body. (We are, of course, not concerned with the theological aspect of this argument, but in such theological contexts one finds the views of the ancient theory of Being uttered, as it were, "under oath"!)

---

[39] I, II, 32, 8.
[40] *Pensées*, no. 172 (according to L. Brunschvicg's numbering).
[41] C.G. 4, 33.

Against this doctrine, according to which full humanity in the corporeal and spiritual sense could not be ascribed to Christ, Aquinas
put forward, among other arguments, the argument from wonder.
Aquinas' argument ran as follows: In the Holy Scriptures (Lk 7:9),
it is reported that Christ was astonished (in the story, a centurion
from Capernaum says, "Lord, do not trouble yourself, . . . but say
the word . . ."; "When Jesus heard this he marveled at him"). If,
however, Jesus was capable of wonder, then—so Aquinas—"beyond
the divinity of the Word and beyond the perceiving soul" (it being
common to both that they are incapable of wonder!) something must
be assumed to be in Christ, in conformity with which wonder might
be predicated of him, and this something is the *mens humana*, "the human intellectual soul".[42] The proximate environment of a sensuously
given reality can become transparent only to an intellectual faculty
of knowledge that does not possess and intuit everything at once—
that is, for the wondering person!—but that does so only gradually
so that ever more fundamental depths become manifest.

This quality of being something distinctively human is also characteristic of philosophizing. "None of the gods are seekers after truth",
so Diotima is made to speak in Plato's *Symposium*.[43] "Nor, for that
matter, do the ignorant seek the truth. . . . And, indeed, what makes
their case so hopeless is that . . . they are satisfied with what they are."
" 'Then tell me, Diotima,' I [Socrates] said, "who are these seekers
after truth, if they are neither the wise nor the ignorant?' 'Why, a
schoolboy', she replied 'could have told you that. . . . They are those
that come between the two.' " This in-between, however, corresponds
to the realm of the genuinely human. It is genuinely human not to
comprehend (the way God does) but also not to become rigid; not
to confine oneself within the presumably fully illuminated world of
everyday life; not to rest content with one's ignorance; not to lose
that childishly fluid openness which is peculiar to the hoping person
and only to him.

The attitude of the philosophizing person, like that of the person in
wonder, is for this reason to be preferred to the despairing provincial-

---

[42] Ibid.
[43] *Symposium* 204a1–b2. [Quoted after the translation by Joyce, in *Plato: The Collected Dialogues*, p. 556.]

ity of a dulled intelligence—he is a hopeful person! But he is, in turn, *inferior to* those who possess something definitively, who know and comprehend—he remains hopeful, a wondering and philosophizing person.

It is also by virtue of this element of hope (among other things!) that philosophy is distinguished from the special sciences. Philosophy has a fundamentally different relation to its object than the individual sciences do to theirs. The questions dealt with in the special sciences can, in principle, be answered definitively, or, at the very least, they are not unanswerable in principle. It can be determined conclusively (or one will presumably someday be able to determine) what the virus causing this infectious illness is. It is in principle possible that one will someday be able to say that it has now been demonstrated in a scientifically irreproachable way that such-and-such is the case and not otherwise. No one, however, will ever be able to answer a philosophical question (what is this "ultimately and in the final analysis"? What is illness as such? What is knowledge as such? What is man?) conclusively and definitively. "No philosopher has ever been capable of completely tracking down the essence of even a single mosquito"[44]—this sentence stems from Aquinas (who at the same time thought, however, that "the knowing spirit penetrates into the essence of things").[45] The object of philosophy is given to the philosophizing person in hope. Dilthey's remark should be understood in this context: "The demands of the philosophizing person are unrealizable. The physicist stands for a comforting reality, useful to himself and others; the philosopher exists like a holy man, as an ideal."[46] It lies in the nature of the special sciences that they emerge from wonder insofar as they arrive at "results". The philosopher, by contrast, does not emerge from wonder.

With these same words both the greatness and the limitations of science are being addressed as well as the station and dubiety of philosophy. To be sure, it is "in itself" better to dwell "under the stars". But man is not so constituted that he can endure such dwelling indefinitely! Certainly, it is a question of greater importance that aims

---

[44] *Symb. Apost.*, prologue (no. 864).

[45] I, II, 31, 5.

[46] *Briefwechsel zwischen Wilhelm Dilthey und dem Grafen Paul Yorck v. Wartenberg 1877–1897* (Halle-Saale, 1923), p. 39.

at the world as totality and at the ultimate nature of things. But the answer is not directly accessible to us the way answers are accessible to the questions of the special sciences.

It is the negative aspect, in particular, that, insofar as it is given along with the structure of hope, has belonged to the concept of philosophy from the very beginning and that indeed, was even more pronouncedly a part of it at the beginning. From its inception, philosophy has in no way understood itself to be a superior form of knowledge but rather has consciously regarded itself as a form of knowing self-abnegation. According to legend—by then an already ancient legend—the terms "philosophy" and "philosopher" were coined by Pythagoras—and that in marked contrast with the words *sophia* and *sophos*: no man is wise and knowing; wise and knowing is God alone. And for that reason man can at best deem himself a loving seeker of wisdom, a *philosophos*. Plato speaks in exactly the same manner: the question is raised in the *Phaedrus* of which epithet Solon and, for that matter, Homer deserve: "To call him wise, Phaedrus, would I think be going too far; the epithet is proper only to a god. A name that would fit him better, and have more seemliness, would be 'lover of wisdom,' or something similar."[47]

These anecdotes are, of course, well known. But we are all too inclined to dismiss them as purely anecdotal, as something that is more at home in the rhetorical realm. Sufficient reason exists, I believe, however, to attempt to exercise more caution here and to take seriously and precisely the implications of this etymology.

What exactly is being said, however? Two points are, above all, being expressed. The first point that is being made is that we do not "have" the knowledge, the wisdom, toward which philosophical questioning aims and that our not having it is not simply provisional or accidental but that we *can*not have it in principle; that our not having it represents an eternal "not yet".

The question concerning essence actually includes a claim to comprehension on the part of the would-be knower. To comprehend something means—so Aquinas argues—to know it insofar as it is intelligible in itself, to transform every type of intelligibility into

---

[47] *Phaedrus* 278d2ff. [Quoted after the translation by R. Hackforth, in *Plato: The Collected Dialogues*, p. 524.]

knownness, to know something through and through and "to its very depths".[48] Now, there is absolutely nothing that man in this way—that is, as something comprehended in the strict sense—could know. Consequently, it belongs to the nature of the question concerning essence, that is, of the philosophical question (insofar as it is articulated by someone), that it cannot be answered in the same way in which it is posed. It belongs to the nature of philosophy that it aims at a wisdom that nevertheless remains unattainable to it, albeit not in such a way that absolutely no relation obtains between the two. This wisdom is the object of philosophy—but as something lovingly sought, not something that is ever had. This, then, is the first point that is being made in the Pythagorean and Socratic-Platonic interpretation of the word *philosophia*. This idea is taken up and made more precise in the *Metaphysics* of Aristotle. It also found its way, partly through Aristotle, into the works of the great medieval thinkers. Some very curious and penetrating variations on these ideas may be found, for example, in the commentary Aquinas wrote on the corresponding sections of Aristotle's *Metaphysics*. There the argument is made that because it is being sought for its own sake, wisdom cannot be the exclusive property of man. We are presumably able to "possess" the data of the special sciences wholly, but it belongs to the nature of these data that they are "means"; they cannot satisfy us in such a way that we are able to seek them entirely for their own sake. What is capable of satisfying us in this way and what is thus sought for its own sake—that is granted to us only in hope. "Only that wisdom is sought for its own sake", so it appears in Aquinas, "which is not owed to man as his property"; rather it is peculiar to the essence of a wisdom lovingly sought for its own sake that it falls to man as a loan ("sicut aliquid mutuatum").[49]

It belongs, then, to the nature of philosophy that it "has" its object in the manner of a loving search. With this, a very important point has been expressed—a point that is in no way uncontroversial. Hegel appears, for example, to contradict explicitly such a determination of philosophy by itself when, in the preface to his *Phenomenology of Spirit*, he declares himself to be working so that philosophy can "come closer

---

[48] *Super Joh.* I, 11 (no. 213).
[49] *In Met.* I, 3 (no. 64).

to the goal of being able to set aside the epithet 'love of wisdom', and become real knowledge—that is the task that I have set myself." This gives expression to a claim that fundamentally transcends what human means allow—a claim that led Goethe to speak of Hegel and philosophers of his ilk in an ironically dismissive tone as "these men who believe themselves capable of mastering God, the soul, and the world (and whatever other names might exist for what no one comprehends)."[50]

In that original construal of the word "philosophy", however, is contained yet a second idea, which only rarely tends to receive explicit attention. Both in the legendary utterance of Pythagoras and in Plato's *Phaedrus*, as well as in Aristotle, the human *philosophos* is contrasted with the divine *sophos*. Philosophy is not man's loving search for just any type of wisdom; it is oriented toward wisdom such as God possesses. Aristotle even goes so far as to refer to philosophy itself as "divine science" because it aims at a truth that only God fully possesses as his own.[51]

This second idea, which is also implicit in the original self-determination of philosophy, is subject to diverse construals. To begin with, the first thought (that is, that philosophy cannot ultimately comprehend its object) may be honed even further: the boundary that has been set here is more precisely defined as the boundary between man and divinity: man is as little capable of possessing that authentic wisdom as he is of ceasing to be a man. It also suggests that philosophy includes, in its essence, an orientation toward theology. Here an openness to theology is being posited as part of the original notion of philosophy. Thus something is being expressed here that clearly contradicts what in the modern age has become the accepted notion of philosophy; for this new conception of philosophy assumes that it is the decisive feature of philosophical thought to disengage itself from theology, faith, and tradition. And yet a third point is raised by the way in which philosophy defines itself in antiquity: the refusal on philosophy's part to regard itself as a doctrine of salvation.

But what is meant with "wisdom such as God possesses"? The conception of wisdom that is being invoked here can be summed up

---

[50] In a letter to Zelter dated October 27, 1827.
[51] *Metaphysics* 1.2.983a6–7.

as follows: "He is absolutely wise who knows the ultimate cause"[52] (whereby "cause" should not be understood only in the sense of an efficient cause, the formal cause being what is primarily meant). Such knowledge, however, in the sense of comprehending knowledge, can be attributed only to an absolute spirit, to God. Only God comprehends the world "from a single point", that is, from within himself, as its single ultimate cause. "He is wise who knows the ultimate cause": in this sense, only God may be called wise.

This, then, is the end toward which philosophy aims: understanding reality in terms of a single unified principle. It belongs, however, to the nature of philosophy that although it is "on the way" to this goal—indeed, in loving and hopeful pursuit!—it is fundamentally incapable of attaining it. The two aspects belong to the notion of philosophy, as it was developed and understood in antiquity.

This suggests, in turn, the critical notion that it is impossible to acquire from the concept of philosophy a rational interpretation of the world based on a single principle and derived from a knowledge of the "highest cause". In other words, there cannot be a "closed system" of philosophy. The claim to have discovered a cosmic formula is, then, by definition nonphilosophy and pseudo-philosophy!

And this notwithstanding, Aristotle[53] recognizes in philosophy, and in metaphysics specifically, the highest of the sciences, precisely because of its goal (that is, to know the ultimate cause), even though this goal is only attainable in hope and as a loan. And in his commentary Aquinas makes the following remark: "The little that is acquired in it [in metaphysics] outweighs everything else that is known by the sciences."[54]

Precisely in philosophy's twofold and Janus-faced structure, precisely in the fact that, in wonder, a path is being taken and tread that is, however, unending—precisely in the fact that philosophy has the structure of hope, it shows itself to be something thoroughly human, it shows itself, indeed, to be the fulfillment of human existence itself.

---

[52] II, II, 9, 2.
[53] *Metaphysics* 1.2.983a5–6.
[54] *In Met.* I, 3 (no. 60).

Man's relatedness to the totality of being is achieved in the philosophical act. Philosophizing is directed toward the world as a whole—that is what we have been arguing. Now, a certain interpretation of reality is given to man prior to *all* philosophy, always already preceding it— "always already", "since time immemorial". And this is an interpretation of reality, a tradition (in doctrine and anecdotes), that concerns and refers to the *entirety* of the world.

Man stands "always already" in a tradition of religious doctrine, which offers a picture of the world in its totality. It belongs to the essence of such a tradition to have "always already" existed and been in force—epistemically and logically prior to all philosophy, to all interpretations of the world that build on experience.

There is a theological view that traces this primordial tradition to a primordial revelation, a communication that occurred at the beginning of human history, an unveiling [*Enthüllung*] of the meaning of the world and the meaning of human history as a whole; a communication, albeit overgrown and encrusted, lives on in the myths and traditions of the different ethnic groups. We cannot explore this in more detail here.

It is important, however, for our purposes to recognize that the great initiators of Western philosophy, which continues to sustain contemporary philosophizing—that Plato and Aristotle, in particular —not only found ready-to-hand and identified a pregiven interpretation of the world but over and beyond this philosophized on the basis of this "always already" existing interpretation. "[T]hey alone [the forefathers] know the truth of it. However, if we could discover that for ourselves, should we still be concerned with the fancies of mankind?"[55] How often are we told in other passages of his that this or that doctrine was "handed down from the ancients" and is for this reason not only worthy of veneration but is also true in an exceptional —indeed, inviolable—way? "God, . . . as the old saw has it, holds in his hands beginning, end, middle of all that is [and] moves through the cycle of nature, straight to his end", as the elder Plato puts it

---

[55] *Phaedrus* 274c1ff. [Quoted after the translation by Hackforth, in *Plato: The Collected Dialogues*, p. 520.]

in the *Laws*.[56] The same thought may be found in Aristotle: "Our forefathers [ἀρχαίων καὶ παμπαλαίων] in the most remote ages have handed down to us their posterity a tradition . . . that the divine encloses the whole of nature"—this is how it reads in the *Metaphysics*.[57]

It is important to recognize this—that is, to recognize that the great paradigmatic figures of Western philosophy appeal "in good faith" to a pregiven interpretation of the world that was handed down to them —especially since the modern history of philosophy, which is dominated by the rationalist belief in progress, has equated the beginning of philosophizing with the self-delimitation of thought from tradition. On this view, philosophizing is based precisely on reason's reaching its "maturity" vis-à-vis tradition; the rebellion against the *religious* tradition belongs most prominently to the essence of philosophy; and this is evident as well in the rise of Greek philosophy: clearly, the Pre-Socratic, pre-Attic philosophers were and continue to be understood as "enlighteners"—and this despite the fact that the latest research has made it appear likely that the Homeric teachings concerning the divinities, to which the Pre-Socratics from Thales to Empedocles were, in reality, sharply opposed, should themselves be considered a kind of "enlightenment theology", which the Pre-Socratics sought to replace with a more primordial, pre-Homeric theology.

What the history of philosophy's beginnings and the first bloom of Western philosophy, which was never again to unfold in this manner, appear to demonstrate, then, is that all philosophizing rests on an interpretation of the world that has been passed down to it as something "always already" communicated in advance and that this tradition ignites philosophizing.

Plato, however, goes one step farther. He not only argues that there is a tradition stemming from the "men of old", which the philosophizing person is obliged to honor, but he is also persuaded that this "knowledge belonging to the men of old" is ultimately of divine origin. "There is a gift of the gods—so at least it seems evident to me— which they let fall from their abode, and it was through Prometheus,

---

[56] *Laws* 715e7ff. [Quoted after the translation by A. E. Taylor, in *Plato: The Collected Dialogues*, p. 1307.]

[57] *Metaphysics* 12.8.1074b1. [Quoted after the translation in Jonathan Barnes, ed., *The Complete Works of Aristotle: The Revised Oxford Translation*, vol. 2 (Princeton, 1984), p. 1698.]

or one like him, that it reached mankind, together with a fire exceedingly bright. The men of old, who were better than ourselves and dwelt nearer the gods, passed on this gift in the form of a saying." So writes Plato in referring to the theory of ideas in his dialogue the *Philebus*.[58]

That "wisdom such as God possesses" is, then, on Plato's view, already known and available to us, even *before* the loving search for this truth, that is, philosophizing, has begun. Without the preexisting counterpoint of a somehow illuminative divine wisdom that offers itself to man as a gift prior to any intellectual effort on his part— without this counterpoint, philosophy, as the loving search for this "wisdom such as God possesses", is not conceivable at all, however much this fact serves to explain, on the other hand, philosophy's autonomy. This independence of philosophizing vis-à-vis the "always already" pregiven stock of tradition, which derives from divine revelation, consists in the fact that the philosophical act begins with the contemplation of the visible, concrete reality of experience that lies before our eyes; that philosophizing begins "from the bottom," with the questioning of the things encountered in everyday experience, which opens up to the seeker ever new and more "wondrous" [*erstaunlicher*] depths. At the same time, it belongs to the essence of the always already existing tradition that it also precedes experience— experience and its conceptual preformation; that it is not a "result" achieved "from below" but a gift, pregiven, always already expressed and revealed.

What is at issue here is the fundamental relation between philosophy and theology (theology being construed here in the general sense of an interpretation of the stock of traditions). If one—in a somewhat simplifying fashion but not unduly so, I assume—wishes to reduce the community of essence between theology and philosophy, as it emerges in Plato and in ancient philosophy, to its basic contours, one might formulate it as follows: Theology "always already" precedes philosophy—and this not simply in the sense of a chronological sequence but rather in the sense of partaking in a relation of logical order. It is a pregiven interpretation of reality, referring to the world as a whole, which gives rise to philosophical questions; philosophy is

---

[58] *Philebus* 16c1ff. [Quoted after the translation by R. Hackforth, in *Plato: The Collected Dialogues*, p. 1092.]

thus linked to theology in an essential way. There is no philosophizing that does not receive its impulse and impetus from a preexisting interpretation of the meaning of the world as a whole. The ideal image of a "wisdom such as God possesses", from which the movement of philosophical thinking in its loving search time and again derives its motive and direction, becomes, independently of experience, visible in the theological realm.

Now this does not imply, for example, that the theologian has what the philosopher seeks. The theologian does not already have in his character as theologian, that is, as the preserver and interpreter of the stock of traditions, the knowledge of Being that the authentic philosopher has. To be sure, that word by which the *logos* is revealed as that by virtue of which everything came into being is also and specifically a statement concerning the structure of reality as a whole, but the theologian, who is called upon to specify, preserve, and defend the meaning of this statement with regard to the total stock of traditional truths of revelation—that theologian does not already possess the wisdom that accrues to the philosopher from contemplating the world "from below". Conversely, the philosopher is able in the light cast by this statement to attain in his questioning of things to a knowledge that would otherwise remain closed to him—a knowledge that is, not of a theological kind, but of a thoroughly philosophical nature, demonstrable *in* the things themselves.

This kind of impartiality with regard to theology is the distinguishing feature of Platonic philosophizing. Plato would have stared, uncomprehending, if someone had called his attention to the fact that he had abandoned the jurisdiction of "purely" philosophical thinking for the realm of theology. In the *Symposium*, for example, he has Aristophanes recount a—to all outward appearance—extremely grotesque and almost burlesque tale of primordial man, who was originally globular in shape, endowed with four arms and four legs and hermaphroditic and who was then later cut into pieces ("just as you or I might chop up sorb apples for pickling"), with each piece now seeking the half that will tally with himself.[59] And this, according to Aristophanes, is precisely what we call "*eros*": "the desire and pursuit of wholeness". Behind the comedic details, however, the basic structure of the story is discernible: Formerly, in the beginning, our

[59] *Symposium* 189d6–193d5.

nature was sound and integral, but man was driven by hubris, by the consciousness of his own terrible strength and his "high thoughts", to displace the gods; and as punishment for the arrogance of wanting to be like the gods, man was deprived of his primeval wholeness. Now there is every reason to hope that *eros*, which is the desire to restore this original state of wholeness, can find its true fulfillment "if we are well-ordered" in our worship of the gods. This is certainly not "philosophy"; something like this cannot be thought up or derived from the experience of reality as a "result"! But may not *that* aspect of the Platonic dialogues which allows us to experience them as something truly affecting be traced back to the fact that the question of what *eros* is ultimately and in the final analysis is being considered in conjunction with the answer given by religious tradition—that is, to precisely this joining of philosophy and theology? Does philosophy, whose nature it is to survey the entire field of human existence, not owe its totalizing character to this?

It is impossible, then, to want to pursue philosophy in conscious and radical abstraction from theology and to appeal to Plato at the same time. One can only philosophize in a Platonic manner and with Platonic aspirations using a theological counterpoint. If one is earnestly inquiring into the origin of things (and that is, after all, what is taking place in the philosophical act), one cannot at the same time for the sake of some ideal of methodological purity put to one side the preexisting religious tradition and its explicit claim concerning the origin of things—unless one no longer accepts this claim. However, to accept them, to believe them, *and* in philosophizing to put them to one side—that one cannot seriously do!

Of course, the question then naturally arises of where here and now the authentic prephilosophical tradition is to be found. What is the contemporary version of that message which, according to Plato, "through Prometheus, or one like him . . . reached mankind" "as a gift from the gods"?[60] To this one would have to respond that since the end of Western antiquity there has been no prephilosophical tradition pertaining to the world as a whole apart from the Christian one. There is today in the West no theology other than the Christian

---

[60] *Philebus* 16c2f.

one! Where could a non-Christian theology in the robust sense[61] be found?

This implies, in turn, that, in the Christian era, it is only possible to philosophize in counterpoint to the Christian interpretation of the world if those aspirations are to be realized with which Plato entrusted philosophy. The question, "how is Christian philosophy possible?" appears to be much less difficult to answer than the converse question of how a non-Christian philosophy is possible—assuming that by philosophy we understand what Plato meant by it.

Of course, this is not to suggest that it suffices to be a Christian or to recognize Christian tradition as valid in order to be able to practice philosophy in the grand sense, which involves investigating the world, immersing oneself in Being, and proceeding "from below", which, in turn, depends for its success on the natural ingenuity of the gaze that is directed at the world. It also does not imply that Christian philosophy is the only one that can be a living philosophy. Living philosophy can also be pursued in opposition to what is Christian. Still, one can only oppose Christian belief with articles of faith, however much they may purport to be "purely rational": rationalism also has its articles of faith, so that the structure of genuine philosophizing remains preserved as a counterpoint to articles of faith. (Where religious tradition has dried up *completely*, so that one no longer understands what is meant when the words "God", "revelation", and "logos" are uttered—at that point even philosophy could not flourish.)

Philosophy acquires its vivacity and its inner tension through its counterpoint to the theological. It is thence that philosophy derives the spice, the poignancy of the existential! It is precisely this fact—that the subject of philosophy, which has shriveled to the status of a specialized discipline, has become shallow, because it fearfully avoids contact with the theological problematic (which is also true in part

---

[61] At the close of the week of higher learning in Bonn in 1947, I was advised that a revival of the theology of *antiquity* could, in fact, today be observed, for example, in the works of Walter F. Otto, so that one can no longer claim that the only theology that exists is the Christian one. To this I would respond that admiration does not amount to belief. Would one seriously want to argue that in this new Greek worship ancient theology in the strict sense has been "assumed as truth"—is so fully "believed"—that, for example, in an extreme existential situation (like that of death) one would pray to Apollo or Dionysus? If this, however, is not true, then one cannot speak here of a "theology in the robust sense".

of so-called "Christian" philosophy)—that explains the stimulating impact of Heidegger's mode of philosophizing. The explosive character of this philosophizing consists in nothing other than the fact that, from an originally theological impetus, it poses with a thought-provoking radicalism questions that demand a theological response— and in the fact that such a response is at the same time just as radically rejected. Suddenly one can again taste the spice of theology on one's tongue! And today in France, if one disregards what is sheer fashion, the situation is similar: precisely because this "existential" atheism is in no way a "purely philosophical" or even a "scientific" affair but rather a theological position, it is able to endow philosophy with a fundamentally theological dimension, which does not make this philosophy any the more genuine, since it is a pseudo- or anti-theology, but, for that, all the more lively; it truly concerns man—because it concerns the whole, in which philosophy by definition is interested. When, for example, Jean-Paul Sartre says that atheistic existentialism concludes from God's nonexistence that there is a being that exists without being subject to a superior will and that this being is man, there is presumably no one who would consider this a philosophical thesis rather than a theological one, no one who would not regard it as an article of faith. But this thesis is, in fact, forcing thought to the level of theology! As long as one proceeds from such a counterpoint, it becomes possible to philosophize in a living manner.

Still, to philosophize in a *living* manner that is at the same time *genuine* is possible only in counterpoint to a genuine theology, and that implies, *post Christum natum*, a Christian theology. But once again let me say that not every factually existing form of philosophizing that appeals to Christian theology accomplishes, in so doing, this unity of truth and vivacity. On the contrary, a philosophy that is at once true and living will either not be achieved at all (and it is certainly possible that we will be left waiting) or, *if* it is realized, then only as a Christian philosophy (in the aforementioned sense!).

This is no longer a "purely" philosophical statement. The nature of philosophy, however, which since its inception has understood itself as the loving search for that "wisdom such as God possesses", makes it inevitable for the philosophizing person to transcend the realm of "pure" philosophy, which, although capable of being theoretically and methodologically delimited and sealed off, is not existentially so—this realm being conceptually distinct but not separable in reality—and adopt a theological position. There is no other way to philosophize! And that because philosophizing, precisely insofar as it constitutes a basic human attitude toward reality, is possible only with regard to the totality of human existence, to which the ultimate standpoints also—and, indeed, primarily—belong.

Now, at the close of our endeavor to respond to the question, "what does it mean to philosophize?" we must devote some remarks to the notion of a Christian philosophy, without, however, in any way suggesting that the extremely complex problem of a "Christian philosophy" has been exhausted or even simply illumined in its essential outlines.

Before doing so, however, we will have to refute a common opinion that asserts that one of the ways in which Christian philosophy (or a Christian philosophy) distinguishes itself from a non-Christian philosophy is that the former finds itself in possession of more polished solutions. This is not the case. Although Christian philosophy reasons from the counterpoint of entirely indubitable certainties, it is nevertheless true that Christian philosophy is able to realize in purer form a genuine sense of wonder, which is, after all, based on not knowing. One of the great thinkers of our age, who takes his guidance from Aquinas, has stated that the most distinctive feature of Christian philosophizing is not that it has at its disposal more polished solutions but rather that it possesses "to a greater degree than any other philosophy" a sense of mystery.[62] It is, of course, by no means so that in matters of faith and theology—the certitude of faith notwithstanding—everything becomes clear to the believer, that every problem appears resolved. On the contrary, as Matthias Joseph Scheeben has pointed out, the truths of Christianity are in a unique way incomprehensible; to be sure, the truths of reason are themselves also incomprehensible, but what is distinctive of the truths of Christianity is that they "remain hidden [to us] despite revelation".[63]

Now one might ask why it is that a Christian philosophy is to be preferred to a non-Christian philosophy, especially if it has not arrived

---

[62] R. Garrigou-Lagrange, *Der Sinn für das Geheimnis und das Hell-Dunkel des Geistes* (Paderborn, 1937), pp. 112f.

[63] M. J. Scheeben, *Die Mysterien des Christentums*, ed. J. Höfer (Freiburg, 1941), pp. 8f.

at more sophisticated solutions, if one still has not come to grips with an answer, if, indeed, problems and questions still remain. Now it is surely conceivable that its claim to greater *truth* might lie in the fact that it perceives the world in its authentic character as mystery and in its inexhaustibility. It is surely possible that in the experience that Being as such is a mystery—not to be comprehended and not to be made palpable in a wide-ranging statement—reality is grasped in a deeper, more profound, and more genuine sense than in a system, however transparent, that bewitches the spirit through its clarity and distinctness. And precisely this is the aspiration of Christian philosophy—to be more genuine, especially in its appreciation of the mysterious character of the world.

In the event, this does not make philosophizing any easier. Plato himself would also appear to have felt and acknowledged this if one interpretation of Plato[64] is correct in asserting that the reason why Plato considered philosophizing to be something tragic is that it remains ever dependent on myth insofar as the philosophical interpretation of the world cannot be rounded off to form a closed circle.

From an intellectual standpoint, as well, Christian philosophizing is not made easier simply because, as one might perhaps think, faith "illuminates" reason. The explicit recourse to theological arguments (as one finds, for example, in Aquinas) is not intended to enable more polished solutions but is intended rather to break through the methodological isolation and restriction to the "purely" philosophical in order to open up and release even more the genuinely *philosophical* impulse, the loving search for truth, the space belonging to the mystery, that space which, by definition, is characterized as being boundless, that is, by the fact that one can continue on into infinity without ever being "finished".

On the other hand, it is precisely the point of these theological truths concerning the world as a whole and the meaning of human existence—it is precisely the "eschatological function" of theology—that it sets a "no" in opposition to the spirit, which naturally pushes for clarity, transparency, and systemic closure (this is the meaning be-

---

[64] The interpretation is that of Gerhard Krüger, *Einsicht und Leidenschaft* (Frankfurt am Main, 1939), p. 301.

hind the familiar observation that the truths of faith are the "negative norm" of philosophical thought).

Philosophizing, then, is not made any "easier" this way! On the contrary, it is so "intended"—and it would have been surprising had it been otherwise—that the Christian philosopher have a more diffi-cult time of it intellectually than someone who does not consider him-self bound to the norm of traditional articles of faith. In Hölderlin's "Hyperion", one can find the verse: "The heart's wave would not foam up to such beautiful heights and become spirit if that ancient mute rock, fate, did not oppose it"—it is the ancient, speechless, unyielding rock of revealed truth, not to be softened, that prevents philosophical thought from flowing as in well-canalized stream beds. It is the convolution of thought, engendered by this resistance, that distinguishes Christian from non-Christian philosophy. A philosophy of history, for example, that reckons with the Antichrist's domination of the world at the end of history, that is, with the fact that human history culminates in what from a mortal perspective is a calamity— a philosophy of history that despite all this does not degenerate into a simple philosophy of despair—in other words, a Christian philosophy of history cannot possibly arrive at an intellectually facile view of his-tory, as opposed to a philosophy of "progress", that is, a philosophy of historical progress, which is made easier (at one time even attrac-tive, something one can no longer say today!) by the fact that it over-looks the "apocalypse"! Philosophical thinking does not become easier when it ties itself to the norm of Christian revelation, but—and this claim is simply self-evident to the Christian—it is more genuine and more in keeping with reality! It is a creative, a productive resistance that revealed truth sets in opposition to philosophical thought. It is a more rigorous type of prerequisite to which Christian philosophizing is subject. Christian philosophizing is uniquely characterized by the fact that it sees itself obliged to endure a tension that goes beyond the realm of purely conceptual problems. Christian philosophizing is more complicated because it forbids itself from arriving at "obvious" formulations *by* overlooking realities, by choosing that and omitting this; because, cast into productive disquiet through its having caught sight of revealed truth, it is forced to think in broader terms and, above all, not to rest content with the blandness of rationalist gener-alizations. It is this welling up of the spirit as it breaks against the rock of Christian revelation that distinguishes Christian philosophizing.

It is, then, by virtue of its being bound to the preexisting counter-point of Christian truth that the content of Christian philosophizing is enriched. At the same time, it is assumed that not only the Christian character of this philosophizing is genuine and powerfully present but also its philosophical character (this must continually be repeated because it so seldom goes without saying). A well-known book on the history of medieval philosophy by Maurice de Wulf concludes with the observation that Scholasticism lapsed into ruin, not from a lack of ideas, but from a lack of minds!

Thus, the "no" that theology, as *norma negativa*, opposes to philosophical thought is anything other than "negative". For one will not want to characterize it as something negative that thought is prevented from lapsing into certain errors in the first place. It may with more justification be regarded as something positive that the human spirit, on the basis of its believing acceptance of the truth of revelation, is able to assent with greater certainty to specific philosophical truths, which are, "in themselves", also attainable and demonstrable by natural means. "States lacking in justice are nothing more than gangs of robbers"—this proposition is certainly self-evident enough; it is arguably, however, no coincidence that it can be found, *not* in a textbook on legal philosophy, but rather in a theological work on the city of God, that is, in St. Augustine.

Now one may ask the question: Is philosophy, then, completely superfluous for the Christian? Is theology not sufficient, or even faith as such? As Windelband says in his *Einleitung in die Philosophie*,[65] "Whoever already has a world view and is determined to continue believing in it under all circumstances has, for his part, absolutely no need for philosophy", and that is arguably also an accurate description of the genuine Christian! Philosophy is, in point of fact, not necessary for one's *salvation*; only one thing is necessary, and that one thing is definitely not philosophy. The Christian cannot expect an answer to the question of human salvation from philosophy, much less salvation itself. He cannot philosophize with such expectations and for the sake of such results; he cannot philosophize in such a way as if his salvation depended on investigating those relationships that make up the world. Being able to lose oneself in problems, which is the hallmark

---

[65] Windelband, *Einleitung*, p. 5.

of a philosophizing that relies entirely on itself—and all the more so, the more serious it is—this existential identification, as it were, with the intellectual problematic is foreign to the believing person. In Aquinas one feels one can almost perceive a kind of cheerfulness that goes along with the inability to comprehend, an attitude that has much in common with humor. Philosophy is just as important and just as superfluous as the natural fulfillment of man's essence is necessary or, as the case may be, unnecessary. For philosophizing is, in fact, the realization of the human spirit's natural propensity toward totality. Now who would want to determine (*in concreto!*) the degree of necessity required for these *potentia*, these possibilities of being, to find their natural realization!

One last observation: up until now, we have been speaking as if what is "Christian" were exclusively or primarily a matter of doctrine, assertion, or truth. And we have spoken of a "Christian philosopher" in an analogous sense, as one is accustomed to speak of a "Kantian philosopher"—by which a philosopher is meant whose philosophical views coincide with those of Kant. When, however, it is asserted of someone that his philosophizing is Christian, that cannot simply mean that his world view is consistent with Christian teaching. For Christianity is, after all, essentially reality, not simply doctrine! Thus the problem of a Christian philosophy does not consist exclusively in determining whether natural philosophy and supernatural faith can be brought together theoretically and, if so, how, but rather in determining whether, through the rooting of the philosophizing person in Christian reality, his philosophizing becomes a Christian philosophizing and, if so, how.

The quotation, "which philosophy one chooses depends on what type of person one is", stems from Fichte—a somewhat unfortunate choice of words, for it is not the case that one simply chooses a philosophy! In any event, what is meant is clear and also correct. Even in the realm of natural knowledge, it is not the case that in order to catch sight of a truth, one need only strain one's thoughts to a greater or lesser degree; this applies all the more if the truth concerned has something to do with the meaning of the world and of life; even here it is not enough to be a "quick study"; one must also be a human being and a person. Now Christianity is a state of being that will transform and mold a person in all his faculties—but particularly in his desire to know—all the more thoroughly, the more he opens himself to it.

This is not the occasion and it is also not my place to speak more specifically to these issues. What has hitherto been said may suffice to render intelligible the existential structure of a Christian philosophizing.

In Aquinas[66] one can find a distinction between two types of knowledge: between genuinely theoretical knowledge, knowledge *per cognitionem*, and knowledge that occurs on the basis of a community of nature, knowledge *per connaturalitatem*, a distinction we prefer to think of as something thoroughly modern. In the first case, the object of knowledge is something foreign; in the second case, what is known is something belonging to oneself. In the case of the first kind of knowledge, a moralist or ethicist, for example, who need not be a good person himself, determines what is good; in the case of the second type of knowledge, knowledge *per connaturalitatem*, the good person recognizes what is good—on the basis of his immediate participation and involvement, on the basis of an inner attunement, thanks to the unerring instincts of the lover (for love is that through which the alien becomes one's own, that through which the *connaturalitas* arises —as Aquinas also notes).[67] Only someone who, to use an expression of Dionysius the Areopagite, is not only "learned in the divine but also experienced in the sufferance of it" can preside over divine things as if they were his own due to a shared community of nature.[68]

Thus, Christian philosophy will be brought to full expression by someone who has not only "learned" and is familiar with what it means to be Christian—someone to whom it is not only a "doctrine" with which he, at a purely conceptual level, brings his conclusions into theoretical alignment and agreement—but rather by someone who allows the Christian to become a reality within himself and who, not simply knowing and learning, but rather "suffering" and experiencing reality, acquires Christian truth for himself on the basis of a genuine community of nature and from this vantage point philosophizes about the natural causes of the world's reality and about the meaning of life as well.

---

[66] I, 1, 6; II, II, 45, 2.

[67] II, II, 45, 2.

[68] Dionysius the Areopagite, *De divinibus nominibus* 2, 4; cited in II, II, 45, 2.

A PLEA FOR PHILOSOPHY

Many grand and necessary things, like the law, are by nature unprotected. They require defense by the powerful who find herein not only their duty but also their legitimacy. The understanding's exercise of power takes, for good or for ill, the form of argumentation.

I.   A topic that is by its nature controversial—The first objection: Has the philosophical question not been answered?—The second: The problematic nature of its object: What does it mean to be "encountered"? Can the incomprehensible be discussed? —The third: The special sciences and the totality of the real— The fourth: For what is the good-for-nothing good?

II. The "philosophical" aspect—Typically, one does *not* philosophize—The shock caused by death and *eros*—Incommensurability with praxis—The reasonableness of the attempt—Brentano's comforting words of consolation. The similarity of the artistic and religious acts to the act of philosophizing. Spurious realizations and counterfeits. Religion and magic. Art and "entertainment".

III. The innocuousness of the "party worker", the perniciousness of the sophists. The "concerns of the day" and the "vanity of opinions" (Hegel).

IV. Against the claim to totality raised by the world of work—In what sense is "only" philosophy "free" (Aristotle)?—Freedom and knowledge in general. Safe haven for the preoccupation with truth—Why is philosophizing in a unique way "theoretical"?— The research scientist does not remain silent but inquires—The gold of philosophical silence in the silver currency of scientific discourse—The "simplicity" of philosophizing as more sublime than scientific "objectivity"—The philosophical way of being "critical"—"Using" and "enjoying" (Augustine)—Philosophy, contemplation, and loving reflection.

81

V. What does it mean to be "meaningful in itself"?—To be good
for something in the whole of one's personal existence—The
problem with this argument—The "achievement" of knowing
within the context of human existence: saturation through being. "See or perish" (Teilhard de Chardin). "What do they not
see . . ."—Philosophical *theoria* and *visio beatifica*—Reality as a
whole and the nature of spirit. Existing in the face of all that
is—"What is it for something to be real?" (Aristotle)—"To
grasp a complete fact" (Whitehead).

VI. "None of the gods philosophizes" (Plato). Philosophy means
nonwisdom—The incomprehensibility of the philosophical object—Knowing and comprehending—"The being-real of things
is itself their light" (Thomas Aquinas)—The lucidity of beings
can be experienced—The difference between this and Marxism
—The creatureliness of the world as the reason for its intelligibility as well as its incomprehensibility—Against agnostic resignation and rationalistic *hubris*.

VII. Philosophy "an embarrassment for everyone" (Jaspers)—"Scientific philosophy"—List of complaints—The unending path
of philosophizing and existence—In what does the perfection of
knowledge consist?—"Exactness is a fake" (Whitehead)—"Insight and wisdom equally dispensable" (T. S. Eliot)—Science as
discovery, philosophy as reflection—Points of contact between
the scientific and philosophical problematics of today.

VIII. Facing the scientific challenge—The language of philosophy and
the "clarity" of speech—The abuse of language by the philosophers—Philosophy and poetry—Distinctness and precision—
Language and terminology—The "wondrous" character [*Erstaunliche*] of reality as "protocol"—The relation of philosophy
to the empirical—Legitimation through recourse to experience.
Leaving nothing out.

IX. The incorporation of suprarational data—Not "the" philosophy,
but the philosophizing person—Revelation, tradition, faith,
theology—The problematic of a "presuppositionless" philosophy—Jean-Paul Sartre's "articles of faith"—The triviality of
academic sophistry—Can the philosophizing Christian leave out
of consideration truths of faith?—Two answers: The believer

cannot philosophize (Heidegger); the philosophizing person cannot believe (Jaspers)—The absolutism of the interrogative nature of philosophizing, the absolutism of philosophy's autonomy: both opposed to the received conception of philosophy
from Plato to Kant—The relationship of the known to the believed, which is established in the philosophizing act, is not easily
described. The analogy to a polyphonic fugue. Seeing and listening. A preparedness for conflict.—The crucial point: achieving
an openness toward the whole.

I

In the following discussion, I shall, as concerns methodology, be orienting myself somewhat on the procedure that for several centuries
was in use in the institutions of higher learning of medieval Christianity. As can be confirmed by a reading of any randomly chosen *articulus* from the great summa, the usual procedure was to put forward a
question for discussion, formulated in as precise a manner as possible,
along with the sometimes only vaguely intuited suggestion of an answer—whereby the questioner would initially fall mute and become
a listener, listening to the opponent and his possible objections. More
precisely put, it is the questioner who gives form to these dissenting
opinions, which are expressed in the most concise and compelling
language. A procedure that is not only very ambitious and complicated but also highly meaningful. On one point, namely, there could
now no longer be any confusion, that is, that the object in question
is something that can be viewed in different ways, a topic that is by
nature controversial—"by nature" here meaning not solely by virtue
of the many-sided nature of an objective state of affairs but also by
virtue of the specific nature of the seeker after knowledge, of the subject, who does not stand for the individual, as he is on his own—not
the one, but the many and, strictly speaking, *all* men. Already through
this procedure, then, the participants are reminded quite emphatically
that the search for truth is a shared human endeavor, which naturally
takes place in the form of dialogue and discussion, perhaps also in the
form of a disputation, but even as a possibly unending dispute, which
can never be mediated so as to yield an ultimate reconciliation—at

least as long as, for example, a genuinely philosophical object is being inquired after.

And precisely the same is true of the inexhaustible subject with which we are concerned here. For just this reason, we intend to discuss it from the very outset in the form of a *quaestio disputata*; that means, in such a way that the presence of alternative points of view will remain palpable at every moment.

The question to be discussed here—or what we might just as well call our thesis—may be expressed as follows: "To philosophize means to reflect on the totality of that which is encountered with regard to its ultimate meaning, and this act of philosophizing, so construed, is a meaningful, even necessary activity, from which the spiritually existing person can absolutely not desist."

Two distinct claims are being raised here—which is also why the objections that might be anticipated tend to run in two different directions: Either they dismiss the definition of philosophy being proposed here as wrong-headed; or they claim that it is, if not nonsensical, then at any rate futile to occupy oneself with philosophy in this sense at all.

At first glance, one might find the definition quite "general," perhaps even extremely vague and all too innocuous. It *should*, however, be "general"; that is intentional. It will soon become evident that it is not vague. And it is so far from being innocuous that, repeated some hundred kilometers east of here,* it would be regarded as an act of sabotage—and rightly so. What is meant by this definition is very much the same as what was expressed by Alfred North Whitehead, with complete spontaneity but with what were hardly unreflected words, at a public symposium held at Harvard University to commemorate his seventy-fifth birthday, namely, that philosophizing means asking the simple question, "What is it all about?"[1] The person speaking is neither a naïf nor a simplistic romantic but the cofounder of modern mathematical logic whose greatness as a philosopher, however, consists not least in the fact that he in the end recognized that the knowing subject's aspirations toward exactitude were a self-deception and

---

* [The reference is to East Germany in the time prior to the fall of the Berlin Wall.—Trans.]

[1] "The philosophy asks the simple question: what is it all about?" in A. N. Whitehead, "Remarks", *Philosophical Review* 46 (1937): 178.

also labeled them as such.[2] In any event, the sober, thoroughly realist attitude of the scientific researcher as well as an extreme almost neuralgic sensitivity to vague "sayings" can be overheard in Whitehead's characterization of philosophy.

Now at this juncture the *first* objection may be raised. Evidently one wants to suggest with this definition—this is how the objection more or less runs—that philosophy is not a "science" concerned with a clearly circumscribed object. In other cases, when one is asked, "What is psychology?" (or "What is sociology?" or "What is physics?"), the answer always begins with the words "Psychology (and so on) is the science of . . ." In this case, however, philosophizing is supposed to be equivalent to questioning, to discussing questions, to "reflecting" on something. Either the formulation is not intended to be fully precise or . . . Here I would interrupt my interlocutor, simply for his own information, to interject, "No, it is not a provisional formulation that was uttered, as it were, in rough draft; rather, what it says is exactly what it means: Philosophizing is concerned with questioning, with the discussion of questions, basically with the contemplation of a single question. But does this question then remain unanswered? Is this questioning not at least directed toward an answer? Of course! Otherwise it would not constitute genuine questioning! But if one understands by an answer information that satisfies the questioning by giving it peace and in response to which the questioner would then have to cease questioning, then it must, in fact, be conceded that the question of the philosophizing person will *not* be answered. How, then, is the conclusion to be avoided—to put it mildly—that philosophy and philosophizing represent a hardly defensible enterprise, at the very least something that is unrelated to science or even to the epistemological endeavor and the search for truth?

This same objection can obviously be raised from different standpoints. It is above all the kind of objection that an empirically minded person would make who wishes to remain close to experienceable reality and who does not wish to preoccupy himself with a problematic that goes beyond it. But there is also a position that understands itself to be thoroughly philosophical and that makes precisely the same argument. I am referring to "scientific philosophy", which supports

---

[2] For more, see section VII below.

the requirement that the philosophizing person cultivate the principles of exact science in his own field. And, finally, the representatives of the great speculative systems of the early nineteenth century were also incapable of accepting the interrogative character of philosophizing— not Schelling,[3] who calls philosophy "the science . . . of the eternal archetypes of things" ["die Wissenschaft . . . der ewigen Urbilder der Dinge"]; not Hegel,[4] who speaks of it as the "apprehension of the absolute" ["Begreifen des Absoluten"]; and not Fichte,[5] who claimed that "philosophy anticipates the whole of experience" ["die Philosophie antizipiert die gesamte Erfahrung"]. Although the grand epoch of philosophical self-confidence is now fundamentally past and over with, it is still good to recall the kind of aspirations that were being nurtured and promulgated here.

The *second* possible objection addresses a completely different point. The questionable aspect of this definition, it is claimed, lies in its characterization of the object with which philosophy is putatively concerned. First, what exactly is intended by the "all" in the question, "what is it all about?" Here I am tempted to repeat my own formulation: It stands for the totality of what is encountered. And what does it mean to be something "encountered"? And further, *who* encounters it? The answer to the last question is quickly given: Clearly, we are speaking about what is encountered by man, that is, by us. "To encounter something" means that something is brought into view in such a way that it offers up resistance. Strictly speaking—this much is true—absolutely nothing can be brought into view that does not offer resistance. Although I can imagine something to myself, I can create fantasies, their unreality shows itself in the fact that they yield no resistance, that they do not hold their ground [*standhalten*]—unless I am deranged. Again, for something to be encountered by me implies that I run up against it, I meet with it, I find it already there, it objects to me—as *ob-iectum*, as an object. I may, misled by a simplifying "theory" or an ideological interest, perhaps ignore, falsify, and misinterpret it for some time. In the long run, however, the encountered

---

[3] *Vorlesungen über die Methode des akademischen Studiums* (1802), ed. H. Glockner under the title *Studium Generale* (Stuttgart, 1954), p. 70.

[4] In a fragment of a letter addressed to H. F. W. Hinrichs in the summer of 1819 (*Briefe von und an Hegel*, ed. J. Hoffmeister, vol. 2 [Hamburg, 1953], p. 216).

[5] *Erste Einleitung in die Wissenschaftslehre*, ed. F. Medicus (Leipzig, 1944), p. 31.

will defend itself, provided I do not simply avert my gaze from it; it recalls itself unpleasantly to memory in the form of reservations and barbs; it yields resistance.

An interpolated question: According to this, then, the philosophizing person is concerned solely with what is encountered as objective reality—and hence not with the subject himself? Answer: Of course, the subject also belongs to the totality of what is encountered. I, for my part, certainly confront my own gaze, when it is directed at myself, as something that I find already there and that offers up resistance, that is, as something toward which I, as a knowing and interpreting subject, very much have to orient myself insofar as I am concerned with finding the truth. Even if I were convinced that there is something in the "I" that can never appear before my gaze as something encountered, this peculiarity of the subject would also be something that was "discovered" to be there and hence something "objective", which withholds itself from me and which I can neither ignore nor change. Of course, we need devote even less time to considering the peculiar notion that the philosophizing person has to avert his glance from everything that surrounds him: "We have not been speaking of anything that is outside you but only about you yourself."[6] On the contrary, in authentic philosophizing, the discussion includes everything that is, both inside as well as outside.

Assuming this to have been cleared up, the objection persists, what, then, is meant by asking, "What *is* it all *about?*" Is that not a rather inexact—a rhetorical rather than a scientific—formulation? What, strictly speaking, is being asked here? To this I would like to suggest straightaway that one not underestimate the everyday language of men, neither its powers of differentiation nor its wealth of content nor its weightiness. The "exegesis of commonplaces" has already yielded some astounding discoveries. For example, someone who wants to know what this or that "is all about" is evidently of the opinion that what on the surface manifests itself to everyone is not everything; rather there would seem to be something else not readily apparent, a hidden whence and why, a depth not easily plumbed, something "beyond" the merely factual. The question of the philosophizing person is directed toward precisely this dimension. He is inquiring after the

---

[6] Ibid., p. 6.

ultimate, "authentic" meaning—not of this or that, but of everything there is.

And precisely that is impossible, if not utterly nonsensical, our opponent argues; it is precisely with this that the objection is taking issue. If, however, one asks for a more detailed explanation, one is given one of two different responses. The first states that the ground of the world is unfathomable; the second asserts that this ground simply does not exist.

In the first case, an appeal is being made to our intellectual discipline. In his programmatic work *Aufstieg der wissenschaftlichen Philosophie* (*The Rise of Scientific Philosophy*), Hans Reichenbach writes, "The philosopher must not make himself the servant of his desires."[7] But is that not entirely appropriate, one would like to add? The desire to know is not, in fact, one of those things over which we have control. Is this not precisely what Plato is saying when he likens the philosophizing person to a lover, that is, that he, too, is transported "beyond himself" by his shock in the face of the *mirandum* that is the world? One may readily agree; the problem is simply that what Plato intends as praise is registered by the adherents of scientific philosophy with disapproval, as a form of disqualification, which, they are persuaded, does not require any further justification. For them it already suggests a lack of discipline even to discuss what is inaccessible to us.

The second response, which asserts that only what manifests itself exists, is, as is well known, the unquestioned key tenet of all forms of positivism; even the "realism" of Marxist orthodoxy accepts precisely this point. Friedrich Engels[8] deemed it a "philosophical quirk" to want to speak of a hidden ground of reality. The most straightforward formulation may be found in the positivist manifesto of the early Vienna Circle, which bears the title *The Scientific World View*:[9] "Everywhere is surface; everything is accessible to man." It is sense-

---

[7] *Aufstieg der wissenschaftlichen Philosophie* (Berlin, 1953), p. 36. [Quoted from Hans Reichenbach, *The Rise of Scientific Philosophy* (Berkeley and Los Angeles: Univ. of California Press, 1968), p. 37.]

[8] *Ludwig Feuerbach und der Ausgang der klassischen deutschen Philosophie* (Berlin, 1946), pp. 17f. The "program for a longer course on dialectical and historical materialism," which was published by the Philosophical Institute of the Academy of the Sciences of the USSR in 1948, devotes a few paragraphs to this idea, to which Lenin also refers. Cf. I. M. Bocheński, *Der sowjet-russische dialektische Materialismus* (Bern and Munich, 1950), p. 95.

[9] R. Carnap, H. Hahn, and O. Neurath, *Wissenschaftliche Weltauffassung: Der Wiener Kreis* (Vienna, 1929), p. 15.

less even to inquire into the "root" of all things and even more so to inquire after their "ultimate meaning". In short, this mysterious object of philosophy simply does not exist; only the objects of science exist; strictly speaking, they are all without exception physical objects.[10] And just this point provides the basis for the *third* objection, which runs as follows: The only means of comprehending the totality of that which is encountered is through the collaboration of the individual sciences. In reality, however, this joint effort presumably undertaken for the purpose of illuminating reality as a whole has been underway for millennia now without such an ambitious claim having been raised on their part; soberly imposing critical restraints on his behavior, the individual researcher adapts himself in keeping with the division of labor to the comprehensive process of epistemological endeavor: each science formulates a particular aspect; each examines only a tiny cross section of the world, but this it examines in a thoroughly precise manner. But—I would counter—does this not amount to corroborating precisely what one meant to dispute, namely, that no science formally poses that question the raising of which is the distinguishing mark of philosophy, that is, "What is the world as a whole about?" Of course, in a certain sense, it might be argued, following Jaspers, that philosophy can "legitimate itself through no object";[11] there is nothing left over, as it were, to provide the justification—unless the totality of objects may itself be considered one object. This, in turn, is partly a matter of definition.

Still, this third objection articulates a problem that, in reality, can scarcely be resolved. On the one hand, the philosophizing person is, of course, not referring to some "other" world; he is referring, just as much as the empirical researcher, to what is encounterable in experience. And when he, unlike the scientist, views the encountered and questions it with regard to its ultimate meaning, he cannot in the process prescind from what scientific research has brought to light concerning the object under discussion. Someone who, for example, wishes to pursue the philosophical question as to the "essence" of matter simply has to rely on a knowledge of modern elementary particle physics. On the other hand, it would seem to be indisputable

---

[10] Cf. R. Carnap, "Die physikalische Sprache als Universalsprache der Wissenschaft", *Erkenntnis* 2 (1931): 463, 465.

[11] K. Jaspers, *Philosophie* (Berlin, Göttingen, and Heidelberg 1948), p. 272.

that there is a dimension of the real toward which the gaze of the philosophizing person is directed and to whose illumination the sciences are able to contribute little or nothing, so that in this respect philosophy remains independent of science and its particular kind of progress. It is even conceivable that the object of philosophical questioning becomes all the less surveyable and all the more unfathomable, the greater the progress scientific research makes in its investigation of the world. "Enveloped by the rapid advance of science", Wilhelm Dilthey wrote around the year 1900, we are still "more helpless than at any time previously"[12] in the face of "the one, obscure, terrifying object of all philosophy".[13]

The *fourth* objection, which is the last to be discussed, derives its force from the world of the practically occupied person; it is not actually concerned with conceptual problems, and, from a purely theoretical standpoint, it is not particularly impressive; its significance lies in its ability to influence the way we lead our lives. One might reduce it to the following formula: It may very well be possible to philosophize, in the sense of contemplating the ultimate meaning of reality as a whole—it may perhaps even be highly interesting or fascinating —but it is not only without purpose; it actually hinders the active pursuit of life's goals. And for this reason it is nonsensical and, even worse, pernicious.

The impact of this "argument" within the context of our contemporary world, which threatens to become ever more consistently a totalitarian world of work (whether it is dominated by the enforced tyranny of centralized production or by the psychological hegemony of the ideal of efficiency)—the impact, I believe, penetrates so deeply that one might almost say that it has a greater influence on philosophy's situation today than does its actual technical problems. This is not to deny, however, that this kind of radicalism comes in different degrees. They range from a naïve and unreflected ensnarement in praxis to a willfully absolutistic attitude toward the pragmatic, toward the "common utility" (*bonum utile*), toward our "daily bread"—from which it is only one additional step to a fundamental indifference toward the truth. At one end of the spectrum is the person who, in the course of his busy everyday life, is only untheoretical in a strictly factual sense;

---

[12] *Gesammelte Schriften*, vol. 8 (Leipzig and Berlin, 1931), p. 197.
[13] Ibid., p. 140.

at the other end of the spectrum is the practitioner of power politics who aggressively closes his mind to "useless" knowledge—for whom a philosophy, for example, that cannot be "put to use" as a guide to political action deserves no more than liquidation.

II

Whoever wants to look at a thing from a philosophical standpoint must, so they say, regard it under a certain aspect. This way of thinking and talking is itself based on a notion that falls short of the essence of the philosophical act. It is the notion that one could, at will, through a clearly circumscribed intellectual operation, set in motion the act of philosophizing. It may be that something like that is possible for the sociological, psychological, and historical modes of contemplation. When one philosophizes, at any rate, it is not the case that one, on the basis of a decision, adopts a certain standpoint and subsequently abandons it; or that a special form of illumination sets in by which what is philosophically interesting in an object is brought to the foreground. Philosophizing is rather a fundamental human disposition toward the world that is largely removed from arbitrary acts of postulation and discretion. To "tackle" an issue in a philosophical way, to philosophize—that is not a technique that falls directly within our powers of determination.

If this is true, philosophizing is evidently not something one could learn—not even roughly the way we learn a foreign language or to use a microscope, that is, through the acquisition of knowledge, through methodically conducted exercises, repetition, and so on. Philosophizing and studying philosophy are two different things, so much so that one may even stand in the way of the other. Even the poetic act cannot really be learned—neither the act by which a poem comes to be nor the act by which the listener or reader grasps a poem in a poetic way, which is the only meaningful way. In his beautiful book *Mysticism and Poetry*, Henri Bremond[14] even goes so far as to say, "We do not 'learn' how to swim"; rather, "one day, in the midst of the first hour or even only at the end of the twentieth hour, we notice that we have lost the ground from beneath our feet without going under and

---

[14] *Mystik und Poesie* (Freiburg im Breisgau, 1929), p. 25.

that we get on without walking"; we swim. "The same thing happens in the poetic experience", writes Bremond. And I would add: The same thing happens in the act of philosophizing!

Generally, man is *not* in the frame of mind to inquire—he simply does not feel like inquiring—into the ultimate meaning of reality as a whole. In the average case, it is thus not to be expected—and quite understandably so—that the philosophical act and philosophical questioning will be set in motion. "How do things stand with the world as a whole?"—we do not ask such questions when we are in the midst of building a house, attending a trial, taking an exam, and so on. It simply does not occur to us as long as our attention is being claimed by the active pursuit of life's goals, with the soul's "objective" fixed on a sharply delimited cross section of the world, that is, to what belongs to the problem at hand, to what is "needed"—and *not* to anything else. (Of course, it is always and at any time possible in educated society to discuss a philosophical "problem" thrown at one like a quiz question from outside. This is not what I am referring to; I mean by philosophical questioning an existential process that is carried out in the core of the soul, an urgent, spontaneous act of our inner life from which one cannot desist.) Thus it probably also requires a shaking up of our everyday "normal" understanding of the world, which—naturally and quite rightly—dominates man's workday; it requires a violent shove, a shock, so that that questioning which aims at the totality of human existence and the world and which bursts forth from beyond the realm of mere subsistence—the act of philosophizing itself—can be set in motion.

One's personal encounter with death is a shock of just this kind. For those who do not close their mind to the experience, the preoccupation with procuring life's necessities (in the broadest sense) loses its urgency from one moment to the next. Instead, the philosophical question about the true meaning of life, which is directed toward the whole, intrudes with unexpected urgency. Plato is clearly familiar with what he is saying when he insists, with an often alienating acuity,[15] that the proximity to death—indeed, the longing for death—and philosophy are closely related. "I had become a vast problem to my-

---

[15] See *Phaedo* 64a4ff.

self" (factus eram ipse mihi magna quaestio) [16]—this is how Augustine concludes his account of the sudden death of a dearly beloved friend. The person bouncing back from such an experience—"back" from where and to what? one might ask—a person who has been so shaken does not immediately succeed in dealing with the exigencies of eking out a living: "Leave me in peace; I'm not of any use to anyone right now." Unlike, say, in the case of an illness, he will never experience such temporary unfitness as a defect or even as a hindrance; instead, he will experience it as an enrichment, as a liberation, as the certainty that comes with being able to understand the things of this world and human existence more deeply and being able to value them more accurately than ever before.

The other existential force, *eros*, which is contrasted with death, is also able to affect and transform man in this way. For someone who has been moved by the power of *eros*—an entirely different kind of person from those who are inflamed by, and desirous of, the purely sensuous—the world has also been transformed unexpectedly. The totality of world and human existence likewise appears before his eyes, but again only insofar as he does not close himself off to the experience. Here, too, the words of Plato should be recalled, who describes the intermediate divinity *Eros* as being himself a philosopher. [17]

The philosophizing person has at least this in common with the person who has been touched by his encounter with death and the person who has been moved by *eros*: he, too, does not accommodate himself unquestioningly to the functionality of our workday praxis; he does not "fit" in this world; he sees things "differently" from the person who is primarily occupied with the pursuit of life's ends. This inconsistency, this incommensurability cannot—so it would appear—be eliminated from the world; it has always existed; and there is much that speaks in favor of the fact that it is steadily becoming more acute.

It has always appeared to me noteworthy that the history of European philosophy is already able to report in its very first chapter about the laughter with which the practical everyday understanding, by no means unjustly, greets the philosophizing person. By contrast, one could have dismissed the tale of Thales, that one-time observer of

---

[16] *Confessions* 4, 4, 9.

[17] *Symposium* 204b2ff.

the heavens who stumbled into a well, and the Thracian maidservant as a harmless anecdote, which owes its preservation to an accident of tradition and which in the end expresses nothing more than a life experience; indeed, one could have done this if Plato had not taken the story so seriously. In the dialogue the *Theaetetus*,[18] Socrates attempts to persuade his interlocutor, Theodorus, of the constitutional unworldliness, as it were, of the genuine philosopher; and when this man, a seasoned mathematician, appears not to understand and asks then what he means by this, the Platonic Socrates gives the following answer: He means the same thing as was demonstrated by the example of Thales, who was scoffed at by a clever and witty maidservant from Thrace for being so eager to know what was happening in the sky that he could not see what lay at his feet; "anyone who gives his life to philosophy is open to such mockery."[19] This is a decidedly forceful statement. And yet Plato could not have known anything of the modern regime of work and its absolutistic approach to utilitarian concerns. As a result, the philosophizing person—that is what is being claimed here—finds himself by his very nature in an irremediable conflict with the industriousness of the practical person. That this is not a distinctively Platonic form of overstatement but simply the truth is demonstrated a hundred times a day.

My path to the university regularly takes me past court buildings; and often I see people assembled in the anterior square, speaking excitedly with one another or oppressively silent, evidently completely taken with the thought of *their* rights, the course of their trial, the prospects for their defense, a sentence that was considered too mild or too harsh, and so on. Sometimes I imagine that Socrates would step forth before these people, whose worries I completely understand, and would attempt, as in the Athenian agora, to begin a conversation, not about whether the one was right in this and the other in that but about what generally and in the final analysis it means to be right and just what law, right, and justice are and why the polity cannot flourish without them. Now one need not further flesh out the scene of how energetically they would turn their backs on him,

---

[18] *Theaetetus* 173c6–174a1.

[19] Ibid. 174a8f. [Quoted after the translation by F. M. Cornford, in *Plato: The Collected Dialogues*, p. 879.]

assuming it did not come to anything worse. That is a completely natural reaction. But it is always to be expected in such cases where a philosophical question is thrust unprepared into the world of practical people (although there is really no way of "preparing" people!) —be it "Why is there something at all rather than nothing?" ("To ask this question is to philosophize", according to Heidegger)[20] or be it, in Aristotle's formulation, the question of what it means to be something real.[21]

The awkwardness of philosophizing, however, becomes all the more apparent—showing itself in its full contours and to its full extent— as soon as it is confronted with the principles and the subterranean motives of the modern world of work. And whoever reflects on the fact that it is, after all, no accident that we now face the task of securing our existence under completely new conditions could easily begin to waver in his defense of philosophy. Not only the struggle against starvation compels us to the ever more intensive technological exploitation of all available forces; even the preservation of freedom in this world, divided and overshadowed as it is by opposing concentrations of power, appears to require all our efforts. Are we right to insist that it is part of a genuinely human existence to keep alive the question of the ultimate meaning of reality as a whole? On the other hand: at no other time, except when nothing else seems to exist but the need to procure bread—at no other time does the insight that men cannot live from bread alone acquire such force. And it is precisely when such a biblical phrase appears outside its customary context in completely modern dress, for example, as the title of a Soviet novel[22] —it is precisely then that it reveals its full and indestructible sense.

---

[20] *Einführung in die Metaphysik* (Tübingen, 1953), p. 10. [Quoted from: Martin Heidegger, *An Introduction to Metaphysics*, trans. Ralph Manheim (Garden City, N.Y., 1961), p. 10.] [In his personal copy of "A Plea for Philosophy", J. Pieper lists further references to Leibniz, Schelling, and Wittgenstein. In a work written two years before his death, "Les Principes de la nature et de la grâce fondés en raison" (*Kleine Schriften zur Metaphysik*, vol. 1, [Darmstadt, 1965], p. 426), Leibniz (whom Heidegger does not mention) describes just this question, namely, "Why is there something at all rather than nothing?" as the "primary question". The references to Schelling and Wittgenstein may be found in J. Choron, *Der Tod im abendländischen Denken* (Stuttgart, 1967), pp. 310f, nn. 28–30.—ED.]

[21] *Metaphysics* 7.1.1028b3–4; 4.1.1003a21.

[22] W. Dudinzew, *Der Mensch lebt nicht vom Brot allein* (Hamburg, 1956).

In any event, nothing is so understandable as the fact that the attempt has been repeatedly undertaken to eliminate the inconsistency between philosophy and the world of work. The result has always been the same: the destruction of philosophy. It is the weaker sister of the two; that is precisely the reason why it stands in need of defense. The question is complicated by the fact that from time to time philosophers themselves attempt to remove this incommensurability from the world—and this also since time immemorial or at the very least since the sophist Protagoras, who defines the business of the wise, in which he sees himself engaged, as teaching men to take proper care of their personal affairs.[23]

It can be shown, in turn, I think, how the dynamics of this kind of self-destruction have become increasingly more radicalized over time up to the present day. One need only, for example, compare the following three sentences (whose sources will remain at first unnamed) with one another. The first sentence states that the old theoretical philosophy must be replaced with a new practical philosophy that would "render ourselves the lords and possessors of nature".[24] The second claims that all human knowledge has the status of a tool within the greater enterprise of "intellectual industry"; that the goal of every intellectual effort is the safeguarding and enjoyment of life; that philosophy is not actually directed toward knowledge of the world but rather toward finding ways of mastering it.[25] The third sentence runs as follows: "A scientist who is concerned with abstract problems must never lose sight of the fact that the aim of all science lies in the satisfaction of society's needs." That in each case basically the same is being said, only each time more pointedly expressed, can be recognized by everyone: The first sentence may be found in Descartes; the originator of the second is a representative of American pragmatism, John Dewey; and the third I have somewhat disingenuously taken from the *Great Soviet Encyclopedia*.[26]

If in the totalitarian work-state not only science but also philosophy (or what is taken for philosophy) is now subjected to the duress of constantly having to respond to the inquisitorial question of what it

---

[23] Plato *Protagoras* 318eff.

[24] *Discours de la Méthode*, chap. 6.

[25] Cf. G. E. Müller, *Amerikanische Philosophie*, 2nd ed. (Stuttgart, 1950), pp. 222ff.

[26] *Großen Sowjet-Enzyklopädie*, 2nd ed. (Berlin, 1952), 2:1317.

has to contribute to the "Five-Year Plan", then this represents nothing more than the ultimate consequence of Descartes' call for a practical philosophy, just as the dictator, with his implementation plans, is nothing more than a contemporary version of the lords and possessors of nature ("maître et possesseur de la nature").

Whoever seeks to eliminate the fundamental incommensurability between philosophy and the world of work only serves to make the philosophical act improbable of achievement or even impossible—the philosophical act whose nature as well as dignity consists in the fact that it not only does not belong to the world of work but actually transcends it, going one step beyond it.

In his introductory lecture held in Vienna in 1874, "On the Reasons for Discouragement in the Philosophical Field" (Über die Grunde der Entmutigung auf philosophischem Gebiete), Franz Brentano, Husserl's teacher and a figure of otherwise inestimable influence, includes among some of the causes for the "universal distrust" of philosophy "the impossibility of practical use": "Philosophy has alone, among all the abstract sciences, failed to prove itself through practical fruits."[27] Brentano himself certainly shares this reservation; he is convinced that it is, in fact, a weighty objection. And the only thing he is able to oppose to it is the hope that for philosophy, too, which is, of course, developing more slowly, "the time of its awakening to fruit-bearing activity" will come.[28] Now this comforting word of encouragement, so it appears to me, no longer moves us today. More important, however, is the question of whether we need it in order to feel neither "distrustful" nor "discouraged" in the presence of philosophy and its genuine fruits, even if uncompensated by anything else.

III

Philosophizing is not the only activity in which the world of work is transcended; it is also transcended in certain other existential acts. They, too, are fundamentally incommensurable with the world of work; and the attempt to remove this inconsistency from the world

[27] F. Brentano, *Über die Zukunft der Philosophie*, ed. O. Kraus (Leipzig, 1929), p. 92.
[28] Ibid., p. 99; see also p. 98.

is, again, synonymous with the destruction of the existential act it-self. I have already discussed the case of *poetry*; it is mentioned here as being representative of the fine arts generally. It should come as no surprise that a truly great poem—a loving appraisal of the world, crafted in rigorous proportions of image, form, and sound—occurring in the midst of a world of actively pursued purposes strikes us as be-ing just as alien and curious as a philosophical question in the midst of a world of actively pursued purposes. The *religious* act breaks forth even more decidedly into that realm beyond the world of utility and productivity. Even the sentence, "Give us this day our daily bread", although it appears to refer to nothing more than the satisfaction of one's basic needs, could not be experienced, in the act of prayer, as the "raising of one's heart to God", if at the same time a step had not been taken beyond the need itself; the hunger would have to have been forgotten for at least a moment.

Thus philosophical, artistic, and religious acts are, in fact, related in a special way. Most importantly, "the inner relation to the mystery of life and world . . . is common to all three", as Dilthey has observed.[29] Dilthey is one of the few who has turned his attention to the structure of the philosophical act—in Dilthey's particular case, in a "philosophy of philosophy",[30] to which he increasingly devoted his attention up to the last few years of his life. This affinity and interrelationship reveals its power, however, in many ways. Thus, without having to know more about a particular society, it may, for example, be anticipated from the start that in a society that dismisses the discussion of gen-uinely philosophical questions as "socially insignificant"—which can, of course, occur in different ways and not only in a political dictator-ship—the fine arts and religion will also not flourish. And it is also likely that in such a society death and *eros* will be trivialized, thereby depriving them of their power to move people. This is undoubtedly true: such shocks are not conducive to our being industrious.

In this age of great social experiments, one can always find here and there confirmation of the fact that the subterranean connection between philosophy, religion, and poetry persists undetected, even in the teeth of hardened opposition. A political regime may one day, for

---

[29] *Gesammelte Schriften* 5:367.
[30] Ibid., 8:204.

example, find it expedient for poetry to be resuscitated in that country—poetry pure and simple (but apolitical, of course)—especially
since the experience of running up against nothing other than the
party platform in novels and dramas has gradually become intolerable. So they encourage writers and film directors to try their hands
at producing a comedy or a love story once in a while. But lo and
behold: it does not work! It could work only if the entire fecund
terrain in which everything else that evades and resists its planned
utility is able to flourish were liberated and not simply this little fleck
of fenced-off earth. A remarkable coincidence, worthy of some reflection, that romantic fiction and comedy spring from the same soil as
philosophy and prayer!

Worse, however, and far more dangerous than undisguised oppres-
sion is the self-induced illusion of favoritism. Baldly stated, there is
a tendency under the hegemony of a purely utilitarian thinking for
forgeries to establish themselves, counterfeits of the genuinely religious, artistic, and even philosophical acts. The danger lies in the fact
that the illusion, or rather self-deception, is hardly noticeable; nothing
seems to be lacking because no place has been left empty.

In lieu of a genuine prayer there now stands, for example, a "magic"
practice, namely, the attempt to invoke superhuman powers, to assimilate even God himself, as a functionary power, to the purposes of a
this-worldly praxis. Magic is in this sense by no means the limited preserve of a primitive cult or clandestine circle; it is a temptation toward
perversion that continually accompanies religious life. The boundaries
separating the two are often hard to make out in the concrete case.
When does a prayer cease to be a genuine raising of the spirit toward
God and thus a release from the confines of life's necessities? The
genuinely religious life doubtless offers possibilities for inner satisfaction and happiness that simply cannot be acquired any other way.
What happens, however, when religion is glorified and practiced for
the sake of its "success", that is, as the means to a happy life? Now,
something like that is not so completely unthinkable. This, it appears
to me, marks the beginning of the conversion—and perversion—of
the religious into the magical; and I would maintain that a natural
affinity exists between such perversion and an absolutism of praxis.

Spurious realizations of the artistic may also manifest themselves in
the most varied of forms—for example, as "entertainment" in which

the "ingratiating" has been elevated to the status of ultimate measure. (According to Goethe, "the greatest artworks are simply uningratiating.")[31] The workday routine has pointedly—and professedly—*not* been transcended; instead, one makes oneself comfortable within its confines—to which nothing could be objected if the confinement did not threaten to become permanent. Even the *littérature engagée* represents a possible form of adulteration, the more dangerous, the greater its technical virtuosity. Texts that in all innocence set themselves the task "of encouraging people to implement the Five-Year Plan"[32] and declare themselves "weapons of socialism"[33] will not easily be confused with genuine poetry. Where, though, does one draw the line between poetry and propaganda in the unique work of Bertolt Brecht?

The most reprehensible thing about such counterfeits lies, again, in the fact that the loss of the genuine article goes unnoticed. One misses what is truly intended with religion and fine art because one believes oneself to be already in possession of them; one does not miss the gift that was intended for us because one is convinced that it has already fallen to one's direct share.

Thus it is very unlikely that a genuine raising of the soul toward God can occur in someone whose "religious" practice is shaped by the discretionary attitude of false prayer—on the basis of which he believes himself to be "pious". Similarly, it is hardly to be expected that in a world dominated by what we shall call "entertainment music" (or by propagandistic poetry) a genuine, artistically inspired act can emerge, especially if one is in the habit of believing that what one has been hearing the entire time is music (or poetry). For exactly the same reason, by the way, erotic emotion becomes in a subtly or brutally sexualized atmosphere increasingly improbable: one takes sex itself for *eros*.

Pseudo-philosophy has many faces, as well. Relatively harmless— "harmless", not in the sense of being easily lived through, and without danger, but in the sense of being easily recognizable—is that face corresponding to "practical philosophy" which allows itself to be systematically exploited for social purposes. When a German professor

---

[31] Cf. F. W. Riemer, *Mitteilungen über Goethe*, ed. Arthur Pollmer (Leipzig, 1921), p. 334.

[32] Presentation at the Fifth Conference of the ZK of the SED. Report in *Neues Deutschland*, March 23, 1951.

[33] Professor Kurt Hager, "Kunst ist Waffe für den Sozialismus", *Sonntag*, October 20, 1957.

of philosophy describes "our comrades the philosophers" as "party workers in that field",[34] then no one is taken in; there is no question here of deception or misrepresentation. It becomes much more difficult to discriminate between the two when such usage is justified in a highly sophisticated philosophical manner with an anthropological theory that is manifestly (if only apparently) directed toward the whole, this being only one of the literally countless possibilities available to that "creative" thinking which is considered the exclusive domain of the sophist.[35] Here the danger of confusion or of self-deception is especially acute: "He *seems* just like a philosopher. He talks just like a philosopher. In fact we may say that he appears even more like a philosopher than the philosopher himself."[36] In other words, it has become infinitely easy—and this is precisely what makes it a "forgery"—for someone *not* to recognize the crucial difference.

The reason for that, however, is that the genuinely philosophizing person, who is completely unconcerned with his own importance, selflessly, in "complete alienation from all pretension",[37] reveals the unfathomable object whose appearance liberates the subject lying beyond all forms of self-validation from the egocentric preoccupation with his own need, however "spiritual" and sublime. By contrast, the sophist, although emancipating himself from the norm of objective truth and who is thus in that sense "free",[38] remains, in his pursuit of originality and in the desperate longing to contribute through terminological and intellectual pyrotechnics to higher entertainment,[39] trapped within the confines of what one "needs".

The bipolar opposition within philosophy of which Hegel speaks ("on the one hand, the spirit's absorption in the vital needs of the

[34] Professor Kurt Hager, Conference report in *Neues Deutschland*, December 17, 1957.

[35] John Wild, *Plato's Theory of Man* (Cambridge, Mass., 1948), p. 280.

[36] Ibid., p. 283.

[37] This was written by Goethe in a letter to Herder, dated November 10–11, 1786, while the former was in Rome.

[38] "Hence sophistry always tends to ignore the intentionality of thought, regarding reason not as the apprehension of an object, but rather as an isolated process of making hypotheses or theories in the mind. This tendency to regard reason as though it had no *object* of its own is common to modern idealism and pragmatism" (J. Wild, *Plato's Theory of Man*, p. 280, n. 36).

[39] Cf. J. Pieper, "Der Verderb des Wortes und die Macht: Platons Kampf gegen die Sophistik", *Hochland* 57 (1964): 12–25.

day and, on the other, . . . the vanity of opinions"[40]) may be reduced to a common root. What they have in common is that, in the one case as in the other, reason, in violation of its true nature, "seeks"— to borrow another phrase from Hegel—"its own" [*das Eigne sucht*].[41] Wherever such "self-seeking" behavior [*Eigensucht*] dominates the existential realm, the philosophical act cannot be expected to flourish, if it ever emerges at all.

IV

Whoever, then, intends to defend philosophy against the charge that it is of no use and is thus a nonsensical and indefensible endeavor —whoever intends to demonstrate why it is nevertheless worthwhile to philosophize—will begin his rejoinder by explicitly affirming the objection, or, at the very least, the first part of it, even reinforcing it and taking it far more literally than perhaps even his opponent himself. Yes, it is true: philosophy is of no practical use; it cannot and should not be used for anything! In Martin Heidegger's words, "It is absolutely correct and proper to say that 'You can't do anything with philosophy.' "[42]

The aggressiveness that emerges here is due, not solely to the formulation, but also to the thought itself. Insofar as I recognize the contemplation of the whole of reality, that is, philosophizing, which is admittedly irrelevant to any conceivable praxis, to be a meaningful —indeed, necessary—human activity, I have already denied the totalitarian claim of the workday world. In so doing, I have already disputed the view that a Five-Year Plan could be raised to the status of an absolute measure; I am, in effect, asserting that there is an existential realm for which the categories of "returns", "practicability", "usability", and "efficiency" have no application and which nevertheless belongs, indispensably, to a genuinely human life.

---

[40] Inaugural address held on October 22, 1818, in Berlin; printed in G. W. F. Hegel, *Encyclopädie der philosophischen Wissenschaften in Grundrisse*, ed. G. Lasson, 4th ed. (Leipzig, 1930), p. LXXIII.

[41] Ibid.

[42] *Einführung in die Metaphysik*, p. 10. [Quoted from Heidegger, *Introduction to Metaphysics*, p. 10.]

Has what at first glance appeared to be an embarrassment, a defect, and an infirmity that had to be conceded, for better or worse, now shown itself to be, on the contrary, a mark of distinction, even a privilege, that is being exercised and asserted?

Indeed, it has. To this kind of privilege we give the name "freedom". Philosophizing is essentially a free activity, and for this very reason, it serves no one and is of no use to anyone!

And with this, the time has come to speak of one very special aspect of the concept of "freedom". Although this aspect has always been thought in conjunction with the traditional Western notion of freedom, it is not so easily grasped. Before all else, it is important to dispose of the error that what is meant with freedom is basically nothing more than the political liberty of the citizen. It is, in fact, not so far removed from that, and it is impossible to set that notion of liberty completely aside, but more than a simple identity obtains between the two. That is one of the reasons why arguments break out whenever this topic is discussed with politicians and sociologists. A lack of obstruction on the part of external powers—in particular, by the public authorities—is not what in the first instance is meant by this special kind of freedom; what is intended is rather a certain inner quality. It is freedom in the same sense implied by the ancient use of the term *artes liberales*, "the free arts", handed down to us from antiquity. "Academic freedom" might also be mentioned in this connection; it, too, originally referred to something more than simply a special case of freedom of political speech or the opportunity granted the student to organize his studies as he sees fit.

It would seem that it was Aristotle who, in a very dense and not easily deciphered passage from the *Metaphysics*,[43] explicitly formulated this aspect of the notion of freedom for the first time. And, in the same connection, he even speaks of philosophy; indeed, he says, that philosophy *alone* is in this sense "*free*". In what sense? Whoever through careful reading attempts to get to the bottom of Aristotle's *Metaphysics* will come up with a curious result, namely, that "free" here is synonymous with "non-practical"! "Practical" is what *serves* the realization of certain purposes. This is exactly what is being denied with respect to philosophical *theoria*. It is "free" insofar as it is not related

---

[43] *Metaphysics* 1.2.982b27.

to something outside itself. Philosophizing is, on the contrary, an activity that is meaningful in itself and that need not be justified first on the basis of "*service*-ability".

One will, presumably, not find this particularly enlightening on a first hearing. More to the point: Is this not closer to an assertion than an argument? And, besides, is not tautology somehow involved in all this?

Many things are at any rate involved here. We find ourselves in our investigation of such topics not far from the hub of a wheel whose spokes practically touch each other. Moreover, one can hardly expect in this realm a demonstration that proceeds *more geometrico*. On closer examination, so it appears to me, there are three different ideas that are connected with one another in the Aristotelian formulation. The first concerns the relationship between knowledge and freedom, the second the unique character of philosophical *theoria*, while the third, the one that goes most to the heart of the matter, is concerned with attempts to answer the question of how philosophizing can be meaningful in itself. We shall briefly discuss these points one by one.

With regard to the *first* point, I would like to relate an experience that some years ago unexpectedly and very dramatically opened my eyes. At that time it was still possible for student groups to come to us, in a semi-legal manner, from the totalitarian state [the former East German republic] for conversation and discussion. In one such circle, the talk casually turned to a then much-discussed but now virtually forgotten novel, questions concerning which our friends from "over there" answered by pointing out that it could not be published at home because it contained major historical errors concerning the Russian Revolution, which, for example, had never interfered with the unfolding of the individual. We countered that such matters could, in the end, be objectively determined—or was that not the case? For that to happen, however, it would be necessary, they said, that one be able to discuss the matter thoroughly in a fully independent manner —not necessarily in public, but at least independently of any official directive. At the very least, they continued, there would have to be a free space in the midst of society in which such a discussion could be conducted unhindered. With this point, which had initially been pursued quite innocently, something essential had unexpectedly become clear to the disputants, and not just the ones from "over there"; to be more precise, two things had abruptly become evident.

First, what it means for a polity to have such a "free space"—a space in which, contrary to other such provocatively proclaimed slogans, "the class conflict [is truly] suspended"[44] as well as the Five-Year Plan, "politics" in general, and all other interest groups, whether collective or private. The ancient term *schole*, which signifies "school" and "leisure" at the same time, designates a space of just this type. What is meant is a safe haven within which, autonomously, that is, without talk of practical objectives entering into the conversation, only one basic question is discussed: "How do things stand?" Secondly, it suddenly became clear to us that such a free space must be protected and guaranteed from outside—by the political authorities—that its freedom is made possible, indeed, even constituted by nothing other than this vehement will to truth, which is exclusively interested, even if only for this particular moment, in one thing—that the state of affairs being discussed be brought to view as it really is.

It should not be difficult for anyone nowadays to imagine a world whose atmosphere is almost completely shaped by an all-pervasive public language that consists exclusively of "catchwords". All speech occurs "so that" or "for the sake of"; it does not communicate anything; it accomplishes something. But is it not at the same time clear that someone who in the midst of such an existential space clogged with proclamations, banners, and reports manages to keep his view unfalteringly fixed on how things really are—someone who, even if it is silently and secretly, is able to express his knowledge of what is in words of the heart (like "The emperor has no clothes")—that that person has managed to preserve for himself a free space!

Here again, the original meaning of a seemingly already familiar word should be recalled: *theoria* and "theoretical" meant, in the original understanding of the ancients, exactly that: an understanding of the world, a turning toward the world, characterized solely by the desire that the reality of that world manifest itself as it is. But by "truth" we mean nothing other than this self-manifesting of reality.

[44] Proclaimed by Professor Scheler at a conference on the current tasks of philosophy; report in *Neues Deutschland*, December 17, 1957.

Consequently, that particular way of understanding the world may also be described as "theoretical" which aims at truth and nothing else—with this, I have again borrowed from Aristotle's *Metaphysics*, this time almost verbatim.[45]

Nowhere else and at no other time, except as practiced in philosophical *theoria*, has there been such a radical independence from any even remotely conceivable kind of employment for practical purposes. And it is just this independence that constitutes the "freedom" of the philosophizing person.

As a result, truth and knowledge, on the one hand, and freedom, on the other, belong together, and that in a very special and quite specifiable sense. Perhaps, then, it will no longer sound so preposterous to hear that, in the medieval sense of that term, "the free arts, the *artes liberales*, include all those that are oriented toward knowledge."[46] In the same way, the old saw about the truth that shall make us free (Jn 8:32) is suddenly given, on the basis of such experiences and thoughts, an unexpectedly fresh and, in an entirely different way, serious interpretation.

Now, however, on to the second question: How is it possible for the "theoretical" to be a *distinguishing* feature of philosophizing at all? Does not every science aim at precisely this? And is not *theoria* to be found in each science as well as that freedom which goes along with it? The answer, as might be expected, cannot be easily formulated or presented in a one-dimensional manner.

Theoria, as an existential act of man, aims, as we have said, at the pure perception of reality, at truth and nothing else. The power to perceive reality is, in fact, nothing other than reason itself; already language makes this clear to us. The nature of reason presents itself unalloyed in just this act of *theoria*; only in such an act is reason entirely itself. Now, however, *perceiving means being silent*. "That's been told many times by now, but there's nothing to stop its being told again":[47] only what is itself invisible is transparent, and only one who is silent hears—so much so that the more radically the will to listen is

---

[45] *Metaphysics* 2.1.933b20.

[46] "Illae solae artes liberales dicuntur, quae ad sciendum ordinantur" (Thomas Aquinas, *In Met.* I, 3 [no. 59]).

[47] Plato, *Gorgias* 508d5–6.

directed toward the whole, the deeper and more complete the silence must be. Thus philosophizing (as the contemplation of reality as a whole and the purest realization of *theoria*) amounts to engaging so completely in listening that this listening silence is not disturbed or interrupted for anything, not even for a question.

This is just what distinguishes philosophy from the special sciences. The sciences do not remain silent; they inquire. It is precisely through this questioning that the special sciences are constituted. Francis Bacon[48] even went so far as to liken the method of the experimental natural sciences to a painstaking interrogation, to a kind of torture, through which an answer is wrung from nature. This is an extreme but certainly not a completely incorrect metaphor. Incidentally, I am in no way implying that it is somehow impermissible or inappropriate to subject nature to such a forceful interrogation. And, of course, it is possible and—if there is to be any knowledge of reality at all— even necessary that the answers obtained are heard in silence, that is, in the attitude of *theoria*. The only difference is that in the case of the sciences, as we have indicated, the silence is not complete; it is interrupted and restricted by the explicit formulation of that particular aspect under which the object "world", which is in itself infinitely multifarious, is interrogated. Here, too, however, it belongs to the nature of the question formulated that it already fixes the direction of the response; in other words, entire provinces of reality are from the outset expressly rejected as being "of no interest". If one looks at the matter this way, then the query of the philosophizing person is, strictly speaking, not a question at all. "What is it all about?": this question is more like the articulation of that silence itself which in full and unlimited openness eavesdrops on the world. To this extent, the objection that has been raised by the exact sciences, namely, that what is here being asked is not a legitimate question at all, is clearly correct. Whoever regards the world "from every conceivable aspect" (whereby even the question of what is meant by a "conceivable" aspect is left open!) obviously does not regard it "under one aspect"! But this is exactly the way in which the philosophizing person actually views his object, the totality of reality and human existence.

Of course, with all this, we are far from implying that the scientific

---

[48] *De dignitate et augmentis scientiarum* 2, 2.

contemplation of the world, which, insofar as it energetically formulates and pursues this special aspect, does not remain completely silent, is not for its part a legitimate endeavor; that would be absurd. It goes without saying that it is, in fact, a vitally important endeavor. There should be no misunderstanding about this.[49] And within scientific research, which is conducted, not by an abstraction like "science", but by living human beings, there occurs, parenthetically, often enough a clandestine philosophizing. This hidden imprimatur, often in the main more sensed than palpably present, appears to me to make up what is genuinely "academic" in science; it suggests that the silver-based currency of scientific discourse is found alloyed with the gold of philosophical silence.[50]

It is clear that this silence is not associated with some kind of neutral passivity, nor does it derive from this kind of passivity. On the contrary, it is nurtured by a real commitment in the depths of the soul, namely, by the concern and worry that not a single thing be left out of its contemplation of reality as a whole. Although there is at the same time no doubt that this whole can never be completely comprehended, in no way should anything be intentionally omitted, covered up, forgotten, or suppressed. This openness to the whole is really something like a criterion of identity; as a *differentia specifica*, it singles out the philosophizing person.

Now it may in addition be said of such openness that it presupposes an impartiality—insofar as it is not identical with it—which extends far deeper into the core of man's existence than that matter-of-factness one labels "scientific objectivity". The search for a means of perfecting a technical procedure or an investigation into the causes of a certain symptomatology—such tasks do not affect me in the core of my being as a person, even if they hold me spellbound day and night. In order for questions of this type to be answered completely and adequately, it does not matter—apart, of course, from my scientific qualifications—what kind of person I am. At any rate, it does not require that impartiality which the philosophical act demands. Its lack does not hinder me from conducting scientific research with great success;

---

[49] As is, for example, the case with O. Seel, *Die platonische Akademie* (Stuttgart, 1953), pp. 45ff. Cf. J. Pieper, *Was heißt Akademisch?* (Munich, 1964), p. 126.

[50] Cf. ibid., pp. 22ff.

but it will most certainly hinder me from genuinely philosophizing, for example, from reflecting with undiminished powers of perception on everything that, in the final analysis, occurs when a human being dies. Here not much can be accomplished simply by using one's head, regardless of how intelligent that head might be. What is necessary is a completely relaxed opening up of the soul's secret responsive powers, which cannot be initiated by an act of will. It seems that the wisdom that has been handed down in the Far East has done more to keep this knowledge alive than the Western *ratio*.

As a first approximation, one might describe this personal precondition for the philosophical act with that brilliant formulation of Goethe's that has already been cited: "complete alienation from all pretension."[51] Even more applicable is the biblical proverb concerning the "singleness" (*simplicitas*) of the eye, which causes the whole body to be filled with light.[52] Only this singleness, which cannot co-exist with any form of reservation, enables us to perceive at all the entanglements of that object toward which philosophizing is directed.

One will perhaps object that this is a prerequisite that no one can, in fact, completely satisfy. This is doubtless true. The significance of this prerequisite, which is nonetheless extremely concrete and portentous, can be recognized in what is formally excluded and contradicted by it.

The time has come to discuss the fact that science not only does not possess *theoria* in the same radical sense as philosophy but that it has a different relationship to freedom, one specific to it. There even appears to be a special form of intellectual captivity that can befall only scientific thought and precisely when it attempts to philosophize or, more carefully put, when it attempts to express in such a manner what the world as a whole is like. Whoever then asserts what goes without saying for the scientific view of the world—that I am now, in my capacity as a philosophizing person, expressly leaving out of consideration everything that cannot be persuasively demonstrated and critically examined, that I am interested exclusively in what is "clearly and distinctly" knowable—has already fallen short of the questioning

---

[51] Letter to Herder dated November 10–11, 1786.

[52] Mt 6:22. In Luther's translation: "If your eye is sound, then your whole body will be light; but if your eye is mischievous, then your whole body will be all darkness."

attitude of the philosophizing person. With this, he would already have forfeited that openness which characterizes the philosophizing person *per definitionem*—that openness to the unforeshortened object of human knowledge, that is, to reality as a whole, which must be considered from every conceivable aspect. How can he be sure, however, that there is no information concerning reality that represents valid information but that can be neither verified nor comprehended "clearly and distinctly"? (Incidentally, no one could live even a single day of his life without accepting as true information of precisely this kind.) How do we know that what is in itself "most evident" is not, as Aristotle suggests,[53] related to our understanding as the light of day is to the eye of the owl? For the philosophizing person, to be "critical" does not mean in the first instance to grant validity only to what is absolutely certain but to be careful not to suppress anything.[54]

Another characteristic of the relationship between science and freedom is that science, on account of its practicality, can be used for specific purposes—and legitimately so, that is, without its worth being diminished in any way. No one has ever taken offense at the notion that medical science is in the service of curative therapy or that chemistry and physics are concerned with accomplishing technical tasks. The concept of "practicality", however, necessarily includes in itself the potential both for use as well as misuse. It is well known that some of the earliest discoverers of atomic energy wanted to prevent the technical exploitation of their findings. That is, however, absolutely impossible—just as impossible, for example, as preventing business from using insights from depth psychology—it belongs simply to the nature of science as such!

Against that "transformation of the world" of which Marx spoke in a famous maxim, there is not the least bit to be objected; on the contrary, it is a positive—even a necessary—thing to transform the world, to transform not only nature but also existing social relationships. We have seen, however, that it is no less positive, no less necessary, to know the world and to "interpret" it from a purely theoretical standpoint, concerning oneself with the truth and nothing else. It becomes hopeless, even impossible, to transform the world meaning-

---

[53] *Metaphysics* 2.1.993b9.
[54] Cf. J. Pieper, *Über den Glauben* (Munich, 1962), pp. 81f.

fully if one has not previously recognized what, in the final analysis, it is. That dimension of the world, however, toward which the gaze of the philosophizing person is directed is fundamentally inaccessible to, and removed from, every conceivable means of transforming the world, from all techniques and uses.

Augustine had distinguished between *uti* (using) and *frui* (enjoying) and, more importantly, between those things one uses and those others one enjoys but does not or should not use.[55] To enjoy a thing means to affirm it for its own sake and to take pleasure in it. By contrast, to use something means "to make something the means for acquiring those things one enjoys".[56] One might say that philosophical contemplation is concerned with those things "man enjoys". Still, this is a formulation that can be easily misunderstood. It becomes more readily comprehensible, however, if one considers something else as well.

The word with which the Romans translated the Greek *theoria* into Latin was *contemplatio*. Even in the Latin translation of the main Aristotelian text, which Thomas Aquinas took as the basis for his *Commentary on the Metaphysics*, it is possible to find the formulation, "theoria id est contemplatio".[57] Whenever, however, the concept of contemplation appears in this Thomistic context, a previously hidden element unexpectedly becomes visible and can be isolated, an element that is undoubtedly also implicit in the ancient Platonic/Aristotelian concept of *theoria* and that now likewise completes our conception of the act of philosophizing and of what it tacitly includes. The act of philosophical *theoria*, at least in its outward manifestation, is, in fact, virtually indistinguishable in structure, or so I am persuaded, from that which later Christian usage in the West dubbed "contemplation."

Contemplation, however, means *loving* contemplation, a beholding of the beloved.[58] It must then be asked whether a philosophizing reflection on reality as a whole does not at the same time presuppose or include an affirmation, however constituted, of this same reality. One

---

[55] *De doctrina christiana* 1, 3f.; *De Trinitate* 10, 10.
[56] Cf. Thomas Aquinas, 1, d. 1.
[57] *Metaphysics* 2.1.993a30.
[58] Cf. J. Pieper, *Glück und Kontemplation*, 3rd ed. (Munich, 1962), p. 74.

shies away from using the weighty word "love" in this context. "Affirmation", on the other hand, is obviously too inexact and too weak. Someone who is simply incapable of ever engaging in philosophical *theoria* because he regards the things of this world and perhaps even men themselves (with the exception of himself) only as raw material, as stuff from which something can be made—someone who is, in short, a *maître et possesseur de la nature*—can also be described as in a certain sense affirming things and finding them good—but good for himself and his purposes. What seems to be required of the philosophizing person, prior to all consideration of individual details, is that he, independently of their utility and usefulness, finds the things good *in themselves*—the things, the world, Being, beings as well as Being itself. But do we not call the affirmation of that which is "good for us and for our purposes" desire (*amor concupiscentiae*)—whereas only the affirmation of that which we regard as "good in itself" constitutes love in the genuine sense? If we analyze the sentence "omne ens ist bonum" (all being is good), which has since become somewhat enigmatic to us, in order to determine its precise meaning, then the upshot is that it cannot be regarded as expressing anything that is in any way defensible unless it be the following: the world, insofar as it is created, is willed by God, that is, loved by him as his creature, and is thus, by sheer virtue of the fact that it exists, good. Of course, it is not simply a matter of a single word (although one should perhaps not refer to such a primal term as a "word"); rather, the point is to force an initially unnoticed presupposition of philosophical *theoria* into the light of day. This is, perhaps, more likely to occur if one formulates the matter negatively and throws out the following question for consideration: Is not philosophizing, as the means of human fulfillment, at least just as threatened by the workday world's claim to totality as it is by the nihilistic dogma that the world as a whole is absurd and that everything that is deserves to perish?[59] Should both threats be presumed to coexist in unspoken collusion with each other?

We are still in the process of trying to interpret those ten incredibly concise lines from Aristotle's *Metaphysics*. In fact, it is impossible to understand a single word of the text if one fails to note and accept its underlying implications. Two have already been discussed—the

---

[59] Cf. F. Nietzsche, *The Will to Power*, no. 24.

first concerns the quite literal sense in which the will to truth is a liberating power, and the second the fact that the will to truth finds its purest fulfillment in philosophical *theoria*. Two things, it is to be hoped, have as a result become clear: first, that "knowledge . . . is then especially liberal . . . when and so far as it is philosophical"[60] and, second, that although the sciences are all involved in the quest for truth, only philosophy is, in the strict sense, as Aristotle himself puts it, the "science of truth",[61] *maxime scientia veritatis*.[62]

<h1 style="text-align:center">V</h1>

Still, all this will, in retrospect, have been called again into question if it is not possible to explain (*point three*) how this kind of reflection on reality as a whole, which is of no use and hence "free" and which aims at truth and is hence purely "theoretical", can be something *meaningful in itself*?

What does it signify to be meaningful in itself? I do not know whether a genuine misunderstanding is possible here; I would like at any rate to call attention to the possibility. "Meaningful in itself" does not, of course, signify meaningful *apart from man*, as if it implied correspondence with some set of norms obtaining in the abstract; human existence clearly provides the referential framework. "Meaningful in itself" is that which in a unique way has relevance to man and his existence.

This by no mean entails an absolutistic conception of man. What is, in fact, being implied is that man is, in a certain respect, also "meaningful in himself". This is precisely what is meant with the complex notion of a "person". One may define a person, if one allows oneself a somewhat permissible simplification, as a being that exists for the sake of its own perfection. However, only the individual is a personal being in this sense. He alone is in reality a "who" and a "somebody";

[60] J. H. Newman, *The Idea of a University*, discourse 5, 5.

[61] *Metaphysics* 2.1.993b19f.

[62] Thomas Aquinas, *In Met.* II, 1 (no. 297). "Si ergo huic conjunxerimus, quod . . . philosophia prima non est practica, sed speculativa, sequetur quod recte debeat dici scientia veritatis" (ibid., no. 290); ". . . *quod philosophia prima maxime consideret veritatem*" (ibid., no. 291).

strictly speaking, it is open only to him to be respected for what he is and in no way to be used as the means for something else outside himself.[63] With this, something momentous has been said, momentous also in terms of the value (and "valuation") of the philosophizing act, which cannot be conceived other than as an act emanating from the person. Wherever society (or the "world-spirit", "matter", "cosmos", or "evolution") is regarded as the decisive engine for attaining to the human, it is *eo ipso* true that the individual person can neither be something meaningful in himself nor can he do something meaningful in itself, whether that activity be philosophizing or something else.

As a first approximation, it may then be said that "to be meaningful in itself" amounts to "being good for something within the totality of a person's existence". As has in the meantime become evident, however, this expression—"good for something"—which has already been used once in contrast to "useful", needs to be defined more precisely. After all, even bread is good for something, that is, for satisfying one's hunger or for the purpose of satiation. To eat to the point of satiation is, in turn, good because it keeps one alive and prevents one from becoming ill. But what is being healthy and enjoying corporeal existence good for? Can that be asked at all? Obviously, we are approaching a boundary here. At least it could still be answered that one is living out an authentically human existence; that one "is becoming what one is"; that one is doing good; that one "glorifies" God; and so forth. But with this, the end of the chain of justification has been reached. And it is meaningless to pose a further question (such as "What is leading a meaningful human existence good for?"). At this stage, it no longer makes sense to refer to what is "good for something"; rather, we should instead speak of the "good" as such, of the *bonum hominis*[64] itself, and, above all, of what is included in this notion.

The earliest proverb to come down to us from the city of Athens, a hundred years before Plato—Anaxagoras' answer to the question,

---

[63] Thomas Aquinas maintains that even divine providence guides the human person "for his own sake"; in asserting this, he takes literally the astonishing biblical formulation (Wis 12:18), according to which God himself governs us "with great lenience" (cum magna reverentia) (C.G. 3, 112).

[64] Thomas Aquinas, *Virt. com.* 9.

Why were you put on this earth?—should be understood in the same light. His response was that it was for the sake of the contemplative observation, *eis theorian*, of heaven and the order of the universe.[65] Now the very same idea is being expressed with the thesis currently under discussion here: Since the philosophical contemplation of reality as a whole is a human activity that is meaningful in itself, it is not simply "oriented" toward "man's good", nor does it contribute to it, but it is rather an essential constituent of the good itself—and that means the common good as well, the *bonum commune*. Philosophical *theoria*, contemplation aimed solely at truth—which, however, can never be realized except in individual persons—is one part of the good centering around man's public life—and that not in the form of a "service" [*Dienst*] or contribution to the common good, but as an indispensable element of that good.[66]

Granted, with this, our thesis has become clearer, but it still remains a mere assertion. The question is how good the arguments that have been adduced in its favor are. What confounds the issue is that the thesis as well as the arguments that are to be brought forward in its favor concern not only philosophy but the characteristics of the philosophical itself; to reflect on this is already to philosophize and, hence, to refer to the precondition for that unique kind of impartiality and simplicity of which I have already spoken. This is not to say that something that is relevant to an "objective" assessment could not be presented at all; however, it does suggest that this could only occur with the simultaneous obligation to allow oneself to be engaged at a deeper level than the superficially rational.

The argument raises two issues for our consideration: *first*, the significance and the function of theoretical knowledge within the framework of human existence and, *secondly*, that very particular relationship which links the object of philosophical *theoria* to the nature of spirit.

First, what is, in effect, happening when man perceives reality, when he sees things as they are? The Western philosophical tradition offers an unexpectedly unanimous response to this question. What is happening, the answer runs, is an appropriation of reality, incomparable

---

[65] Cf. Aristotle, *Eudemian Ethics* 1.5.1216a15. Clement of Alexandria, *Miscellanies* (*Tapestries*) 2, 130, 2. Diogenes Laertius, *The Lives and Opinions of Eminent Philosophers* 2, 3 (no. 10).

[66] Cf. Thomas Aquinas, 4, d. 26, 1, 2.

in its intensity with anything else, a "conquête de l'être,"[67] a participation in the world, an assimilation, a swallowing whole, a taking possession—literally, nourishment and satiation through Being.
When, in the midst of Plato's vision of the great feast that occurs in
"that place beyond the heavens", it is said of the soul that when it
in bliss beholds true being, it *is nourished* at the same time,[68] this is
just as little intended as allegorical speech as when Aquinas refers to
knowledge as the noblest means of possessing something ("nobilissimus modus habendi aliquid").[69]

Moreover, such figures of speech are not so far removed from those
with which we are already familiar as might initially be assumed. For
example, we ourselves know quite well in principle—and we do not
need anyone to tell us, specifically—that we do not turn something
into our real "possession", which we can refer to as "mine" or "ours",
simply by purchasing it or through any legal procedure. Rather, regardless of what we might wish or believe ourselves to possess—a
garden, a book, a sculpture, but also a friend, a teacher, a lover, or
even what has befallen us only once as an encounter or event—we
"have something" from them only to the extent that we keep them
present before us through a continually renewed seeing, contemplating, reflecting, and remembering. In no other way can we gain access
to our true riches, the genuine possessions of this life. To be certain
of this, we hardly require corroboration through that "wisdom belonging to the men of old".

Incidentally, one need not turn for such corroboration only to the
men of old. Pierre Teilhard de Chardin began his book on the phenomenon of man[70] with a surprising "prologue", which at first hardly
seems to belong to it; it carries the title "Seeing". In a certain sense,
so he writes there, "all life is enclosed" in seeing; "the gaze's acuity and field of perception [are] the criteria for perfection"; indeed,
the principle of ascent guiding the evolution of all that lives might
be summarized in the formula: "the emergence of ever more perfect
eyes" (élaboration d'yeux toujours plus parfaits). "See or perish"—

---

[67] P. Rousselot, *L'Intellectualisme de Saint Thomas* (Paris, 1936), p. XVI.
[68] *Phaedrus* 247d3–4.
[69] *De causis* 18 (no. 339); see also 4, d. 49, 3, 5, 1 ad 2.
[70] *Le Phénomène humain* (Paris, 1955). German translation: *Der Mensch im Kosmos* (Munich,
1959).

that is across all environmental niches "the situation dictated by the mysterious gift of existence".[71]

The dismaying alternative formulated by Teilhard de Chardin, "voir ou périr", entails another challenge that might easily be overlooked. It prompts one to ask whether the utmost counterpart to "decay" could at the same time be defined as the utmost extremity of "seeing"—who would, by implication, be the wholly saved one, the ultimately perfect one, the one who has arrived at the goal as seer (see-er) in the highest conceivable sense. We all know how emphatically just this is asserted in the traditional notion of a blissful life. It almost appears as if whoever undertakes to describe the ultimate perfection will speak of absolutely nothing else but the act of beholding: "What do they not see who see him who sees all?";[72] "our whole recompense: see-ing";[73] "if . . . man's life is ever worth the living, it is when he has attained the vision of the very soul of beauty . . . ; he shall be called the friend of god, and if ever it is given man to put on immortality, it shall be given to him";[74] "the happening [Glücken] of theoria is man's happiness [Glück]";[75] "And eternal life is this: to know you. . . ."[76] This chorus of voices, in which the Holy Scriptures of Christendom and the theology founded on them resonate with the philosophers of antiquity, might actually be augmented with many more voices.

It should be borne in mind, however, that these expressions do not refer exclusively to an "eschatological hereafter"; rather they are as-serting that a person on this side of history longs at all the differ-ent levels of his nature to know and to see. "We prefer sight to al-most everything else."[77] The author of this sentence, Aristotle, even acknowledges an explicit connection between vulgar onlooking and philosophical theoria: If we are already willing to spend great sums of

---

[71] Le phénomène, p. 25; Mensch im Kosmos, p. 3.

[72] "Quid est quod non videant qui videntem omnia vident?" (Gregory the Great, as cited by Thomas Aquinas, Ver. 2, 2).

[73] "Tota merces nostra visio est" (Augustine, Sermones 302. Migne, PL 39, 2324; see also De Trinitate 1, 9).

[74] Plato Symposium 211d1f.; 212a6f. [Quoted after the translation by Michael Joyce, in Plato: The Collected Dialogues, p. 563.]

[75] W. Szilasi, Macht und Ohnmacht des Geistes (Freiburg im Breisgau, 1947), p. 154. This sentence is intended as an interpretation of Aristotle.

[76] Jn 17:3.

[77] Aristotle Metaphysics 1.1.980a25.

money to travel to Olympia for no other reason than to see games, contests, and displays, then how much more intent must we be on beholding Being itself and truth.[78]

Still, there is no need for concern: it would never have occurred to me to equate philosophical *theoria* with the *visio beatifica*. The contemplation of reality as a whole with respect to its ultimate meaning, that is, philosophizing as such, takes the form of a questioning rather than a beholding. But we were supposed to be discussing how philosophizing can be something "meaningful in itself", and, when viewed from this standpoint, there is, in fact, a connection. Nowhere else, it appears, does the intensity of a spiritual existence as such and the hunger for the uncurtailed possession of this life, which finds its goal and its ultimate incomprehensible fulfillment in the *visio beatifica* —nowhere do they appear so purely and so intrepidly, as it were, as in the simplicity of the philosophical questioner, who, no less than the ultimate beholder, has only one thought in mind: truth, the self-manifesting of the infinite object.

We turn now to consider the *second* issue, namely, the object of this philosophizing and, more particularly, the special correspondence between it and the nature of spirit as such.

Curiously, whoever inquires in contemporary handbooks and reference works after those features that distinguish spiritual from non-spiritual beings will only rarely find mentioned there a characteristic that was apparently regarded by the great tradition as being more basic than "immateriality" or "consciousness". I am referring to that universality which attaches to spirit by virtue of its nature: the intellectual soul is in a certain sense itself "the all" (quodammodo omnia)[79] and is from birth so constituted as to "come together with every type of being" (convenire cum omni ente).[80] Strictly speaking, this faculty or constitution, which allows it to come into relation with absolutely everything that is, cannot even be said to be a property, something that the spirit "possesses"; the spirit *is* itself this power, this relating faculty that is directed toward the *totum* of reality. It is the essential and distinguishing feature of spirit that it is not confined but also not

[78] Aristotle Fragment 58 (ed. Rose).
[79] Aristotle *De anima* 3.8.431b21, as cited by Thomas Aquinas, *Ver.* 1, 1.
[80] Thomas Aquinas, *Ver.* 1, 1.

adapted to the cross-sectional milieu of an "environment" but that it relates itself to *the* world; this explains its superiority in relation to all other nonspiritual beings; it is what distinguishes man, for example, from the animals. And it is this same totality of Being that is the object of philosophizing; indeed, with philosophizing, nothing more is meant than the contemplation of reality *as a whole*.

Still, something does not seem quite right here. In any event, it is difficult to suppress a certain unease in light of the last few sentences. Have we not spoken all too magnificently of man and, by implication, of the possibilities of philosophy? There are, in fact, good reasons for this suspicion. Nevertheless, it is not completely justified.

Of course, one is not giving a complete description of man when one characterizes him as a spiritual (an "ensouled") being. On the contrary, he is at the same time so fundamentally corporeal that one might even go so far as to assert that there is nothing "purely spiritual" in man at all (but also nothing "purely material"). As a result, he is factually incapable of living simply and continuously "in the face of all that is". If only to still his hunger, he needs to set up shop in the narrow domicile of the "environment", in which his gaze is quite predictably restricted to what is of use and serviceable, to what one "needs to live". It remains nonetheless true that if such confinement (to the realm of planned utility, to the straightforward concern with earning one's daily bread, to "servile" labor, and so forth) becomes permanent, so that it can no longer, for whatever reason, be broken through, then human existence threatens at that very moment to become inhuman. It must be expected of the man who is establishing himself—naturally and rightly—in the world (and he must expect it of himself) that he will realize time and again in some manner not to be prescribed the inherent power of spirit, that he will allow himself to shake off the fortifications built into the bustle of praxis (so sheltering and even comfortable, despite all the talk of "bother" and "hectic"), that he will place himself in question—and that he, then, in wonder, will catch sight of the true extent of "his" world, which amounts, in fact, to no less than everything. It is in precisely this that the necessity and dignity of the philosophical act is to be found— what in the philosophical act is meaningful in itself.

Of course, the "totality of the real" need not always be made the object of formal inquiry. This notwithstanding, the philosophizing person is directly concerned with the overall structure of that same world, it should be noted, with which our daily praxis must also come to terms. The well-known proposition from Aristotle's *Metaphysics*[81] to the effect that the philosopher investigates Being as Being, which appears all too readily understandable, has two meanings. The first is that nothing "other" is involved in the philosophical contemplation of Being than what lies before every man's eyes, the real and reality in general. More unsettling is its second meaning: what lies before everyone's eyes is viewed *as* something real. One may well ask, " 'As' what else, then?" But, in reality, such a form of contemplation is the most unlikely in the world. The fountain pen with which I write will naturally be viewed by everyone as just that particular writing instrument we tend to use nowadays. To the question of what am I holding there in my hand, we normally expect information about the special properties of this fountain pen—for example, the volume of ink, the brand, the manufacturer, and so on. If I were to answer instead: Don't you see, what I have here in my hand is an industrial product, something designed and produced by man, a *res artificialis*, as the ancients called it—that would be, to put it mildly, a rather unexpected answer. At the same time it would be fully correct; it would even be giving expression to things that are worth considering more deeply. But one does not typically view a fountain pen or any of the thousands of other technical (or artificial) products with which we continually have intercourse as *res artificialis*. If it had been my intention to provoke my questioner even more, then I would have said something like "This is a piece of matter." What kind of perplexed thoughts would have come to him everyone can picture for himself at his own leisure. Incidentally, that, too, would have been a highly significant answer, one whose sense could not have been easily exhausted. And despite all this, I still would have failed to view and characterize my writing instrument *as something real*. With all this, I would, arguably have inspired only laughter—which, in turn, would have possibly reminded me of the tale about the Thracian maiden. "This is something real." Now one might not perhaps have disputed the fact that this is a thoroughly correct answer—but is it really saying anything?

---

[81] *Metaphysics* 3.2.1003a21.

The ancients, for their part, who in this were only claiming to articulate and to interpret what the ordinary man in any event already
thought and knew, did not find that in this sentence so little was being
expressed. Among the things being expressed, for example, is the fact
that there is something that engages in the activity of "being", an *ens*
(present participle, *participium praesens*, of *esse*!); that it, moreover, is
something structured in such and such a way, a *res*, and determined
by "an ensemble of properties" (ensemble de qualités);[82] that it is at
the same time an *aliquid*, something formlike that is distinct and that,
through its limits, sets itself apart from everything else. With this,
only the very first steps in the direction of an answer, steps that were
in any event tentatively undertaken, have been intimated—hints at an
answer to the question, "What is it to be something real?"

Regardless of how it might be answered specifically, however, our
original question, which has unexpectedly become a philosophical
question, no longer concerns only that concrete thing which gave
rise to the question in the first place. All of a sudden, even if no
express mention has been made of the fact, one is inquiring into the
structure of reality in general, into the structure of everything that is.

Alfred North Whitehead has said, appealing incidentally to Plato,[83]
that the problem that, in reality, poses itself for the philosophizing person is "to grasp a complete fact".[84] In the same moment, however,
that the philosophizing person sets out to accomplish this and thus to
conceive of the extremely concrete, undoubtedly experienceable, and,
after all, by no means unfamiliar fact of "death" in a complete manner
and to state what befalls a man in death, not only in physiological and
biographical terms but with a view to the whole—from that moment
on, I say, he is speaking no longer solely of this punctual event but—
whether openly or tacitly—of the entire context of human existence,
of reality as a whole, of "God and the world", as they say. In this
respect, the philosophizing person (again, whether he knows it and
likes it or not) also distinguishes himself at a very basic level from
the empirical researcher who qualifies as such by virtue of the fact

---

[82] Jean-Paul Sartre uses these words to circumscribe the concept of *essentia* (*L'Existentialisme est un humanisme* [Paris, 1946], p. 18).

[83] *Sophist* 248e.

[84] *Adventures of Ideas* (New York, 1956), p. 203.

that he observes his object under a clearly specified aspect and who is
thus not even entitled to speak of "God and the world". To do this
would be just as unscientific as *not* to do it would be unphilosophical.

When, however, those questions that are either gradually or all too
spontaneously ignited by the concrete given become philosophical
ones, this is the result of a multi-textured process. Not only does one
distance oneself ever more from what is "practically" relevant, as can
be inferred from the example of the fountain pen; the horizon of
the original question is at the same time widened to precisely the
same extent so that its boundaries can no longer be made out. Significantly, this question proves to be all the more unanswerable, the
more it comes to encompass the totality consisting of both the world
and its ground.

VI

If, however, the question of the philosophizing person is really unanswerable, does this not imply that its object is unknowable? And is it
still supposed to be meaningful to ask this question?

In his *Symposium*, Plato has Diotima say, "None of the gods are seekers after truth."[85] This is supposed to indicate that ultimate knowledge
and philosophizing exclude each other. Clearly, Aristotle is expressing
exactly the same thought in the thoroughly unmythological diction of
his *Metaphysics*;[86] there it is said that the question of the philosophizing
person ("what is being?" "what does it mean to be real?") is a . . .
question. And Aquinas wrote the astonishing sentence (astonishing
because it is not found in Kant's *Critique of Pure Reason* but rather in
the *Quaestiones disputatae* of this great teacher of Christendom, whom
some had tried to turn into a rationalist who knows the answer to
every question): "Rerum essentiae sunt nobis ignotae" (the essences
of things are unknown to us).[87] How can that be, however, if what
characterizes the philosophizing person is precisely to inquire after

---

[85] *Symposium* 204a1. [Quoted after the translation by Joyce, in *Plato: The Collected Dialogues*, p. 556.]

[86] *Metaphysics* 7.1.1028b2ff.

[87] *Ver.* 10, 1. Similar remarks may be found in the commentary on Aristotle's *De anima* I, 1. (no. 15); *Spir. creat.* 11 ad 3; *Ver.* 4, 1 ad 8.

the essential cause of beings and of the world in general? The same duality is present in the very meaning of the word *philosophia* itself: and from the very beginning—indeed, especially at the beginning—this meaning was clearly recognized and also articulated (by Pythagoras and Plato, for example).[88] It has two key aspects: "Philosophy" is in the *first* instance actually a negative epithet, clearly signifying a *lack* of wisdom. No one—no mortal, at least—can possess a definitive knowledge of things in their depth and breadth; such knowledge, if we had it, would make us unconditionally "wise" and "knowing". The *second* semantic element in the epithet "philosophy" has a positive connotation. In its affirmative sense, philosophizing means precisely this: staying on the hunt, persisting in the "loving" search for what is simply worth knowing—for that wisdom which makes us absolutely wise—while at the same time being aware of the impossibility of an ultimately satisfying answer.

But is that not heroic nonsense? I think not. For the time being, at any rate, I am persuaded that this characterization of philosophizing and its object offers a completely sober and precise description of the matter at hand, which cannot be expressed any other way.

As regards the "unknowability" of the object with which the philosophizing person is concerned, this does, in fact, require a more precise definition: "unknowable" can mean many things, and of course only one can be meant here.

Whoever says that the stars are invisible by day is referring, strictly speaking, not to a specific feature of the stars themselves, but rather to the conditions under which alone the eye is capable of perceiving them. No one will dispute the fact that the stars "in themselves" are just as visible by day as by night; they are, regardless of lighting, possible objects of sight. "Invisibility" can, however, also refer to a quality of the object and would then imply that the object is, in itself, so constituted that it cannot be perceived by the eye; in this sense an effort of will is just as invisible as a melody. Thus, if "unknowability" is predicated of the object of philosophical *theoria*, then one must be clear whether something is being asserted about the possibility and conditions of (subjective) knowledge or about the constitution of the object itself.

---

[88] *Phaedrus* 278d3ff.

For the same reason, one should be clear in advance about the difference between knowledge (*cognoscere*) and comprehension (*comprehensio*). Comprehension is, of course, a special form of knowledge, but it is the exact nature of this special quality that is in question. One might argue that the comprehending form of knowledge is synonymous with creative knowledge, a "knowing to the very end". A still more precise formulation may be found, it appears to me, in Aquinas: To comprehend a thing means to know it "so well", as to know it "as it is in itself".[89] An object is then comprehended when, on its side, there is nothing left over from the purely knowable, no remainder, that could be transformed into something known. If there were such a remainder, however, would it still not have to be called "knowable", although unknowable in fact? Or could there possibly be things, states of affairs, contexts, structures, that are unknowable "in themselves", that is, not only factually unknown by man, but simply inaccessible to knowledge as such, just as a melody is absolutely unattainable by sight?

This, as cannot easily be concealed, is a question that goes to the very heart of the matter, affecting one's world view from the bottom up. Whoever attempts to answer it will immediately recognize that he must declare in favor of an ultimate position. We are again, or perhaps still, confronted with the hub of the wheel, where everything connects up with everything else. This need not in itself imply that the answer cannot in any way be justified on empirical grounds, our answer here being that there are no objects "unknowable" in themselves, either in philosophy or elsewhere. On this view, reality, to the extent that only it is involved, is accessible to knowledge in all its realms and structures—this accessibility can be designated by many names: "manifestness", "unconcealedness", "perceivability", "brightness", "lucidity". "The being-real of things is itself their light."[90]

The proposition asserting the "truth" of all things ("omne ens est verum") must also be rescued from its obscurity for it asserts nothing other than that everything that possesses being is by nature, that is, by virtue of its being real, at the same time intelligible. It is, however, not completely accurate to describe the proposition as asserting nothing

---

[89] "Comprehendere autem proprie dicitur aliquis aliquam rem cognoscendo, qui cognoscit rem illam quantum in se cognoscibilis est" (*Super Joh.* I, 11 [no. 213]).

[90] "Ipsa actualitas rei est quoddam lumen ipsius" (Thomas Aquinas, *De causis* 6 [no. 168]).

"other" than this. In reality, that "other" which it asserts in addition
to this is even more important than the aforementioned. That "other"
is the *reason* why the things are intelligible and have names: the reason is that everything that is emerges from the creatively designing
knowledge of God and *consequently* possesses "in itself", as something
thought and, in fact, uttered,[91] "word-character",[92] that is, the characteristic of being in principle comprehensible and intelligible. "We
see the things you have made because they are. But they are because
you see them."[93]

Now it will be said that this is not a question to be settled by
empirical data. That is correct. And, of course, one cannot persuade
anyone to accept this world view—this point will prove decisive in
another context. Still one must recognize that this proposition concerning the truth of all beings loses not only its poignancy but also its
entire sense if one isolates it from the thought of the createdness of
the world. Now, after precisely this happened in the modern systems
of rationalism, up to and including the systems of Neoscholasticism,
it should not be in the least surprising that the wretched remainder
should have completely vanished from all living philosophizing. One
should not deceive oneself, however: the straightforward denial of
the createdness of the world also has unforeseeable consequences for
the philosophical understanding of the world that are perhaps truly
"realized" only in stages. With this denial, one distances oneself not
only from the holy tradition of Christianity but also from the Greek
world view,[94] which means also from those origins that inevitably
shape one's own thinking, in terms of both its problematic and its
terminology. Although it is open to discussion whether, as Jean-Paul
Sartre has claimed,[95] the very conception of a "human nature" has
already become meaningless, it is certainly impossible to deny consistently that things were thought out by a creative, designing spirit and

[91] Cf. J. Pieper, "Was heißt 'Gott spricht'?", *Catholica* 19 (1965): 189f.

[92] R. Guardini, *Welt und Person* (Würzburg, 1940), p. 110.

[93] Augustine, *Confessions* 13, 38. [Quotation from Saint Augustine, *Confessions*, trans. Henry Chadwick (Oxford, 1991), p. 304.] See also *Confessions* 7, 4.

[94] For more on this, see J. Pieper, *Über die platonischen Mythen* (Munich, 1965), pp. 53ff.

[95] "Il n'y a pas de nature humaine, puisqu'il n'y a pas de Dieu pour la concevoir" (Jean-Paul Sartre, *L'Existentialisme*, p. 22). [In English: "There is no human nature, since there is no God to conceive it" (Jean-Paul Sartre, *Existentialism and Human Emotions* [New York, 1957], p. 15)].

—as if this had no consequences—to continue to find comprehensible and meaningful the notion that the intelligibility of these very same things is an empirically verifiable fact.

Does, however, the intelligibility of Being really present itself to us *empirically*? Shortly before his death, the logician Heinrich Scholz confronted me, not without an ironically critical emphasis, with the question of whether the heavens would really cave in if it should turn out in light of the structure of reality that there are, in fact, "obscure" and inaccessible states of affairs. Can "structure"—I countered—be conceived at all without thinking *eo ipso* of something that, despite its possibly infinite complexity, is somehow determinable and comprehensible? Something that is real and at the same time not identifiable in principle—that not only stretches our imagination, it pushes it to the breaking point. "But modern physics has apparently turned up just such a state of affairs!" I fired back with the question of whether at this juncture, then, one had broken off and permanently abandoned further research along these lines. "No, naturally not!" How can this conclusion be "natural", though, unless one is convinced, perhaps even in opposition to one's own philosophical thesis, that states of affairs exist that are "in themselves" unknowable?

The sentence "omne ens est verum" can in fact be reformulated in this way: It makes sense to continue doing research.

As is well known, even orthodox Marxism makes the same point. "The world and its regularities [are] eminently knowable"; there are "no unknowable things, but there are certainly things that are not yet known": these sentences are taken from Stalin's programmatic work *On Dialectical and Historical Materialism*;[96] and since he can appeal to Engels and Lenin for support, it may be assumed that they have ceded none of their official validity. Do they express the same idea as the ancient proposition asserting the truth of all that is real? If not, where does the difference lie?

The difference consists in the fact that, first, Stalin is referring, strictly speaking, not to a quality in things, but rather to a capacity for human knowledge (although the two aspects can, of course, not be completely separated from each other). Secondly, the capacity for

---

[96] J. Stalin, *Über dialektischen und historischen Materialismus*. Complete text with critical commentary by I. Fetscher, 4th ed. (Frankfurt, Berlin, and Bonn, 1957), pp. 8of. See also n. 8 of section 1.

"an exhaustive knowledge" of the world[97] is being asserted of human reason; and as proof, one is referred to an argument from praxis, an argument by way of "experiment and industry", that is, that there is nothing in the world that could not also be produced by men. As we know, this is a notion that is by no means restricted to Marxism; in fact, it is not all that far removed from Sartre's thesis that man is nothing other than what he makes of himself.[98] I do not dispute the fact that in the realm of the technical and artificial but also in that of the moral and historical, man is engaged in "creative" activity— as long as one does not fail to recall that man has never succeeded in anything other than transforming a pregiven reality. Here however something else is at issue, namely, the irremediability of the distinction between what man has made and what he has not made, between *res artificiales* and *res naturales*, that is, between such things that take their measure from human design and which, for precisely this reason, we can completely know and those things that owe their measure to divine design and that we for that reason can never "know to the very end" because no finite faculty penetrates to the archetype that resides in the divine spirit.

Here again it becomes evident how impossible it is to set aside one's basic convictions when engaging in the act of philosophizing. I am *not* saying, let it be noted, that the philosophizing person will, insofar as he philosophizes "in the proper fashion", arrive with a certain necessity at a specific interpretation of reality. I *am*, however, saying that, provided he continues to inquire philosophically with complete openness, he will ultimately arrive at a point where he cannot avoid raising very basic questions regarding the world and human existence. This may, however, be the point at which he finds himself compelled expressly to accept or reject the interpretation of the world embodied in the tradition.

The sentence "omne ens est verum"—even its so optimistic sounding translation, which one is almost tempted to regard as a kind of slogan for scientific policy ("it makes sense to continue doing research")—has then, surprisingly, two aspects. The one enables us to recognize an ever deepening access to all existing things; the other,

---

[97] Cf. F. Engels, *Ludwig Feuerbach und der Ausgang der klassischen deutschen Philosophie*, pp. 17f.

[98] Jean-Paul Sartre, *L'Existentialisme*, p. 22.

the impossibility of ever reaching rock bottom. Both aspects—not just "the view from daylight" [*Tages-ansicht*] to borrow from Fechner, but also the "view by night" [*Nacht-ansicht*], that is, the inexhaustibility of the real—both are empirically verifiable facts. That, however, both may be traced back to the same origin; that they are even in a certain sense identical; that, more specifically, the things are, taken for themselves, knowable in their ultimate constitution because they originate in the infinite *brightness* of the divine *logos* and that they are at the same time unfathomable to us precisely because they originate in the *infinite* brightness of the divine *logos*—this is not empirically verifiable.

The philosophical act begins at the boundary where intelligibility and unfathomability intersect; it is initiated by a recognition of the incomprehensibility of the world and human existence.

This boundary has not, parenthetically, been fixed for all time, and one cannot specify *in concreto* where it runs. It can also be displaced —so it would appear—depending on the degree of openness or drive for clarification on the part of the individual spirit in a manner that cannot be determined in advance. Here again lies one of the differences between science and philosophy, that is, that in philosophy the individual person and his ability to listen counts for so much more. It is meaningful to speak of "the sciences" as if they made up a single enterprise with its own division of labor extending over centuries, almost as if it were a collective subject. "The sciences have shown . . .": one may legitimately describe its findings in this way. It is, by contrast, nonsense to say that philosophy has discovered or explained this or that. However true it may be that philosophizing as a living activity takes place in the dialogue between spirits, precisely as dialogue, there can be no "teamwork" in philosophy. No philosophizing person can in any way profit from the "results" of Plato's philosophizing unless he thinks through Plato's thoughts for himself. In the special sciences, by contrast, the results at which an individual researcher has arrived may be used by everyone without their being compelled to retrace the lines of inquiry pursued by this one person.

What is above all uncharacteristic for philosophizing is a form of progress where the more it penetrates into its object, the more the "white spots on the map" are made to vanish. On the contrary, as eminently suitable as this metaphor may be for the scientific investigation of the world, the metaphor is exactly inverted in the case of philosophizing: the deeper and more comprehensive the insight, the more overwhelmingly the unanticipatable field of what has still to be known dominates one's view. This, however, is related in a very direct way to the endlessness of the design that the philosophizing person, insofar as he philosophizes, undertakes to decipher.

With regard to the answerability of the philosophical question and the knowability or nonknowability of its object, the following may be said in summary: It may well occur that the impartiality of the philosophizing person may become clouded, or his intellectual energy may suffer fatigue and fail. Two things, however, cannot happen to him on his way. He will never come across barriers that lie in the object itself and that simply prevent him from moving forward; nor will he ever come to the end of his path, that is, to that point at which the question that originally set him thinking has been answered conclusively.

The world view, on the basis of which this may be asserted, and the only one on the basis of which it may be made plausible, is of course vulnerable to attack on two fronts: by various forms of agnostic resignation and by various forms of rationalist hubris. Both types of position are extremely topical far outside the realm of academic philosophy. Ironically, this same world view is constantly in danger of being confused with its opposite numbers and even of changing over into them. One need only guard against this for as long as it takes one to realize that this world view is indeed characterized by incomprehensibility, but it is the incomprehensibility of a world that is lucid in itself and to its very depths, and that it is indeed intelligible, but it is the intelligibility of a world that is illuminated by a (for us) "inaccessible light".

VII

In 1960, in the midst of an academic lecture, Karl Jaspers made the remark that philosophy had become "an embarrassment for everyone".[99] With this, he was referring, not to the inconsistency that naturally arises with regard to the world of use-oriented praxis, but rather

---

[99] *Wahrheit und Wissenschaft* (Basel, 1960), p. 20.

to philosophy's status within the modern university. Even this embarrassment, it appears to me, however, could only fully be eliminated from the world by simultaneously eliminating philosophy itself. Here, again, a natural incommensurability is involved, this time that between philosophical and scientific thought. And it was only to be expected that the university would subordinate itself all the more exclusively to the criteria of exact science as this incommensurability became ever more pronounced. There are, however, good reasons for this tendency toward exclusivity, which may readily be observed; indeed it is virtually unavoidable. In philosophizing something occurs that, when viewed from a scientific standpoint, is highly objectionable, even impossible—assuming, that is, one understands by philosophizing what Plato and Aristotle understood by this term and what it meant in the great philosophical tradition extending up to Karl Jaspers.

Still, scientific research and philosophy have never stood in each other's way per se. Strictly speaking, it is not they who have been the interlocutors in that dispute which has been quite audibly underway for some time now; rather, the catcallers have been those who declare the exact sciences to be the only binding norm-setting model for any reflection on reality and truth that aspires to be taken seriously —with which, of course, not an intrascientific thesis, but a theoretical one, one originating in the philosophy of science and hence a properly philosophical thesis, is being advanced. This argument is, in fact, broadly invoked—for example, by the defenders of a "scientific philosophy". And on the other side? Naturally those under attack do not dispute the inherent lawfulness of science. They, do, however, strongly insist on there being other equally indispensable forms of the human epistemological endeavor, which, although different from science, are correlated with it in many ways and which are even dependent on it—for example, philosophy.

This kind of dispute does not break out wantonly. Instead, it should from the outset be presumed that it is associated with specific changes in the total fabric of historical existence. This necessitates from time to time a revision and reformulation of positions. This should not be taken to imply—just the opposite!—that conflicts are at bottom misunderstandings that can be removed through further clarification. On the contrary, some disagreements will be made even more acute through a clear statement of the problem. Of course, it is impossible to specify in more detail here what the principles of scientific research are and what it means, conversely, to philosophize. But a kind of catalogue of points of contention should in any event be attempted, at the very least a short list of their "differences" (in the twofold sense), which, with a certain predictability, have tended to inflame the controversy.

First, allow me to recall the metaphor of the unending way, which I have used with some circumspection to designate the inner state of the philosophizing person; this analogy has a more precise sense than might perhaps have initially been realized. More importantly, it points up the most radical difference between philosophizing and scientific research, the one that most distinguishes the one from the other. While it is true that one sometimes says of the sciences that they are "always on their way to new goals", this is not meant in the same sense as in philosophy.

In tackling a problem that has been put to him, the physicist is certainly not entering on an endless path. At some point, perhaps even after a long period of time, he has covered the entire path. The question is then answered; the corresponding hope is fulfilled; the goal achieved. At the same time, however, still other questions announce themselves, but that is, then, another story. Whoever sets himself the task of reflecting on the entirety of world and human existence, that is, of philosophizing, has already set his foot on a path whose end he, in this world, will never reach. He remains "underway"; the question is never conclusively answered; the hope never laid to rest. Perhaps he succeeds in making understandable to someone after a fashion that in this way, *in* the living enactment of question and hope, one at least keeps oneself open to the infinite object, the totality of the real. One remains at its heels, as it were, and keeps it—the object—in view, whereas otherwise its existence must simply be forgotten. This remains, however, in essence a highly vexing and intolerable mode of expression, not for the scientist, but for the "scientific world view", which "recognizes no insolvable problems";[100] "all knowledge of being is obtained as a matter of principle through the method of the special sciences; any other 'ontology' is idle chatter."[101] In one word:

[100] R. Carnap, *Wissenschaftliche Weltauffassung: Der Wiener Kreis*, p. 15.
[101] M. Schlick, "Erleben, Erkennen, Metaphysik", *Kant-Studien* 31 (1926): 157.

the absolutism of exactitude and perfection and that which by nature has the character of a "not yet" mutually exclude each other; nothing is as evident as this.

Now, as everyone knows, there is an old proverb that says that man himself likewise remains his whole life long "unfinished" [*unfertig*] and "on the way", a *viator*—regardless of the many other ways in which he arrives at his goal and regardless of how much he otherwise, in the realm of knowing and in the praxis of making and doing, succeeds in finishing [*fertig bringen*]; for this reason human existence itself has the structure of hope—just like the act of philosophizing itself. And I wonder whether, in fact, one must already have perceived and accepted this relationship between the inner structure of existence itself and the philosophical act, which admittedly cannot be grasped very precisely, in order to be able to acknowledge the hopeful and inquiring philosophical act as a turning of one's attention toward the mystery of the world, not only as something that is "also possible", but as something that one cannot abstain from or dispense with.

Another point of contention between philosophy and science that is difficult to reconcile is their fundamentally different conception of what at bottom constitutes the relative perfection of human knowledge. From the standpoint of science, one can say that science is perfect only insofar as a state of affairs, regardless of type, can be grasped in clear conceptual terms and precisely formulated. By contrast, the philosophizing person, as fascinated as he perhaps is by the formal perfection of scientific thought, is incapable of perceiving in this feature the perfection of knowledge at all.

It appears to me to be not only a personally moving fact but one highly relevant to the technical problem at hand that Alfred North Whitehead, whose career began under the star of *Principia Mathematica*,[102] a work of such formal exactitude that it is probably intelligible to and reproducible by only a very few, could say at the end of his life, as a philosopher in the manner of the great tradition and with a legitimacy like that of no other: "The exactness is a fake", that is, a will o' the wisp, a phantom. This is the final sentence of the eighty-year-old's valedictory address (on the topic of immortality), held at

---

[102] This is the title of a three-volume work, written together with Bertrand Russell, which has become a classic in modern mathematical logic; it was published between 1910 and 1913.

Harvard University in the spring of 1941.[103] Nathaniel Lawrence, the author of a pathbreaking work on Whitehead's philosophical development,[104] auditor at and witness to this memorable lecture, reported to me that Whitehead gave this, his last public speech, "with the entire energy to which his high, faltering voice was capable, and with such a radiant goodness that one thought he was on the verge of saying, 'The Lord is my shepherd', and perhaps he really was." There can be no hint of a suspicion here that, with this sentence, some kind of irrationalism is being proclaimed or even simply conceded. No, what manifests itself here is a transformed conception of what it means for our knowledge to be perfect, one no longer determined by science, that is, the distinctly philosophical conception.

We have already said once that being "critical" for the philosophizing person amounts to making sure that not a single thing is left out. The totality of the real, however, toward which this concern is directed, is not identical with that sum which is obtained by addition and which contains each thing and all things; rather, what is meant is the *totum*, the articulated fabric of the world, in which there is a hierarchy, organized according to greater and lesser plenitude of being, and above all a highest that is simultaneously the deepest ground and origin for every individual thing and for the whole. I realize that this is, for the time being, only an assertion, indeed, a very bold and very "vulnerable" one, which urgently requires justification. Still, I do not intend to discuss it further here or even to justify it. I am more concerned now with making plausible why someone who reflects on the whole of reality, that is, the philosophizing person, must necessarily have a different conception of "perfect knowledge" than the special sciences and that for him knowledge is only then perfect if the totality of the real and that in which it is best represented is brought into view. What is crucial is the ontological status of what is brought into view, not the *modus* of what is brought into view.

The principles of scientific methodology, by contrast, do not by themselves enable us to distinguish between things of "higher" and "lower" ontological status or even between what is worthier of being

---

[103] A. N. Whitehead, "Immortality", delivered as the Ingersoll lecture at the Harvard Divinity School on April 22, 1941. Printed in P. A. Schilpp, ed., *The Philosophy of A. N. Whitehead* (New York, 1951), p. 700.

[104] N. Lawrence, *Whitehead's Philosophical Development* (Univ. of California Press, 1956).

known and what is less worthy of being known; far from allowing us to make such distinctions, it seems rather to forbid them. That is, of course, completely appropriate; there is nothing wrong with that. It becomes objectionable, however, when the making of such distinctions is generally dismissed as impossible or even as simply meaningless on the basis of a pseudo-philosophical absolutism concerning the principles of scientific methodology. T. S. Eliot reports that his philosophical studies were at the beginning overshadowed by a feeling of inferiority in relation to the exact sciences, in which context he also happens to mention *Principia Mathematica*; in the meantime, however, he continues, it appeared to him that the overemphasis on formal precision in philosophy had its counterpart in certain movements in modern art; the latter afford a means "of producing works of art without imagination", the former, "a method of philosophizing without insight and wisdom".[105]

By contrast, it is only on the basis of a "loving search for truth", that is, on the basis of genuine *philosophia*, that one might be tempted to say, "The little knowledge that we may be able to acquire concerning the most sublime things is more desirable than the most certain knowledge of inferior things"; "even if our contact with eternal beings is slight, none the less because of its surpassing value this knowledge is a greater pleasure than our knowledge of everything around us, even as a chance, brief glimpse of the ones we love is a greater pleasure than seeing accurately many other and greater things." The first of these two texts stems from the *Summa Theologica* of Thomas Aquinas.[106] The author of the second is Aristotle,[107] from whose sober mind one had not perhaps expected such courtesy of formulation.

"The result of philosophy is not a number of 'philosophical propositions,' but to make propositions clear."[108] This thesis from Ludwig Wittgenstein's *Tractatus Logico-Philosophicus* is also intended to mark

[105] T. S. Eliot, Introduction to J. Pieper, *Leisure: The Basis of Culture* (London and New York, 1952; 7th ed., 1964). A German translation appeared as a postscript to J. Pieper, *Was heißt Philosophieren?*, 5th ed. (Munich, 1962), pp. 116f.
[106] I, 1, 5 ad 1.
[107] *De partibus animalium* 1.5.644bff. [Quoted from Aristotle, *On the Parts of Animals*, trans. James G. Lennox (Oxford, 2001), p. 13.]
[108] L. Wittgenstein, *Tractatus Logico-Philosophicus*, 5th ed. (London, 1951), p. 76 (4.112). [Quoted from Ludwig Wittgenstein, *Tractatus Logico-Philosophicus* (London, 1922), p. 77.]

a fundamental distinction between philosophy and science. We can set to one side for the time being the question of whether Wittgenstein meant to say, as might reasonably be assumed, that the task of philosophy consists primarily or even exclusively in logically analyzing those propositions in which the findings of science are expressed. In any event, his assertion, as it stands, actually points to—contrary, perhaps, to the intention of its author—an essential peculiarity of philosophizing, which again, when compared with the methodological principles of the sciences, must appear to be scarcely comprehensible, indeed, even scandalous.

All the findings of science have in essence the character of a discovery, that is, the revelation of something that had hitherto been concealed and unknown. The glory of the sciences consists in investigating the world in this manner. Clearly, however, philosophy cannot lay claim to the same kind of glory for itself. With this, a verdict appears to have already been passed. Strangely enough, in philosophy precisely this "deficiency" is elevated to the status of a program. Philosophy, it has been said, aims at something entirely different from a broadening of our knowledge of the world. But what then otherwise? A provisional answer might be: recollecting something already known but forgotten, something that, however, should not remain forgotten.

Whoever examines in a philosophical manner, that is, under every conceivable aspect, phenomena like guilt, freedom, and death or whoever considers the basic question concerning the structure of Being in general ("what does it mean to be something real?") will certainly experience a progressive illuminating of reality, in keeping with the depth of his commitment to conceptual clarification and the impartiality with which he opens himself to reality and allows himself to be affected by it; and he will naturally be interested in doing precisely this. Nevertheless, it would actually be wrong to assert that the philosophizing person in this way comes face to face with something absolutely not yet known, never before thought, something new and unknown. On the contrary, what occurs is more akin to the growing distinctness of something already, albeit obscurely, known, the taking possession of something that has almost been lost, precisely that kind of retrieval of what has been forgotten that we call memory. Even the truly "new" achievements of the great philosophers, like Aristotle's discovery, for example, that, contrary to Parmenides' view, there is a third thing between being and nonbeing, namely, that which is oriented toward actualization, that which awaits its accentuation, the *potential* (*dynamis*)—even this discovery, which had never before been expressly thought and formulated, was accepted and recognized as true, not on the basis of a confrontation with empirically determined facts, but solely on the basis of *re*-cognition. In philosophy, it is always the case that something that is already "naturally understood" is raised through a "secondary" effort to the status of reflectively explicit knowledge.[109]

This must necessarily appear a less impressive achievement when compared with the triumphant performance of the sciences, which every day deliver new facts, structures, and relationships to man's view and even more so into his hands—most importantly, the increasingly perfect, scientifically proven techniques of mastering nature. Are, by contrast, the philosophizing subject and philosophy not always asserting the same thing? Are they not dealing with the same eternal problems? An objection of this kind was already raised against Socrates' discussions; Alcibiades brings the issue up in Plato's *Symposium*.[110] And even before that, how do we measure progress in philosophy? Does such a thing exist at all? Doubtless, the posing of such questions may be orchestrated with all the deprecation which in fact accompanies the activity of the philosophizing person time and again —and this legitimately in those areas where the criteria of scientific methodology rightly possess or lay claim to absolute validity.

This, incidentally, should be conceded immediately: "Progress" is in fact a problematic category in the philosophical realm if what is meant by progress is a steady enrichment of our collective knowledge that increases *eo ipso* in a manner commensurate with the passage of time. In this respect, there is an analogy, again, with poetry. No one asks whether Goethe came farther than Homer. Philosophical progress certainly exists, but not so much across generations as in the inner life experience of the philosophizing person—and that in the same proportion in which he, silent and attentive, catches sight of the depth and breadth of his at once new and primeval object.

How little the sciences find themselves by nature in fundamental op-

[109] C. Nink, *Ontologie: Versuch einer Grundlegung* (Freiburg im Breisgau, 1952), pp. 6f.
[110] *Symposium* 221e5f.

position to philosophical questioning has seldom been so clearly perceivable as in this—our—age. The scientific investigation of reality
appears today to have arrived at an extreme point—at least in certain
fields—which is already almost identical with the standpoint of the
philosophizing person. And this standpoint, if only the gaze remains
directed impartially enough at that which manifests itself, is usually
entered into without hesitation. So, for example, the *elementary particle
theorist*, insofar as he inquires, from a purely physical standpoint, into
the elementary structure of matter, may run up so hard against the
philosophical problematic, "what is material reality, ultimately and in
the final analysis?" that the boundaries between physics and the philosophizing person may appear to have been virtually annihilated. The
fact that particularly among modern nuclear physicists not a few have
felt themselves called upon to make what are essentially philosophical utterances may, in part, be explained by this unusual occurrence.
The empirical researcher in the field of depth psychology also tends
to encounter existential facts of such a kind that, already in his very
first attempt to interpret the "material", he is inevitably caught up in
the question of the ultimate meaning of human existence. And even
homo faber can from time to time, in the face of scientific technology, be brought into a situation where he likewise catches sight of
that extreme point. That was, for example, precisely the case at that
moment when the mastery of natural forces, which had been sought
since times immemorial, reached its zenith. The experience of such
inherent power appears at the same time to compel reflection on human existence as a whole. For confirmation, one need only consult
the documentary report on the first atomic explosion in the desert
of Alamogordo: "Even the most unrepentant atheists were so shaken
that they could describe their impressions only in religious images."[111]
Robert J. Oppenheimer's remark to the effect that science has now
known sin has often been cited. And the first session of the Atomic
Energy Commission was opened by its chairman with the last words
of the traditional formulaic oath, which had never before held such
significance for him: "God help me!"[112] Even if one wanted to see
in all this only a helpless romanticism or even mere sentimentality,

---

[111] M. Boveri, *Der Verrat im 20. Jahrhundert*, vol. 4 (Hamburg, 1960), p. 205.
[112] Ibid., p. 206.

one point cannot be denied: from one moment to the next they no longer found themselves within that "special" province with which science and technology are otherwise exclusively concerned. Clearly, they now found themselves confronted with the totality of world and human existence!

As soon as the scientist—whether he be a nuclear physicist, a depth psychologist, or whatever else—crosses this boundary, everything that otherwise applies to the philosophizing person also applies to him with equal force. The questions that now pose themselves can no longer be answered with the exactitude that, a moment before, when one still spoke as a seasoned specialist, came naturally. And whatever information may have been acquired will not become our disposable possession, as is the case with the findings of science; suddenly, it becomes comprehensible why the men of old spoke here of a "loan".[113] Perhaps, if things are as they should be, perhaps, since one can hardly ignore the relationship of those questions that now unexpectedly aim at the whole and one's own inner existence, there may even come to light at the same time a new understanding that both philosophizing and human existence itself possess the same basic structure—that of hope?

VIII

Although the "scientific world view's" claim to exclusivity has set it on a false path, ending in sterility, the philosophizing person can do nothing healthier than to confront this challenge. It would spell his own doom if the philosophizing person were to choose to withdraw from the clarifying disputes and infinite dialogue through which the unveiling of the world and man's understanding of himself have always taken place and in which, not coincidentally, the exact sciences now have a dominant voice. As scientific methods became increasingly more differentiated, it was only to be expected that the critical demands placed on philosophizing and on the exactitude of philosophical utterance would become more acute. The request made of the philosophizing person that he reflect on philosophy's own possi-

---

[113] Thomas Aquinas, *In Met.* I, 3 (no. 64).

bilities includes an opportunity that it would simply be impermissible *not* to exploit—at least if philosophy is not to be dismissed as an "intellectual sideshow" on the margins of the "recherche collective de la vérité",[114] of that magnificent endeavor that has been described as knowledge of reality.

The philosophizing person should, it seems to me, subject himself to the "scientific" critique, even if it is unjustified on two points: first, with respect to *language* and, second, with respect to philosophy's relation to the *empirical*.

We have, however, all too often had the Wittgensteinian dictum thrown up at us as both a caution and a rebuke: "What can be said at all can be said clearly; and whereof one cannot speak thereof one must be silent."[115] Under closer scrutiny, this aphorism yields far less than the grandiloquent diction would seem to imply. The reason that the imperative it contains does no harm lies in the questionable nature of the preceding indicative. How is it supposed to be determined whether there is something that cannot be said at all? More importantly: What does "clearly" mean here?

Whitehead has written, "Clarity always means 'clear enough'."[116] Clarity is not something absolute; it assumes that something has been made "*sufficiently* clear" to *someone*. Still, sufficient to what purpose? Is "saying something clearly" synonymous with saying something in such a way that the object under discussion is now made to appear before one's eyes in sharp relief and fully distinct? Or must that statement perhaps also be deemed "clear", that tells me I am confronted with a reality whose extent is, in fact, simply *not* measurable and that consequently can never be brought clearly and distinctly before my eyes? Obviously, it is possible to speak of an object that cannot be exhaustively understood and hence can also not be adequately described in such a way that this impossibility can itself be given clear expression and perhaps even supplemented with information on the degree of incomprehensibility and the reasons for the object's being so. The philosophizing person finds himself in just such a situation; this is precisely what singles him out, that is, that he is obliged to

---

[114] M.-D. Chenu, *Introduction à l'étude de Saint Thomas d'Aquin* (Paris, 1950), p. 291.

[115] L. Wittgenstein, preface, *Tractatus Logico-Philosophicus*, p. 26. [Quoted from Ludwig Wittgenstein, *Tractatus Logico-Philosophicus* (London, 1922), p. 27.]

[116] "Remarks", *Philosophical Review* 46 (1937), p. 179.

speak of something undeniably encountered but that cannot be expressed exactly in words. And his specific problem, insofar as it lies in the linguistic realm at all, consists in allowing the ultimately inexpressible, along with what is being positively asserted, to become distinct in his utterances.

The scientific researcher is not expected to submit himself to such constraints—which make it somewhat more understandable that he often all too easily allows himself to criticize the language of philosophical scholarship. It is a triumph, all too cheaply won, to tear one of Hegel's sentences from its context and to challenge the uninitiated to examine critically "the so-called philosophical language", as in a showcase, as it were, and "in the same way that the zoologist looks at a rare kind of beetle".[117]

This is not to deny, however, that, conversely, the philosophizing person has much to learn from the language of science. Even in the case of the most obscure scientific utterances, it remains true that language, by its very nature, is primarily oriented, in its communications, toward making reality known. In other words, we are concerned here, not with issues of "general comprehensibility", but with the natural function of language. Even if, as in the case of Albert Einstein's last papers on general relativity, only a very few are at all capable of deciphering them and of following them comprehendingly, it is never the language as such, strictly speaking, that obfuscates the understanding; on the contrary, it affords access to an object that is in itself difficult to comprehend. By contrast, the difficulty in reading a book on philosophy lies often enough, as everyone knows from his own experience, in nothing other than the misuse of language, so that language itself is the impediment, nothing else. This, however, not only runs counter to the spirit of science; it is just as much at odds with the intellectual and linguistic style of the great Western philosophers themselves, from Plato to Nietzsche. Not only are the concrete and decisive metaphors of a Socrates, who, fully unconcerned with his own importance, speaks of cobblers and fullers, or—in clarifying the notion of *idea*—of a broken shuttle, employed specifically for the sake of distinctness and clarity and—what amounts to largely the same thing—for the sake of establishing dialogical contact

---

[117] Reichenbach, *Aufstieg der wissenschaftlichen Philosophie*, pp. 13, 82ff.

with the listener; Plato, Aristotle, Augustine, and Aquinas all held
what basically amounts to the same view. In fact, they made recourse
to everyday linguistic usage a matter of principle. "The usage of the
multitude is to be followed in giving names to things"[118]—and by
no means simply as a didactic device, but because otherwise thought
itself would lose its binding character. In those cases where a linguistic conformity, whether expressly agreed or tacitly enforced through
convention, has been replaced by the arbitrariness of a personal terminology, the individual speaking in this manner has in so doing abandoned the essentially shared human endeavor to acquire knowledge—
which, far from ruling out the formation of fraternities, encourages
them. "Death, as the shrine of nothingness, is the mountain peak of
Being" (Der Tod ist als der Schrein des Nichts das Gebirg des Seins).
The worst thing about a sentence like that, it seems to me—apart
from the impossibility of translating it into any foreign language,[119]
which should itself not be taken lightly—is not the ambiguity surrounding what is meant; worse still is the defensive posture, unmistakable in itself, which forbids a clarifying question.

Perhaps one is reminded here of the old notion according to which
philosophy and poetry are related. Even such "unromantic" thinkers
as Aristotle and Aquinas have, in fact, spoken of such a relationship;
both the philosopher and the poet, they claim, are concerned with
the *mirandum*.[120] While this relationship is, in its consequences, naturally not without significance for philosophical language, it should
nevertheless not be so construed as if the philosophizing person were

---

[118] Aristotle, *Topics* 2.2.110a15–18. Aquinas quotes this sentence in the *Summa contra gentes*
1, 1. See also *Ver.* 4, 2.

[119] In Kyoto, I asked a university professor who translated the author of this sentence into
Japanese what the translation for *das Gebirg des Seins* would be within the context of that same
sentence; to which I, who speak no Japanese, was given the rapid and matter-of-fact reply:
"the mountain of being". That this no longer has anything to do with the German text is
clear, but it remains an open question to what extent the original formulation forces one to
adopt such nonsensical translations. Or to take another example: "À partir du jeu de miroir
du Tour encerclant du Souple, le rassemblement propre à la chose se produit"—who would
have realized that this is the French translation of the following German sentence: "Aus dem
Spiegel-Spiel des Gerings des Ringen ereignet sich das Dingen des Dings"? ["Out of the
ringing mirror-play the thinging of the thing takes place", quoted from: Martin Heidegger,
"Language", in *Poetry, Language, Thought*, trans. Albert Hofstadter (New York, 1971), p.
178.]

[120] Cf. Thomas Aquinas, *In Met.* I, 3 (no. 55).

thereby relieved of the obligation of striving for utmost clarity in
his use of words. It is quite manifestly in their choice of object that
philosophy and poetry, according to this conception of their relation, agree; in contrast to the practical understanding of everyday
life, both keep their gaze fixed on the realm of the wondrous, which
unexpectedly opens itself up beyond the putatively matter-of-course
and in the midst of it. Not to cover up the world's unfathomable
ground [*unergründlichen Grund*] with language, but to bring it before
one's view through language—this is the task that confronts both the
philosopher and the poet. With this, however, the distinction between
the two has not in the least been blurred; the method of philosophy,
unlike that of poetry, is not one of representation through sensuous
forms (sound, rhythm, repetition, figure) but rather one of capturing
reality in nonintuitive concepts. In this attempt to give the incomprehensibility of Being expression in clear conceptual terms lies the
specifically linguistic difficulty involved in philosophizing.

   Clarity of expression is thus very much required by philosophy, no
less so than by the other sciences. But clarity is not synonymous with
"precision". At any rate there is a degree of precision to which the
philosophizing person not only factually never attains but to which he
does not even aspire. This would seem the appropriate point at which
to discuss a proposal that tends to constitute a recurring element in
every "scientific" critique of philosophy. I mean the proposal, usually formulated somewhat apodictically, that the philosophizing person dispense with the use of the natural, organically evolved, historical language and instead invent a "symbolism liberated from the dross
of the historical language",[121] that is, a formalized symbolic language,
an artificial terminology. The mathematical symbol and the artificial
term possess, in fact, that special type of precision in which is manifested that which makes science science: the deliberate restriction of
one's attention to a particular aspect. For precisely this reason, however, an artificial technical language is unsuitable for use in philosophy.
"Precise" means literally "to cut off". The precision of a term consists in the fact that, proceeding from a particular aspect, it cleanly
cuts out a partial phenomenon from a complex state of affairs and
presents it, as an isolated specimen, for observation. Again, it is com-

---

[121] R. Carnap, *Wissenschaftliche Weltauffassung: Der Wiener Kreis*, p. 15.

pletely appropriate that science make use of an artificial terminology. To philosophical utterances, by contrast, it brings at best a semblance of exactitude; in reality, it occludes the object with which philosophy is concerned and lets it fade into oblivion, whereas the power of a natural language consists in its being able to hold the object present before one. The term *exitus*, which is sometimes used by physicians and which denotes the physiological state of cardiac arrest, is precise; the expression "death", which belongs to the natural language, is not a term but a word; it possesses less precision but more distinctness because "death" signifies and designates the entirety of what befalls a man in death.

Of course, it can once in a while be meaningful or even necessary for philosophy, especially in a propaedeutic field like formal logic, to employ an artificial language, which is then only comprehensible to a specialist or expert. Within his own proper domain, however, the philosophizing person speaks of things that by their very nature concern, not just specialists, but human beings in general, meaning everyone. What he says certainly need not be readily comprehensible to a casual listener, nor need it be available, as it were, at no additional cost; on the contrary, great difficulties in understanding may be involved— to whose resolution the rigors of conceptual thought may perhaps be less necessary than that meditative silence which cannot be brought about through exertion but can certainly be destroyed by it. What is crucial for philosophy is that it make palpable through an extremely cautious handling of language, as distinct from terminology, those powers of expression that arise from the natural and organic evolution of words and with which everyone is basically already familiar so that—beyond all questions of precision—the object of man's search for wisdom, which is of concern to everyone, becomes and remains clear.

Paradoxically, this object may sometimes show its unexpectedly wondrous character precisely to the one who at first undertakes to describe it in the precise "protocol" language of the exact sciences. This attempt leads to a kind of alienation effect, to which, however, those will remain impervious who insist on regarding what has been registered this way as capturing absolutely everything. If someone like an experimental physicist, for example, were to record as a mechanically measurable process in protocol language what transpires when two human beings extend their hands to one another—they stand, faces turned toward one another, at a specific distance from one another; the underarms are lifted, as if through the action of a lever, from their previous almost vertical position in such a way that the hands of both parties are in contact; then, for a measurable period of time, the hands clasp one another whereby an equally measurable degree of pressure is exerted; and so on—if this person were to perceive and describe the handshake in this way and at the same time to recognize and reflect on the fact that, with this press of the hands, as registered in the protocol language, the reconciliation of two opponents, say, had found its confirmation, then an entirely new way of experiencing the inexhaustible *mirandum* of being human would have been revealed to him.

Apart from the lack of linguistic precision, what appears to be most offensive to the scientific critics of philosophy is its questionable relation to the empirical. Of course, the demand here being made of philosophy is far from unequivocal. It is doubtless justified, however, to the extent that it implies that philosophizing, like all other claims to knowledge, must prove itself by keeping its connection with experience transparent. Although the philosophizing person, when discussing, for example, the implications of the concept of Being, transcends the realm of the empirically given, this movement of transcendence must, naturally, if it is not to lapse into the groundless and fanciful, take its departure from the immediately experienced or at least experienceable. Granted, what is at issue here is the depth structure of the real, which is no longer to be found simply on the surface and which can also perhaps not be expressed completely and adequately in words; still, it must be possible to show that it has the same structure as that which lies before every man's eyes and how the two can be the same. The somewhat aggressive sounding sentence, which was clearly so intended, "There is no path to factual knowledge apart from that offered by experience",[122] can also be understood in a manner thoroughly acceptable to the philosophizing person. On the other hand, it is hopeless—and, incidentally, not worth the effort—to want to defend the many essayistic or systematic forms of purely constructive-speculative thought as "philosophical".

---

[122] Ibid., p. 28.

On the other hand, it represents a by no means rare misunderstanding to think that a particular proposition concerning experience is itself a proposition drawn from experience. That there is a difference should be clear, if not at first glance, then certainly on reflection. Whoever accepts it as a truth has already conceded, in so doing, that our fundamental convictions necessarily—and probably also legitimately—rest on something other than experience, as well as on experience itself.

What, however, does "experience" mean? My tentative answer, offered by way of suggestion, is that experience is knowledge based on immediate contact with reality. Experience occurs primarily but —as hardly anyone now doubts—not solely through that sense perception in which, literally, "the objects affect our senses", as the first sentence of the *Critique of Pure Reason*[123] rightly states. We not only "experience" something when our hand feels the tangible or our eyes see the self-manifesting; the entire living bodily person is an infinitely differentiated and sensitive reflector of such immediate contacts with reality and, to that extent, a single organ of possible experience.

Here, undoubtedly, lies one of the sources of all knowledge. Nothing that is grasped by this organ, insofar as it is in contact with reality —either the external world or the reality that we ourselves are—may be left out of consideration, when our purpose is to arrive, "on the path of experience", at a more comprehensive and more penetrating knowledge of what is. Whitehead expressed this same idea in almost solemn terms:

> Nothing can be omitted, experience drunk and experience sober, experience sleeping and experience waking, experience drowsy and experience wide-awake, experience self-conscious and experience self-forgetful, experience intellectual and experience physical, experience religious and experience sceptical, experience anxious and experience care-free, experience anticipatory and experience retrospective, experience happy and experience grieving, experience dominated by motion and experience under self-restraint, experience in the light and experience in the dark, experience normal and experience abnormal.[124]

---

[123] I. Kant, *Critique of Pure Reason*, B, introduction.
[124] A. N. Whitehead, *Adventures of Ideas*, pp. 290f.

And what is more, he adds, these evidential findings do not disappear with the end of the experiential act; they are stored and "preserved" in the great institutions, in whatever men do, in language and the great works of language,[125] and above all, as everyone knows, in the treasure houses of science.

In insisting that the *corpus* of human experience includes nothing less than all this and perhaps considerably more, I accept at the same time the critical demand that philosophizing justify itself through recourse to experience. With this attempt to loosen up the concept of experience and render it less doctrinaire, however, a demand has clearly been raised that now unexpectedly takes aim at the positivistic critics of philosophy themselves.

On the other hand, the philosophizing person, who has, with this, been assigned an unsurveyable evidential basis, now finds himself truly confronted with an almost superhuman task. How could a single individual, however brilliant, ever be in a position to incorporate in his philosophizing even that fraction of the empirical data concerning the world which are preserved in the sciences? In fact, "the demands placed on the philosophizing person are unrealizable";[126] the intuition behind Dilthey's deep sigh here is completely sound. The requirement cannot be satisfied in a positive way. It can, however, be "respected", as it were, in another way—by way of omission, as it were. And this kind of respect may certainly be expected of the philosophizing person; he is not permitted formally to exclude even a single possibly relevant datum concerning reality from his deliberations. Were that to occur, the philosophizing person would in that moment cease to exercise that task which is most properly his own and which consists in reflecting on reality as a whole, and this under every conceivable aspect.

---

[125] Ibid., p. 291.

[126] *Briefwechsel zwischen Wilhelm Dilthey und dem Grafen Paul Yorck v. Wartenburg 1877–1897*, p. 39.

There is not much disagreement about the fact that the philosophizing person must respect the findings of science; the bone of contention lies elsewhere. Who today would care to deny that someone who is inquiring, philosophically, into the "essence" of man (whatever that might mean in detail) can no longer ignore the fact that, for example, man is an "evolutionary phenomenon", to whom falls an irreplaceable role in the evolution of the cosmos and life and who, according to everything we now know, could not have appeared either earlier or later on this earth than when he actually did. In philosophical anthropology, evolutionary theory has already forced the expulsion of "putative philosophical knowledge, which is, in fact, nothing of the sort".[127] The same is true of the other empirical sciences: psychology, behavior research, sociology, and so on. No one can dispute the fact that it is simply unphilosophical to ignore deliberately even a single one of their findings under the pretext that at the moment one is solely concerned with the "metaphysical nature" of man.

Would it be any different, however, if one were to insist that a philosophical discussion of man could just as little afford to ignore the information that in the earliest moments of man's history something extremely important and portentous—something like crime and punishment—befell him and that its consequences have fundamentally shaped his historical existence up until the present day? Plato, at any rate, is to be numbered among those who believe something of the kind. In the course of discussing the highly germane anthropological question concerning the ultimate sense of *eros* in the *Symposium*, he considers first the contributions of psychology, sociology, and natural science to that question before going on to mention with great matter-of-factness the mythical narrative of man's self-incurred fall from a primordial state of well-rounded perfection. Evidently, he is of the view that the philosophizing person has to consider not only the cognizable knowledge of this world but also holy tradition. When the attempt is undertaken in the *Republic* "to define . . . whom we mean by the philosophers", the first criterion that is mentioned is

---

[127] N. Luyten, "Zum Evolutionsproblem in philosophischer Sicht", in *Naturwissenschaft und Theologie*, vol. 2 (Munich, 1959), p. 168.

that the philosopher is fond of *all* wisdom.[128] A genuinely keen appetite is always for the whole; someone who is really hungry never says he likes only one part and not the other.[129] In this way, the soul of the genuinely philosophizing person "is ever to seek integrity and wholeness in all things human and divine".[130]

Still, it is not the purely historical that is of interest here; we are not really concerned with Plato per se and of course not with a particular mythical account of man's fall, either. The question that is being raised here extends much farther than that; and it is directed, by no means toward a past, albeit "glorious", epoch of philosophy, but toward the contemporary philosophizing person and his inner situation.

The question runs as follows: Does it belong to the genuine philosophical task of the philosophizing person to consider evidence on the world and human existence that derives *not* from experience and rational argumentation, but rather from a realm that can be denoted with the terms "revelation", "holy tradition", "belief", and "theology"? Is it possible legitimately to include such statements that are neither empirically nor rationally demonstrable in one's philosophizing? To which I would answer: It is not only possible and legitimate; it is necessary.

This thesis must now be secured against possible misunderstandings. Above all, it must be clear how it is *not* meant.

First, we are speaking, not of "philosophy" as such, but—just as in the previously cited passage from Plato's *Republic*—of existential philosophizing and the philosophizing person. In other words, the question is not whether, for example, theological propositions should also be treated in a systematic presentation of the substantial problems of philosophy. It is perhaps true that even this question cannot simply be answered in the negative, but that is not what is under discussion here. What is open to discussion is the following assertion: If the philosophizing person regards certain forms of supernatural evidence concerning reality and human existence as genuine data, that is, if he

---

[128] Plato *Republic* 474b5. [Quoted after the translation by Paul Shorey, in *Plato: The Collected Dialogues*, p. 713.]

[129] Ibid., 475c3. [Quoted after the translation by Shorey, in *Plato: The Collected Dialogues*, p. 714.]

[130] Ibid., 486a5; 485b5. [Quoted after the translation by Shorey in *Plato: The Collected Dialogues*, p. 722.]

—not uncritically, of course, or to the point of naïveté—accepts their validity as being beyond doubt, then, in the event he would deliberately omit them from his discussion, he would at that very moment cease to philosophize in earnest because from then on he would no longer be contemplating his object, the totality of world and existence, "under every conceivable aspect".

Such an attempt at inclusiveness does not in the least imply that the philosophizing person would be working at cross purposes to theology; he is not automatically doing physics when, inquiring into the "nature" of matter, he considers the findings of quantum mechanics. Generally speaking, however, the real opportunities for philosophizing are determined, not by the degree to which knowledge of scientific research findings has been disseminated, but by the degree of truth to which the underlying articles of faith may lay claim.

It is a crucial question, of course, whether such superhuman evidence really exists and on what basis we can be certain that it does. That, however, is a different question from the one being entertained here. The conviction *that* there is in fact something like a *theios logos*, a communication from God to man, and that this revelation is distinct and perceptible for us—this conviction will not be discussed here; it is simply assumed. This notwithstanding, it is possible to specify more precisely what is meant by the term "revelation", in this connection.

"Revelation" stands for that original act of communication that lies quite simply beyond all conceptual understanding and in which alone divine speech "lets itself be heard"; it is what Plato has presciently described as the bringing of the divine message by an unknown Prometheus.[131] By "holy tradition" is meant the process of passing down and receiving from one generation to another, in which a revelation once received is kept historically alive.[132] "Faith" is the personal act of assent through which the divine communication that has reached our ears in this way is accepted as truth on the basis of its origin. Finally, "theology" is the attempt to interpret the superhuman data, which are accepted on faith as true, in terms of what they actually mean.[133]

---

[131] Plato *Philebus* 16c5ff.

[132] Cf. J. Pieper, *Über den Begriff der Tradition* (Cologne and Opladen, 1958), pp. 13ff. (See also sections 2 and 3 of the essay on "Tradition" in this volume.)

[133] Cf. J. Pieper, *Hinführung zu Thomas von Aquin*, 2nd ed. (Munich, 1963), pp. 205ff.

Secondly, a preponderance of evidence suggests that whenever the philosophizing person attempts to gain clarity about the meaning of the totality of world and existence, he inevitably has recourse to data that are "superhuman" insofar as they are confirmed neither by experience nor by rational argumentation. This is not any the less true because the individual is unaware of this appeal to the superhuman or expressly denies it. The uniqueness of a "presuppositionless" philosophy, so conceived, consists in precisely the fact that, as T. S. Eliot notes in connection with "some philosophers", its presuppositions are "concealed from both author and reader".[134]

But even in those cases where the rejection of holy tradition has been elevated to the status of a principle—by this, I mean not only its methodological "exclusion" but the unequivocal rejection and denial of its content—I say, even in those cases, this act of negation, whether one is aware of it and approves of it or not, inevitably has the character of an article of faith.

It never ceases to amaze me how little Sartre, for example, seems to notice this. As is well known, he quite explicitly construes existentialism as the attempt to think through to the end the consequences of God's nonexistence.[135] He is evidently unaware of the fact that he simply presupposes uncritically, without any trace of a justification, God's nonexistence—and this with far more "faith" than the thought of creation was ever presupposed in traditional philosophy. While it is true that he proceeds from an interpretation of the traditional concept of "creation"—and one cannot even begin to discuss his position without at the same time presenting this (grotesquely incorrect) interpretation[136]—I suspect that Sartre, who for his part expresses his repudiation of God and the creation with the greatest matter-of-factness, would declare the counterargument to his position to be "philosophically impermissible", although it belongs, logically speaking, to the same conceptual realm. (A double standard that is customarily found elsewhere as well.) And despite all this, Sartre's thought possesses precisely on account of its resolutely straightforward commitment to those underlying articles of faith, which for it

---

[134] T. S. Eliot, "Insight and Wisdom in Philosophy" (*Einsicht und Weisheit in der Philosophie*), postscript to J. Pieper, *Was heißt Philosophieren?* ("What Does It Mean to Philosophize?").
[135] Sartre, *L'Existentialisme*, p. 94.
[136] Ibid., pp. 19f.

lie beyond discussion, that immediate existential relevance which will always be the distinguishing mark of an earnestly lived philosophizing; whereas academic sophistry, which regards it as a dictate of discretion to hold its crucial positions, if it has any, in obscurity, remains necessarily and essentially irrelevant.

Thirdly, although I am convinced that every philosophical interpretation of the world and human existence is based, at least unconsciously, on assumptions that aim at the whole and that one does not so much "know" as "believe", in what follows only that case will be considered in which the philosophizing person is a professed believer, who appeals to a holy tradition, expressly acknowledged to be true, and who knowingly attempts to reflect on the information contained therein. In the civilized societies of Western Europe, such a believer will typically be a Christian. While it is fair to say that the truths of Christian belief amount in the first instance to a doctrine of salvation and not to a picture of reality or a hermeneutic of existence, at the same time they also imply certain very basic propositions that have a direct bearing on the object of philosophy, the totality of world and human existence.

Still it is *not* the problem of a "Christian philosophy" that we intend to discuss here; rather the actual thesis we shall be discussing may be formulated as follows: A Christian cannot put to one side the truth of revelation he accepts in faith as divinely authenticated insofar as he purports at the same time to be in earnest with his philosophizing.

In the philosophical literature, two weighty objections have been raised against this view, each of which is argued differently, but both of which are highly representative. These objections were voiced by Martin Heidegger and Karl Jaspers.

Heidegger argues that the questions of the philosophizing person must remain "like an empty and unwarranted brooding"[137] to whoever accepts the biblical account of creation as truth, all the more so as the believer claims already to have the answer to the very question the raising of which constitutes philosophizing itself:[138] Why is there something instead of nothing? "From the standpoint of faith

---

[137] *Einführung in die Metaphysik*, p. 5. [Quoted from Martin Heidegger, *An Introduction to Metaphysics*, trans. Ralph Mannheim (Garden City, N.Y., 1961), p. 5.]
[138] "To ask this question is to philosophize", (ibid., p. 10). [Quoted from Heidegger, *Introduction to Metaphysics*, p. 10.]

our question is 'foolishness'. Philosophy is this very foolishness. A 'Christian philosophy' is a round square and a misunderstanding."[139]

Jaspers likewise affirms the irreconcilability of religious belief and philosophy but for another reason, as was already indicated: "No upright person can refrain from choosing between religion and philosophy"—between "either the renunciation of autonomy or the renunciation of revelation".[140] Faith is here quite correctly understood as a reliance on someone else, whose authority one accepts. This is precisely what the philosophizing person is debarred from doing. Authority is "the true enemy of philosophizing"; every reason that might be cited for submission to an authority "denies liberty".[141] This, I hasten to add, reflects only one (partial) aspect of Jaspers' much more nuanced conception of the relation between philosophy and religion ("Philosophy emerges factually from the soil of a religious substance, whose outward expression it at the same time combats")[142] but this element, which is of primary interest in our context, is clearly also a very decisive part.

Reduced to a simple formula, both Heidegger and Jaspers are asserting, first, that the believer cannot simultaneously be a philosophizing person and, second, that the philosophizing person cannot believe. If one inquires somewhat more deeply into the characteristic elements of philosophy that stand behind these theses and that are reflected in them, it is a striking fact that both emphasize an aspect that plays scarcely a role, if any, in the conception of philosophy that has dominated from Plato to Kant.

It is true that Heidegger's formulation also provides substance for further reflection: Does it not miss, for example, the very essence of the concept of "faith"? Revelation notwithstanding, faith means the very *opposite* of certain knowledge and sure possession, so that, as the theologians tell us, the truths of faith "still remain concealed" to us.[143] And as for the question of why there are beings at all, it acquires the utmost acuteness and urgency, inflamed rather than chastened by revelation and faith. But all that need not be discussed here.

---

[139] Ibid., p. 6. [Quoted from Heidegger, *Introduction to Metaphysics*, p. 6.]
[140] Jaspers, *Philosophie*, p. 258.
[141] Ibid., p. 265.
[142] Ibid., p. 269.
[143] M. J. Scheeben, *Die Mysterien des Christentums* (Freiburg im Breisgau, 1941), pp. 8f.

What interests us is the provocative radicalism with which Heidegger insists on the absolute character of philosophizing as a form of questioning: "The unsecured holding of one's ground in questioning amid the uncertainty of Being as a whole" is even reputed to be "the highest form of knowledge".[144]

Perhaps one will at this point look up with some surprise and respond by asking whether I am not in fact saying exactly the same thing. Have I not also spoken of the structure of hope that underlies the act of philosophizing and of the inquiring contemplation of reality as a whole that can never be brought to rest by a final, comprehensive answer? That is all true; and yet the agreement is only superficial. The answer lies, briefly and somewhat aggressively formulated, in the fact that "questioning" in the one case means to be in search of an answer despite being aware of this ultimate incomprehensibility and to be open to it, whereas for Heidegger "questioning" would appear to mean essentially warding off every conceivable answer and closing oneself off to them (because through them the interrogative character of this questioning would be violated).

Jaspers' formulation is also problematic in a variety of ways. For example, I ask myself what could possibly be meant by a "renunciation of revelation", if revelation means that God has spoken to man? Still, this, too, must be put to one side; instead we propose to examine Jaspers' own particular conception of philosophy. Its specific character derives, it seems to me, from the special weight it places on the philosophizing person. While he is certainly desirous of an answer, his desire is, on the other hand, not so unconditional that he would allow it to be communicated to him by another. Although this emphasis is, I believe, not alien to the ancient conception of philosophy, it plays virtually no role there.

Common to both positions, Jaspers' as well as Heidegger's, is an almost envying vigilance in ensuring that the formal character of the philosophical act is not violated or compromised. Here the methodological "purity" of the philosophizing act appears to be considered almost more important than any possible answer to the philosophical question. This represents a crucial departure from the great Western philosophical tradition. One might even go so far as to say that Plato

---

[144] M. Heidegger, *Die Selbstbehauptung der deutschen Universität* (Breslau, 1933), pp. 12f.

and Aristotle were not interested in philosophy at all (at least not in this sense), that is, as a formal, carefully delineated academic discipline, and certainly not for the sake of the delineation itself. They were interested instead, with an intensity of questioning that fully absorbed their attention, in directing their gaze toward, and keeping before their eyes, the question of what ultimately human virtue and *eros* are—what the real is in general. They were hardly concerned with anything else but an answer to these questions, regardless of how vulnerable and fragmentary those answers might be: the most important thing was that they were forthcoming, no matter from where.

The Platonic Socrates never shies away from acknowledging those ultimate truths that shape human existence; he knows them, not on his own, but *ex akoes*, by hearing.[145] This is also suggested by the close juxtaposition of rational argumentation with mythological tradition, typical of almost all Plato's dialogues. In the much more "scientific" philosophy of Aristotle, such attentive devotion to a suprarational source occurs less often; still it has been convincingly demonstrated that "the *credo ut illegam* stands . . . behind his *Metaphysics*, as well."[146] The same tradition is still at work in Immanuel Kant, although it is not readily apparent. Thus one is surprised to find, eight years after the *Critique of Pure Reason* was published, Kant referring to the New Testament as a "perennial guide to genuine wisdom" from which reason "receives new illumination in the face of that which . . . remains perpetually obscure to it and from which it nevertheless requires instruction".[147]

How exactly the relationship between the known and the believed that is to be established in the philosophical act might be given theoretical expression—that is another extremely difficult question, which we can discuss at least briefly here.

When we said that the philosophizing person must "respect", "include", and "reflect on" the truth of revelation, if he is at the same time to be an existentially engaged believer—at the very least, he

---

[145] Cf. *Phaedo* 61d9; *Phaedrus* 235d1; *Timaeus* 20d1. This expression, which is repeated verbatim in the Greek of the New Testament ("faith comes from what is heard", Rom 10:17), is rendered as "from hearsay" in the German translations of Plato, which clearly represents, not merely an inaccuracy, but an actual distortion.

[146] W. Jaeger, *Aristoteles* (Berlin, 1923), p. 404.

[147] (Draft of a) letter to Heinrich Jung-Stilling in the spring of 1789 (*Briefe von und an Kant*, ed. E. Cassirer, pt. 1 [Berlin, 1918], p. 381).

should not deliberately "ignore" it or "exclude" it "from considera-tion"—these were certainly meaningful ways of circumscribing what we meant. But they might possibly also work to conceal how infinitely complicated a legitimate conjoining of the two kinds of data can be. On the one hand, the difference between natural knowledge and faith remains unaffected; they are clearly two distinct things, which can be joined with one another—and that in such a way that neither of them compromises its own distinctive form and value. It should not then be conceived as a shapeless diffuse mixture. On the other hand, the idea of methodologically staking out a subject area and hence of not cross-ing a subject boundary is not only uncharacteristic for both philoso-phers and theologians, it is hardly practiced by them. Neither the one nor the other is authorized, as it were, to say what for the individual researcher is a simply a matter of fact: This is of interest to me; that is not. Both are directly concerned with investigating the "integrity and wholeness in all things human and divine".[148] One must, then, be prepared from the outset to encounter almost insuperable difficulties if one sets out to describe adequately what is unique to that relation-ship.

The use of intuitive images in this connection should in no way be disparaged. A genuinely felicitous analogy has the advantage of setting a simple form before the mind's eye, without allowing that *arcanum* in which everything that is genuinely real is soaked to fade into for-getfulness.

Thus, the metaphor of a contrapuntal symphony, in which distinct voices mutually reinforce, challenge, and perhaps also quiet one an-other so that a new, unexpectedly rich tonal pattern emerges, which can no longer be explained in terms of the sheer addition of its ele-ments, is immediately intelligible as a means of illustrating the juxta-position of known and believed.

Perhaps it is already something more than a "metaphor" when we refer to someone who believes as a "listener"? Is it at all possible to characterize him more precisely? He is really someone who neither knows himself nor sees with his own eyes; he is someone who allows himself to be informed by someone else. No small portion of what he, as a believer, has heard discussed concerns the same world that

---

[148] Plato *Republic* 486a5. [Quoted after the translation by Shorey in *Plato: The Collected Dia-logues*, p. 722.]

presents itself to his gaze and that he, using his own eyes, observes as both empirical researcher and philosophizing person. And possibly through what is heard his gaze will be made more acute for, or diverted toward, something that he now abruptly sees for himself with his own eyes and that would otherwise have been concealed from him, if he had not heard and reflected on that message which has reached his ears from elsewhere. The clarifying power of such an image is evident. It makes it immediately apparent that the dichotomy that Jaspers proclaimed between philosophy and faith and that was characterized by him as being inevitable does not exist as such. Why should one be compelled to choose hearing over the use of one's own eyes, or vice versa? What is to prevent one from doing both—seeing and hearing, philosophizing and believing? Conversely, who of us is in a position to say, even in the natural life of the spirit, according to what pattern or blueprint what is seen and what is heard penetrate each other and are intertwined?

In fact, nowhere does it stand written that it must be at all possible to specify a valid norm for the relation of known to believed. Besides, more is involved than simply a difficulty in conception. This relation strives toward realization and that under the endlessly variable conditions of concrete existence. Conflicts are not only possible here but are absolutely unavoidable as the natural concomitant of spiritual progress. One might see precisely in the preparedness for such disagreements and in the willingness to endure them patiently without rash attempts at reconciliation or premature resignation the hallmark of a genuinely philosophical education. And one is reminded of the platitude according to which the superiority of a philosophy that truly incorporates all attainable data manifests itself, not in its ability to offer more refined philosophical solutions, but rather in making the mysterious nature of reality more intuitively apparent to our eyes.

In the end, it is perhaps not so important to have worked out a formal theoretical structure, in which faith, knowledge, and philosophizing are each assigned their distinct roles as precisely as possible. More critical is the living realization of that unlimited and all-encompassing openness to everything that is, something that is not so much an attitude or a virtue of the spirit as it is its very essence—in short, its nature.

ON THE PLATONIC IDEA OF PHILOSOPHY

Garbed as I am in the raiment of academic ceremony, there is little I would not undertake to forestall an encounter with Socrates—that character through whom Plato most forcefully expressed his views concerning the essence of philosophy, views expressed, not in the manner of an abstract character or after the fashion of a definition, but—more poignantly, polyphonously, indeed, inexhaustibly—in the form of an exemplary figure. Were it to come to such an encounter with Socrates, I would have to ready myself for a greeting of the following sort: "What enviable fate that you should cross my path, O radiantly bedecked one! For you evidently belong to those extremely fortunate ones who dispose over wisdom as a priceless possession, for which philosophy is the search, since you even go so far as to style yourself, with such winning certainty, a teacher of philosophy. Begrudge me not, therefore, the favor of taking part in your wisdom. For mine, baldly stated, is hardly worth the speaking of; it is a highly dubious affair, akin to a dream.[1] To be a teacher thereof—that appears to me to be something extraordinarily grand,[2] but as for myself, I know naught of it. And I must confess straightaway that I have, in no wise, been anyone's teacher."

With this fictitious Socratic greeting, we find ourselves squarely transported to the very heart of our subject. Incidentally, the wording is far from being completely fictitious; I have attempted to render the greeting as authentically as possible. For example, the final sentence ("I have, in no wise, been anyone's teacher") may be found word for word as part of Socrates' legal defense;[3] uttered in the face of death, this suggests that it was spoken with great earnestness by a man whom medieval Christianity mentioned in the same breath with Jesus Christ as one of humanity's greatest teachers (common to both

---

[1] *Symposium* 175e3.

[2] *Apology* 19e1.

[3] Ibid., 33a5

was the fact that they left behind no writings).[4]—But I said we were already in the midst of our subject, and what is to be discussed is nothing less than the object of philosophical questioning. First off, though, it should be clear that what prompts Socrates' "I know that I do not know" is neither a nondescript form of "modesty" nor a kind of intellectual coquetry. This all-too-often quoted—and mostly misunderstood—maxim of Socrates' should also not be interpreted as a mere therapist's trick practiced by an expert molder of souls and intended to move one's interlocutor to self-critique. Finally, the sentence is not asserting that man is incapable of any kind of knowledge. Socrates would not dispute the claim of a single physicist, historian, or independent researcher to be able to arrive at certain results. And when he himself is asked, "Is there something you know?" he answers very emphatically: "But of course, absolutely! In fact, I know a great deal! However, what I know are only details!"[5] (And this is something that the sciences—and perhaps the exact sciences most of all —must learn from Socrates/Plato as well, namely, that their findings lack perforce the kind of significance that answers to human beings in their deepest need; they may make one learned and perhaps even industrious, but they do not make one wise—a claim, incidentally, that the greatest of scientists have never made!) Those things that are ultimately important, those great things the knowledge of which would make one "knowing" or just plain "wise"—what is in the end worthy of being known, this is precisely what man is incapable of knowing, at least in its totality: this was exactly Socrates' experience, which he never grows tired of relating. But that is only part of the picture; the other part is this: for Socrates/Plato, philosophizing means simply being on the hunt for that which is worth knowing, for that wisdom which makes one unconditionally wise—and this despite the impossibility of its possession and despite knowing that its possession is impossible. The words *philo-sophia* and *philo-sophos* are explicitly interpreted in this way:[6] not even Homer and Solon were in possession of this type of wisdom; this belongs, rather, to God alone; and for that reason even the wisest among men can at best be

---

[4] Thomas Aquinas, III, 42, 4.
[5] *Euthydemus* 293b7.
[6] *Phaedrus* 278b7–d6.

called *philosophoi*, loving seekers of wisdom—*that* wisdom which is, however, God's possession.

With this still sketchy characterization of philosophy, Plato is not only giving expression to something that has been passed down to him from long ago (Pythagoras would be the first name to mention here) but is at the same time imparting to that tradition, now firmly entrenched, a powerful impetus, so much so that his great disciple, the more "critically" and "pragmatically" minded Aristotle, will explicitly take up this thought and elaborate on it: Not only is the wisdom sought in philosophy actually the property of God alone, but what the philosophizing person is actually inquiring after is God himself.[7] Already, in this still very compressed formulation, however, the fundamental greatness of the philosophical project, as well as its dubiety, has been brought clearly into the open: its unrivalled superiority no less than its futility, its considerable promise no less than its inevitable inadequacy. More importantly, it can already be inferred from this definition that, in the act of philosophizing, something occurs that from a "scientific standpoint" appears highly offensive—indeed "unbelievable"—something socially nonconformist, something irritatingly unorganizable, and so on. And Socrates, as has already been said, would be the first to acknowledge these objections and reservations and, for his part, to corroborate and reinforce them.

I will now undertake to analyze this Socratic observation concerning the essence of philosophy—or, better said, the Platonic observation that is presented through the figure of Socrates and through his verbal disputations—more precisely with regard to its constituent elements while at the same time endeavoring to adhere as closely as possible to Plato's own language. As is well known, Plato's works do not develop their own technical vocabulary, and that, too—I note here in passing—has its justification in the subject matter of philosophy, as Plato himself, in looking back on his life, points out: "[T]here is no way of putting [philosophical insight] in words like other studies."[8] But already when, in lieu of the words ἰδέα and εἶδος, which in the Greek of Plato's time were vivid, sensuous expressions, meaning

---

[7] *Metaphysics* 1.2.983a8–9.

[8] *Seventh Letter* 341c6. [Quoted after the translation by L. A. Post, in *Plato: The Collected Dialogues*, ed. Edith Hamilton and Huntington Cairns (Princeton, 1961), p. 1589.]

roughly "the inward appearance of things, visible only to the eye of
the soul, but still something visible"⁹—when, instead, we say "idea",
we are already one step removed from natural language and one step
closer to the artificial one of terminology.

If we now begin to inquire more closely into the individual con-
stituents of the Platonic conception of philosophy, we find, as a first
approximation, that the philosophizing person is concerned with *reality as a whole* and with *wisdom in its entirety*. This is the first feature
to which Socrates calls attention when in Plato's great dialogue the
Republic, he attempts to "define . . . whom we mean by the philosophers":¹⁰ in every case, he says, it may be observed that a truly strong
desire aims at the whole;¹¹ thus one who is truly hungry is not dainty
about his food, taking "only a part and a part not".¹² "Then the lover
of wisdom, too, we shall affirm, desires all wisdom, not a part and a
part not."¹³ "[His is] a soul that is ever to seek integrity and wholeness (τοῦ ὅλου καὶ παντὸς) in all things human and divine."¹⁴

These sentences from Plato's *Republic* contain an insight of momentous import, one that is much more accurate than might be presumed
at first glance: Whereas each science constitutes itself as the particular
science that it is by formulating a certain "aspect"—a very specific
question—one that is concerned explicitly and exclusively with *this*,
and expressly not with *that*, no science asks how the world is as a totality. But it is precisely in this—in the world as a totality, the world
in all its aspects—that philosophy is interested. The philosophizing
person is so much eye and ear that he does not even dare interrupt this
attentive silence with a straightforward question. Only one thought
consumes him, that nothing from the *totum* of reality be omitted, overlooked, covered up, kept secret, or forgotten. This concern is something so distinctive—is so much a *differentia specifica*—that one can say
that it singles out the genuinely and seriously philosophizing person.

---

⁹ Cf. P. Friedländer, *Platon*, vol. 1 (Berlin, 1954), pp. 16ff.

¹⁰ *Republic* 474b5. [Quoted after the translation by Shorey, in *Plato: The Collected Dialogues*, p. 713.]

¹¹ Ibid., 475c3.

¹² Ibid., 475b5. [Quoted after the translation by Shorey, in *Plato: The Collected Dialogues*, p. 714.]

¹³ Ibid., 475b8. [Quoted after the translation by Shorey, in *Plato: The Collected Dialogues*, p. 714.]

¹⁴ Ibid., 486a5; 485b5. [Quoted after the translation by Shorey, in *Plato: The Collected Dia-logues*, p. 722.]

It would be downright unphilosophical, in other words, to exclude formally any attainable data concerning reality. Here, however, we need to speak more concretely. Whoever inquires, in a philosophical manner, after, say, the philosophical nature of man would destroy the philosophical character of this questioning were he to say, for example, "The medical, psychological, and genetic facts do not concern me (since, after all, I am inquiring after the 'metaphysical essence' of man)." He would, however, just as much cease to philosophize if he were inclined to say, "It does not concern me that religious tradition insists that man, after a certain primeval event, is not what he actually could and should be." The philosophical character of this interrogative stance would also be compromised if one said, "What interests me exclusively is what is 'clearly and distinctly' knowable, what can be critically examined; I want to know only what can be made compellingly obvious and is thoroughly demonstrable." To limit oneself to certain types of evidence would defeat the very purpose of philosophical questioning.

The act of philosophizing requires that one's gaze be completely uninvolved, a state of complete unaffectedness that is inconsistent with any form of conditionality. Philosophy betrays itself at the very moment it begins to construe itself as an academic subject. The philosophizing person is not characterized by the fact that he is interested in philosophy as a "subject"; he is interested in the world as a totality and in wisdom in its entirety. Such is Plato's conception of philosophy! How is this reflected in the dialogues? In the *Symposium*, the question is put before those present at the banquet: What is love—ultimately and in the final analysis? And then it is discussed from the standpoint of the physician, the natural scientist, the psychologist, and the sociologist, until someone else speaks up who says: No one can understand *eros* who does not reflect on what, soteriologically, has transpired between gods and men—at which point he begins to recount the myth of original sin and of man's fall and of the unquenchable yearning to regain this original state of wholeness. And finally Socrates conjures up the priestly figure of Diotima, from whom knowledge of the mysteries of *eros* has been handed down: "This . . . was the doctrine of Diotima [and] I was convinced. . . ."[15]

---

[15] *Symposium* 212b1. [Quoted after the translation by Michael Joyce, in *Plato: The Collected Dialogues*, p. 563.]

It is clear that it is the relationship between philosophy and theo-logy, in particular, that is being addressed here. It is impossible not to touch upon this—neuralgic—point in an explanation of the Pla-tonic conception of philosophy. It is all the more important, then, to formulate this thesis as precisely as possible. I am not claiming that the philosophizing person is, on Plato's view, compelled by the very nature of the philosophical act to revert to a theological world view. Rather my thesis is this: The philosophical approach to inquiry, as Plato understands it, not only does not require, it actually forbids that supernatural evidence concerning the world as totality be rejected from the outset. Such a rejection would be unphilosophical because —to repeat—the philosophizing person is *per definitionem* concerned with the whole, with the totality of what is in all its aspects.

A *second* element belonging to the Platonic conception of philosophy can be found in the following thought, which recurs several times in the dialogues: the philosophizing person, insofar as he philosophizes, is on the hunt for "the Idea of Being".[16] I have already argued this point above: a simple transliteration of the Greek sets us all too easily on the false path—on the path of pompous bombast and unreal ab-straction—whereas Socrates and Plato speak in an incomparably con-crete manner when they attempt to clarify what they mean by ἰδέα and εἶδος. Among Socrates' interlocutors in these philosophical con-versations there was arguably not a one who would not have known what the shuttle with which the weaver runs the thread through the warp looks like. "And suppose the shuttle to be broken in [the] mak-ing", so runs Socrates' maieutic questioning. "Will he make another, looking to the broken one? Or will he look to the form (εἶδος) ac-cording to which he made the other?"[17] The answer, of course, is that the carpenter will look to the form. In this context, we prefer to speak of the "*idea* of the shuttle"—against which nothing is to be objected, as long as we do not allow ourselves to forget that what is meant is not only something inordinately precise and almost intu-itive but also something that is, in fact, not otherwise distinguishable from what men normally say and think. What is meant is clearly the

---

[16] *Republic* 486d10; *Sophist* 254a8.

[17] *Cratylus* 389b1-3. [Quoted after the translation by Benjamin Jowett, in *Plato: The Col-lected Dialogues*, p. 427.]

pattern, the design, the "prior image" [*das vorgehende Bild*] (as it was known in German mysticism). In what follows, however, the realm of the intuitive and generally known is left behind. According to Plato, a pattern, an original form, a design informs and precedes *all that is*, not only the shuttle and all artificially produced things, but even the natural things of this world, including man himself; there is an archetype of the good, proper, orderly man, in relation to which one can and should orient oneself, against which empirical human reality is constantly measuring itself and against which it must rectify itself —just as a carpenter must orient himself toward a plan, if a useable, a "proper" shuttle is to emerge. If one were to know the design for man, then one would know exactly what it means to be a man. This is precisely what is being claimed with regard to the philosophizing person—not that he actually *succeeds* in achieving this insight, but that, insofar as he philosophizes, he inquires after the archetypes, not after the design of this or that being, but after the pattern of reality as a whole, after the primordial sense of being real. In Plato's metaphor, philosophizing amounts to being on the hunt for the "Idea of Being".

Insofar as Jean-Paul Sartre has recently attacked the Platonic world view in an extremely radical and, in its radicalism, revealing manner, we have, somewhat unexpectedly, been given the opportunity to bring the general contours of that world view into sharper relief. Sartre's existentialism consists, by his own definition, in the following: *No* design precedes or informs natural beings, least of all man; and since there is no design, no "prior image", there is also no point in speaking of the nature or essence of man. Sartre is equally explicit about why he thinks this should be the case: because the God who could have conceived of this design does not exist![18] In pursuing this contrast, it becomes possible to penetrate more deeply into the innermost meaning of the Platonic world view. Arguably, Plato did not entertain the thought of creation in the strict sense, but he consistently assigned the archetypes of things—"ideas"—to the realm of the divine. He also said that apart from the eye and the presence of visible things, yet a third element is necessary if we are truly to see

---

[18] Jean-Paul Sartre, *L'Existentialisme est un humanisme*, p. 22. [Cf. the English translation, "Existentialism", by Bernard Frechtman, in *Existentialism and Human Emotions* (New York, 1957), p. 18.]

things, namely, sunlight; in the same way a divine light is required if
the eye of our soul is to perceive the archetypes.[19] Even more relevant
to the present context are the mature words of the later Plato to the
effect that God is the measure of all things,[20] whereby the concept
of measure is to be understood as being closely related to the concept of archetype. Sartre's thesis, which shows its geniality by way of
negation, dramatically exposes the deeper significance of this Platonic
idea for contemporary thought and makes palpable the subterranean
connection that links this idea to a thought that for Plato was still
inconceivable. In a single stroke, one realizes how it was possible for
Augustine to see in the Platonic theory of ideas a presentiment of the
wisdom of the divine *logos*, conceived as the ultimate embodiment of
all the archetypes.

Of course, these necessarily oversimplified remarks on "totality"
and the "Idea of Being" are far from exhausting the infinitely many
strands of thought that constitute Plato's response to the question of
what it is that concerns the philosophizing person. There are a multitude of other epithets with which he seeks to express that toward
which philosophy directs its efforts at knowledge: the "idea" is the
"eternally same" and the "unchangeable";[21] it is the "one", and not
the many;[22] it is "that which makes a man happy";[23] it is "order";[24]
it is the "divine".[25] Even after such a fragmentary listing, it is already
clear for what reasons Socrates insists that the wisdom after which
the philosophizing person inquires and which he seeks cannot possibly enter into his possession. And we have no difficulty concurring
with him in this: the precise design of the world cannot be known
—not in the way we know exactly and conclusively at what tem-
perature heat melts a specific metal. But there is a second difficulty
here: What is the point of hunting for a wisdom that cannot, as a
matter of principle, be hunted down? And is it not absurd in the first
place to pose, and elaborate on, a question that by all accounts cannot

---

[19] *Republic* 507d11–509b10.
[20] *Laws* 716c4.
[21] *Republic* 484b3; 500c1; 525b5; *Philebus* 58a1.
[22] *Gorgias* 526c3.
[23] *Euthydemus* 282d1.
[24] *Republic* 500c9.
[25] Ibid.; *Sophist* 254b1.

be answered definitively? Nowadays, this objection has been put forward quite emphatically by the so-called "scientific philosophy" and
with ever-greater influence, especially in the Anglo-Saxon world. It
strikes at every form of philosophizing that derives from Plato, and
that means virtually everything that has been associated here in the
West with the name of "philosophy" for the past two thousand years.
This is a highly explosive topic, which, however, cannot be explored
further here. I only wish to make the Socratic/Platonic conception
of ignorance slightly more intelligible. What is being referred to as
philosophy here is something whose high profile makes it assailable on
many fronts. It has its exact counterpart in presumptive knowledge,
that form of ignorance against which the political philosopher Plato
cautions, adding that as soon as such ignorance is accompanied by
power, it will become a source of monstrous crime.[26] The ignorance
of the genuinely philosophical man is based on a positive experience
in which he actually comes to view his object—even if only as something that transcends his powers of comprehension. This knowing ignorance includes and therewith embodies a well-founded view of the
world, namely, that the world is unfathomable, a statement that reflects a finding based on personal experience. Only someone who has
had this experience can be a knowing nonknower. Socrates says that
it was apparently because of the intensity of this experience, to which
he himself had been privy, that the Delphic oracle pronounced him
one of the wisest among men. "Gentlemen, please do not interrupt"
—this is how, during his legal defense,[27] he begins this provocative
story. It is, indeed, disquieting—and not just for Athenians! But if
one takes a look at the history of philosophy, it becomes evident that
this conceptual paradigm—ignorance as the highest form of knowledge—has from that time on never quite disappeared from the Western tradition. For example, there is a proposition in Thomas Aquinas
that reads: "That is the uttermost extremity of man's knowledge of
God: to know that we do not know God."[28] The German cardinal
Nicholas of Cusa, in particular, passionately defended this Socratic
notion. The *docta ignorantia*, he explains, presupposes that this learned

---

[26] *Laws* 863c7.
[27] *Apology* 21a6.
[28] *Pot.* 7, 5 ad 14.

ignorance actually encounters its object: only someone who has stared into the sun knows that its light transcends the ability of our eyes to see.[29]

Now one might object that this experience does not represent something uniquely philosophical. Even the exact sciences find themselves increasingly running up against their own limits. As proof, one might adduce a letter in which Albert Einstein, a few weeks before his death, writes: "If I have learned anything from the ruminations of a long lifetime, it is that we are much farther away from acquiring a deeper insight into the elementary processes than most of our contemporaries believe."[30]

To this it might be answered that the difference consists in the fact that science comes to an end at the limits of knowledge, whereas philosophy begins with those very limits. This is, of course, an overstatement. But one must recognize that already the very first philosophical question could not be answered adequately—and that is in keeping with its very nature. As for Einstein's comment, it was hardly meant to be so understood as if the findings of modern physics should now be cast into doubt. On the other hand, I wonder whether, perhaps, that "deeper insight", which Einstein describes as having been denied us does not refer to precisely that which attracts the philosopher's interest to these "elementary processes". Insofar as the philosophizing person deals, albeit in a formal manner, with the element of incomprehensibility in the world, a definition of philosophy can never begin with the words, "Philosophy is the doctrine of . . .". For this very same reason there can never be a closed system of philosophy. Plato would presumably have acknowledged, with the greatest of sympathy, the Hegelian critique of his dialogic—that is, nonsystematic—form of philosophizing (Plato's "philosophical education" was described in Hegel's *Vorlesungen über die Geschichte der Philosophie* [*Lectures on the History of Philosophy*][31] as "not yet so developed" "for genuinely scientific work"). On the other hand, no one would have been capable of formulating the kind of ironic barbs that Socrates would, over

[29] *Apologia doctae ignorantiae* 2, 20ff.

[30] Letter to Max von Laue (dated February 3, 1955), published in the *Frankfurter Allgemeine Zeitung* of April 23, 1955.

[31] *Sämtliche Werke*, ed. by H. Glockner (Stuttgart, 1928), 18:186.

thousands of years, have aimed at the great systematic philosophers —unless, of course, it were Plato himself.

In the times when philosophical self-awareness, which was apotheosized most notably by Hegel as the Absolute, was at its zenith—in those times, irretrievably past, one had almost forgotten that philosophy, as a concept, is more of a negative than a positive determination and that it has, since its inception, consisted more of questions than of answers. For us it is not only the bold answers provided by the speculative systems that have become unconvincing; we are now hardly able to go on recognizing the philosophical *question* itself as meaningful. What does it mean for a questioning, a seeking, a "being on the hunt" to be genuinely philosophical? Plato wants us to understand that what it means, above all, is to recognize that there is a dimension of reality that is simply not accessible to our rational approach. This kind of questioning is not the intellectual game in which the sophist is so well versed, but rather the way—and, in fact, the only way—in which the knowing mind can keep its unfathomable object in sight, in which it can remain close to the cosmic mystery, fast on its heels, as it were. By contrast, whoever says, in agreement with "scientific philosophy" that unanswerable questions are meaningless questions—he is no longer dealing with the world as a totality, he has already lost sight of it!

In this there is an intimation of the type of demand that is being placed on the philosophizing person in Plato's view and how one goes about recognizing the "philosophical man". It is, above all, the energy of the soul that allows it to persist implacably in its questioning, which, as a living spiritual act, is directed toward the world in its totality and depth; it is an openness for that which arouses wonder —wonder at the fact that something exists at all—an openness that must continually be reconstituted anew. And all this, coupled with the crucial demand for utmost precision.[32] Plato makes explicit mention of the fact that the effort required is like that of contestants in a physical competition.[33] And the often misunderstood statement that mathematics should serve as a propaedeutic to the study of philosophy must also be understood in this context. It does not mean that the

---

[32] *Republic* 504e2.
[33] Ibid., 504a1; 504d1.

"results" of philosophy must (or even could) be acquired and presented *more geometrico*;[34] rather, Socrates expressly describes a training
in mathematics as "the prelude of the strain that we have to apprehend",[35] which, however, is another way of saying that without the
discipline and precision of a formally stringent thinking, its actual object could not be reached. It can, however, very easily happen that
its actual object is not achieved *despite* the most precise intellectual
techniques—because the soul lacks the ability to let itself be affected
and its questioning gaze lacks simplicity, without which the object of
philosophizing cannot be brought to light and kept in view.

There is an astonishing remark in Plato's *Republic* concerning those
factors that might pose a threat to this kind of openness. What Socrates
calls "the most surprising fact of all"[36] is that precisely what we might
consider beneficial could prove to be deleterious. In this connection it
does not especially surprise us to find cited as the primary obstacles
to philosophizing such "so-called goods" as beauty, wealth, bodily
strength, "connections", and the like.[37] And, of course, it is not this
which Socrates finds so surprising. Still, it takes one somewhat aback
to hear with what directness Socrates says of a young companion—
one who might perhaps even have been present—that he was fortunate to have had reins placed upon him (his sickliness) that made him
stick with philosophy so that he was, for example, unable to go into
politics. Although this was probably not meant in complete seriousness, it is also true that it was not said entirely in jest. What, however, is most surprising is now said in undoubted earnest, that is, that
bravery, prudence, and other virtues of this kind might interfere with
the act of philosophizing and philosophical contemplation as such—
although these virtues belong to the very notion of an orderly man!
What is the point being made here? The point is that perfection is not
synonymous with self-made ethical perfection. Something, however,
is also being said about the innermost nature of the philosophical act.

We have spoken of the spiritual energy that drives the kind of pure

---

[34] For more on this, see H. Scholz, *Was ist Philosophie?* (Berlin and Vienna, 1940), esp. pp.
8f.

[35] *Republic* 531d8. [Quoted after the translation by Shorey, in *Plato: The Collected Dialogues*,
p. 764.]

[36] Ibid., 491b7. [Quoted after the translation by Shorey, in *Plato: The Collected Dialogues*,
p. 727.]

[37] Ibid., 491c1–4.

questioning that holds out to the end, the kind that inquires after the meaning of the world, after reality as a whole, after the archetypes, and so on. This way of putting the matter was not completely free from misunderstanding. It could be so understood as if what were meant were primarily or even exclusively the strenuous, arbitrary activity of a thinking that keeps itself under control. In reality, however —and it is this to which Socrates appears to be alluding with his talk about being "surprised"—it is not so much a question of doing as it is one of receptivity, of being willing to let something befall oneself. What is meant is an extreme—a seismographic, as it were—ability to be attentive, which does not require exertion so much as it does a silence that penetrates one's innermost being and that cannot be induced by any activity, no matter how disciplined, but that can very well be disrupted by it.

The "difficulty" involved in philosophizing is not of the kind that could be overcome through sheer "intellectual labor"—which again does not mean, of course, that one is spared the "exertions of the concept". In the "Seventh Letter", Plato describes a kind of test procedure for recognizing the genuinely philosophical person, one based on the way in which the person in question responds to any type of difficulty. Plato himself had tried out the test on the tyrant Dionysius. "One must point out to such men that the whole plan is possible and explain what preliminary steps and how much hard work it will require, for the hearer, if he is genuinely devoted to philosophy and is a man of God with a natural affinity and fitness for the work, sees in the course marked out a path of enchantment, which he must at once strain every nerve to follow, or die in the attempt."[38] The unsuitable candidates, however, will either fail and give up on the plan or they will conclude that they are well-informed enough already.[39]

Again, one will perhaps argue that the same might be found true of every type of research and of the sciences as a whole. In what way does this express something peculiar to philosophy? I would answer: What is at issue here points to the "erotic" character of philosophizing, and that is something that is uniquely different. The analogy between the erotic encounter in the narrower sense and the

---

[38] *Seventh Letter* 340b4–c5. [Quoted after the translation by Post, in *Plato: The Collected Dialogues*, p. 1588.]

[39] Ibid., 340d5–341a3.

philosophizing person is drawn explicitly in the Platonic dialogues the *Symposium* and the *Phaedrus*. This appears to be Plato's own personal discovery. *Eros* himself, the daemon, is described as "a lifelong seeker after truth",[40] and in the myth concerning the ascent of the soul, in which man elevates himself to the place of the gods, the lover and the person who seeks "in innocence" (ἄδολως) after wisdom are the only chosen ones among all the remaining human beings.[41]

What, however, is the significance of this quaint form of mythical expression? The first thing to note is that it is not unintentionally "poetic". Just as in the erotic convulsion something happens that does not simply lie within man's free disposition, so the philosophical search for wisdom cannot be understood as an act set in motion exclusively by man. In the act of philosophizing a sovereignly planning reason does not face a world of "possible objects" to which it then freely devotes itself in accordance with the goal it has set. Rather philosophizing arises from an insatiability we cannot master but which demands satisfaction over and above our bodily needs. When Hans Reichenbach, one of the leading architects of the "scientific philosophy", writes that "the philosopher . . . appears incapable of mastering his desire to know",[42] he is expressing Plato's view exactly. The difference between the two consists simply in the fact that Reichenbach considers this a fatal argument *against* the Platonic conception of philosophy. One sees immediately that, inevitably, very profound issues are involved here—for example, whether man must perhaps by virtue of his very nature ask questions that transcend his ability to comprehend, whether man, perhaps, as Pascal put it, transcends himself to an infinite degree.

At this point, philosophy's proximity to *eros* can also be reinterpreted: in the erotic encounter with sensuous beauty a passion is awakened that cannot be quieted; one shaken by *eros* catches sight of a promise in whose nature it lies that it cannot be kept in what for it would evidently be the appropriate way. Similarly, in the earliest

---

[40] *Symposium* 203d7. [Quoted after the translation by Joyce, in *Plato: The Collected Dialogues*, p. 563.]

[41] *Phaedrus* 249a1.

[42] *Der Aufstieg der wissenschaftlichen Philosophie* (Berlin, 1953), p. 36. [Quoted from Hans Reichenbach, *The Rise of Scientific Philosophy* (Berkeley and Los Angeles: Univ. of California Press, 1951), p. 25.]

moment of philosophical wonder, a question (what does it mean for something to be real?) already comes alive that cannot be satisfied in the finite realm, or, alternately expressed, cannot be answered "scientifically".

The unsatisfiable nature of philosophical *eros*—Diotima speaks of the "illiberal" *philosophia*[43]—this essential insatiability extends beyond the realm of corporeal existence. That means the philosophizing person, insofar as he philosophizes, is in a tragic as well as a comic way in disproportion to "this" earthly reality. And this disproportionateness cannot help but affect philosophy's situation within human society— about which one closing observation has still to be made.

One knows how much pleasure Socrates appears to take in using ever-new and hyperbolic turns of phrase to portray the awkwardness of the philosophizing person: such a person barely knows where even the town hall is; he has no knowledge of the powerful interests competing for government office; he is completely unaware of things like the difference between noble and common birth; "he is not even aware that he knows nothing of all this" (this last is a piece of self-description offered in ironic reflection!).[44] The laughter of the Thracian maidservant who mocks Thales for having tumbled into the well while observing the heavens—this same laughter has always been reserved for those who devote themselves to philosophy. I need not belabor here what is generally well known. Incidentally, Socrates does not speak only of the laughable behavior of the philosophizing person; he himself also knows how to laugh. When, for example, "flowery language is spoken" or when one praises tyrants, then it is his turn —the philosopher's—to laugh and then "in all seriousness"![45] But enough of this. In the end it is not overly important to know who laughs over whom or with what justification.

It seems more important to ask, after everything that has already been said, what positive role can be assigned to philosophy in human society. Of course, what is meant by "philosophy" is not a specific group of human beings, not a body consisting of "representatives" of the subject, whose social function would then have to be explained.

---

[43] *Symposium* 210d6.

[44] *Theaetetus* 173e1. [Quoted after the translation by F. M. Cornford, in *Plato: The Collected Dialogues*, p. 879.]

[45] Ibid., 174d2–3.

Socrates has said that the face of the genuinely philosophizing person cannot easily be recognized—it is "hardly easier to discern than the god"[46]—and it is worth keeping in mind here his bitter remark to the effect that philosophy has suffered the worst form of calumny from those who call themselves philosophers.[47] We are asking here, not about the performance of a particular institution or group, but rather about the value of philosophizing—wherever it finds itself realized— for human society.

Aristotle the Platonist gave philosophy's own estimate of itself in a formulation that appears in the *Metaphysics*: All the sciences are more necessary than it, but none can lay claim to a greater dignity ("necessariores omnes, nulla dignior").[48] The "dignity" of philosophy and the station proper to it in human society derive from the fact that it alone is able to incite an indispensable disquiet in the face of the following question: After we perform, with a wondrous expenditure of intelligence and labor, all that is necessary—responding to the exigencies of life, making the essential provisions (in every sense), and securing one's livelihood—what is a truly human life, once it has been so enabled, now supposed to consist in?

To voice this unsettling question amid all the satisfactions of men making themselves at home in the world and to keep this question alive with an incorruptible and precise intellectual effort—this marks the real achievement of philosophy and its genuine contribution to the common good, even if it is incapable on its own of providing a complete answer.

---

[46] *Sophist* 216c3. [Quoted after the translation by Cornford, in *Plato: The Collected Dialogues*, p. 959.]

[47] *Republic* 489d1.

[48] 1.2.983a10.

CREATURELINESS AND HUMAN NATURE

Reflections on the Philosophical Method of Jean-Paul Sartre

Few would fail to acknowledge how right Sartre was to observe—in a remark penned as early as 1946—that the term "existentialism" had by then been applied to such a wide variety of things that it no longer meant anything at all, *rien du tout*.[1] And yet more than a few rather precise formulations may be found in Sartre's own writings, which, if nothing else, leave little doubt as to what he himself understood by "existentialism". Although it is just as difficult to reduce these rejoinders to a single common denominator, the context in which they are embedded is unambiguous, and one formulation may be used to interpret the other and to make it clear. Allow me to cite three such "definitions" of existentialism.

First: "Existentialism is nothing else than an attempt to draw all the consequences of a coherent atheistic position."[2] Atheism—that, indeed, is Sartre's starting point, which he "presupposes" with barely a hint of argumentation.

Second: "[T]here is no human nature. . . . Man is nothing else but what he makes of himself. Such is the first principle of existentialism."[3] Sartre constantly reverts to this point, regarding it as "given that . . . there is no human nature for me to depend on."[4] And in a discussion with an interlocutor, who at several points advances an opposing opinion, he is at pains to note that "we are united in one point: there is no human nature."[5]

---

[1] Jean-Paul Sartre, *L'Existentialisme est un humanisme*, p. 16. German translation in J. P. Sartre, *Drei Essays* (Frankfurt, 1960), p. 9. [Quoted from Jean-Paul Sartre, *Existentialism and Human Emotions* (New York, 1957), p. 12.]

[2] *L'Existentialisme*, p. 94. [Quoted from Sartre, *Existentialism*, p. 51.]

[3] Ibid., p. 22. [Quoted from Sartre, *Existentialism*, p. 15.]

[4] Ibid., p. 52. [Quoted from Sartre, *Existentialism*, p. 30.]

[5] Ibid., p. 136.

Third: "Existential philosophy is above all a philosophy that asserts that existence precedes essence."[6] While it is true that Sartre distinguishes between "two kinds of existentialist,"[7] the Christian and the atheistic, there is one thing, he claims, they both share, namely, the conviction that existence precedes essence. Although it is highly doubtful whether this applies to the "Christian existentialists", among whom he numbers Gabriel Marcel and Karl Jaspers, there is at the same time no uncertainty as to *what* he means here.

This last characterization appears to me the most fundamental, even apart from the fact that it is the one that most readily explains the choice of the epithet "existentialism". It also represents, parenthetically, the earliest definition that Sartre was to offer of existentialism. He enunciated this principle for the first time during the Second World War, in a still relatively unknown interview with the Communist weekly '*action* that appeared in the edition of December 29, 1944: "Have you already explained existentialism to your readership? It is very simple."[8] A year later, in a lecture published in 1946,[9] Sartre once again made an attempt at a general characterization; here, too, the existentialist doctrine, although clearly intended for specialists and philosophers, is described as "easily defined".[10]

Although it has been said of the lecture—by historians of philosophy, primarily—that it is actually too journalistic and too superficial to be taken seriously,[11] I would argue, conversely, that this nonacademic, spontaneous, and unrehearsed attempt at self-interpretation is much more interesting and even more instructive than a heavily fortified treatise that comes replete with technical jargon and conceptual apparatus.

Granted, then: Existence precedes essence. What does that mean?

The two crucial nouns, "existence" and "essence", are used by Sartre in their received classical sense, a fact that has, incidentally, earned him the reproach that he remains too wedded to the tradi-

---

[6] Ibid., p. 101.

[7] Ibid., p. 17. [Quoted from Sartre, *Existentialism*, p. 13.]

[8] The original text was not available to me. The quotations stem from L. Richter's *Jean-Paul Sartre* (Berlin, 1960), pp. 18f.; individual expressions are cited there in the original French.

[9] It is the essay, "Existentialism", from which we have been quoting.

[10] Ibid., p. 16. [Quoted from Sartre, *Existentialism*, p. 12.]

[11] Cf. J. M. Bocheński, *Europäische Philosophie der Gegenwart*, 2nd ed. (Munich, 1951).

tional theory of being.[12] By "essence", Sartre understands an enduring juxtaposition of attributes, a "community" of specific qualities,[13]
"the ensemble of . . . the properties which enable it to be . . . defined."[14] This does not, in fact, sound that much different from the
following proposition to be found in Aquinas' *Summa theologica*: "Essentia proprie est id quod significatur per definitionem."[15] And what
about the meaning of "existence"? Sartre's answer is that it corresponds to actual presence in the world,[16] to "presence . . . in front of
me".[17] Again, the term is being defined in a way that is thoroughly
traditional and, for that matter, extremely plausible.

However, the same cannot be said of the way in which Sartre relates
the two concepts, "essence" and "existence", to each other. Indeed,
it is his avowed intention not only to oppose the traditional world
view but to transform it into its opposite. By his own admission, his
purpose in beginning with a detailed interpretation of the traditional
view is to highlight his own thesis by way of contrast. Of course,
it may be questioned whether this interpretation is correct. In this
context, Sartre refers to the *vision technique du monde*, with which he
associates the view that God created man and world, and he goes on
to point out that, contrary to his own thesis, the "technical view of
the world"[18] implies that essence precedes existence.

As an example of this type of creation, Sartre famously introduces
the manufacture of a paper cutter or letter opener: The artisan knows
in advance what he plans to make; he is aware of "what" a letter
opener is; he is familiar with that particular juxtaposition of properties; in a word, he knows the *essence* of a letter opener—and hence the
essence of a letter opener must precede its existence! But, on closer
examination, is it really the essence, the whatness, the nature that

---

[12] Cf. M. Müller, *Existenzphilosophie im geistigen Leben der Gegenwart* (Heidelberg, 1949),
pp. 69ff.

[13] "L'ensemble constant de propriétés", in *L'Action*; cf. L. Richter, *Jean-Paul Sartre*, p. 18.

[14] "L'ensemble . . . des qualités, qui permettent de la définer" (*Existentialisme*, p. 18).
[Quoted from Sartre, *Existentialism*, p. 13.]

[15] I, 29, 2 ad 3.

[16] "Une certaine présence effective dans le monde", in *L'Action*; cf. Richter, *Jean-Paul Sartre*,
p. 18.

[17] "La présence en face de moi" (*Existentialisme*, p. 18). [Quoted from Sartre, *Existentialism*,
p. 13.]

[18] Ibid., p. 18. [Quoted from Sartre, *Existentialism*, p. 13.]

come first? Or is it rather the design in the mind of the artisan—the plan, the blueprint, the pattern, the model?

Strictly speaking, there is in reality neither an existence that would predate a being's essence, nature, or whatness nor an essence that would predate existence; being, in abstraction from essence and whatness, is just as inconceivable as whatness and essence in abstraction from being and existence. This notwithstanding, it is certainly true that an intimate and critical relationship obtains between essence, whatness, and nature, on the one hand, and plan, blueprint, pattern, model, on the other. And whoever knows the design of a thing knows at the same time its essence or nature; indeed, he is the only one who knows its essence and nature *completely*.

Thus, according to Sartre, the traditional religious world view, which he dubs the *vision technique du monde*, is based on (or may even be equated with) the notion that there is a divine artisan, who, in a fashion analogous to that of the manufacturer of a letter opener, confers upon man and world their essence and whatness. In point of fact, though, Sartre hardly mentions the world after that but speaks exclusively of man, who is the sole object of his interest.

At this point, one might raise the question parenthetically whether this conception of creation does not miss the crucial point. For while it is certainly true that creation is an essence- and whatness-conferring act, is it not before all else existence-positing? If so, then there is no analogy to human activity that could correspond to it.

But, as I have already remarked, Sartre is using what he calls "the technical view of the world" merely as a contrasting foil, against which he intends to highlight his own thesis and clarify it. His own thesis, which he is alone concerned to prove, runs as follows: From the fact that man has no essence and whatness designed and conceived in advance that could have been invented and then imparted to him by a divine manufacturer, it may be inferred that in the case of man, existence precedes essence.

Whether this inference is legitimate from a purely logical point of view or whether opposites are here being confused—a "contrary" being taken for a "contradictory" (as when one infers from the fact that something is not black that it must then be white)—or whether the most that a valid inference from Sartrean premises could assert would be that there is no essence that precedes human existence— all these questions we will set aside for the time being.

What primarily interests us is how Sartre himself construes the sig-nificance of his problematic inference and interprets it, and, in fact, he undertakes several such attempts at self-interpretation—three, at the very least. *First* interpretation: "What is meant here by saying that ex-istence precedes essence? It means that, first of all, man exists" and, "only afterwards, defines himself";[19] "man defines himself little by little."[20] *Second* interpretation: "Man . . . is indefinable";[21] the defini-tion of man "remains forever open".[22] *Third* interpretation: "There is no human nature."[23]

I cannot come up with a single reservation that would prevent me from fully acquiescing in the first and second interpretations. Sartre is quite simply right, I think—contrary to the kind of rationalistic misunderstanding of man and world that ignores not only the reality of evolution but also the crucial distinction between artificial things, that is, those things that are designed and produced by man, and what we shall cautiously term "nonartificial" things, those things whose de-sign was not conceived by man and whose essences, for precisely this reason, are far less familiar than those of artificial things.

On these points, then, one finds oneself in full agreement with Sartre: man cannot ultimately be defined. I would even go so far as to say that not a single *res naturalis*—no nonartificial thing whatsoever —can be defined by us in a rigorous way for the simple reason that we cannot know its design, its pattern, its prototype [*Urbild*]. This view does not in any way represent a form of "agnosticism". We do, in fact, know a great deal about both man and the natural world. What has been denied us is only a final comprehensive definition. In Sartre's words, the definition of man "remains forever open."

Still, what in the world does all this have to do with the third and clearly crucial interpretation, by means of which Sartre explains his initial thesis and which asserts that there is no human nature at all? One thing at least is immediately obvious: this interpretation derives from Sartre's atheism, from which he intends, by his own admission, to draw the ultimate consequences. The complete formulation reads as follows: "[T]here is no human nature, since there is no God to

[19] Ibid., p. 21. [Quoted from Sartre, *Existentialism*, p. 15.]
[20] *L'Action*; cf. Richter, *Jean-Paul Sartre*, p. 19.
[21] *Existentialisme*, p. 22. [Quoted from Sartre, *Existentialism*, p. 15.]
[22] *L'Action*; cf. Richter, *Jean-Paul Sartre*, p. 19.
[23] *Existentialisme*, p. 22. [Quoted from Sartre, *Existentialism*, p. 15.]

conceive it."²⁴ To the inevitable follow-up question, "What, then, is man if there is really no human nature?" Sartre gives a thoroughly consistent response: "[A]t first, he is nothing."²⁵ And later? Later, he "is nothing else but what he makes of himself".²⁶ Man invents and makes himself without the benefit of any pregiven design.²⁷ This is precisely what Sartre means by freedom in his terminology.

This concept has, however, lost all the triumphant connotations that it possessed in the eighteenth century; it inevitably had to lose them, once freedom came to be understood as denying the existence of any form of obligation or limitation and even more emphatically of any point of reference, whether this be some kind of "aid" or something more akin to a means of support. Sartre himself repeats this several times: "There are no omens in the world";²⁸ "man is forlorn, because neither within him nor without does he find anything to cling to";²⁹ "the existentialist does not think that man is going to help himself by finding in the world some omen by which to orient himself."³⁰ It is that now familiar form of freedom to which man has famously been "condemned".³¹

All the other well-known concepts that belong to Sartre's philosophy of existence have their origin here as well. *Forlornness (délaissement)*: "[W]e are alone, with no excuses";³² "forlornness implies that we ourselves choose our being."³³ *Anguish:* "Forlornness and anguish go together."³⁴ *Despair:* "[T]he term has a very simple meaning. It means that we shall confine ourselves to reckoning only with what de-

---

²⁴ Ibid., p. 22. [Quoted from Sartre, *Existentialism*, p. 15.] The French text runs: "puisqu'il n'y a pas de Dieu pour la concevoir". This thought appears to me to be distorted, if not falsified, by the British translation: "because there is no God to have a conception of it" (Jean-Paul Sartre, *Existentialism and Humanism* [London, 1948], p. 28).

²⁵ *Existentialisme*, p. 22. [Quoted from Sartre, *Existentialism*, p. 15.]

²⁶ Ibid. [Quoted from Sartre, *Existentialism*, p. 15.]

²⁷ "Man is condemned . . . to invent man" (*Existentialisme*, p. 38). [Quoted from Sartre, *Existentialism*, p. 23.]

²⁸ Ibid., p. 47. [Quoted from Sartre, *Existentialism*, p. 28.]

²⁹ Ibid., p. 36. [Quoted from Sartre, *Existentialism*, p. 22.]

³⁰ Ibid., p. 38. [Quoted from Sartre, *Existentialism*, p. 23.]

³¹ Ibid., p. 37. [Quoted from Sartre, *Existentialism*, p. 23.]

³² Ibid. [Quoted from Sartre, *Existentialism*, p. 23.]

³³ Ibid., p. 49. [Quoted from Sartre, *Existentialism*, p. 29.]

³⁴ Ibid. [Quoted from Sartre, *Existentialism*, p. 29.]

pends on our will."[35] *Absurdity of the world and human existence:* "[T]o say that we invent values means nothing else but this: life has no meaning *a priori*."[36]

The radicalism of this mode of thinking, which one may legitimately admire, compels us for our part—or so it appears to me— to rethink certain fundamental concepts in our own tradition. I am referring above all to the intimate relationship between the concept of "creatureliness" and the concept of "nature", and, more specifically, to the question of whether "by nature" must always and necessarily be synonymous with "by virtue of creation" or "on the basis of creation". Sartre rightly polemicizes against those philosophers of the eighteenth century who refused to go on speaking of God and who even openly denied the creation of man and all beings while continuing to refer to the "nature" of man and the "essence" of those beings as if nothing had changed.[37] The point behind Sartre's objection is clear: One cannot legitimately speak of a "human nature" unless one is willing to acknowledge that there is a God who, as Creator, imagined and designed it. What we are obliged to reconsider and rediscover here is nothing less than the implicit connection between the concept of a "design", a pattern, a model, or, as Meister Eckhart called it, a "prior image" [*vorgehendes Bild*], on the one hand, and the concept of a nature, an essence, or a whatness, on the other. It seems likely that Sartre's thesis is correct: Where there is no design (and hence no designer), there is also no essence or nature. In Aquinas' *Summa theologica*, there is a sentence that expresses virtually the same thought: "For the fact that a creature subsists according to a certain standard and certain limits indicates that it comes from some source" [*Nam hoc ipsum quod creatura habet substantiam modificatam et finitam, demonstrat quod sit a quodam principio*].[38] Might one not also express it this way: There is no human nature unless there is a Creator who could have designed it (or, rather, who actually designed it)? Astonishingly, this fundamental conviction is shared by both Jean-Paul Sartre and Saint Thomas Aquinas.

---

[35] Ibid. [Quoted from Sartre, *Existentialism*, p. 29.]

[36] Ibid., p. 89. [Quoted from Sartre, *Existentialism*, p. 49.]

[37] Ibid., pp. 19f. [Quoted from Sartre, *Existentialism*, pp. 21–22.]

[38] I, 93, 6. [Quoted from St. Thomas Aquinas, *Summa Theologicae*, Blackfriars English transl., ed. Edmund Hill O.P., vol. 13 (London: Eyre & Spottiswoode, 1964), p. 69.]

And the same conceptual relationship between man's "nature" and his createdness or "creatureliness" is also at the bottom of many of the debates that concern us today—for example, the debate over "natural law" and the "natural" moral law, but also the debates over eschatology and the future, over hope and evolution.

In the contemporary self-understanding of Christian theology there is a tendency, a trend, to believe that being a Christian means nothing more than to be open to the future (a view that comes close to quoting Rudolf Bultmann almost verbatim)[39] or to believe that the whole of Christian theology amounts to nothing more than eschatology and that hope is the only Christian virtue. All this may be legitimate and defensible in a certain, limited sense; it can, moreover, be understood as a necessary reaction to the hegemony of rationalism and traditionalism. Even so, I find it an alarming sign when a representative existentialist Marxist and a leading participant in the Christian-Marxist debates over the last few years (in Marienbad and Salzburg) like Roger Garaudy, who has studied the writings of some "progressive" theologians with tremendous care, can come to the conclusion that the meaning of human existence, as construed by the "new" Christian theology, is to liberate oneself from one's own nature and one's own past and so be free to make one's own decisions.[40] And Garaudy does not find it difficult from his standpoint to embrace this idea fully. If I were a Christian theologian and I were to find myself understood in this way, then I could only view this agreement with profound mistrust; and I would feel myself obliged to review and revise my own formulations. In reality, the agreement is, of course, more than apparent. There is, in fact, a real commonality, namely, the more or less explicit disinterest in what man is "by virtue of creation"—regardless of whether the reason for this disinterest is a general (atheistic) repudiation of the notion of man's createdness or the assumption that human nature is fully corrupted (by original sin), which, in turn, implies an extremely problematic conception of creation and creatureliness. In any event, it is a discomforting thought that atheism and supernaturalism are able to come together in a common conclusion at all.

---

[39] Cf. "Neues Testament und Mythologie", in *Kerygma und Mythos*, vol. I (Hamburg, 1967), p. 29.

[40] R. Garaudy, *De l'anathème au dialogue* (Paris, 1965), p. 44.

And this in itself could—and, perhaps, should—be impetus enough to rethink the concept of "nature" (particularly, the nature of man) and that of creatureliness.

The problem of a "new" ethic—or, rather, the problem of whether one can meaningfully speak of a "new" ethic at all—should also be viewed in this context. Even in the "old" ethic (by which is meant, not the purely contingent conventionality associated with knowing what "one" should and should not do, but rather the norms derived from the great tradition)—even in the traditional moral teachings of Christianity, understood to be traditional in just this sense—there has certainly always been a place for "creativity", for the "new" and individual response to unforeseen situations; there is even a place for the "invention" of which Sartre so often speaks. Perhaps there is something to be rediscovered here as well. I am thinking of the rank that Thomas Aquinas, for example, assigned to the virtue of prudence; one has spoken—not unjustly, I think—of the "suppression" of this teaching by the moral theology of the previous century.[41] But, of course, "invention" (in the sense of beginning from scratch) could never be a core concept of a Christian ethics as it is for Sartre. The former teaches that all human morality has the character of a "continuation", the furthering of something that has already begun and is in progress. And what has already begun is that which we, "by nature", that is, by virtue of creation, have always been and always have.

It is assuredly no mere coincidence that the question concerning human nature takes on greater urgency the moment the topic turns, for example, to birth control. And the widely misunderstood hesitation and reserve shown by the Catholic Church certainly have their origin, not in a "conception of nature that is confined to biology" (as is sometimes maintained in discussion),[42] but in nothing other than a profoundly responsible earnestness, which attempts to do justice to man's status as creature. Closely related to the aforementioned problem of a "new" ethic is the problem of man's manipulation by man and, no less important, the problem of consciously engineered evolution. Teilhard de Chardin has said that we are now called upon, in

---

[41] It is R. Garrigou-Lagrange who speaks of a "quasi-suppression of the virtue of prudence" (quasi-suppression du traité de la prudence) in his essay "Du caractère métaphysique de la théologie morale de Saint Thomas", *Revue Thomiste* 8 (1925): 345.

[42] See, for example, G. Scherer, *Anthropologische Aspekte der Sexwelle* (Essen, 1970), pp. 92ff.

entering a new stage of evolution, to lay our own human hands on the genetic life-force. But where, then, does it end? What are the limits? One need not look, though, as far as Aldous Huxley's *Brave New World*; it suffices simply to acknowledge the proposals that were made with the appropriate "scientific" gravitas at a London symposium on "man and his future" held in 1962[43]—for example, those concerning artificial insemination (for example, that we must rid ourselves of the old-fashioned prejudice that father and child should be blood relations, and so on).[44] Why not breed a new kind of human being?

Of course, I am far from being in possession of a magic formula by means of which all these problems might be resolved. On the contrary, I am well aware that the concept "human nature", which, in truth, has never been capable of exhaustive definition, must be thought out anew. But I remain at the same time convinced that mankind risks dehumanization as well as denaturation the moment human nature fails to be understood as something created, as something that has been designed and brought into being by a creative spirit absolutely superior to man. Viewed from this standpoint, the cautionary example of Jean-Paul Sartre is rather typical—or so it appears to me—of one core position.

I would like to close by adding a few remarks on what might be described as Sartre's unwitting "proof of God's existence". As is readily apparent to any reader, Sartre's starting point is a decidedly vehement atheism, which is more a matter of faith than it is a product of rational argumentation. At the same time, Sartre's thought is governed by an especially profound appreciation for the superfluity of the world. Here is this Antoine Roquentin sitting on his bench in a public park at "6:00 P.M." and all of a sudden he realizes how accidental, how "contingent", he himself is, along with all the things around him: "We were a heap of living creatures, . . . embarrassed at ourselves, we hadn't the slightest reason to be there, none of us."[45] "The essential thing is contingency. I mean that one cannot define existence as necessity. To exist is simply *to be there*; those who exist let themselves

[43] G. Wolstenholme, ed., *Man and His Future* (London, 1963).

[44] Ibid., pp. 247ff.

[45] J. P. Sartre, *Der Ekel* (novel) (Hamburg, 1963), p. 136. [Quoted from Jean-Paul Sartre, *Nausea*, trans. Lloyd Alexander (New York, 1964), p. 128.]

be encountered, but you can never deduce anything from them."[46] "Every existing thing is born without reason, prolongs itself out of weakness and dies by chance."[47]

The last formulation already suggests that all this is not being proffered as a theoretically neutral account of the real contingency of man and world. Rather, the intent is to expose and denounce contingency as something absurd. "All is free, this park, this city, and myself. When you realize that, it turns your heart upside down and everything begins to float . . . : here is Nausea" (voilà la nausée).[48] "It was there, in the garden, toppled down into the trees, all soft, sticky, soiling everything, all thick, a jelly. And I was inside. . . . I was frightened, furious, I thought it was so stupid, so out of place, I hated this ignoble mess. . . . I choked with rage at this gross, absurd being."[49] "I had learned all I could know about existence. I left, I went back to the hotel and I wrote."[50]

Now my question is this: Is this not exactly the same claim that is being made in the old argument for God's existence, what in Hegel's philosophy of religion is still called the *argumentum e contingentia mundi*, that is, that the world—precisely because of its obvious contingency, its sheer nonnecessity—would indeed be absurd were it not for the existence of an absolute, necessary being that sustains it?

Perhaps Sartre would counter here by asking, "Why should it not be possible for there to be a completely meaningless world? What precludes the possibility that reality and human existence are, in fact, absurd?" "It is absurd that we are born, and it is absurd that we die."[51]

My response to that would be two-tiered. First, no one in the world —not even Sartre himself—is able to think through consistently this notion of the absurdity of everything that exists. Otherwise how could one continue to speak—as Sartre does—of freedom, justice, responsibility, and so on? Second, if one were nevertheless to insist that

---

[46] Ibid., p. 139. [Quoted from Sartre, *Nausea*, p. 131.]

[47] Ibid., p. 142. [Quoted from Sartre, *Nausea*, p. 133.] The German translation, which is highly questionable in some regards, has here: "dies through external causes" (*durch äußere Einwirkung*). The phrase in French is *meurt par recontre*, which can probably best be rendered as "dies, as it so happens".

[48] Ibid., p. 139. [Quoted from Sartre, *Nausea*, p. 130.]

[49] Ibid., pp. 142f. [Quoted from Sartre, *Nausea*, p. 134.]

[50] Ibid., p. 143. [Quoted from Sartre, *Nausea*, p. 135.]

[51] *L'Être et le Néant* (Paris, 1949), p. 631.

absolutely everything in the world is, in reality, absurd, then one would, *eo ipso*, no longer have any "grounds" whatsoever for believing anything; for "ground" [*Gründ*] here means *ratio, raison,* reason. It should be clear that, if that were the case, one could no longer "give grounds" [*begründen*] for anything—not even God's nonexistence.

HEIDEGGER'S CONCEPTION OF TRUTH

"The essence of truth is freedom"[1]—this sentence of Martin Heidegger's, an extraordinary and astonishing sentence—is to be subjected in what follows to a critical examination. This thesis forms the centerpiece of a short essay, "Vom Wesen der Wahrheit" (On the essence of truth), published in 1943, which purports to lead "the question of the essence of truth beyond the confines of the ordinary definition provided in the usual concept of essence".[2] The essay takes up a question with which Heidegger had already dealt extensively in his most voluminous work up to that time, *Sein und Zeit* (Being and time), published in 1927. But even in that work the essence of truth had *not* yet been identified with freedom, although there are certain hints that already point in this direction. A more unequivocal anticipation of this thesis may, however, be found as early as 1929 in the monograph *Vom Wesen des Grundes* (On the essence of reason).

It would be difficult to argue that, in equating freedom with the essential attribute of truth, the restriction typically placed on such definitions has been observed, namely, that the *definiendum* be better known than the *definiens*. Is an inquirer after the meaning of truth not being referred with such a formulation to something much less evident, something even more convoluted? But it is not at all in keeping with the Heideggerian mode of philosophizing to offer textbook definitions. And in his discussion of truth he further admits to having no interest in "furnishing concepts", as he somewhat pejoratively puts it.[3] Metaphysics is, for its part, "not a division of academic philosophy", but "the basic occurrence of *Dasein* [human existence]", indeed, "it is *Dasein* itself",[4] and for that reason the disclosure of truth's essence

---

[1] *Vom Wesen der Wahrheit* (Frankfurt am Main, 1933), p. 14. [Quoted from Martin Heidegger, "On the Essence of Truth", in *Basic Writings*, ed. David Farrell Krell (New York, 1977), p. 125.]

[2] Ibid., p. 27. [Quoted from Heidegger, "Essence of Truth", p. 139.]

[3] Ibid., p. 28. [Quoted from Heidegger, "Essence of Truth", p. 141.]

[4] *Was ist Metaphysik?* (Frankfurt am Main, 1943), p. 22. [Quoted from Martin Heidegger, "What Is Metaphysics?" in *Basic Writings*, p. 112.]

involves "a thinking, which, instead of furnishing representations and concepts, experiences and tries itself as a transformation of its relatedness to Being."[5]

Such efforts at self-understanding are, however, of little use to someone who, in the end, simply wants to know how Heidegger formally defines "truth" and "freedom" and how freedom can be related to truth at all, much less how it can be presumed to constitute its very essence. Only with difficulty can the desire for clarification of a statement's plain sense come to terms with this thinking, which conceives of itself in terms of human existence's coming to an understanding of itself and which is rife with powerful tensions of both a conceptual and affective nature—to say nothing of the at times almost willfully playful neologisms, which make no concession to normal parlance.

What, then, does the proposition, "The essence of truth is freedom", mean? To begin with, it is clear from the outset that the proposition is, in fact, being offered as a definitional attribute in the strict sense and not merely as a possible distinguishing mark. While it is true that whoever utters "a" truth or assents to one must be free to do so, this is not, Heidegger maintains, the point of his thesis; "rather, the proposition says that freedom is the *essence* of truth itself. In this connection 'essence' is understood as the ground of the inner possibility of what is initially and generally admitted as known."[6]

Heidegger explicitly takes as his starting point something "admitted as known", that is, the common and familiar conception of truth, and offers a sustained analysis of this notion in its dual character as *adaequatio intellectus ad rem* and as *adaequatio rei ad intellectam*, truth as *propositional* truth and truth as *material* truth. *Propositional* truth means "the accordance of what is meant in the statement with the matter"; *material* truth means "the consonance of a matter with what is supposed in advance regarding it". Thus genuine gold is that which is in accordance with "what, always and in advance, we 'properly' mean by 'gold' ".[7] With respect to the latter formulation—a statement of the common understanding of material truth—it is important to note that it represents a watered-down version of what had originally been a theological conception, later sanitized in line with Enlightenment

---

[5] *Wesen der Wahrheit*, p. 28. [Quoted from Heidegger, "Essence of Truth", p. 141.]

[6] Ibid., p. 13. [Quoted from Heidegger, "Essence of Truth", p. 125.]

[7] Ibid., p. 7. [Quoted from Heidegger, "Essence of Truth", p. 119.]

ideals. Heidegger clearly recognizes this, and he himself openly traces the current conception of truth to "its most recent (that is, the medieval) origin".

Heidegger's exposition of the medieval theory of truth is worth considering for a moment insofar as it exhibits two common misrepresentations or misunderstandings—common in the sense that both may be traced to the same root, from which Heidegger's *own* conception of truth derives as well.

The *first* misunderstanding arises in the following way: Heidegger says that the medievals—he does not provide any further information about a specific author or school—construed material truth in terms of correspondence to the idea, as preconceived in the mind of God. In this sense, material truth meant something like conformity with the idea. Now the *intellectus humanus*, which, after all, also belongs to the realm of created beings, shows itself to be "idea-conformable" "only by accomplishing in its propositions the correspondence of what is thought to the matter".[8] And it is this, he argues, that constitutes "the tracing back of propositional truth to material truth" by means of "a theological explanation".[9]

In other words, Heidegger is making the following claim: According to the medieval view, the *intellectus humanus* is "true" (in the sense of being materially true) insofar as it—in conformity with the preconceived idea of the *intellectus humanus* in God's mind—realizes logical truth, epistemological truth, and propositional truth. Now this is incontrovertibly Scholastic doctrine—*only* that the medievals by no means saw in this teaching a reduction of propositional truth to material truth. *Never* did the medieval theory of being attempt to reduce in this way the logical truth of the statement to the ontological truth of the *intellectus humanus*; *never* during the Middle Ages was propositional truth justified with reference to man's faculty of knowing, where being in conformity with its idea would have consisted in just this—realizing true knowledge. Such a claim would have been understood as indicating that the grounding provided for the objectivity of scientific knowledge and of subjective veracity was to be taken in more of an ethical sense and not as an ontological justification for logical truth. On the contrary, the truth of the proposition was grounded in

---

[8] Ibid., p. 8. [Quoted from Heidegger, "Essence of Truth", p. 120.]
[9] Ibid., p. 10. [Quoted from Heidegger, "Essence of Truth", p. 120.]

the Middle Ages exclusively though recourse to the *ipsa res*, whose intelligibility, however, rested on its having been known previously by God the Creator. It is this recognition by God and its *resulting* intelligibility for man that *together* constitute the medieval conception of material truth. And it is material truth, *so construed*, to which the medievals reduced logical truth. Thus Scholastic doctrine does *not* assert that there is logical truth because—and insofar as—the *intellectus humanus* is ontologically true, *but rather* propositional truth holds in logic because the object of knowledge, Being itself, is ontologically true.

A *second* difference between the medieval theory of truth and the interpretation given to it by Heidegger relates to the concept of *adaequatio* itself; here misunderstanding is inextricably interwoven with formal objections and counter arguments: "To say that an assertion '*is true*' signifies that it uncovers the entity as it is in itself. Such an assertion asserts, points out, 'lets' the entity 'be seen' . . . in its uncoveredness. The *Being-true* . . . of the assertion must be understood as Being-uncovering. Thus truth has by no means the structure of an agreement between knowing and the object in the sense of a likening of one entity (the subject) to another (the Object)."[10] Consequently, the familiar notion of an *adaequatio rei et intellectus*, which dates back to the medieval theory of truth, does not extend as far as the essence of propositional truth—at least, according to Heidegger.

This objection overlooks two points: *First*, it ignores the fact that Heidegger's equation of Being-true with Being-uncovering *is a medieval* thesis both in the formal sense and literally, the two coinciding with one another even in their choice of expression. Historically, the sentence "verum est manifestativum esse" (the true is revelatory of being), which stems from Hilary of Poitiers, along with Augustine's statement, "veritas est qua ostenditur id quod est" (truth is that by which what is shows itself), stands at the very beginning of medieval reflection on the essence of truth, and the two expressions—presumably translations of similar formulations from antiquity, like Heidegger's own turn of phrase—were a part of the standard repertoire of those *auctoritates* continually cited in the medieval *quaestiones*.

---

[10] *Sein und Zeit*, 5th ed. (Halle an der Saale, 1941), pp. 218f. [Quoted from Martin Heidegger, *Being and Time*, trans. John Macquarrie and Edward Robinson (New York, 1962), p. 261.]

Secondly, Heidegger does not recognize the extent to which it is a distinguishing feature of the medieval theory of truth that in it the two conceptual elements (truth as disclosure of being and truth as *adaequatio*), which Heidegger viewed as being mutually contradictory or as completely unrelated, are expressly and *formaliter conjoined*: *to the extent that* the knowing mind "un-covers" something real, it receives its measure from just this real thing; *insofar as* reason comes to know being, it is inwardly molded by the latter so that knowledge is a matter, not simply of accommodation, but of outright identity.

At this point an additional remark—a caveat—must be made. A precursor to the Heideggerian objection had already been raised in the Middle Ages, by Duns Scotus, to be specific, a for that time no longer very typical medieval thinker. Like Heidegger, Duns Scotus, too, had rejected the notion of an *adaequatio passiva*, the passive accommodation of the faculty of knowing to its object in the act of knowledge—*veritas non recipit adaequationem passivam.*[11]

We will have opportunity later to note a second, more profound affinity between the Heideggerian conception of truth and that of Duns Scotus (whose theory of the categories Heidegger, incidentally, made the subject of his *Habilitation* thesis). The specifically modern notion of truth is already implied in the decisive emphasis that Duns Scotus places on the subject's activity in the process of knowing. It is also the common denominator at the bottom of the misunderstandings to which the genuine medieval theory of truth is subjected in Heidegger's presentation: it represents a diminution of the form-conferring, molding, mensural function that—on the medieval view —is to be ascribed in knowing to objective reality and to the *veritas rerum* inherent in it. And this, it appears to me, is precisely one of the sources for Heidegger's own conception of truth—and this despite the undeniable fact that it is a primary concern of this thinking to confront man with the Being of existing things.

Before we proceed farther, however, it still has to be asked *which* conception of truth—propositional truth or material truth—it is that Heidegger is defining as freedom. His answer is neither one. Heidegger is seeking the most primordial, most authentic form of truth that grounds every other type of being-true. From the very beginning, he is convinced that "the thesis that the genuine 'locus' of truth lies

---

[11] *Op. Ox.*, I Sent., d. 19, 6, 6.

in the judgment . . . fails to recognize the structure of truth";[12] the essence of truth must "be sought at more primordial level . . . than the traditional characterization of it as a property of assertions would allow";[13] "truth does not originally reside in the proposition."[14] Such formulations recur throughout all his writings. For those who are inclined to recognize already in this point a certain affinity with the ancient theory of being, such an interpretation would appear to be confirmed and reinforced initially by the fact that Heidegger openly traces logical truth back to material truth as the more primordial form of truth: "Propositional truth is rooted in a more primordial truth . . . in the prepredicative manifestness of Being, which is here termed 'ontic truth'."[15] This turn toward what is objective in the world of material being, which is enacted in so decisive a manner, ends up then falling back even more emphatically on the subject.

Even ontic truth in the sense of the manifestness and uncoveredness of beings does not yet represent for Heidegger the primordial form of truth. He argues that entities uncovered within the world "are 'true' in a second sense. What is primarily 'true' . . . is *Dasein*."[16] "[O]nly with *Dasein's* *disclosedness*", that is, with the truth of *Dasein*, "is the *most primordial* phenomenon of truth attained."[17] In *Sein und Zeit*, it is asserted that " 'there is' truth only in so far as *Dasein* is and so long as *Dasein* is."[18]

The notions of *Dasein* and disclosedness, which are essential to Heidegger's philosophizing, stand in need of a more precise explanation. *Dasein* for Heidegger is *human being*: "this entity—man himself—" "we denote by the term '*Dasein*'."[19] What distinguishes *Dasein* from what is "non-*Dasein*-like"[20] is that *Dasein* "not only finds itself in the midst of Being, it also relates itself to Being and through Being to

[12] *Sein und Zeit*, p. 226. [Quoted from Heidegger, *Being and Time*, p. 269.]
[13] *Vom Wesen des Grundes*, in *Festschrift Edmund Husserl zum 70. Geburtstag gewidmet: Ergänzungsband zum Jahrbuch für Philosophie und phänomenologische Forschung* (Halle an der Saale, 1929), pp. 78f.
[14] *Wesen der Wahrheit*, p. 12. [Quoted from Heidegger, "Essence of Truth", p. 125.]
[15] *Wesen des Grundes*, p. 76.
[16] *Sein und Zeit*, p. 220. [Quoted from Heidegger, *Being and Time*, p. 263.]
[17] Ibid., p. 220. [Quoted from Heidegger, *Being and Time*, p. 263.]
[18] Ibid., p. 226. [Quoted from Heidegger, *Being and Time*, p. 269.]
[19] Ibid., p. 11. [Quoted from Heidegger, *Being and Time*, p. 32.]
[20] *Wesen des Grundes*, p. 105.

itself."[21] "What is distinctive of *Dasein* is that it relates itself to Being as the understanding of Being."[22] Heidegger calls this being able to understand Being, this "being as uncovering" the disclosedness, or truth, of *Dasein*; ontic truth, the manifestness of existing things, is based on this.

At this stage, one need not interpret the thesis in a subjectivist manner; and, taken for itself, this thesis need not be at variance with the conception of truth underlying the medieval theory of being. Heidegger himself explicitly invokes the name of Thomas Aquinas, who, likewise, if not quite so fastidiously, asserts "*Dasein*'s ontico-ontological priority".[23]

Such an appeal is, I believe, not entirely misplaced. For Aquinas does, in fact, say that the truth of existing things could not be an overarching characteristic of beings as such "if a being were not postulated which by its very nature is so constituted as to come together with everything that is" (nisi accipiatur aliquid quod natum sit convenire cum omni ente; hoc autem est anima).[24] This being able to come together with all that is ("posse convenire cum omni ente"), which Aquinas ascribes to the intellectual soul, is not so far removed from what Heidegger, who cites this turn of phrase,[25] understands by the disclosedness of *Dasein*. Aside from the fact that, according to Aquinas, in the relation of coming together (*convenientia*) between soul and entity it is the entity that impresses itself on the intellect, that *confers* form and measure, while the soul is essentially form-*accepting*— apart from this, another crucial difference is that Aquinas speaks of a *natum esse* (that is, this coming together with all things belongs to the soul *by its very nature*, just as our faculty of knowing is directed toward being as its *natural* state of reference)[26] whereas Heidegger posits the essence of *Dasein*'s disclosedness as freedom.

As has already been mentioned, though, the identification of truth with freedom is made only in Heidegger's *later* writings. In *Sein und Zeit*, he can still be found arguing that "[w]e *must* presuppose truth . . . as *Dasein*'s disclosedness." "We must 'make' the presupposition

---

[21] Ibid., p. 104.

[22] Ibid., p. 78.

[23] *Sein und Zeit*, p. 14. [Quoted from Heidegger, *Being and Time*, p. 263.]

[24] *Ver.* 1, 1.

[25] Cf. *Sein und Zeit*, p. 14. [Heidegger, *Being and Time*, p. 34.]

[26] *An.* 13 ad 11.

of truth because it *is* one that has been 'made' already with the Being of the 'we'."[27] The only qualification that Heidegger makes in this regard is to add that "[t]his belongs to *Dasein*'s essential thrownness into the world. *Has Dasein as itself ever decided freely whether it wants to come into 'Dasein' or not, and will it ever be able to make such a decision?*"[28]

Even as early as *Sein und Zeit*, however, one can come across a formulation like the following: "*Dasein*, in so far as it *is*, has always submitted itself already to a 'world.' "[29] The fact that man himself submits to the world of existing things, rather than already finding himself naturally and by nature referred to them, points the way toward the conceptual determination of truth as freedom. And here Heidegger's thought, which was originally understood and hailed as a "turn to the object", begins to reverse direction toward the subject.

Still, Heidegger is right to defend himself against a superficially subjectivist interpretation of the thesis that truth is freedom—as if in this way truth would be abandoned to man's caprice. He is justified in doing so because, given the way Heidegger conceives of truth, it is *per definitionem* a "letting beings be",[30] or, as he referred to it in an earlier work, a "letting world reign".[31] By implication, then, I, in encountering the world as disclosing *Dasein*, let "beings be as the beings which they are".[32] Here there is—or so it would appear—no trace of subjectivism.

At the same time, however, freedom also implies a giving oneself leave [*Sichfreigeben*]: the kind of letting be [*Seinlassen*] involved in leaving-oneself-open [*Sicheinlassen*]. On this view it is an autarchic, self-empowered subject who gives himself leave to leave himself open to beings. Heidegger argues this explicitly: "To let be is to engage oneself [*sich einlassen*] with beings."[33] And this engagement is such that it "withdraws in the face of beings"[34]—a formulation in which

---

[27] *Sein und Zeit*, p. 228. [Quoted from Heidegger, *Being and Time*, p. 271.] [The first quotation is an abbreviation of two sentences that read in full: "We *must* presuppose truth. *Dasein* itself, as in each case my *Dasein* and this *Dasein*, *must* be; and in the same way the truth, as *Dasein*'s disclosedness, *must* be."—ED.]

[28] Ibid., p. 228. [Quoted from Heidegger, *Being and Time*, p. 271 (italics in original).]

[29] Ibid., p. 87. [Quoted from Heidegger, *Being and Time*, pp. 120–21.]

[30] *Wesen der Wahrheit*, p. 17. [Quoted from Heidegger, "Essence of Truth", p. 127.]

[31] *Wesen des Grundes*, p. 102.

[32] *Wesen der Wahrheit*, p. 15. [Quoted from Heidegger, "Essence of Truth", p. 127.]

[33] Ibid., p. 15. [Quoted from Heidegger, "Essence of Truth", p. 127.]

[34] Ibid. [Quoted from Heidegger, "Essence of Truth", p. 128.]

the distance implicit in the subject's free standing apart [*Gegenübersein*] from those beings finds especially clear expression. "The going beyond to the world is freedom itself."[35] As a result, transcendence— just that "overcoming" in which Heidegger recognizes the "essence of the subject" or "the basic structure of the subject"[36]—"does stumble across" world; rather "freedom holds itself out to [world]."[37]

One only becomes cognizant of the special coloring and tone that are peculiar to the definition of freedom as the "letting be of man" and the "letting reign of world" when one views it against the background of that general relation to Being and world that Heidegger presupposes. Only then does it become clear, for example, how this thinking differs from Aristotle's saving of the appearances ($\sigma\dot{\omega}\zeta\varepsilon\iota\nu$ $\tau\dot{\alpha}$ $\phi\alpha\iota\nu\dot{o}\mu\varepsilon\nu\alpha$), which also implies something like a letting be of beings.

The relation to Being postulated by Heidegger has nothing of the straightforwardness of that receptive way of looking at things, nothing of the easy unaffectedness and accepting simplicity associated with immersion in Being—something that can flourish only on the basis of an affirmation of Being as a whole. Instead, Heidegger experiences himself in the world of existing things as if at their mercy; beings are lived through as an imperiling of *Dasein* itself. The attitude of the knowing subject may be characterized as one of self-assertion and the forceful overcoming of resistances.

As a result formulations become possible such as Heidegger's definition of the sciences as the "unsecured holding of one's own ground in questioning amid the uncertainty of Being as a whole".[38] Knowledge, as "the most acute imperilment of *Dasein* in the face of the superiority of Being", is unfavorably contrasted with the "calm acceptance of essences and values as they are in themselves".[39] Reference is made to Greek philosophy as that "through which Western man rose up for the first time against the hegemony of Being"[40] and

---

[35] *Wesen des Grundes*, p. 101.

[36] Ibid., p. 81.

[37] Ibid., p. 101. [Where Pieper, deviating from the original wording of the text, inserts the expression "world", it literally says in Heidegger that transcendence does not "stumble across the 'for the sake of' as a preexisting value and end".—ED.]

[38] *Die Selbstbehauptung der deutschen Universität* (a speech delivered on Heidegger's acceptance of the position of Rector at the University of Freiburg im Breslau on May 27, 1933) (Breslau, 1933), p. 13.

[39] Ibid., p. 17.

[40] Ibid., p. 8.

to the passionate desire of the Greeks "to remain close to Being as such and under its duress".[41] More significantly, however, his remarks on the obdurateness of knowledge[42] may legitimately be construed as self-descriptions.

The basic features of such an attitude may be brought into sharp relief through a comparison with its extreme counterpart, Goethe's openness to Being: "my schooling: to see and read off all things as they are; my pledge: to let the eye be my light; here, enveloped in total silence, my complete alienation from all pretension leaves me content"—so the Italian traveler writes in a letter to the poet Herder dated November 10–11, 1786.

Heidegger's definition of the truth of *Dasein* as the freedom involved in the letting-be of beings is reminiscent of his discussion of yet another kind of freedom, his call for "*an impassioned* **freedom towards death**—*a freedom which has been released from the Illusions of the 'they,' and which is factical, certain of itself, and anxious.*"[43] And it is almost impossible to overhear in the one expression or the other his strained insistence on the autonomy of the subject.

Regardless, however, of how freedom is defined, its association with the act of *willing*, encouraged by long-standing patterns of thought and speech, is bound to reassert itself in any attempt at a definition. It is fair, then, to say that Heidegger, with his thesis "truth is freedom", makes truth depend on the will. And thus, when truth, defined as freedom, is presented as being the ground of the inner possibility of any type of truth whatsoever, the wellspring of all Being—of propositions as well as of things—indeed, the very possibility of knowledge and the essence of the knowing subject itself are at the same time assumed to lie in the will.

Here again, the affinity with Duns Scotus becomes apparent: the maxim *voluntas est superior intellectu* asserts that the will is not constituted by anything other than the will itself and that freedom is the ground of the possibility of the intellect's knowing (whereas, conversely, Thomas Aquinas understands freedom to be grounded in knowing). And so one would like to classify Heidegger as a Scotist in this respect—were it not for the fact that this epithet has lost much

---

[41] Ibid., pp. 9f.

[42] Ibid., p. 9.

[43] *Sein und Zeit*, p. 266. [Quoted from Heidegger, *Being and Time*, p. 311 (italics and bold print in original).]

of its discriminating force, insofar as the *whole* of modern philosophy might aptly be so described, beginning with Descartes, for whom logical affirmation and negation—and even his Method of Doubt—are essential forms of willing, *modi volendi.*[44]

It would exceed the scope of this study to examine Heidegger's conception of truth from the standpoint of its opposite, "untruth", as well—or, in Heidegger's terminology, the "inessentiality" [*Unwesen*] of truth—despite the not inconsiderable increase in understanding that such an undertaking promises. If the essence of *truth*, Heidegger argues, is not confined to *propositional* truth, then *un*truth—except when it occurs in knowing—must also reside in *Being* itself. On the basis of this argument, which even from a purely formal point of view is highly vulnerable, Heidegger arrives not only at the notion of the untruth of Being but also at the juncture where his theory of truth connects up with one of the central tenets of his philosophy, his theory of the nothing. Unfortunately, we cannot devote more space to this topic.

One further aspect of the Heideggerian theory of truth, however, should be emphasized before we conclude. The question that prompts Heidegger to respond with the thesis that truth is freedom is a very pointed one: "Whence does the presentative statement receive the directive to conform to the object and to accord by way of correctness?"[45] In short, whence does *Dasein* receive its "directedness toward beings"?[46] More specifically, the question is asking about the origins of that orientation toward Being which characterizes the faculty of knowing.

It is possible to respond to this question with a makeshift answer, one in keeping with a formal and self-imposed restriction to what is pregiven in experience and one that is—to that extent—offered more in resignation: The faculty of knowing derives its orientation toward beings from the same place it derives its nature, for it is, in its innermost nature, directed toward Being. It is, however, also possible to answer the question the way Plato and Aquinas chose to answer it. Plato answered it by pointing to the divine and to the Idea of the

---

[44] *Principia philosophiae* I, 32. [This pointed observation comes as something of a surprise insofar as only more recent scholarship has unequivocally established the decisive influence of Scotism on the problematic of modern philosophy.—ED.]

[45] *Wesen der Wahrheit*, p. 13. [Quoted from Heidegger, "Essence of Truth", p. 125.]

[46] Ibid., p. 21. [Quoted from Heidegger, "Essence of Truth", p. 134.]

Good, which is the authentic source of truth and reason.[47] Aquinas answered that the *intellectus divinus* made the soul knowing and the things knowable and related the one to the other so that they are "by nature" linked to one another.* Heidegger's answer is that *Dasein* receives its "directedness toward beings"[48] from *freedom*. From whose freedom? From "the freedom of Da-sein".[49]

There are philosophical questions to which there can be given either no answer at all or only a theological one. Among those questions is the one concerning the origin of *Dasein*'s directedness toward beings. To them may be reckoned as well that primordial question which Heidegger deems "the basic question of metaphysics":[50] "Why are there beings at all, and why not rather nothing?"[51]

Precisely herein lies, it seems to me, the exciting, affecting, and explosive character of Heidegger's philosophizing, that is, in the fact that, motivated by what is at bottom a theological impulse, questions that in themselves would require a theological answer are posed with a provocative radicalism and that, at the same time, such a response is just as radically rejected, without the theological answer finding its replacement in a confession of ignorance and in what Goethe calls that calm reverence before the unfathomable.

It is also in this sense that Heidegger's shocking description of human inquiry is to be understood: Man's questioning is, he says, not directed toward an answer at all, but the questioning itself, as an obstinate holding of one's own ground in the absence of any reply, is "the highest form of knowledge".[52] And one might, in fact, argue that in Heidegger's work, as well, the question of truth—the question of its *essence*—has been left unanswered.

---

[47] *Republic* 517b8–c5.

* [*Ver.* 1, 2.—ED.]

[48] *Wesen der Wahrheit*, p. 21; see also p. 17. [Heidegger, "Essence of Truth", p. 134; cf. also "that inner directive for correspondence of presentation to beings", p. 129.]

[49] Ibid., p. 20. [Quoted from Heidegger, "Essence of Truth", p. 132.]

[50] *Was ist Metaphysik*, p. 22. [Quoted from Heidegger, "What Is Metaphysics?", p. 112.]

[51] Ibid., p. 22. [Quoted from Heidegger, "What Is Metaphysics?", p. 112.]

[52] *Selbstbehauptung der deutschen Universität*, p. 12.

LANGUAGE AND THE
PHILOSOPHIZING PERSON:

Aperçus of an Aquinas Reader

"General Linguistic Usage"

In one of the first sentences of his *Summa contra Gentiles*, Thomas Aquinas reflects on Aristotle's observation in the *Topics* (II, 2, 110a, 15–18) that "the usage of the multitude is to be followed in giving names to things"—which, of course, does not mean that one should also orient oneself toward the multitude in one's *interpretation* of the things so named or even that it would be permissible for one to do so. What it does mean, however, is that one should distrust any "original" definition that sets itself too far apart from ordinary language use and that one should, at least initially, adhere to the living speech of human beings, the *communis usus loquendi*.[1] "One should use names the way the many (*plures*) use them."[2] It goes without saying that general linguistic usage, which is here vested with a certain authority, refers neither to the hackneyed and impoverished jargon of the street nor to the paper-bound technical language of "experts". What is meant is the speech of "educated" people ("educated" in the best sense of that word), insofar as that speech has emerged organically from its original linguistic roots: it is this toward which the philosophizing person must orient himself in naming things—not for purely didactic purposes, but simply because one would otherwise wind up in a world of nonbinding utterances, with the certain ground of reality swept from under one's feet.

Still, one should in no way be deceived into believing that it is easy to determine how every word is meant in normal language, especially when it is a question of such fundamental notions as "guilt", "love", and "happiness". I would even go so far as to say that it is virtually impossible for absolutely everything to be "realized" in the reflective

---

[1] I, 83, 2.
[2] *Ver.* 4, 2.

consciousness that the average person—including the reflecting individual himself—really means when, in everyday speech, he uses words
like the ones just mentioned. Probably the same applies to words with
far less existential relevance. At first glance, for example, it may appear fully appropriate and even relatively accurate to demarcate the
concept of "similarity" from that of "identity"—and so define it—
in such a way that it signifies agreement only in several features but
not in all respects. This definition may also be found in philosophical lexica.[3] Linguistic usage, however, does not just embody positive
dicta as to what can legitimately be said; it also stipulates that a word
can*not* be used in a certain context. Thus Aquinas calls attention to
the fact that it is clearly not possible to say that God is similar to
his creatures or that the father is similar to the son or that a man is
similar to his portrait—which implies that in the concept of similarity
yet another semantic element is at work, namely, that relating to the
notions of descent and dependence.[4] Archetype and copy, father and
son, may, when the two are considered together, very well "agree in
several respects"; only the son, however, is "similar" to the father,
and only the copy is similar to the original, but never the father to
the son or the original to the copy.

Word Origin (Etymologia) and Word Sense (Significatio)

Aquinas owes his discovery of this undoubtedly important aspect of
the concept "similarity", not solely to a penetrating analysis of what
human beings normally say when they use the word "similarity"—
that is, to the attentive analysis of linguistic usage—but also to the contemporary understanding of the word's origin, which, for a change,
just happens to be correct this time, that is, to the word's etymology. Thus, in his commentary on the Sentences,[5] Aquinas writes, "The
essence of the image lies in imitation, from which fact it derives its
name, for *imago* means virtually the same as *imitago*." As one can confirm by consulting the Oxford Dictionary, the kinship between these
two words has at least been correctly identified—for a change, as
I have already said. For the most part, the medieval elucidations of

---

[3] Cf. J. Hoffmeister, *Wörterbuch der philosophischen Begriffe* (Hamburg, 1955), p. 19.

[4] I, 4, 3 ad 4.

[5] 1, d. 28, 2, 1.

words, including even some of those found in Aquinas, are hopelessly wrong. One need only recall how often Aquinas explains the name of the stone *lapis* by reference to the fact that one might injure one's foot striking against it (*laedere pedem*). On the other hand, it cannot be denied that this rather extreme example makes especially clear what Aquinas is here concerned to demonstrate, namely, that our names for things never extend to their essence, nor are they ever capable of expressing them.

This notwithstanding, it is possible to cite another fortunate exception. Again, the word *aliquid*, with which one of the most universal (and, in this sense, "transcendental") concepts is designated, one that encompasses all genera and is predicated of every being, is quite correctly interpreted by Aquinas as *aliud quid*. With this etymological explanation, Aquinas has very precisely isolated the word's essential core: that each being within the totality of this essentially multiform world has by virtue of its "being other" its own essential form, that is, by virtue of the limits that separate it from all other beings. Both Joseph Gredt[6] and Edith Stein[7] failed to understand and so misinterpreted this very clear Thomistic proposition, thus denying their readers the fundamental insight expressed therein and falling short of it themselves.

Incidentally, a word meaning that is from an etymological standpoint utterly fantastic can be significant at another level, as it were— for example, when in the ninth century the Frank abbot Paschasius Radbertus, in the conviction that hope (*spes*) has something to do with foot (*pes*), asserts that the despairing lack the feet to advance on the path of Christ.[8]

Aquinas, however, distinguishes very clearly for his part between the idiomatic sense of the word, as intended by the average speaker, and its etymologically inferred origin: "The etymology of a word is one thing, its meaning another."[9] Still, Aquinas does not merely distinguish, he also evaluates, and that in a manner which is no less clear. For example, he is, of course, naturally familiar with the word

---

[6] *Die aristotelisch-thomistische Philosophie* (Freiburg im Breisgau, 1935), 2:12.

[7] *Endliches und ewiges Sein* (Louvain and Freiburg, 1950), p. 270.

[8] *De fide, spe et caritate* 2, 4; Migne, PL 120, 1430.

[9] "Aliud est etymologia nominis et aliud est significatio nominis" (II, II, 92, 1 ad 2). See as well in this connection I, 13, 2 ad 2.

"person", which in Greek originally designated the masked actor;
that, however, does not prevent him in the least from predicating of
God as well the concept of person, which in the interim had come
to signify "the spiritual essence that exists in itself".[10] "In assessing
a word, one should orient oneself, not toward its origin, but rather
toward what it means."[11] In short, an etymological argument possesses
"at best little weight".[12]

Whoever reflects on the demonstrable futility of Heideggerian etymology can only concur. What does it after all contribute to the clarification of the concept *Erörterung* [discussion] when he points out that
the name for "place", *Ort*, originally meant the point of a spear?[13]

Language and Terminology

In the course of a lecture presented before an audience of "Thomists"
on the modernity of Thomas Aquinas' thought, I once argued that
one reason for his contemporary relevance is that no "-ism" could
legitimately be derived from his work. Of course, that was an exag-
gerated formulation, offered as a provocation; it was aimed at a kind
of textbook "Thomism" that is predicated on the error that one can
compress the thoughts of the Common Doctor into a system of the-
orems that could be propagated within a school. In the subsequent
discussion, which was, understandably, quite heated, I raised two key
objections against this view: *First*, the proposition, "The essences of
things are unknown to us",[14] which occurs a dozen times in Aquinas
himself, cannot be found in the "Thomistic" textbooks; *second*, "textbook" Thomism has recourse to a terminology unlike Aquinas himself, who speaks a living language. Although the two objections are
implicitly related to one another, only the second will be the subject
of the following discussion.

The answer to the question of how terminology differs from language and term from word is that term and terminology are "made",

---

[10] *Pot.* 9, 3 ad 1; 1, d. 23, 1, 2 ad 1.

[11] "Iudicium de nomine non debet esse secundum hoc a quo imponitur, sed secundum id
ad quod significandum instituitur" (1, d. 23, 1, 2 ad 1).

[12] II, II 1, 6 ad 3.

[13] Cf. Martin Heidegger, *Unterwegs zur Sprache* (Pfullingen, 1969), p. 37.

[14] *Ver.* 10, 1.

artificial, and, by virtue of a convention, restricted and affixed to specific meanings; by contrast, language and word have evolved historically, naturally, and cannot be tied to an unequivocal sense. Terminology is the legitimate vehicle for understanding in science, especially in the natural sciences. Terminology makes possible that precision and accuracy which first transforms a sentence into a scientific statement. Philosophy likewise requires clarity of expression. Still, clarity is not the same as precision. "Precise" literally means "cut off". The precision of scientific terms consists in cleanly extracting a partial phenomenon, in keeping with a specifically determined aspect, from a complex state of affairs and, as it were, presenting it as in the form of an isolated preparation for investigation. The term occasionally used by doctors to refer to the physiological state of heart arrest and respiration, "exitus" (or any arbitrary fact X), is thoroughly precise. But the word "death", which as a part of natural language exhibits a low degree of precision, can lay claim to an incomparably higher degree of clarity, because "death" signifies all that which takes place in the process of a person's dying, including the incomprehensibility of it.

Aquinas distinguished between two types of tool; there is—so he argues—the kind of tool that is joined corporeally to man, for example, the hand, which he, following Aristotle,[15] dubs "the tool of tools";[16] beyond this there are nonattached or "separate" tools, like the hammer or the axe.[17] In keeping with this distinction, one might describe language as an attached tool and terminology as a separate one. With this, three claims are being made: first and foremost, that we are just as little capable of fashioning language as we are of fashioning the hand; second, that we always remain dependent on the evolving natural language; and finally, that we are able to employ and even understand the artificial terminology only on the basis of a nonterminological, that is, a linguistic, agreement, just as we can only "hand-le" an axe with the help of the hand.

Now, as far as Aquinas is concerned, there is no real terminology to be found in his work, despite all appearances to the contrary. He has not created his own univocally defined jargon to which he himself has

---

[15] *De anima* 3.8.432a1–2.

[16] I, 91, 3 ad 2.

[17] III, 64, 5 ad 3.

then consistently adhered; on the contrary, he prefers to use several synonyms consecutively (as has been shown in a very detailed study by the Frenchman F. A. Blanche).[18] Thus, ten distinct formulations are used to circumscribe the notion of "relation", and just as many different words refer to what is meant by *forma*; in one passage the *causa efficiens* is referred to as *causa agens*, and in another it is referred to as *causa movens*. If nothing else, F. A. Blanche's study proves that all this is not evidence of a certain linguistic laxity in Aquinas but is rather the expression of a conscious attitude. It is just this attitude that causes him to shy away from the attempt to define such fundamental concepts as "knowledge" or "truth" precisely. Despite his having made every effort to ensure clarity of diction, Aquinas never forgot that man does not know the essences of beings and that all reality remains, at bottom, a mystery.[19]

Inauthentic Word Usage

In the case of languages that have undergone a historical evolution— one might even say, within the jurisdiction of "language" as such— there naturally occurs a phenomenon whose emergence is completely ruled out in those cases where artificial idioms are tied by individual convention to clearly circumscribed meanings, that is, in the case of terminology; it is, in fact, the express purpose of these artificial languages to preclude precisely such phenomena. I am referring here to "inauthentic" word usage. "Inauthentic" here is in no way synonymous with "vague" or "meaningless"; it means that a word is not to be taken in its primary sense, the one that is "authentically" associated with it.

The actual state of affairs is, however, somewhat more complicated than that, not least because the field of "inauthentic" word usage extends farther than one might perhaps suspect at first.

A highly relevant example—relevant on material grounds as well— is the word "believe". When someone says, "I believe that tomorrow it will rain", he is clearly not using the word "believe" in its authentic sense; instead of "I believe", he might just as well have said, "I suspect", "I hold it to be true", "I think"—and so forth. As already

---

[18] F. A. Blanche, "Sur la langue technique de St. Thomas d'Aquin", *Revue de Philosophie* 30 (1930).

[19] For more on this, see M.-D. Chenu, *Introduction à l'étude de St. Thomas d'Aquin*, p. 102.

mentioned, this way of using the word is not at variance with its sense; there is even a legitimate reason for using the word "believe", here. The reason is that all these expressions have a semantic component that they share with the "authentic" sense of "to believe": They all express the idea that, in any event, one does not *know* with certainty (that is, whether it will rain tomorrow).

In man's ordinary factual way of speaking, there is even a meaning of the word "to believe"—and this is what makes the matter so much more complicated—that involves a false ascription of truth, a false taking-to-be-true: When someone exclaims, "I was of the belief that today is Monday, but it is really Tuesday!" he could equally well have said, without altering the sense of the sentence, "I imagined" or "I wrongly thought".

Precisely herein lies the difference between "authentic" and "inauthentic" word usage: the crucial criterion for deciding whether the word "believe" is being used in its "authentic" sense, that is, in its full and unqualified sense, is that, in such cases, no other word can be found to replace it. Let us assume that a friend tells me in confidence some very surprising, perhaps even terrible things about someone who stands very close to me; and the question is whether I should take what I have heard to be true, whether I, better said, should *believe* the other who earnestly vouches for the accuracy of his account. In this case, *no* other word can do proxy for the word "believe". A believer in the strict sense is someone who accepts the testimony of someone else as true and genuine: "To believe" always means to believe *someone* about *something*—whether this someone is another person or God himself. "Ad fidem pertinet aliquid et alicui credere."[20]

Incidentally, inauthentic word usage may also occasionally be encountered, without being explicitly acknowledged as such, in scholarly writings. An attempt has even been made to construct an entire theory around the relationship between belief and knowledge (in the sense that belief in the possibility of the facts to be investigated is necessarily presupposed a priori in every fact-based inquiry—for example, in archaeology).[21] And it is possible that one could accept the truths of Christianity as valid, not on the testimony of the divine

---

[20] II, II, 129, 6.
[21] S. Thompson, "A Paradox concerning the Relation of Inquiry and Belief", *Journal of Religion* 52 (1951).

204 FOR THE LOVE OF WISDOM

logos, but because one is impressed by the marvelously self-contained nature of its worldview and the intellectual depth of its conception. Perhaps such a person would consider himself, in an uncritical mood, a believing Christian, but, as Aquinas points out, in this way he would be grasping the truth that is the legitimate object of belief in a way other than that of faith: "Ea quae sunt fidei alio modo tenet quam per fidem."[22]

Translatability

When Thomas Aquinas, by order of Pope Urban IV, undertook to write a small treatise, completed in 1263, on the disagreements between the Roman Catholic Church and the Eastern Orthodox Church of the Byzantine Empire, from which the former had been separated for centuries, he experienced in a very dramatic manner the difficulties that naturally attend any type of translation. Nevertheless, he agreed to take on the task and mastered it. In so doing, he formulated the principle that it is absurd to substitute a specific word in one language for a specific word in the other; rather a good translator must take into account what was, in fact, meant and must endeavor to "carry it over" [*hinübertragen*] into his own language. Evidently, he was working with texts that were not untranslatable in principle. And what he himself set down is doubtless itself translatable, which, of course, does not imply that it is easy to translate a sentence of Aquinas' into German without altering its sense. Here, too, the operative principle is not to simply translate a Latin word by a German one. For example, an appropriate translation of the short sentence, "virtus est ultimum potentiae",[23] one that is in keeping with its sense, would run as follows: "Virtue is the utmost that one can be."

In the meantime, mankind, as has become painfully evident at international congresses, is fast approaching the limits of mutual understanding on account of the variety of languages being spoken today. Thus even an author as competent as Günther Anders has ventured the opinion that in order for communication to remain possible at all, we have to agree, for better or worse, to a kind of voluntary linguistic impoverishment that is the result of renouncing "the ideal of

---

[22] II, II, 5, 3.
[23] *Virt. com.* 9 ad 15.

the depth of the mother language and that of the breadth of cultured speech". "We have to learn . . . in our language how to speak translatably." "Medieval Latin was also a comparatively poor language, but it provided the surety for the rise of Europe."[24]

Aquinas' *Quaestiones* show, however, that language, even that of philosophy and theology, can, in principle, be translated transparently without sacrificing either depth or breadth or even the occasional spark of poetic radiance, especially when the simplicity of its outer form only has the appearance of having been achieved effortlessly. Again this should, of course, not be taken to mean that the *Quaestiones* are "intelligible to all" or that it is easy to translate them adequately. And when Günther Anders says of "contemporary German philosophers" —for the most part correctly—that none is actually translatable, then the reason is by no means always to be found in the "depth" and "breadth" of their language but more often than not in their arbitrarily inconsistent use of words. Just one example: "the thinging of the thing takes place" ("[*Es*] *ereignet sich das Dingen des Dinges*")[25]—how can this rather cryptic phraseology of Heidegger's be translated into a foreign language, if it is already questionable whether it may really be considered German at all. In any event, the curious endeavor to produce a French translation[26] has proven an utter failure, as might have been expected from the start.

Enlightening, "Illuminative" Speech

If language is essentially "communication", then this concept necessarily entails not only a listening interlocutor but also someone to whom something is really being communicated—that is, something that he does not already know and with which he is not already familiar. Only then, evidently, is language in the true sense realized. But it is equally evident that there must be a hierarchy or sequence of stages corresponding to different levels of realization. Genuine speech, for example, also takes place when I call to my neighbor from over the garden fence, "Today we finally have good weather!" Although, in

---

[24] Günter Anders, *Der Mann auf der Brücke* (Munich, 1959), pp. 59ff.

[25] M. Heidegger, *Vorträge und Aufsätze*, p. 179. [Quoted from Martin Heidegger, "Language", in *Poetry, Language, Thought*, trans. Albert Hofstadter (New York, 1971), p. 178.] Further examples may be found in J. Pieper, "A Plea for Philosophy" (in this volume).

[26] *Essais et conférences*, p. 215.

saying this, I am not telling him anything that he does not already know as well as I do—still, this is clearly a case of speech in the strict sense. An entity that was not ensouled would in no way be capable of such an utterance; the ability to make such utterances presupposes the kind of unbounded spiritual potentiality on the basis of which language is first able to become language at all. Although they occupy the lowest rung in the hierarchy, the significance of such "meaningless" chats should not be underestimated; the muting of such speech would be nothing less than inhuman, but, fortunately, it is hardly to be feared. Even if I were to call my neighbor's attention to something that was really new to him—say, my previously undisclosed decision to emigrate to Australia—it would indeed, strictly speaking, constitute a form of communication, but it would still be far from achieving the ultimate in what language is expected (and able) to perform or bring about in human existence, something that is necessary if the ultimate purpose of language is to be unconditionally fulfilled.

At this point, we might do well to recall a distinction on which Aquinas elaborates in a corner of the *Summa Theologica* where one would hardly expect to find it, namely, in the treatise on the discourse of angels, "De locutionibus angelorum".[27] I am referring to the distinction between *locutio* and *illuminatio*, between "mere" speech and "illuminative" speech. A greeting addressed to the neighbors, even if it were to communicate something as yet unknown and "new", still constitutes genuine speech, but it is not—or not yet—"illuminative" speech. Although it is undoubtedly an act of *locutio*, that does not, in itself, make it an act of *illuminatio*. Not all *locutio* is *illuminatio* ("Non omnis locutio est illuminatio").[28]

With "illuminative" speech, a communication is meant that is instructive in the broadest and best sense of that term, a communication that causes a light to go off (*"einleuchtend" macht*) in the interlocutor with regard to a certain state of affairs or a specific aspect of reality. Not only is the spirit of the person who listens and now for the first time sees and understands illuminated or "enlightened", but also that cross section of reality that is being discussed. The latter, in turn, presupposes that reality, which encompasses not only God, the world, but also man himself, is in its very being such that in the

---

[27] I, 107, 2.
[28] Ibid.

act of knowing it is possible for it to become "enlightened" at all. Alternately expressed, it is being assumed not only that human understanding is capable of receiving truth but also that there is a *truth of material things* and that the being of the world is in itself by virtue of its createdness—that is, by virtue of its having originated in the knowing design of the divine *logos*—bright and pellucid down to its very core—that, as Aquinas wrote, "its being-real is its light."[29] This light, however, is only the reflection and radiance of the divine light and its truth.[30]

Since, however, the creation is an object of knowledge that, in its pellucidity, can never be exhausted by any one human being, every particular person stands in the position vis-à-vis every other of being able to communicate something not yet known to the other. In other words, there is no one from whom one could not—or, indeed, should not—let oneself be instructed in the form of an enlightening, "illuminative" talk.

The Language of Poetry, the Language of Philosophy

Both Aristotle and Aquinas have spoken of the affinity that binds the philosopher to the poet. It is at first glance a somewhat unsettling circumstance to find this same thought expressed by two such uncommonly sober thinkers. In his commentary on Aristotle's *Metaphysics*, Aquinas notes that the philosophizing person may be likened to the poet insofar as both are concerned with the wondrous [*mirandum*]: "uterque circa miranda versatur".[31] What is meant by the wondrous, however, is not that about which human beings generally tend to wonder [*staunen*]—and certainly not the extraordinary, that rare eruption of the sensational beyond all normalcy. On the contrary, the wondrous refers to the astounding fact [*das Erstaunliche*] that there is something real at all; it points to a dimension of non-everydayness in the things themselves that one is inclined to dismiss by force of habit as something that is in fact natural.

Now the question is whether this affinity with poetry, which is based on a common gesturing toward the *mirandum* (or wondrous), also has consequences for the *language* of the philosophizing person,

[29] *De causis* 1, 6 (no. 168).
[30] I, 107, 2.
[31] *In Met.* I, 3 (no. 55).

and, if so, which ones. This is, of course, not to say that philosophy is, by nature, a type of "conceptual poetry"; such a conception is absurd. Rather, it would be more appropriate to say, and to acknowledge beforehand, that affinity and comparability are not the same as identity and so that a difference remains between philosophy and poetry. The language of poetry is sensuous form, image, rhythm, and sound; the language of the philosophizing person is nonintuitive conceptualization and abstraction (whereby it is worth recalling that "abstraction" clearly includes recourse to what is intuitive and concrete). This is not to deny the fact that great poets have often enough proven themselves to be adept philosophers. One need only recall Goethe's *Maxims and Reflections*, the *Fragments* of Novalis, or the great line from Hölderlin's *Notes to Antigone*, which appears amid a philosophical theory of man: "It is a remarkable make-shift of the clandestinely operating soul that at the highest level of consciousness it eludes consciousness."[32]

By contrast, it is typical of philosophers that they have far more rarely written memorable poems. It is part of their stock in trade to transpose conceptual knowledge into clear language—into language, let it be noted, and not into terminology! There is no path that leads from the scientific term to the poetic expression, the latter having, in turn, little in common with the obscurantism of such musically euphonious sound impressions (language "as the peal of stillness")[33] as occasionally go by the name of "philosophy". For utterances to emerge as genuinely philosophical, they must in careful collusion with language make its powers of expression—those that arise from the natural evolution of words and with which everyone is basically already familiar—palpable to such a degree that the truth sought by every man is brought before his eyes and not allowed to disappear from view.

---

[32] *Sämtliche Werke* (Frankfurt am Main, n.d.), p. 919.
[33] Heidegger, *Unterwegs zur Sprache*, p. 30. [Quoted from Heidegger, "Language", p. 207.]

WHAT IS INTERPRETATION?

Fully mindful of the difficulty of the subject on which I am now embarking and of how great the explosive potential that has built up in an almost unmanageable scholarly apparatus, I would like to begin by reducing the expectations for the following discussion. My purpose is *not* to develop a theory that illuminates its object from all sides but at most to grasp somewhat more keenly certain of its aspects—an approach I certainly expect *will* serve to clarify the general situation. On the other hand, it would not surprise me if certain theses that I intend to defend incite controversy and a discussion—a productive one, I hope—ensues.

What, then, is interpretation? The most precise definition I have up to now encountered was furnished by the Canadian theologian Bernard Lonergan.[1] He wrote: "An interpretation is the expression of the meaning of another expression." As is readily observed, it is a formulation of almost deceptive simplicity, as is not seldom found among definitions that hit the nail square on the head. The first difficulty presents itself as soon as one attempts to translate this definition into German, that is, to subject it, in turn, to interpretation. (Translation is, in fact, a fundamental form of interpretation, and, in a certain sense, all interpretation may be considered translation.) In the present case, the difficulty lies in the fact that the word "expression", which is used twice in Lonergan's definition, does not mean the same thing each time: the first time it denotes an activity, a bringing-to-expression, whereas the second time it is being used in the sense of a substantive, that is, to refer to what is being expressed. In other words, interpretation consists in bringing to expression something that was intended by what someone else has already brought to expression.

I propose now to turn my attention to the fact that the interpreting subject is at the most minimal level concerned with a very specific type of expression, namely, with an expression by which the person

---

[1] B. J. F. Lonergan, *Insight* (London, 1957), p. 586.

expressing himself means something; in short, the interpreter is concerned with a meaningful, or, better said, meaning-laden expression. Of course, one may in a very broad sense speak of an "expression" whenever something that would not be self-evident moves outward. If "expression" is so construed, the symptom of an organic illness and the blush of someone caught in a lie may both be considered "expressions", which can, in turn, be made the objects of possible interpretation. In the precise sense of the term, however, a meaningful or meaning-laden expression may be assigned the quality of interpretability only when an ensouled being actively refers by means of sensuously perceptible signs to something distinct from those signs and thus makes that thing intelligible to others. Unquestionably, the *word*, whether spoken or written, has a prominent place among these sensuously perceptible signs; and of course we shall be discussing the word in what follows. But the bodily gesture—the shaking of one's head, for example, or the greeting conveyed by an outstretched hand —belong just as much to the realm of meaning-laden expressions as all man's other symbolic activities. When Columbus came to Cuba and found in the settlements of the indigenous peoples that cornstalks were lain across the doors of their huts, which meant the equivalent of "entrance forbidden", he saw himself confronted by a manifestly meaning-laden expression that first had to be interpreted with regard to what it meant—"interpreted" in the precise sense of that term. And, of course, musical or sculpted works of art are likewise meaning-laden expressions that are actively communicated.

Incidentally, the active nature of the communication need not imply that the meaning must be consciously conveyed. An unconscious smile or wrinkling of the brow on the part of the person expressing himself, as distinct from blushing or symptoms of illness, is likewise an active expression that refers to something else. Even in the case of linguistic expressions, it is possible for the speaker through the use of a specific word to mean something intentionally of which he himself is unaware—something that may possibly first become clear to him when he feels he has been misunderstood. Perhaps we are completely incapable of coming to a full understanding of what is actually meant with each of the words used in daily conversation—even the ones meant by ourselves (the ones "subjectively" meant). Who considers the fact, for example, that the concept of "similarity" not only means,

as it says in the dictionaries,[2] agreement with respect to certain features, but that it also includes a semantic component relating to the
notions of descent and dependence (which is why we can say that the
son is similar to the father but not that the father is similar to the
son).[3]

Now it is difficult to conceive of the "thing" to which a meaningful expression refers—something distinct from the sign—as being
anything other than what is in some way real. Thus an expression, to
the extent that it is meaningful, may also be interpreted in terms of
the fact that it refers to reality. If, for example, someone claims, "The
sentence, 'The world is created', is not a meaningful expression but
a meaningless statement", then what he is trying to say with this is
that there is no real thing to which that sentence corresponds and for
that reason it is neither capable of interpretation nor in need of it.

In light of the preceding argument, it is now possible to distinguish
the concept of interpretation, in the strict acceptation of that term,
from connotations that are either too broad or too narrow—both of
which may be encountered in actual linguistic usage—by focusing on
the *object* of interpretation. The view that the concept of "interpretation" is too narrowly construed when, as is prominently the case
with both Schleiermacher[4] and Dilthey,[5] it is limited exclusively to
the interpretation of a spoken or written expression—to a "text"—
can, I think, very plausibly be defended. In what respect, after all, can
"the language of gestures", construed as a meaningful form of expression, that is, one that refers to reality, be said to differ essentially from
speech or writing? Far more challenging is the attempt to delimit the
concept of interpretation from the other side. One would immediately agree with Emilio Betti, who considers it an abuse of the word
when, by interpretation, "any 'inference' from a given set of signs
is understood";[6] and one would presumably find the notions of that

---

[2] J. Hoffmeister, *Wörterbuch der philosophischen Begriffe*, 2nd ed. (Hamburg, 1956), p. 19.

[3] Cf. Thomas Aquinas, *De div. nom.* 9, 2 (no. 832).

[4] F. Schleiermacher, *Hermeneutik*, ed. H. Kimmerle (Heidelberg, 1959), p. 124.

[5] *Die Entstehung der Hermeneutik*, in *Gesammelte Schriften*, vol. 5, pt. 1 (Stuttgart and
Göttingen, 1964), p. 317. Cf. also W. Babilas, *Tradition und Interpretation* (Munich, 1961), p.
37.

[6] Emilio Betti, "Zur Grundlegung einer allgemeinen Auslegungslehre", in *Festschrift für
Ernst Rabel*, vol. 2 (Tübingen, 1954), p. 96.

Spanish author rather curious who says that someone who drinks a glass of water "interprets" this water as being something potable.[7] But what about when Bacon[8] and Galilei speak of an "interpretation of nature" or when a commemorative volume in Guardini's honor[9] is made to bear the title *Interpretation der Welt* (Interpretation of the world)? Even more problematically, however, what are we to make of the "classic" case, as it were, of *dream* interpretation, which is described as a form of "interpretation" not only in psychoanalysis[10] but also in the Bible (in the Vulgate translation of the Book of Daniel alone, the word occurs over twenty times)? To this objection I would reply that in all the cases mentioned the word "interpretation" is, in fact, being used in the strict sense, *given certain assumptions*. And I will now attempt to enumerate some of these assumptions. As long as natural science could understand itself, however vaguely and noncommittally, as being engaged in a "reading of the book of nature", that is, as interpreting a text with which an author intended to express something; and, if the things, insofar as they represent *creatura* that have emerged from the divine *logos*, really have "word-character", as Guardini put it,[11] then the quality of interpretability can rightly be ascribed to nature and to the world as a whole—whereby the question to be considered remains *by whom* what is "in-itself" interpretable is actually to be interpreted (after all, the stars have the quality of visibility whether on a bright day or behind a cloudy sky, although our eyes may not be able to see them). Moreover, individual natural events like a thunderstorm, the flight of a bird, or the curdling of sacrificial blood may also legitimately be classified as "interpretable" (albeit perhaps only by competent and especially qualified interpreters) —provided these events are all regarded as the revelation of a superhuman spiritual power. And perhaps even the neurotic symptom itself is intelligible and interpretable in the strict sense, insofar as the psychotherapist is able to apprehend it as an expression of the soul, which

---

[7] J. Marias, *Reason and Life* (London, 1956), pp. 186f.

[8] Cf. the entry on "interpretation" in the Oxford Dictionary: " 'Interpretation of Nature' —a phrase used by Bacon to denote the discovery of natural laws by means of induction."

[9] *Interpretation der Welt* (Würzburg, 1965).

[10] P. Ricoeur, *Die Interpretation: Ein Versuch über Freud* (Frankfurt, 1969), p. 39.

[11] *Welt und Person* (Würzburg, 1940), p. 110.

"at bottom knows what it wants".[12] Finally, as regards the interpretation of dreams, the attempt to interpret one may involve one of two things: a causal "explanation" arising, say, from the interaction of the libido with the need for recognition and early childhood experiences and an unabashedly non-"explanatory", hermeneutic interpretation of the dream as divine message, which, however, is only possible for the prophetic spirit; in its biblical usage dream interpretation has only this latter sense.

If, at this juncture in our discussion, we cast a glance backward and ask ourselves what, then, has been explained, the result may appear somewhat thin. Up to this point, the discussion has after all centered exclusively around what is to be recognized as interpretation in the strict sense. But in what interpretation consists and with what justification it is deemed valid—these are questions that, in fact, I have not even expressly formulated. All this is true. But at any rate it has now become possible to answer them more precisely: To interpret an expression validly means to determine what is meant by what is being expressed, to understand it and to communicate it further, to make it intelligible. With this, however, we have uncovered a highly ambitious project.

Already, the first-mentioned and crucial component of the concept of interpretation—understanding what is meant with a meaning-laden expression—presupposes for its realization that a multitude of requirements are satisfied that can hardly be perfectly fulfilled and that probably cannot even be fully listed. For this reason, it is not especially difficult, as it were, to compile a negative anthology of classic blunders. We, too, shall be contributing a small chapter to that anthology —not out of a lust for polemic, but because the violations of a norm are more readily recognized, while the norm itself is more likely to elude a positive formulation. Moreover, I shall be restricting myself to that field with which I am personally and professionally most familiar, that field which is roughly circumscribed by the catchwords "Plato" and "Scholasticism" and which includes, say, the border area between philosophy and theology.

---

[12] A. Görres, *Methode und Erfahrungen der Psychoanalyse* (Munich, 1958), p. 274.

Schleiermacher has captured one of the most important requirements in the pithy observation: "Every understanding of the particular is conditioned by an understanding of the whole."[13] But what
exactly is included in this idea of the "whole"? First of all, a meaning-
laden expression is always wedded to a larger intellectual context, and
indeed it has almost descended to the level of a commonplace—albeit
a completely accurate one—that, if one is not to misconstrue a sentence's meaning, one should not "take it out of context". This appears
to be so obvious that one might easily conclude that there is nothing
more to be said. In fact, the presumably impermissible happens all the
time, not only in the journalistic skirmishes of daily politics, which
live almost exclusively from it, but in literary endeavors that present
themselves as serious work, with a claim to genuine scholarship. An
almost incredible example is the newly edited, multi-volume work by
Carl Prantl, *Geschichte der Logik im Abendlande* (History of logic in the
West),[14] which was first published over a hundred years ago and was
reprinted, unchanged, in 1955. It continues to be considered a standard work and has been praised—for example, in Heinrich Scholz's
short *Geschichte der Logik* (History of logic)[15]—precisely for the "ad-
mirable mastery of its material" and "the exemplary multiplication of
its source texts".[16] In reality, it is precisely these positive features in
which Prantl's work is so decidedly lacking. The author has barely
understood, for example, the most basic aspects of Thomas Aquinas'
logic, to which he devotes an extensive discussion—not only because
he takes individual sentences "out of context", but because he supports his assessment and condemnation with sentences that can in
fact be found in the *Summa Theologica* but as "objections", that is,
as the formulation of positions that Aquinas himself expressly rejects.
This misleading use of Aquinas citations has since been perpetuated
in numerous treatises over several generations and has given rise to

---

[13] F. Schleiermacher, *Hermeneutik*, ed. H. Kimmerle (Heidelberg, 1959), p. 467; see also p.
141 for a similar thought.

[14] Carl Prantl, *Geschichte der Logik im Abendlande* (Leipzig, 1855–1870). The volume referred
to here is the 2nd edition, 1927.

[15] Heinrich Scholz, *Geschichte der Logik* (Berlin, 1931).

[16] A notable exception to this praise is J. M. Bocheński, who writes, "It is best to disregard
him [Prantl] completely" (*Formale Logik* [Freiburg and Munich, 1956], p. 10).

an entire array of utterly irremediable errors.[17] The "whole", which Prantl would have had to understand prior to interpreting individual sentences, would not have amounted to more than is contained within the typical one-page format of a Scholastic *articulus*, a thorough reading of which would not have been too much to expect from a historian.

But of course the idea of the "whole"—a knowledge of which is required of the interpreter—extends much farther than this. A meaning-laden expression is, first and foremost, incomprehensible apart from its linguistic fabric (language conceived here in the broadest sense). And only someone who "masters" this particular language, which is spoken at a certain historical location at a certain time, is equipped, after a fashion, to understand something that has been expressed concretely in that language. This mastery begins—to the extent that one focuses primarily on verbal utterances—with a knowledge of vocabulary and grammar; with this, though, a prerequisite has been singled out that is, in turn, far less often fulfilled as a matter of course than one might perhaps suspect. For example, Socrates' statement to the effect that he does not know for himself why it is not legitimate to do oneself violence, rather he knows it only *ex akoés*,[18] by hearing (or *ex auditu*), as Marsilio Ficino, in his translation of Plato, and the Vulgate, in its rendering of the very same expression from Romans 10:7 ("faith comes by hearing"), both write—this, one would assume, easily translatable word appears in all the translations of the Platonic dialogue *Phaedo* known to me (Schleiermacher, Apelt, Rufener)—clearly falsely interpreted—as "by hearsay"!

This implies, it should be noted in passing, that the interpreter should be familiar with and "master" not only the "foreign language" in which the statement to be interpreted is expressed but also the language—typically his own—in which he articulates his interpretation and gives others to understand in what it consists—something that is not regarded as being equally obvious and which, far from deserving only a parenthetical remark, is actually worthy of an entire treatise. Any interpreter of Aquinas who writes that virtue is a "behavior"

---

[17] Cf. J. Pieper, *Wahrheit der Dinge*, 4th ed. (Munich, 1966), pp. 35, 122f.
[18] *Phaedo* 61d9.

[*Gehaben*][19] or even a "habit" [*Verhabung*],[20] by which the word *habitus* is supposed to be translated—his aptitude for interpretation may legitimately be called into question on the grounds that his relationship to his mother tongue is problematic at best. Again, if the authorities responsible for the official newly reworked version of the German Bible seriously wish to defend the view that the word "blessedness" [*Seligkeit*] signifies in the "common vernacular" of contemporary German "a state that is peculiar to children, lovers, the inebriated, and finally the dead as well"[21] and that this is why the customary translation of a phrase from the Sermon on the Mount as the "praises of the blessed" is linguistically unacceptable, then the critical question may be allowed of whether someone who is so little at home in the vocabulary of his own language has not at the same time proved himself unqualified to be a translator and interpreter.

The "whole", however, in which every expression that is to be interpreted is embedded, also includes, of course—beyond vocabulary, grammar, and intellectual context—the undiminished wealth of metaphoric and assonant nuances peculiar to that language. This includes, at one extreme, an ingrained sobriety of diction and, at the other, a preference for the finely honed exaggerations of intuition. It is possible, for example, that the sentence, "If any one strikes you on the right cheek, turn to him the other also" (Mt 5:39), means, in the sense intended by the speaker, something other than what is literally being said. On this point Aquinas[22] offers a very basic observation, which may be applied quite generally as a rule of interpretation: this particular dictum, as well as many others stemming from the New Testament, can be interpreted correctly only from the standpoint of Christ's actual behavior, which in such cases in no way consisted in offering the other cheek but in objecting, "If I have spoken wrongly, bear witness to the wrong; but if I have spoken rightly, why do you strike me?" (Jn 18:23).

Still, whoever wishes to understand and interpret validly a specific meaning-laden sentence must be familiar with far more than the

---

[19] The German Aquinas edition, vol. 11 (Salzburg and Leipzig, 1940), pp. 103f.

[20] Thomas Aquinas, *Summe der Theologie*, ed. J. Bernhart, vol. 2 (Leipzig, 1935), pp. 329f.

[21] *Gottesdienst* 6 (1972), p. 153.

[22] *Super Joh.* XVIII, 4, 2 (no. 2321).

peculiarities of a particular national language. More importantly, in *every* conceivable historical language there are an infinite number of modalities in which to express the same thought; and they, too, are an essential component of that whole which must be co-thought with each sentence. I am thinking, for example, of the famous aphorism in the last chapter of Augustine's *Confessions*, ". . . we see the things you have made because they are. But they are because you see them",[23] and I wonder whether someone can fully comprehend what is meant by this who does not understand that this hymnlike exhortation to prayer is saying the same thing as the dryly conceptual proposition of Thomas Aquinas, according to whom the things we find in this world are by their very nature "situated between two faculties of knowing" —the divine and the human.[24] A good interpreter must also be aware of the fact that the question, "Who is my neighbor?" can be answered not only with a definition but also by reference to the parable of the man who was on his way down from Jerusalem to Jericho and fell into the hands of brigands (Lk 10:30).

Anyone who lacks firsthand knowledge from his own experience of the fact that poetry, along with the factual proposition, necessarily belongs to the total sum of our fundamental modes of expression —the "whole"—and who does not understand what the purpose of poetry is must inevitably remain shut off from entire realms of the humanly expressible and not simply the poetic realm in a narrower sense. Thus it might easily occur to one to ask how much a learned translator and commentator has actually understood of the biblical Song of Songs' meaning and how he would go about making it intelligible if that commentator is working on the assumption that it was "originally" about "an invitation for admission to a spiritual association".[25] Of course, someone who is to be capable of arriving at valid interpretations must also know that something like irony exists, and he must be able to recognize it as well. Otherwise he will suffer a fate similar to that of the famous Goethe philologist Gustav von Loeper, who comments on the dictum in the elder Goethe's *Maxims and Reflections*, "The Hindus of the desert pledged to eat no fish", by

---

[23] *Confessions* 13, 38. [Cited after Saint Augustine, *Confessions*, trans. Henry Chadwick (Oxford, 1991), p. 304.]

[24] *Ver.* 1, 2.

[25] Riessler-Storr, *Die heilige Schrift des Alten und des Neuen Bundes* (Mainz, 1959), p. 1358.

observing that Pythagoras also forbade his disciples to consume fish,[26] without realizing that what is meant is no more real than the oath (of my own invention) that poachers in the marshlands of Lüneberg take never to shoot a chamois. And how is an overly serious, perhaps foreign, interpreter, who is unprepared for playful twists of language, to understand a "gallows song" [*Galgenlied*] by Christian Morgenstern or make it intelligible to others ("Jaguar, zebra, mink, mandrill . . ." —just imagine all the things with which one must be familiar if one is not to stand completely helpless before such a verse!). At the same time, of course, he must also prepare himself for the possibility of sophistic misuses of words, propagandistic lies, and the near-total ubiquity of business-driven advertising, whose slogans do not so much mean as motivate. ("The Stuyvesant generation goes its own way.") The possibilities are—literally—legion.

To sum up: The expert who specializes in one form of human expression or even in a single text, however important (and in the literature surrounding this text), is clearly *not* well equipped to offer a proper interpretation, arguably not even one of the text under study. In order to be able to interpret validly, one would actually have to know from experience all the forms of human revelation within whose totality a particular expression is to be imagined as being situated. One "would actually have to"—with this, the in fact crucial question has already announced itself and has at the same time all but been answered: whether interpretation, insofar as it deals with those great objects that are truly worthy of understanding and being made understood, is not by its very nature a never-ending task.

At this point there is something else to be considered that, although it is one of the prerequisites for understanding, has not up until now been formally addressed. As we have said, a meaningful expression, the only object of an interpretation in the strict sense, refers essentially to reality. The interpreter must, then, focus his attention primarily on this connection with reality and must seek to understand it. One can also express it this way: he must consider the claim to truth raised by the expression to be interpreted. (Truth is, after all, the same as coming face to face with reality!) Simply stated, the interpreter must truly "listen" to the expression to be interpreted and

---

[26] *Goethes Sprüche in Prosa*, ed. J. Hofmiller (Munich, 1959), p. 149.

what is expressed therein. That sounds perhaps all too obvious. In reality, however, the very opposite of "listening" usually occurs in the encounter with significant philosophical and poetic expressions of the past: One acknowledges them with great fanfare but without noticing the reference to reality embodied therein, that is, without reflecting on the primary sense of what is expressed, that is, without really "listening".

Before we proceed farther, a word should be said about such *non-attentive* engagement with an expression; in an effort to be as precise as possible, I would like to put forward three examples. The *first* is completely unliterary and anything other than "learned." During the Second World War, I was employed for some years as a "military psychologist". The process for assessing future officers, airplane pilots, and specialists was such that applicants were initially asked to present their personal circumstances before a commission (parental background, educational history, favorite subjects, pastimes, and so on). One of the experts led the discussion, while all the others followed the report with rapt attention and zealously took notes. The young narrator likely gained the impression bit by bit that what he was revealing about himself had found an entirely uncommon degree of interest. If, however, he could have cast a glance at the jottings of the psychologists, in which lively or stiff facial expressions, relaxed or cramped body posture, predominantly vowel- or consonant-based speech were duly noted—then he could have said, with absolute justification, "You're not even listening to me!" He would have been disappointed and would even have felt—baldly stated—that his dignity had been violated. For everyone who speaks with someone else expects as a matter of course that one listen to him, that is, that one not—or at least not primarily—attend to the peculiarities of his form of expression, to the origin of his metaphors and vocabulary; he also does not want the other to rest content with simply trying to discover what he, the speaker, thinks. Normally, he is also not simply seeking approval, but he naturally hopes that his thoughts will be considered and examined as to whether they are true or false, appropriate, illuminating, fruitful, and so on. All this, however, is equally true of our engagement with authors like Plato or Thomas Aquinas.

My *second* example is borrowed from Platonic exegesis. One may —and it is completely legitimate to do so—study a Platonic dialogue

220 FOR THE LOVE OF WISDOM

(say, the *Gorgias*) solely as a linguistic specimen of Attic Greek after the Peloponnesian War; one may, alternately, focus one's attention on the phenomenon of "sophism", which is presented there; one may instead attempt to determine from specific stylistic features as well as from the dialogue's thematic whether, from a biographical standpoint, it must be a work of the transitional period, written before the mature masterpieces; or, finally, one may ask with regard to the closing myth concerning the final judgment whether this unique version of the story of the subterranean judges derives from Orphism or from the Egyptian Book of the Dead, and one can pursue, in this connection, the question of why Plato places this myth at the end of the hopeless dispute between Socrates and that practitioner of *Realpolitik* Callicles—to which one may, in turn, answer with Werner Jaeger: Because Plato "felt as an artist that a proper transcendental background was needed for the heroic loneliness of Socrates' fighting soul".[27] Of course, no one will argue that it is meaningful, important, and relevant to pose and discuss such questions, all of which, incidentally, were taken from the scholarly literature on Plato. Only it should be clear that whoever proceeds in this manner is not concerned with the reference to reality that takes form in Plato's expressions, not with what is genuinely meant. On the contrary, everything *other than* listening is involved here.

I would like to cite as a *third* example of such a *non*-attentive engagement with an author and his work a voluminous book on Aquinas' ethics that was published in 1933. Significantly, the introductory motto already suggests a dual misinterpretation (first, the manifestly ironic tone of the quotation has been overlooked; and secondly, it has been "torn out of context" through the omission of an essential rider; the motto reads as follows: "It is a pleasure most sublime / To immerse oneself in the spirit of the time / To behold how, among us, a wise man ponders.—Goethe's *Faust*." As is well known, however, it is neither Goethe nor Faust who speaks these lines but rather the medical student, Wagner, and the suppressed line reads as follows: "And how we have come so very far yonder"). Nevertheless, the

---

[27] Werner Jaeger, *Paideia: The Ideals of Greek Culture*, vol. 2: *In Search of the Divine Centre*, trans. Gilbert Highet (Oxford Univ. Press, 1943), p. 151.

work, which was written by Michael Wittmann,[28] may be adjudged, despite the somewhat inauspicious start, a meticulously developed historical exposition that remains absolutely indispensable even up to the present day. Whoever wishes to be reliably informed about the origin of Aquinas' source materials remains dependent, in any case, on this book; each of its chapters begins with a "summary",[29] which clearly distinguishes in each case the Aristotelian and Augustinian elements, Plato's influence, the sprinklings of Stoic thought, and the aftereffects of the later Peripatetics. Anyone expecting, however, an interpretation, that is, an exposition of that which Aquinas himself intended with his own ethical conception (one that was, in fact, molded from all these source materials) and of those ideas that he wanted to make known and communicate will be completely disappointed—because the historian did not think through their connection to the underlying reality, or because, alternatively expressed, he did not, despite all his scholarly research into sources, listen to his author. Only someone who listens is in a position to interpret. We may make the same point differently, borrowing a maxim of Rudolf Bultmann's: "Interpretation always presupposes a living relation to the things" that are being discussed.[30]

It should, however, be clear that, with this, the relationship between interpretation and history, however tentatively formulated, has already been broached—an extremely difficult, even delicate subject, concerning which I would like to make some remarks, which are offered here more in an aphoristic than in a systematic vein.

There is no doubt—and hence it might just as soon be admitted—that the interpretation of an expression whose meaning is not immediately evident is inconceivable without recourse to history. On the other hand, the relation between interpretation and history is not a proportion of such a kind that an increase in the one side *eo ipso* would necessarily translate into an increase in possibilities on the other side. There are significant examples of ingenious interpretations developed in the face of very restricted historical knowledge and sometimes even on the basis of erroneous historical conceptions. Thus it

---

[28] *Die Ethik des heiligen Thomas von Aquin* (Munich, 1933). Cf. my review in the *Theologische Revue* 33 (1934).

[29] See, for example, pp. 216, 274f., 344f., 362ff.

[30] "Das Problem der Hermeneutik", *Zeitschrift für Theologie und Kirche* 47 (1950): 54, 62.

appears to me to be a highly significant fact that a commentary on Aristotle's *Metaphysics* that has even today hardly been surpassed has, as its author, a man who had virtually no knowledge of Greek and who, more significantly, had no idea of how the book was composed; he took it to be a systematic work that had been thoroughly planned from start to finish, as if originating from a single mold, whereas historical research has in the interim taught us that it consists of a rather accidental collection of very diverse texts. The man to whom I am referring is Thomas Aquinas. Of course, one might argue that he could have achieved a far better commentary if, instead of relying on a more or less adequate Latin translation, he had had the Oxford critical edition of Aristotle's works by Sir David Ross. Still it should be borne in mind that it is, in any event, not impossible genuinely to listen to even an indistinctly perceived voice and that a hearing directed primarily toward the expressed thought's relation to reality and hence toward what the author meant can bear such fruit as has seldom been associated with the significantly more advanced accomplishments of historical and philological textual criticism.

The relationship between interpretation and history is, however, problematic to a degree that extends far beyond this. This becomes evident when one realizes that tradition, which implies translation—insofar as the latter holds the sense of something once said identical over time—and the transferring of that sense into the language of the living present, can occur only in the form of valid interpretation and that the relationship between history and interpretation must be thought in analogy to that of history and tradition. Just as, however, the paradox of historical thinking lies, for Theodor Schieder,[31] in the fact that it, "on the one hand, preserves memory while dissolving it, on the other", that it "wants to be passed down, on the one hand, but imperils this passing down, on the other", so the historical way of looking at things can hinder or outright preclude an interpretation in the strict sense—interpretation, construed here as the act of ascertaining what is meant by an expression, its connection to reality, and hence its truth (or untruth).

Now the time has come to remove the previously mentioned "tentativeness" implicit in the formulation "history *and* interpretation"

---

[31] Cf. J. Pieper, *Über den Begriff der Tradition* (Cologne and Opladen, 1958), p. 43.

and to make the relation between the two more precise. The "historical way of looking at things"—the kind of "historical thinking" of which Theodor Schieder speaks (he also uses the word "historicism" in this connection)—all this, although perhaps indicative of the occupational hazard of the historian, is, of course, something distinct from history itself. On the other hand, it remains true that anyone who regards the meaning-laden expressions encountered in intellectual history from an exclusively "historical perspective" is by the same token incapable of genuine interpretation. On this point we cannot help but agree with that Mephisto, made wise by long experience, whom C. S. Lewis introduced to the world of literature under the name of "Screwtape". Lewis' *Screwtape Letters*, first published in London in 1942, presents a brilliant if inverted anthropology, as humorous as it is profoundly earnest (in the Anglo-Saxon world it has circulated in numerous editions and is known to every educated person; here in Germany it is available to us only in a mediocre translation entitled *Dienstanweisung an einen Unterteufel* (User's manual for a devil's apprentice).[32] This *opusculum* consists of the tips with which Mr. Screwtape instructs a still relatively inexperienced novice in the art of seduction; and one time, when the latter, genuinely concerned, points out the fact that intelligent people, in particular, tend to read the wisdom-drenched books of the ancients, his master comforts him with the thought that the historical point of view to which the scholars of the Western world had fortunately been converted by the spirits of hell had just this consequence: that the only question one could be sure would not be posed was the one concerning the truth of what they had read. Rather than doing that, they would prefer to inquire into influences and borrowings, about the personal evolution of the writer concerned, about his contribution to posterity, and so on.[33] No less thought-provoking, however, than these devilish efforts at silencing man's conscience, it seems to me, is a real-life fact I have been able to confirm through reliable authorities: in the Communist-dominated German provinces, the readily available editions of works from the Western tradition (for example, the works of Plato or Dante) are invariably prefaced by an introduction, which is intended to impart

---

[32] *Dienstanweisung an einen Unterteufel*, 18th ed. (Freiburg, 1978).
[33] *The Screwtape Letters*, 15th ed. (London, 1965), pp. 139f.

to the reader a historical understanding of the author and so deliberately (albeit hopefully not always with success) prevent him from
taking what he reads in absolute seriousness. Of course, such explanations need not be genuine examples of history as such. Still, what
is actually being said is of less import—or so it seems to me—than
the intentional diversion of attention away from the work's content
and connection with reality itself to the author and the conditions
surrounding his act of self-expression; alternately expressed, what is
crucial here is the suppression of that genuine listening which is a
prerequisite for understanding and interpretation.

Clearly, anyone who attempts to determine what is meant by a
meaning-laden expression never has to deal *exclusively* with an objec-
tivated expression—with a text, for example—but necessarily at the
same time with the particular person who is expressing himself. Indeed, it is he who, insofar as he expresses himself, means something,
that is, wants to make a state of affairs intelligible and so communicate it. In addition, there is always among the interpreted as well
as among the interpreters an all-embracing commonality—insofar as
all ensouled entities share a nature specific to them as ensouled[34]—
without which understanding and interpretation would, in fact, be
impossible.[35] As a result, one can more or less justifiably regard it
as inconceivable that there could be a meaning-laden expression that
absolutely defied all understanding. Indeed, in the absence of such
commonality, understanding and interpretation would be impossible.
On the other hand, an interpretation that is not only correct after a
fashion but that actually grasps the core of the expression is possible
only if a personal affinity exists that goes beyond the commonality
of being ensouled; I am referring to that *connaturalitas* which makes
possible an immediate apprehension of its ultimate meaning that is superior in precision to logical inference and that allows what is other
than oneself to appear almost like one's own. Arguably, the unfailing
certainty with which Aquinas, in interpreting Aristotle's *Metaphysics*,
penetrates to the depths of what is meant can be attributed to the
connaturalitas that joins both thinkers to each other. Sooner or later,
all theories of interpretation have recourse, at least once, to this kind

---

[34] F. Ast, *Grundlinien der Grammatik, Hermeneutik und Kritik* (Landshut, 1808), p. 172.
[35] O. F. Bollnow, *Das Verstehen* (Mainz, 1949), p. 29.

of affinity. Dilthey refers to the necessity of there being an "affinity, magnified by a protracted living with the author".[36] Here, too, one might recognize that "divinatory" element which Schleiermacher[37] sees at work in every interpretation as the intuitive feminine side corresponding to the "discriminating", rational, male side and which alone is capable of picking up with an unerring scent on what, because of its obviousness, has been left unsaid in the said.[38] It remains, however, an open question, one hardly permitting of a conclusive answer, how exactly such a quasi-personal relationship like the one between Aristotle and Aquinas, that is, between the subject of interpretation and his posthumous commentator and interpreter, is supposed to arise over a distance of some one thousand five hundred years—and that despite the fact that the authors are separated by differences of not only language but culture.

Before bringing these reflections to a close, however, we must discuss a much more complicated matter, that is, the case of a person who finds himself obliged to interpret an expression whose author cannot only not be encountered empirically and identified but who does not even appear to be the same "one" over time. Admittedly, that sounds exceedingly cryptic. But the matter will be illustrated forthwith by means of a highly intuitive example. Allow me to quote a passage from a posthumously published volume of essays by the actor Ernst Ginsberg,[39] who relates a curious encounter:

Early on a rainy Zurich morning, at around 6 A.M., there was a ringing at the door. When I opened it, there stood Else Lasker-Schüler, visibly irritated and upset, her wet hair hanging in her face. She excused herself for her early visit and bade my permission to present a poem that had been composed that very night. She seated herself, dripping wet as she was, with coat and tiger-fur mittens, on the couch, and read me the poem "Those Driven Away" [Die Verscheuchte]. . . .[40] Then, suddenly, she asked, "How do you find dat?" I gave voice to my emotion, but she immediately interrupted me, "No! No! Not if you like it but . . ."—and she pointed to a specific verse—"what does dat mean here? Dat here?"

---

[36] *Entstehung der Hermeneutik*, pp. 329f.

[37] Ibid., p. 109.

[38] Cf. M. Heidegger, *Platons Lehre von der Wahrheit* (Bern, 1947), p. 5.

[39] Ernst Ginsberg, *Abschied: Erinnerungen, Theateraufsätze, Gedichte* (Zurich, 1965), pp. 154f.

[40] Else Lasker-Schüler, *Gedichte 1902–1943*, ed. F. Kemp (Munich, 1959), p. 347.

On the assumption that the poetess was simply looking for confirmation that her words had been clear, I explained what I understood to be the content of that passage. Then she stared at me with her great big eyes and said, astonished, in the sing-song tone characteristic of Elberfeld dialect, "Yes, lad, dat could have been how dat was meant!"

On the one hand, it is clear that this verse was written by no other than just this Else Lasker-Schüler, in her own hand; on the other hand, it can hardly be disputed that it was not she alone—and perhaps not she at all—who had intended something quite specific with this expression. Who else should it be, though? Else Lasker-Schüler, whom no less sober a critic than Bertolt Brecht calls a "a great poetess",[41] says of herself, "It composes itself through me. . . . The poet never intends anything. . . . The more devoutly she listeningly eavesdrops on her angel, the deeper her poetry. People give to this condition the name 'inspiration'."[42] Here again it becomes evident what a loss it is for us not to have a philosophical/theological doctrine of the fine arts, which, however, under the conditions of contemporary thought is becoming ever more difficult to develop (as is true of philosophy and theology, in general). In the period shortly before his death, Reinhold Schneider incessantly inquired into the nature of poetry; despite all this, his experience was that "from year to year it becomes more and more difficult to find an answer."[43]

Unbeknownst perhaps to Else Lasker-Schüler herself, her words fall within a long, grand tradition. This tradition extends from Plato—who says of the poets that they express themselves in a fit of "divine madness",[44] in a disposition of soul, at any rate, that is more akin to a being beyond oneself than to a being at home within oneself—to Goethe, who describes poets as having "truly lost their senses".[45] But even Gottfried Benn, however, who was infamous for dismissing any sort of romanticizing talk about poetry with his rude Berlin dialect—"a poem very rarely 'arises'; a poem is made"[46]—is forced to the realization that "the essence of poetry is perfection and fascination": "I

[41] Ginsberg, *Abschied*, p. 153.
[42] Ibid.
[43] *Soll die Dichtung das Leben bessern?* (Wiesbaden, 1965), p. 27.
[44] *Phaedrus* 245a5ff.
[45] F. W. Riemer, *Mitteilungen über Goethe*, ed. A. Pollmer (Leipzig, 1921), p. 334.
[46] Gottfried Benn, *Essays, Reden, Vorträge* (Wiesbaden, 1959), p. 495.

am not claiming that it is a perfection that derives from itself."[47] The common experience of creative people that forces itself to expression here mirrors that of the attentive reader and listener, including that of the so-called "moderns". Granted, the psychoanalytic approach and, more importantly, the broad, albeit superficial, dissemination of obvious pseudo-poetry (in the form of fashionable make-believe, literary artistry, political propaganda, and sheer "entertainment") have in a certain sense left this reader/listener without any illusions, but, even Plato was obliged, on the basis of his experience with the sophists as manufacturers of fictive reality,[48] to distinguish very sharply between "divine" poets[49] and those not worthy of the name. Anytime, however, the sound of true poetry reaches and moves the contemporary reader or listener, as with the work of Gottfried Benn or Franz Kafka or Georges Bernanos, he knows in that moment that, strictly speaking, it is not the Berlin dermatologist Dr. Benn or the two insurance agents Kafka and Bernanos who have had such an effect on him. And, possibly at that moment, the now old-fashioned but presumably not so misguided device for citing verse forcibly suggests itself to him, "as the poet says": "the poet"—who else could it be otherwise, if not the dermatologist Dr. Benn? Who else is involved? To whom else are we listening? And who otherwise could have intended something with the poetic expression that is now supposed to be given a valid interpretation?

There is a response to this question, which on account of its all too simplistic bypassing of the issue cannot seriously be entertained. The answer can be found in a biography, published in 1941, which argues, with regard to Rilke, that he is "a purely poetic figure in this simple sense: a vessel for divine revelation. One must accept this on faith if one is to be true to Rilke."[50] "Divine revelation", "faith"— clearly, these are very lofty words. Else Lasker-Schüler talks instead of "inspiration"—by which she simply chooses the next best alternative, which is more or less universally accepted. Anyone, however,

---

[47] Ibid., pp. 593, 590.

[48] Cf. J. Pieper, "Mißbrauch der Sprache—Mißbrauch der Macht", in *Über die Schwierigkeit, heute zu glauben* (Munich, 1974), p. 277.

[49] *Meno* 81b2.

[50] C. Osann, *Rainer Maria Rilke* (Zurich and Leipzig, 1941), p. 7.

who thoughtfully accepts the concept of "intuition" has already conceded that a genuine poem like any other work of art, requires, on the part of the observer (listener, reader) a special sensorium, a specific "antenna", as it were, that enables him alone, on the basis of an intellectual-spiritual affinity, to establish contact with that sphere beyond the realm of the rationally comprehensible from which the artist receives his "revelation". Only an artistic man—this is what is here intended and here being expressed—is able to assimilate the work of art adequately, to understand it, and to interpret it validly. The "message" contained therein is perceptible to him alone, and its message is communicated to him alone.

Now, the concept of inspiration has in Christendom been given a predominantly *theological* interpretation. Although it can—unlike, say, "artistic" inspiration—be precisely defined, namely, as the divine authorship acting through a human composer on a text, which, for this very reason, is considered "holy", it also extends far more deeply into that which can no longer be rationally illumined. Of course, it would transcend the scope of the topic to be treated here as well as my own area of expertise to present the concept of theological inspiration in more detail. The single most important aspect of this concept is for us the question of how the conditions for a valid interpretation are modified in the transition to a theological interpretation. Alternately expressed, it is the question of the inner constitution of theology —whereby theology is understood as the attempt to interpret these "holy" texts, that is, to listen, to understand, and to make intelligible what was truly intended by the divine author over and beyond the words of their human author. That, as a result, the demands that have been placed on a valid interpretation must necessarily be all the more severe is evident; one would almost like to say that they have become virtually unsatisfiable.

Now, in order not to end up in the gray of abstraction, I will attempt to illustrate with two concrete examples in what this tightening of the requirements consists and how these requirements might be satisfied.

My *first* example: the eschatological myths, recounted by the Platonic Socrates, concerning the trial of the dead, which awaits every man and which, with its infallible judgment, assigns reward and punishment. Perhaps one will, with some perplexity, ask why this is being adduced as an example of the interpretation of an "inspired" text. In response I would like to offer several thoughts for consideration. First of all, neither Socrates nor Plato raises any claims to authorship with regard to the myths they have narrated; in each case it is a preexisting myth that is being *re*told. I hold the view to be demonstrably false,[51] even though widespread in the academic literature, that Plato, "the mythmaker", invented and composed these stories for the purpose of more effectively presenting his ideas.[52] Moreover, in the *Seventh Letter*, Plato is explicit in tracing this account of the last days back to those "ancient and holy doctrines", *tois palaioís te kaì hieroís lógois*, in which it is, "in fact" (*óntos*), appropriate to believe.[53] Those who express themselves through such doctrines are for Plato in the end "the ancients",[54] by which he means, not the "gerontic", not the men with snow-white hair, but rather those who "dwell close to God",[55] "the truly wise",[56] the first recipient and transmitter of a message brought down from the divine abode by some unknown Prometheus.[57] I do not know of a single definitional attribute by which the ancients, who, in Plato, however, remain unnamed, could be distinguished from what Christian theology understands as an "inspired" author (the prophets, the hagiographers).

Now the very first thing that the Platonic Socrates, a rational, not otherwise easily satisfied disputant, does in the face of such holy traditions, backed by the testimony of the ancients, is to accept their truth on faith. ". . . [Y]ou, I suppose, will consider [it] fiction, but I consider [it] fact, for what I am going to tell you I shall recount as the actual truth."[58] This Socratic faith, however, the affirmation of which binds the believer over the centuries into a single community, not only with the ancients, but above all with that superhuman power

---

[51] Cf. J. Pieper, *Über die platonischen Mythen* (Munich, 1965), pp. 25, 86f.

[52] Typical for this view is O. Apelt's translation of the word *mythos* (*Phaedo* 114d7) as a "fabricated account" [*erdichtete Schilderung*] (Philosophische Bibliothek 147:128).

[53] *Seventh Letter* 335a2–4.

[54] Cf. J. Pieper, *Überlieferung, Begriff und Anspruch* (Munich, 1970), pp. 45ff (included in this volume as "Tradition: Its Sense and Aspiration").

[55] *Philebus* 16c5–9.

[56] *Phaedrus* 274c1.

[57] *Philebus* 16c5–9.

[58] *Gorgias* 523a. [Quoted after the translation by W. D. Woodhead, in *Plato: The Collected Dialogues*, ed. Edith Hamilton and Huntington Cairns (Princeton, 1961), p. 303.]

which speaks through them,[59] a community that might be described (as Karl Jaspers also calls it in a necessarily vague way)[60] as a *corpus mysticum*. This belief creates, and at the same time bears witness to, that affinity, which is, in turn, the prerequisite for an understanding of what is truly meant and hence for a valid interpretation of that meaning. Thus Plato is engaged in theology in the strict sense when, in his interpretation of the myth, he passes from the metaphorical language of the judge's sentence uttered at the crossroads in the underworld meadow to what it actually means, that is, that the real upshot of our existence here on this earth is ultimately made manifest on the other side of death in just this event, which is as inaccessible to our imagination as it is to our experience and which in symbolic language is known as the "final judgment". The fact that Plato, in his attempt at interpretation, throws in contemporary ideas about the structure of the earth and its subterranean waterways is completely to be expected and almost inevitable. Even a modern theologian, when he earnestly undertakes to interpret a received tradition as true, absolutely cannot afford to ignore our contemporary knowledge of man and the world. What alone is important is that the supraempirical gospel of the divine, despite all historical conditioning of its message—a message that can only be heard by the faithful—is made present in identical form to consciousness and kept present before it.

My *second* example is the following sentence from the biblical account of creation: "The LORD God formed man of dust from the ground, and breathed into his nostrils the breath of life" (Gen 2:7). Just as was the case with the eschatological myths recounted by the Platonic Socrates, the question that precedes all else is the following: Does one regard it as "a mere tale" or as "a saying that the gods let fall from their abode"? The question is the same, but the situation of the person attempting to answer it has changed fundamentally since the time of Socrates. First, we now have such reliable information on the history of religion and culture in general and on the history of this text in particular that we can in the meantime say with certainty that, for example, this biblical passage simply repeats an explanation of man's origin that is typical for primitive agrarian societies. Infor-

---

[59] Cf. J. Pieper, *Über den Glauben* (Munich, 1962), pp. 45f.

[60] *Philosophie*, p. 259.

mation of this kind is certainly of interest to theologians, but it does not, of course, by itself constitute theology. Secondly, paleontology and evolutionary theory have provided such basic knowledge on the emergence of man that one can easily arrive at the thought that the biblical account of creation should be dismissed as something completely irrelevant to our times and argue that man is nothing more than an evolutionary phenomenon, no different from fish or other mammals. Again, it must be conceded as a matter of course that a contemporary theologian cannot excuse himself from acquainting himself with, and deliberating on, the findings of these sciences. Even so, this would in no way compel him to declare the human soul to be nothing more than an evolutionary phenomenon and the biblical account of creation to be an irrelevant story. This will be obvious to him, however, only if he believes that this account contains a divinely guaranteed message that transcends everything that is humanly knowable. It is precisely with regard to this point—with regard to the possibility of faith—that the situation has transformed itself radically since the Platonic Socrates' time—something that cannot be discussed without appealing to one's own deepest convictions. The difference consists primarily in the fact that the Christian, unlike Socrates, is no longer obliged to point to an unknown Prometheus or to such anonymous personages as the "ancients" or to strictly functional, albeit venerable, doctrines [*logoi*]; rather he can invoke the *logos* itself, as it has manifested itself in history and in which that community of souls which encompasses the Divine Speaker, the witnesses to his truth, and the faithful—the aforementioned *corpus mysticum*—is personified.

It is, however—just as it was in the case of Socrates and Plato —the self-assimilation to a community through which that affinity and *connaturalitas* are established on the basis of which one is capable of hearing and interpreting what the superhuman Author says and means, above and beyond the humanly composed text (for example, that in the midst of evolutionary change the human soul itself is *not* likewise evolving but rather, inexplicably, represents a transitionless, new reality, which does not actually "become"[61] but rather emerges

---

[61] With this, Plato's conception of the soul as being not only eternal but also unbecoming (*agénetos; Phaedrus* 246a11) acquires a new significance. Cf. J. Pieper, *Begeisterung und Göttlicher Wahnsinn* (Munich, 1962), pp. 122f.

"finished" [*fertig*] from its creative origin and remains immediately bound to it). One can also express the point another way: True theology is possible only on the assumption of such a self-assimilation to that *corpus mysticum*. Just as it is impossible for an unartistic person to understand and interpret a poem, so there can be no unbelieving theologian—as long as, as has already been stated, theology is construed as the attempt to interpret revelation validly.

Interpretation—by this we still mean the task of understanding and making intelligible that which the person who is expressing himself wants to make known and communicate, but it is a task that has now truly been shown to be endless.

TRADITION

Its Sense and Aspiration

*We live now only from our own inconsistency, from the fact that we have not yet really silenced all tradition.**

I. Is tradition something counterhistorical? Not transformation, but preservation—Pascal: two genera of science. Physics and theology—The difficulty of arriving at a preliminary orientation. The silence of the philosophical lexica. Disregard for linguistic usage.

II. Elements in the concept of "tradition"—The interlocutor in the act of handing down. The *tradendum*. Tradition is not discussion —Tradition and teaching. "*Transmettre*" and "to hand down". Learning versus accepting what is handed down—Historical knowledge of the *tradita* may stand in the way of tradition. The inexhaustibility of tradition—Tradition and cultural progress. The maintenance of purity and recollection.

III. Tradition and authority—Who are the "men of old"? The Platonic response: The first recipient of a divinely authenticated message—Revelation and holy tradition. The contents of tradition—The "ancients" and the prophets. The binding character of tradition.

IV. Is there only *holy* tradition? The obligating force of "mundane" tradition—Tradition and traditions—A genuine understanding of tradition frees one and makes one independent of "conservatisms"—The task of theology: the interpretation of holy tradition—The primordial revelation and the myths of pre- and non-Christian peoples—The faithful are not interested in theology but in the divine word.

---

* The motto stems from a work by Gerhard Krüger, *Geschichte und Tradition* (History and Tradition) (Stuttgart, 1948), p. 28.

233

234 FOR THE LOVE OF WISDOM

V. Where has the holy tradition been historically realized? First:
the Christian doctrinal tradition. Second: Myths as an echo of
the primordial revelation. On what basis does Socrates place credence in the "men of old"? The seminal power of the divine
word. Third: the unconscious existential certainties. *Memoria*:
transpsychological and supraindividual—Language as *traditum*.
"Traditionalism"—gratitude and consciousness of tradition.

VI. Holy tradition and philosophy: incorporating the *tradita*—Philosophizing represents neither the fulfillment of tradition nor
its interpretation—Contemporary philosophy and the *tradita* of
holy tradition. Two forms of exclusion: Jean-Paul Sartre's anti-
tradition and the "scientific philosophy"—"Empty seriousness"
(Karl Jaspers) and "empty freedom" (Viacheslav Ivanov). The
unifying power of holy tradition.

I

In the bewilderingly diverse network of that process we call "history", numerous strands may be discerned, among them that of the
"received"—that is, tradition. But tradition is not only fundamentally different from all the other strands; it seems, at first glance, to
be completely alien and unrelated—so much so that one might even
ask whether it is not, in fact, something counterhistorical.

   The most readily visible strands are doubtless those that relate to
our continually advancing inquiry into man and world and to our
ever more intense exploitation of natural forces, which is conditioned
and propelled by that inquiry. For such progress to be possible and
to persist over time, what has been wrested and retrieved through inquiry must be passed on and appropriated without disruption. In the
process—perhaps inevitably—the particular is forgotten or lost. So,
it has been said that certain tints in the glass windows of the cathedral
of Chartres can no longer be reproduced; and during the [postwar]
reconstruction of our cathedrals and town halls, it is reputed to have
been difficult at times to find a craftsman who still knew how to cut
a window arch or the capital of a column from stone. But even society itself is subject to continuous change, whose ultimate direction,

however, it may be difficult to determine: Hegel speaks of progress in the emancipation of consciousness; other prognostications foretell the gradual transformation of mankind into a worldwide army consisting of the working class. Sometimes, the pace of development may accelerate to the point of an explosion; even revolutionary overthrow is a historically recurring phenomenon, and its aftereffects are, it would appear, for the most part, equally ambivalent. Within the same epoch and, as it were, perpendicular to the temporal process, cultures exert reciprocal influences through which states of dominance, dependence, and foreign determination [*Überfremdung*] are created that, in their turn, arouse the resistance of countermovements. The role of the French language in Germany at the time of Frederick the Great is a famous example, but the Americanization of everyday German after the Second World War is in principle a fully analogous process. Again and again, "renaissances" occur that systematically undertake to retrieve the forgotten or the suppressed and bring them again to bear on the present, with the result that they are unwittingly, during the course of such "rebirths", turned into something completely new. The antiquity envisaged by the Carolingian Renaissance has a different face from that of Winckelman's Greece, and neither has much to do with historical reality.

One thing, however, is common to all these (in themselves radically) different forms of historical occurrence: without exception they point in the direction of change, transformation, upheaval, and revolution; they all "go with the times"—things should not remain as they have been up until now. Not only is tradition different in this respect —or at least so it appears initially—in tradition, this aspect appears exactly inverted. To all appearances, tradition is not oriented toward something new, toward either development or change, but rather it is oriented toward keeping something that has always already been given in advance and is logically prior identical against the passage of time and in opposition to it. All of a sudden, programmatic slogans with an entirely different intent can now be heard; instead of "reorientation" and "progress", now the catchword is: "That word above all earthly powers abideth"; "a new gospel" is vehemently rejected (2 Cor 11:4); and even the Marxists refer to "the teachings of the classics", which, although they were composed more than a century ago, are supposed to hold unconditionally even today. Remaining within the vicinity of such thoughts, one runs up against concepts like "deviation" and "orthodoxy", "accommodation", *aggiornamento* and "revisionism", "reformation" and "demythification". In fact, all these terms have a legitimate sense only within the realm of tradition where the preservation of something primordially given is regarded as a vital and elementary task.

Already at this point, the question may be raised whether, perhaps, tradition, the concept as well as the thing itself, has its legitimate place only within the realm of religious belief and "world views". This question strikes, I believe, at the very heart of the problem; it cannot be answered with a simple "yes" or "no". It has, parenthetically, time and again been passionately debated in intellectual history —in a particularly constructive fashion during a somewhat dramatic discussion at the beginning of the scientific age, which, if only because of the greatness of its interlocutors, is worth recalling here. Figures like Galileo, Descartes, and Pascal were participants in this discussion. Pascal played a particularly significant role; he had not only debated with the others but had also attempted to draw a conclusion from the entire exchange with a precisely formulated thesis on the proper jurisdiction of tradition.

This thesis is to be found in a treatise by the then twenty-four-year-old, whose title at first give rises to a completely different set of expectations. The title runs *Fragment of a Preface to a Treatise on Empty Space*,[1] a treatise that was then never written. "Empty space", that is, the abhorrence of empty space, the *horror vacui*, provides, in fact, the actual occasion and the topic of this dispute. In what was the traditional philosophy of nature at that time, the *horror vacui*[2] was considered one of the elemental forces of the material world. "You know", Pascal writes in a letter from the year 1647, "what the philosophers think about this topic: they take it as an axiom that nature abhors a vacuum."[3] Among the contemporary philosophers who subscribed to this belief was also, surprisingly, Descartes. There is certainly a bit of objective irony in the fact that in the same work in which he enunci-

---

[1] *Oeuvres de Blaise Pascal*, ed. L. Brunschvicg and E. Boutroux, vol. 2 (Paris, 1908), pp. 129–45.

[2] For details, see Ersch-Gruber, *Allgemeine Enzyklopädie der Wissenschaften und Künste*, vol. 3 (Leipzig, 1839), pp. 486ff.

[3] *Briefe des Blaise Pascal*, trans. W. Rüttenauer (Leipzig, 1935), pp. 33f.

ates the principle of doubting all tradition, the traditional conception of a *horror vacui* is declared a compelling reason.[4] Even Pascal, as ready as he is to refute this dogma, writes in a letter that he does not yet dare "abandon the principle of the *horror vacui*".[5] Incidentally, he also formulates a general principle, which, however, differs from that of Descartes in a manner typical for him. Whereas Descartes argues that one should not accept anything as valid unless it is completely certain, Pascal finds it neither "correct" nor "permitted" "simply to abandon the maxims handed down from antiquity if we are not compelled to do so through indubitable and irrefutable proofs".[6] Not even a man like Galileo Galilei can, with regard to the *horror vacui*, exempt himself from the force of tradition. Although the common view at the time appeared to find its validation in experience, for example, in the empirically verifiable fact of a pump or siphon's sucking action, as well as that of other hydraulic devices, more decisive for its acceptance was doubtless a *metaphysical* argument: since "nothing" cannot exist, there can also be no space in which sheer "nothingness" is presumed to be.[7] But later new and more accurate experiments were conducted, which again cast doubt on this very argument. Around 1640, the well builders of Florence posed this now famous question to their fellow citizen Galileo Galilei, then seventy-five-years-old: Why, then, is the sucking action of the water pump able to raise the water level up to only a certain height so that not *all* the "empty space", is filled—to which Galileo knew no other answer than to offer a slight modification of the principle of the *horror vacui*. But then his student Torricelli conducted the now famous experiment by means of which —for the world at large, at least—the problem was solved and the

---

[4] In the *Principia Philosophiae* (1644), he writes, for example, that "we know with absolute clarity [*perspicue intelligimus*]" that there is a matter which fills out every conceivable interval; its nature consists "exclusively in being extended substance"; "we do not find in ourselves an idea of any other kind of matter" (*Principia Philosophiae* 2:22). For similar arguments, see *Météores, Discours* 1.

[5] *Briefe*, p. 35.

[6] Ibid.

[7] The question of whether a "void" can exist had already been discussed by the Pre-Socratic philosophers. In the late Platonic dialogue the *Timaeus* (79b1, 79c1), the question is answered in the negative. The medieval commentators on Aristotle devoted considerable space to the question, including Thomas Aquinas, *In Phys.* 4, 13 (nos. 535f.), who takes up the arguments of Averroes.

ancient thesis refuted; with the aid of mercury-filled glass pipes that were then turned upside down, he created experimentally an "empty space" which, from the standpoint of metaphysics, had been thought to be impossible and which, even up to the present day, continues to be named after him, the "Torricelli vacuum".

The pamphlets of this period as well as Pascal's letters attest to the unusual vehemence of this dispute. One can only understand them if one bears in mind the fact that a fundamental conception regarding the structure of the material cosmos had now been undermined and that with this, a fundamental dispute over methodology, already underway for centuries, was forcing its way to a conclusion.

And it was, as we have already pointed out, Pascal, who sought to derive from the dispute, quite apart from sheer polemic, a differentiated *instrumentarium* for the purpose of clarifying the general problem of "tradition", which from the outset lay at the very heart of this debate. Although Pascal does not attempt to conceal his anger over the sterile methodology, which "makes of every opinion of the ancients an oracular saying and recognizes even in its obscurities holy secrets",[8] he explains at the same time that he does not intend to "replace one vice with another and to show the ancients no respect at all, simply because one had had too much respect for them".[9] One might rather summarily describe Pascal's own constructive proposal this way: There are two distinct genera of human science: the one rests on experiment and reasoned argument, the other on tradition and authority. A paradigm example of the first genus is physics, within whose realm an appeal to authority and tradition is meaningless. The second genus is represented by theology; here only the revealed word is acceptable.[10] In physics, as in all sciences that rest on empirical data and rational argumentation, there is no point in referring to the "ancients". Strictly speaking, Pascal notes, it is the contemporaries and the moderns who, in comparison with those of previous epochs, are "the ancients". "Those whom we call 'the ancients' are, in reality, in

---

[8] *Oeuvres* 2:129. See also *Briefe*, pp. 18ff., 43ff.

[9] *Oeuvres* 2:129.

[10] It is true that Pascal initially mentions—besides theology—history, geography, jurisprudence, and languages; and apart from physics he also cites geometry, music, and architecture. In his subsequent discussion, however, he speaks exclusively of theology, on the one hand, and physics, on the other.

all things the beginners; in them the youth of mankind is in fact represented. In us, by contrast—because we have added the experience of the subsequent centuries to their knowledge—is to be found that 'old age' which we revere in them."[11]

On the basis of this distinction, Pascal then critically examines the intellectual plight of his own age:

> Once we have perceived this distinction clearly, we will protest the blindness of those who in physics want to allow tradition to stand alone in the place of reason and experiment; and we will shrink back from the impropriety of those who set rational argument in the place of the tradition of the Scripture and the Church Fathers. . . . Still, the confusion of this century is so great that one comes to hear many new opinions in theology that were unknown to the whole of antiquity, while one should immediately regard new opinions in physics, as few as they, in fact, are, as false as soon as they contradict in the least the traditional views.[12]

The fragment closes with a powerful sentence: "Whatever weight may be attached to antiquity, the truth must always have priority, however recently it may have been discovered. It is older than any opinion that one may harbor concerning it. One misconstrues its nature if one believes that it first comes into being when it comes to be recognized."[13]

What, precisely, is meant by "translation", then? What does it mean to be "handed down"?

These questions, one would think, should be of fundamental interest to the philosophizing person. If, however, in seeking a preliminary orientation, one turns to the usual (German) philosophical lexica,[14] then one will make the astonishing discovery that the word does not even appear in them as an entry. Oddly enough, "traditionalism" is mentioned, but not "tradition". Perhaps, one will conclude, as a result, that the concept falls within the exclusive province of theology, and one will then consult the theological reference works. There one will not, in fact, find oneself at a loss for information; still, they do

---

[11] *Oeuvres*, 2:141.

[12] Ibid., p. 133.

[13] Ibid., p. 145.

[14] For example, those of Walter Brugger, Johannes Hoffmeister, and Rudolf Eisler.

not provide one with very much assistance insofar as the concept is usually restricted to its theological meaning, more or less in isolation from its other connotations—as if there were not in the human language, as it is spoken and understood by everyone, a much more comprehensive concept of tradition that, for all that, can be made more precise. Instead, the theological controversy over "Scripture and tradition" is usually treated early on in the article, that is, in those cases where tradition is not exclusively understood to mean "the *oral* transmission of Christian truth".[15] Even the normally so wonderfully informative *Theological Dictionary for the New Testament* by Kittel offers only an uncharacteristically brief and meager entry, which cannot be compared with the richly documented treatises— richly documented both from the standpoint of the history of religion and often also from the standpoint of the history of philosophy—that it dedicates to other such fundamental concepts. Quite apart from this the article on *paradosis* appears under the entry "*didomi*", which both from an objective standpoint and from the standpoint of ease of reference makes about as much sense as subsuming "tradition" under the rubric of "giving". Incidentally, whoever entertains the notion of interrogating Pauly-Wissowa's time-tested *Real Encyclopedia of Classical Antiquity* must, unless he is, coincidentally, well-versed in Roman law, steel himself for a special surprise. While it is true that he will find under the entry *traditio* a clear and extensive presentation, only the legal concept designating "the transfer of property with the intention of transferring ownership" is discussed, again without any explicit reference to the use of nontechnical language.[16]

II

One must, then, start at the very beginning and attempt to list the individual elements in the order in which the living concept of "tradition", as it appears in the everyday thought and speech of man, may be constructed from them—whereby we will be using the words "tradition" and "reception" synonymously in what follows.

---

[15] According to the *Dictionnaire de théologie catholique*, vol. 15, 1, col. 1253.

[16] Cf. R. Sohm, *Institutionen: Geschichte und System des römischen Privatrechts*, 12th ed. (Leipzig, 1905), p. 309.

What is immediately evident is that in the concept of "tradition", insofar as it designates a process, two interlocutors are involved. The one hands down something; the other receives it. This "something", which is sometimes referred to by the word "tradition", will be designated in the following as the *traditum*, the "handed-down" or "received", or as the *tradendum*, the "to-be-handed-down". It can be found in every conceivable realm of human existence. The *traditum* can be a piece of knowledge or a doctrine, but a legal principle can also be handed down just like a song, a skill, a custom, a prayer, an institution, a power of attorney, a ceremony, or even a behavioral norm—for example, the way in which we address and greet one another, the way in which we behave at religious services, the way in which we receive a guest, and so forth. Our attention, however, will be focused on the handing down of *truth*, in which the *traditum* is a doctrine, a statement concerning reality, an interpretation of reality, a piece of wisdom—whereby it should be noted at the same time that a custom, a legal principle, or a ceremony may also, whether implicitly or explicitly, embody a doctrine.

One feature is common to all the forms of *tradita* mentioned: they all involve something that is fundamentally capable of being received through a deliberate act of the person and transmitted. That sounds perhaps all too obvious. There are, however, definitions of the concept of "tradition", even at the formal level, that appear to overlook this common aspect. If, for example, one defines tradition as "the enduring persistence of life amid changing generations or changes in the stages of life" or as "the repetition of the same"[17] through which "the identity of beings"[18] is preserved, then evidently what is meant by the "to-be-handed-down" here is the unchangingly human, maybe even human "nature" itself—in other words, something that, in the strict sense of the term, we, as the persons handing it down, can neither transmit nor, as the persons to whom it is handed down, receive (or reject).

First, however, more should be said about the interlocutors who are brought together in the process of handing down. Regardless of

---

[17] G. Krüger, *Geschichte und Tradition*, p. 22. See also, by the same author, "Die Bedeutung der Tradition für die philosophische Forschung", *Studium Generale* 4 (1951): 321.

[18] Krüger, *Geschichte und Tradition*, p. 13.

whether the interlocutors being considered are individuals or generations of individuals, they are evidently being construed in such a way
that they do not stand in a relationship of mutual influence. There
is no back and forth; strictly speaking, no exchange of opinion occurs and, in fact, no exchange at all, not even a conversation or a
simple dialogue. But—it might immediately be objected—are there
not talks between father and son (assuming we are dealing with a
normal situation), in which both participate on an equal footing? To
which I would reply: Of course, there are many things that typically
pass between the generations that are *not* part of tradition! Even the
process of handing down itself may, when viewed from an external
standpoint, seem virtually indistinguishable from a discussion; on the
empirical level, the two may be intertwined with one another and
may even coalesce into one another. Still, tradition is, in principle,
very different from a discussion. Between the generations a learning
process normally takes place; and perhaps this process makes up the
largest part of all that which transpires between them. Still, learning is
one thing, but there is a major distinction to be made—a difference
that will be discussed in more detail later—between having something
handed down to one and accepting something that has been handed
down. As was already mentioned, however, the distinction can be so
slight as to be almost imperceptible in the concrete case.

Even in the Platonic dialogues, which may be considered the classic
example of a discussion or a "common inquiry", as Socrates prefers
to call it, it is very easy to read past the point at which critical mass is
suddenly reached and the conversation, in which friends, opponents,
and students participate with equal right, despite marked differences
in status, unexpectedly turns into an act of handing down. When, for
example, Socrates, at the end of the dialogue *Gorgias*, recounts the
myth of the court of final judgment or when in the *Symposium* Diotima initiates Socrates into the mysteries of the soul's ascent to the
archetypal idea of the beautiful, that is something which, by virtue of
its inherent structure, is utterly different from the preceding debates.
Although it is true that Socrates does not turn completely mute in
the presence of Diotima, he does not speak to her as an equal; he
asks and receives an answer; he is rebuked; he is, strictly speaking,
one who hears and listens. What is taking place is not a conversation
but an act of tradition.

The interlocutors who encounter one another in the process of handing down do not therefore stand on an equal footing—which does not in itself imply that they must be at differing levels of intellectual ability. The person handing down is the one who speaks; the one who receives what is handed down is at the same time a listener. Moreover, the two are not, in a certain sense of the word, contemporaneous with one another; they are not, as it were, the same age. Of course, even a conversation, an exchange of ideas back and forth, takes place over time; and, in fact, the answer always comes after the question, and the objection before the rejoinder. Still, something else is meant by this. Whoever attentively receives a *traditum* receives it as a member or representative of the coming generation; even if, in point of fact, he is greater in years than the one handing down the tradition, he is still the "younger" and the heir, to whom what is to be handed down is to be entrusted far into the future. Thus Paul calls those who accept his gospel his "sons" (1 Cor 4:14).

Does not the same apply to the relationship between the teacher and his pupils? And is "handing down" really not the same in principle as "teaching"? It must be conceded that this does, in fact, correspond to one use of the word; in Latin, as well as in Greek, one occasionally finds the words exchanged for one another. "And when he hands them over, we call it 'teaching' "[19]—this is how it stands in Plato. And in Latin it is the same, "from Cicero and Caesar to today's papal bulls".[20] Nevertheless, I think it will prove worthwhile to attend very closely to the meaning of these key concepts, as determined by linguistic usage, even if we sometimes run the risk of losing our patience. Here is an example of how an apparently negligible lack of precision can lead to an extremely momentous obfuscation of whole clusters of concepts. The number of examples can be multiplied indefinitely; there is simply no possibility of clarification or understanding except on the basis of linguistic usage as factually given. Whoever offers a divergent definition, one that at first glance may even appear seductively exact, remains inevitably bound in his

---

[19] *Theaetetus* 198b4. [Quoted after the translation by F. M. Cornford, in *Plato: The Collected Dialogues*, ed. Edith Hamilton and Huntington Cairns (Princeton, 1961), p. 904.]

[20] Cf. A. Deneffe, *Der Traditionsbegriff* (Münster in Westfalen, 1931), pp. 17ff. An entire chapter of this book is entitled "Tradere gleich lehren" (Handing down is the same as teaching).

spontaneous thinking and speaking to linguistic usage—with the result that he himself is continually violating the univocity of his own
terminological convention. Since, however, linguistic usage, as factually given, includes an incalculable multitude of things—for example,
the fact that a word can*not* be used in a specific context—it is by
no means easy to circumscribe explicitly the full sense of a word, as
given by linguistic usage, although everyone, as speaker and hearer,
has it steadfastly in mind and intends it.

To put the question another way: Is tradition, insofar as what is
meant is the handing down of truth, not the same in essence as the
didactic communication of the known from generation to generation?
In short, are not the words "tradition" and "teaching" synonymous,
after all? In response, I would like to submit the following for consideration: The sheer fact that a synonym can be substituted at all
for a certain word without changing the sentence's meaning suggests
already from the outset that what is at issue is not authentic but inauthentic word usage. As long as I can exchange "mean", "suspect", or
"assume" for "believe" (in a sentence like "I believe that it will rain
tomorrow"), I have not yet used the word "believe" in its strict and
authentic sense.[21] As soon as I do this, however, from that moment
on there is no longer any substitute or synonym at my disposal. Undoubtedly any "handing down" (in the strict sense) may be characterized as a "teaching" (in the inauthentic sense), if one understands
by "teaching" nothing more than bringing something to someone's
attention that he had not previously known. In the same way one also
says that someone who describes an incident to me "informs" me of
what has happened—although, as everyone knows, "teaching" and
"instructing" mean something different, strictly speaking, from "re-
porting". And even "handing down" and "teaching" are two fundamentally different things, if one understands each concept in its strict
sense.

This becomes even more apparent if one examines the composition
of the word a little more closely. In the word "tradition", is concealed
the preposition *trans*. The French language, which, in contradistinc-
tion to Latin and German, has, of course, no verb directly derived
from "tradition", brings this out clearly insofar as it designates the

---

[21] Cf. J. Pieper, *Über den Glauben* (Munich, 1962), pp. 26f.

act of "handing down" or "tradition" as *transmettre* ("transmit"). This "*trans-*", however, when it is combined with a verb that expresses a goal-oriented motion, contains, it seems, a clear reference to *three* different locations. Even the word "transport" (to take one example) implies not only that something is being brought somewhere but also that something is being brought from one location, at which the transporting person does not yet find himself, to another, that is, a third, location. This implies that one can speak of an act of "handing down" or tradition in the strict sense only if the person handing down derives what he is communicating, not from within himself, but "from somewhere else".[22] This same conceptual element also comes to the fore in the verb with which the English language designates the activity of transmission. I am referring to the verb "to hand down". Although this "down" would be worth a separate and independent investigation (handed *down* from a still *up*coming event?), it seems to me to be even more instructive to reflect on the two directions to this activity, as implied by linguistic usage: "to hand down from . . ." and "to hand down to (a person)". Here, too, there are the three locations: someone who is at a particular location hands something from somewhere else "down" to another person. "To hand down" does not mean simply to give, bring, communicate, or hand out something to someone; rather it means to hand something out [*aushändigen*] that had previously made its way into one's own hands [*in die eigene Hand Gelangtes*], something handed-over [*etwas Eingehändigtes*]; to communicate something that has come into our possession [*etwas Bekommenes*], something that has come down to us [*etwas Überkommenes*]; to pass something received on so that it, too, can, in turn, be received and passed on.

"I have received from the Lord what I also delivered to you"; "I

---

[22] A. Deneffe, in a very clear and clarifying study of the concept of tradition, asserts that it does "not [belong] to the concept of *traditio* that something received is transmitted" (pp. 13 and 5), and he appeals to the words of Jesus, "Omnia mihi tradita sunt a Patre meo" (Mt 11:27). To this I would reply that there is, of course, here, in the specific case of the word *tradere*, the possibility of an inauthentic usage as well; in the Bible, *tradere* sometimes also means the same as "to betray" or "to be delivered unto the mercy of". As far as the German is concerned, one could hardly render the *tradere* in Jesus' words as cited above with "handing down" (*überliefern*) but could only correctly translate it as "conferred" (*übertragen*) or "entrusted" (*übergeben*).

delivered to you as of first importance what I also received"; "what they received from the fathers they passed on to the sons" (quod a patribus acceperunt, hoc filiis tradiderunt). These three sentences, the first two of which are citations from Paul,[23] the last stemming from a work by Augustine,[24] express relatively precisely the inner form of the act of "handing down".

At the same time, a crucial difference vis-à-vis the act of teaching has become evident. If a researcher communicates to his students what he has worked out on his own—his personal results and findings—it is clear that learning in the strict sense is clearly taking place, but that is not tradition.

To the process of teaching corresponds a process of learning on the part of the listener. And here again it must be emphasized that the act by which something handed down is received is something completely different in structure from learning. It is, however, clear that just as learning does not actually take place when one is addressed only from the lectern and the listener has not in reality learned anything but goes off, having been "lectured" to, so the process of "handing down" can only then be completely realized when the last in the series, the younger generation in each case, accepts and receives the tradendum. If that fails to happen, for whatever reason, then, strictly speaking, there is no carrying on of tradition. One reason for its not having been received may very well be the style in which what is to be handed down is presented and offered. And obstacles of this kind are continually being erected by that generation which happens to find itself at the rudder. One can hardly engage in a more hopeless endeavor, for example, than to respond to a young person's critical question of why (and for what reason) something that has been handed down should continue to be upheld with the observation that it is "just that way". Such a dodge already proves, incidentally, that the paternal generation is no longer able to bring about the living presence of what has been handed down and that this is already a case of what has been called "poor preservation" [schlechte Bewahrung].

I was once the guest of a family in Calcutta, who, through the services of a Brahmin, had the rituals of orthodox Hinduism performed day by day in a room especially reserved for that purpose. The sons,

---

[23] 1 Cor 11:25, 15:3.
[24] Contra Julianum 2, 10, 34; Migne, PL 44, 698.

university students, only laughed in my face as I inquired after the purpose of specific procedures. And when I turned to the father, he shrugged his shoulders and said, "This has been done for a thousand years." When, shortly thereafter, I left the house with one of his sons, he complained to me bitterly that he had never received any other kind of explanation.

Whoever wishes to hand down something cannot simply speak of tradition but must take care to ensure that the content of what is to be handed down—the "old truths" (assuming they are really true) —is kept alive, primarily and paradigmatically through a living language, but also through creative rejuvenation and the "casting off" of its old skin, as it were, through an unrelenting confrontation with the immediate living present and particularly with the future, which in the human realm is the genuinely real. With this it should already have become obvious what an ambitious activity the act of handing down traditions is. An ancient Hebraic proverb has it that "it is more difficult to learn the old than to learn something new."[25] Above all, however, it has become evident how little a genuine handing down resembles something purely static and how wrong it is to think of the concept of "tradition" in connection with inertia or even stagnation. The living transmission of a *traditum* is, in reality, a highly dynamic process.

Still, in what follows, we shall be speaking less about the act of handing down and more about the act of receiving. How is it possible that the last in the series really comes to share in the tradition? Evidently by accepting and receiving what is offered him by the person involved in the process of handing down. But what kind of act is this act of accepting and receiving? In any event it is not simply an act of ac-knowledging [*Kenntnisnehmen*] and of having knowledge [*Kenntnishaben*]. Just as the person handing down (and perhaps even the true teacher as well) does not wish simply to "inform", so acceptance of the *tradendum* is not consistent with the attitude of someone who takes in information. The enactment of tradition does not in any way take the form of "information."[26]

---

[25] L. Ziegler (*Menschwerdung* [Olten, 1948], 1:46) quotes this maxim from P. Vulliaud, *La Clé traditionelle des Évangiles.*

[26] On the other hand, it is at the very least problematic to define tradition as "the ability to preserve and transmit noninformational knowledge" the way Lezcek Kolakowski does ("Vom Sinn der Tradition", *Merkur* 26 [December 1969]: 1086).

It is possible for someone—a historian, for example—to possess a very detailed and extensive knowledge of the *tradita* without accepting them; in such cases he stands outside the tradition. Perhaps it is precisely this knowledge that acts as an impediment. "The tradition is vanishing even though all the documents might still be there."[27] This phrase of Karl Jaspers' raises the issue of the relation between history and tradition, a multi-layered problem. The acceptance of the *tradita* naturally presupposes that one knows what they are; and it is certainly true "that we through the historical and philological labors of the past century have a more direct and perhaps even richer share in the teachings of the 'ancients'—and not just those of the European world—than any previous epoch in recorded history".[28] The acceptance of the *tradita* is in itself not only something fundamentally different from historical knowledge; it is directly threatened by it.[29] Thus, it may be said in all seriousness that the blame for the modern "loss of tradition" and for "traditionless thinking" should be laid to the account of "historical consciousness".[30]

Whoever casts his glance at the historical record, which points up the various problems with the individual material elements out of which, say, the ancient myth of the last judgment is composed, will understandably find it difficult simply to accept the "message" concerning the last judgment expressed in Plato's myth as truth: In that myth, there are at first three judges; then four judges are named; the name *Minos* comes from Crete, where, however, it appears to have been, not a proper name, but a royal title; *Aiakos* derives from a completely different tradition, which is associated with the founding of Troy, but it also appears in the local public sayings of Agineta; the ambiguous word *Hades* refers to a person as well as a place; *Acheron*

---

[27] K. Jaspers, *Von der Wahrheit* (Munich, 1947), p. 838.

[28] Joachim Ritter, conversational comment in J. Pieper, *Begriff der Tradition*, p. 47.

[29] "In fact it is a genuine paradox surrounding the plight of historical thought in the nineteenth century that it preserves memory, on the one hand, but dissolves it, on the other; . . . that historicism would like to pass down tradition, on the one hand, but destroys this tradition, on the other" (Theodor Schieder, conversational comment in J. Pieper, *Begriff der Tradition*, p. 43).

[30] G. Krüger, "Bedeutung der Tradition", p. 325; see also p. 322. For more, see J. Ritter, "Aristoteles und die Vorsokratiker", *Felsefe Arkivi* (Istanbul), 1954, p. 21; reprinted in revised form in J. Ritter, *Metaphysik und Politik: Studien zu Aristoteles und Hegel* (Frankfurt am Main, 1969), pp. 34ff.

is the name of a river in Epirus, which at some points disappears below the earth's surface. Whoever allows this to run through his mind
will be more inclined to regard the entire myth as "a mere tale", just
as Callicles does in the Platonic dialogue *Gorgias*. Socrates, however,
says, "I believe it to be true."[31] And he assumes its truth; he allows
himself to be informed of it, *although* he knows and also asserts that
no reasonable man ought to insist that the facts are exactly as he
has described them.[32] In other words, the materials from which the
message is shaped, molded, and formed and the covering in which it
is conveyed are not decisive. What is decisive is the message itself,
whose point it is that there occurs on the other side of death an event,
transpiring between the divine and mortal realms, in which the real
upshot of one's existence here on earth will finally be made manifest
and which is known in symbolic terms as the day of judgment. Only
this message is of significance for Socrates. In fact, he considers this
message to be of such authenticity that he is willing to orient his life
with regard to it.[33]

Now the act of accepting a *traditum*, into which we are inquiring
here, has precisely this structure. This is what the act of handing
down a *traditum* looks like when it is first brought to a conclusion
and completed, and it is only by virtue of this act that one "stands
in a tradition" and so comes to have a share in it. It is a "receiving"
in the strictest sense of the term, a listening and an allowing oneself
to be informed. I accept something that others offer and extend to
me; I allow myself to be given it by them; this means that I do not
take it for myself; I do not procure it by my own means. Conversely,
I accept the *traditum*, not "because it has been handed down", but
because I am convinced that it is true and authentic. I am unable,
however, to determine, either through experience or through rational
argumentation, whether this is actually true. Here I find myself in
fundamentally the same position as Socrates when confronted with
the prophecy of the last judgment. If it were not so, then I would
not have to let myself be informed of the message by someone else:
indeed, I would already know it myself.

---

[31] *Gorgias* 523a8–b1.
[32] *Phaedo* 114d1.
[33] Ibid., 114d6.

Taken together, all this implies that the acceptance and receipt of what has been handed down has the structure of belief: it *is* belief. For belief means accepting something as true and authentic, not on the basis of one's own personal insight, but insofar as one relies on someone else. It is still too early to discuss who, in the process of handing down a *traditum*, this "other" is, whether the penultimate in the series or perhaps the first.

Thus tradition is, as we have argued, something other than learning; and to accept something that has been handed down is not the same as learning. But does not the learner, according to Aristotle's well-known dictum,[34] also have to believe? That is true. But it is only true of the first stage in learning. It is not critical reflection, which stands at the beginning of all learning,[35] but rather an act of trust that allows one to adopt uncritically what the teacher says; this is, of course, even more true of the relationship between the child, before he reaches maturity, and his mother. Without this uncritical beginning, that critical autonomy could never be achieved which transforms what is simply assumed into something one knows oneself. And only someone who has accomplished that has really "learned" something in the strict sense. Consequently, one could claim with some justification that in its earliest stage the process of learning is similar to that of handing down a *traditum*—similar, but not the same. An important difference is already to be found in the fact that the teacher is familiar with what he teaches and knows it through his own efforts, whereas the person handing down the *traditum* grasps it just as little as the one who receives it. No "older generation" knows more about the day of judgment than the last in the series, to whom they hand down this *traditum*.

It belongs to the nature of tradition that what is being handed down cannot be superseded by any experience or by any revelatory insight. And in those cases where such supersedure takes place, where something hitherto believed is converted into something demonstrated and known through critical reflection, the process loses in that same moment its character of being handed down (if it ever had it). The col-

---

[34] Aristotle, *Sophistic Refutations* 2.165b3–4.

[35] Cf. J. Pieper, "Platonische Figuren: Die Lernenden", in J. Pieper, *Tradition als Herausforderung* (Munich, 1963), pp. 269ff.

lective learning process, which occurs over generations and epochs, should also not be included in the notion of tradition. These are, in reality, two completely distinct strands in the historical fabric.

This seems the appropriate point at which to consider Alexander Rüstow's suggestion that tradition be construed as "the inheritance of acquired properties and achievements";[36] this is also reputed to be what distinguishes men from animals. In one of Wolfgang Köhler's famous experiments in animal psychology, a chimpanzee, Sultan, succeeded on his own in taking down a banana suspended in his cage by using two bamboo shoots—one inserted within the other—but it proved impossible for him to pass this achievement on to his offspring. "What is missing in animals, as distinct from men, is, strictly speaking, not spirit, but tradition—tradition as the possibility of propagating what has been generated from the spirit and so of multiplying and enriching it from generation to generation."[37] This sentence, which may perhaps at first appear somewhat plausible, is rife with inaccuracies. It is, for example, precisely the spiritual faculty that enables human beings to pass on not only the innate but also the acquired, and animals are incapable of this for the simple reason that spirit is "missing". Tradition, too, is only conceivable as a spiritual act. Still, the transmission of "achievements" is no more synonymous with tradition than "multiplying" is synonymous with "preserving".

This introduces yet another element in the concept of tradition into the discussion. It is precisely *this* element that distinguishes tradition from cultural progress. Cultural progress is tied to learning (in the strict sense) in the following manner: Something that is simply assumed at first is worked out by the next generation, "taken over" in critical autonomy on the basis of its own experience and intellectual labor, and then—in revised, diversified, and enriched form—passed on so that it can be learned, in turn, by the successor generation; in short, it is received at first uncritically but is then tested, corrected, supplemented, and enriched. In order to recognize more clearly what is unique about this process, one need only contrast it with the experience one occasionally has in the so-called "developing" countries where the available stock of cultural goods is simply

---

[36] A. Rüstow, "Kulturtradition und Kulturkritik", *Studium Generale* 4 (1951): 308.
[37] Ibid.

"adopted" but not actually "learned". The cultural autonomy of a people, on the other hand, is proved precisely in the ability to penetrate critically into the newly acquired and to progress beyond (and enlarge) the existing stock of cultural possessions. Only in this way does that continuous enlargement of a transmitted cultural stock occur which we call "progress".

Tradition, however, is something fundamentally different. Here the concept of "progress" is completely out of place; at any rate, it fails to capture the essence of the actual process. The notions of individual originality and creative autonomy also stand at several removes from this process. The definition already proposed—tradition is the transmission of something received, so that it can be received and transmitted in turn—should be taken more literally than one is perhaps initially inclined to do. In the aforementioned sentence from Augustine, in which I said the structure of the traditional act is precisely described—"quod a patribus acceperunt, hoc filiis tradiderunt"—the word *hoc* plays a role of some importance. It is precisely what is received that is transmitted and nothing else so that even the last in the series receives exactly the same *traditum* from his "father" that the first in the series handed down to his "son". The *traditum* is something that in the process of handing down simply does *not* grow. As long as the intention that is given along with the concept of tradition itself is able to persist undiluted, there is no accumulation, no enrichment, and no progression. This intention explicitly aims at ensuring that nothing is added to what was originally received; at the same time, nothing from the original content should be left out or forgotten.

This particular semantic element in the concept of tradition, as will soon become evident, has never been completely lost to linguistic usage or conventional patterns of thought. We are absolutely incapable of imagining "*holy* tradition", in particular, as the transmission of self-acquired "achievements", which have accumulated over the course of history. This impression appears even more plausible if one considers more closely some basic words and ideas that have always been thought in conjunction with tradition. The most important of these are the ideas of *preservation* and the *maintenance of purity*, which imply that the initial content, whether it be a doctrine, a directive, or an institution, should be preserved over time without loss of content or addition, unadulterated and unalloyed with alien and unrelated material, and kept present and, as it were, available. The Hebrew word for the appropriation of what has been handed down has the same meaning as "to repeat".[38] And the Indians of Asia refer to this act of appropriation with a word meaning "to repeat after someone else". Both designations convey, in turn, one thing above all else: that any type of deviation should be avoided, that nothing should be omitted, and that nothing should be added. Even the guiding metaphor behind the *thesaurus* of a treasure worth protecting has a similar sense, although it is perhaps not as unequivocal. The concept of the *depositum*, of the entrusted good, also belongs to this penumbra of ideas; one of its semantic elements suggests that it is something that cannot be violated by the preserver of the *traditum* but rather remains beyond his power of disposal. What is learned becomes our property; what has been handed down, however, we possess as a kind of a loan. The concept of *memory* is related to that of tradition and is classed together with it; common to both is the notion that something that was once experienced or said or something that once happened is kept present in consciousness or "re-presented" [*vergegenwärtigen*]. This has been pointed out many times. Tradition has even been called "the memory of society"[39] and "the ontological memory of cultures",[40] and the *mnemosyne* that mnemonic retention which ensures that "the present and the future do not lose their fullness of being."[41] To remember implies not only that one does not forget but also that one does not "add" anything. It would represent a nonsensical use of the term if one were to say that one "remembers" something that goes beyond the content of what was really experienced. Such a distortion of memory would be worse than simply forgetting.

The vital importance of tradition consists in the fact that, just as an old truism has it, "As Dr. Johnson said, 'people need to be reminded more often than they need to be instructed.' "[42] Human existence can

---

[38] W. Bacher, *Tradition und Tradenten in den Schulen Palästinas und Babyloniens* (Leipzig, 1914), p. 20.

[39] W. Solowjew, *Deutsche Gesamtausgabe*, ed. W. Szylkarski, vol 7 (Freiburg im Breisgau, 1953), p. 268.

[40] W. Iwanow, *Das Alte Wahre: Essays* (Frankfurt am Main, 1954), p. 160.

[41] J. Ritter, "Aristoteles und die Vorsokratiker", p. 49.

[42] Cf. C. S. Lewis, *Christian Behaviour* (London, 1943), p. 16.

come to harm not only by failing to learn more but also by forgetting and losing something indispensable.

III

If the way in which what has been handed down is accepted has the structure of "faith", that is, of relying on someone else, then this amounts to saying that tradition cannot be thought without reference to authority. Indeed, throughout the entire Middle Ages, "authority" was virtually synonymous with tradition itself. *Auctoritas* and *ratio*— these were the labels for the two means of proving oneself in Scholastic debate, that is, by having recourse to either tradition or reason. Goethe, in his *Materialien zur Geschichte der Farbenlehre* (Materials for a history of the theory of color), once examined this relationship, in which the concept of tradition is associated with that of authorization, from each side and formulated it this way: "Insofar as we will now be speaking of tradition, we are immediately called upon to speak of authority as well. For, strictly speaking, every authority is a kind of tradition."[43] The same thought may be found, clearly expressed, in Karl Jaspers, albeit more by way of a declarative statement and, as will soon become apparent, not without reservation: "The crystallization of tradition into fixed authority is inevitable; it is . . . existentially necessary because it [tradition] is the primary form of existential certitude for every awakening human existence."[44]

As to the reason for this identity—or, better said, essential connection—between tradition and authority, one might, as a summary first response, submit for general consideration the thought that someone who accepts a *traditum* as true and valid evidently does not himself possess access to that of which he allows himself to be informed by others. It belongs, so it would appear, to the very nature of the process of handing down a tradition that not only the final member but *all* the members of the series depend and rely on someone whom it is assumed was directly present at the origin of the *traditum* and so

---

[43] *Goethes Farbenlehre*, ed. G. Ipsen (Leipzig, n.d.), p. 553.

[44] K. Jaspers, *Philosophie*, p. 263. Hans-Georg Gadamer also describes tradition as "a form of authority" (*Wahrheit und Methode*, 2nd ed. [Tübingen, 1965], p. 264).

can give witness to and vouch for its authenticity. Thus it is through a greater immediacy of possession that the one handing down the tradition proves and justifies the authority of what is being handed down—not just the authority of the penultimate in the series, but the authority of the very first member.

Up until now, we have been speaking about the content of what has been handed down, first by implication and then increasingly by way of example; at this point it is still a matter of purely formal determinations, which are simply given along with the structure that governs the process for handing down traditions. But it has already become clear what kind of resistance is to be expected—and it was, in fact, clear from the very outset.

"Tradition stands in contradiction to rationality"—so writes Theodor W. Adorno in his otherwise inaccurate *Thesen über Tradition* (Theses on tradition).[45] This is a very Cartesian-sounding sentence.[46] From a purely formal standpoint, one need not automatically construe it—as the previous classification of *auctoritas* and *ratio* attests—as if it were simply denying the validity of tradition. If, however, the claim to "rationality" is construed as denying—as must at the very least be suspected—that there are existentially relevant facts that are on principle closed to critical examination by human thought, then all tradition is at the same time being consigned to the realm of the preliminary and provisional. Tradition in some absolute sense, that is, that tradition which can never be overtaken through an exercise of our reason and which can never be invalidated or superseded by an advance in science —such a conception of tradition could, in fact, never be accepted by someone who believes that it goes against the nature and dignity of man's spirit to hold any information concerning reality for true and valid that cannot be "verified" either by experience or rational argument. The affirmation of the reason's autonomy and the recognition of tradition exclude one another. If it is really true, as Karl Jaspers claims, that "the actual enemy of philosophizing" is authority,[47] then —despite all his magnificently formulated insights to the contrary— tradition is simultaneously being rejected as something unacceptable

---

[45] T. W. Adorno, *Ohne Leitbild: Parva Aesthetica* (Frankfurt am Main, 1967), p. 29.

[46] On this, see Gadamer, *Wahrheit und Methode*, p. 261.

[47] *Philosophie*, p. 265.

to the philosopher, both as a critically reflecting and an authentically spiritual person.

What exactly is it that one is relying on when one accepts a *traditum*? How is the authority that vouches for the authenticity of the *traditum* to be conceived concretely? In what historical form is this authority to be found embodied?

One of the epithets with which this authority has historically been designated is that of "the men of old" (*palaioí, archaîoi, antiqui, maiores*). So it might naturally be asked to whom this name refers: Who, then, are "the men of old"? Certainly it does not refer to the elders, the *senes*, the advanced in age, the experienced, the men "with snow-white hair"; the young Pascal had confused this meaning of the word with its actual meaning. It has occasionally been argued that at the very least "reverence for the aged" must be involved.[48] I do not believe that this is the case. It may very well be that the initiator of a series of *tradita* or, more precisely said, the first in this series, possesses at the same time the venerableness of old age; it may even be that he cannot so much as be imagined without this quality of venerableness. Still, the decisive element in the concept of "men of old" is not their many years, and "reverence for the aged" is something fundamentally different from reverence for the *palaioí*. The essential element in this concept is the proximity to origin, to primordiality, to what is earliest, to what marks the onset—the beginning. The counterpart to "the men of old" are the later-born, who no longer possess the immediacy of the origin; they are thus not the "young", regardless of whether, as in Pascal's formulation, what is accentuated in this concept is their inexperience or their still untapped potential for the future. Moreover the epithet "the men of old" is clearly intended as an honorific title; it connotes the exact opposite of someone who has outlived himself, whose time has passed. On Plato's view, which carries some weight on this topic, the "wisdom of the men of old" is the undyingly topical that "lives in the words of all".[49] "[T]hey alone know the truth of it. However, if we could discover that for ourselves, should we still be concerned with the fancies of mankind?"[50] Incidentally, this is also what distinguishes the "men of old" from pioneers and groundbreak-

---

[48] Cf. Pieper, *Begriff der Tradition*, p. 52.

[49] *Laws* 881a2.

[50] *Phaedrus* 274c1. [Quoted after the translation by R. Hackforth, in *Plato: The Collected Dialogues*, p. 520.]

ers in the scientific arena. It is true that they continue to be held in high esteem, and one commemorates their achievements when once again the hundredth anniversary of their birth or death is indicated on the calendar. They are, however, no longer really topical. They are outdated, and their achievements have in the meantime been revised in many ways—by the progress that they themselves helped initiate. Their results and data are now of only "historical" interest. By contrast, one may say of the "men of old" that they occupy within the realm of traditional knowledge the same place that the men making the latest discoveries have earned in the realm of research.

It has also been argued, following Aristotle, that the "men of old" are the poets; he even calls them the *pampalaioí*, the primordial "men of old".[51] I am not so certain that Aristotle really regards the "poetic" as what is decisive here. Plato, moreover, made a distinction between the "divine" poets[52] and all the others, to whom he evidently denied this attribute. The former he reckons among those "who are wise in divine things"; the latter, however, he does not rank among them (I am thinking of personages like Agathon). This notwithstanding, one would have to say that although the "men of old" might very well be thought of as poets, it is by no means the "poetic" that determines membership in that circle consisting of the "men of old". There is even less cause to identify the "men of old" with the great philosophers, those "noble spirits" of whom Hegel said that they "have through the boldness of their reason penetrated into the nature of things, of man, and of God, revealed to us their depth, and acquired for us through their effort that treasure which is the highest form of knowledge".[53] The status attaching to "the men of old" is grounded, not in the geniality and boldness of their thoughts, but rather in the fact that they are, in a thoroughly unusual manner, the recipients of a thoroughly unusual gift.

In Plato, who refers to the "men of old" several times[54] by this

---

[51] J. Ritter, "Aristoteles und die Vorsokratiker", p. 44.

[52] *Meno* 81b1.

[53] *Vorlesungen über die Geschichte der Philosophie*, vol. 1, Sämtliche Werke: Kritische Ausgabe, ed. J. Hoffmeister (Leipzig, 1940), 15a:6.

[54] It seems to me somewhat problematic that only a single source text is listed in Apelt's *Platon-Index*, 2nd ed. (Leipzig, 1923) when one could easily count roughly thirty. In this respect the (unpublished) study by Heinrich Rumphorst, then a student in Berlin, has proven useful to me (*Überlieferung bei Platon*, 1953).

258   FOR THE LOVE OF WISDOM

epithet in his dialogues, they remain anonymous; they do not figure
in them as living presences the way Crito and Phaedo do. As already
indicated, they are generally referred to as the *palaioí* and the *archaíoi*,
but they are not given proper names. Frequently, their presence is concealed even more unrecognizably behind the expression *pálai légetai*,
which is translated as "it has been said since ancient times" or "there
is an ancient doctrine." This implies, first of all, that we are initially
being referred to the obscure early days of a *pálai*, of the primordial
beginning, of a primeval age, which is neither imaginable nor datable.
This should not be taken to reflect some romantically vague notion.
Rather we have been furnished with a reasonably precise account of
who, in Plato's opinion, the "men of old" are and what the significance of their achievement is. This information can be found in a
relatively well-known and patently influential[55] passage of the dialogue
Philebus. There the conversation turns around the question of how the
one and the many are intertwined in the being of things. Neither the
technical problem nor its actual significance need be addressed here; it
is enough to recognize that, in the event, it concerns the inner structure of reality; even in the medieval theory of being this problem
is closely associated with the subject of "creation".[56] What for our
purposes is alone important, however, is that Socrates, in examining,
with uncommon radicalism, the origin of this insight into the one
and the many unexpectedly alludes to the "men of old". "There is
a gift of the gods . . . which they let fall from their abode, and it
was through [a certain unknown] Prometheus, or one like him, that
it reached mankind, together with a fire exceeding bright. The men
of old [*palaioí*], who were better than ourselves and dwelt nearer the
gods, passed on [*parédosan*] this gift in the form of a saying."[57] This is
the definitive Platonic statement on the status and authority of "the
men of old". Their claim to dignity lies in the fact that they received
a message, a *phéme*, something uttered, from the divine wellspring and
that they have passed down what has been received in this way. This
alone is the reason why they are called the "men of old".[58]

---

[55] Cf. K. Reinhardt's article on *Poseidonius* in Pauly-Wissowa, *Real-Encyclopädie der classischen Altertumswissenschaft*, vol. 22, col. 572.

[56] See, for example, Thomas Aquinas I, 47, and *Comp. theol.* I, 102.

[57] *Philebus* 16c5–9. [Quoted after the translation by R. Hackforth, in *Plato: The Collected Dialogues*, p. 1092.]

[58] There is, however, in both the general and the specifically Platonic idiom, a *broader* no-

With this statement of Plato's, something else has at the same time become clear, that is, a still more precise answer to our original question concerning the origin of tradition. This was our question: On whom does the last in the series depend and rely? Whom is he actually "believing" when he accepts what has been handed down as true and authentic? What ultimately provides the surety for what is handed down? The attention of anyone raising this question is naturally directed toward the beginning of the series for a specific tradition, to the first member in that chain. If it truly belongs to the notion of a tradition that what is transmitted by each of the members involved in handing down that tradition, including the first in the series, is something received, meaning that it can neither be acquired nor superseded by original insight, then how and where does this first receive the *tradendum* that is to be handed down from then on? Insofar as Plato responds by pointing to the gods and to the message that has come down to us from them, he is giving us to understand that whoever accepts what has been handed down and "believes" is not ultimately or in the strict sense relying on "the men of old" but rather on the gods themselves—and on the fact that what has been given in the earliest communication within the series of *tradita* (traditional sequence) has really reached him undistorted by time and by the passing of generations.

Incidentally, Plato is far from being alone in holding this view. Not only does the Roman belief in the proximity of "the men of old" to the gods respond to Plato's concerns in much the same terms, perhaps having even been inspired by him ("antiquitas proxime accedit ad deos", writes Cicero,[59] antiquity stands in utmost proximity to the gods), but what is truly exciting about this view—in which we are interested now not as Plato exegetes or even more generally as intellectual historians—is that Plato's position on this issue broadly coincides with the answer that Christian theology, for its part, offers to the same question; through this answer, however, the wisdom of antiquity receives for the backward-looking observer a new significance, one that the ancient philosophers themselves could hardly have anticipated. If one considers the individual elements of the Platonic

---

tion according to which the "men of old" includes all spirits of the past whose thoughts and doctrines are nourished by the tradition of truth that goes back to the divine wellspring. For more on this, see J. Pieper, *Was heißt Akademisch?* (Munich, 1952), pp. 76ff.

[59] *De legebus* 2, 27.

characterization—the "men of old" are closer to the divine realm than the average person could be; they are "better" (*kreíttones*) than we are ("better" referring here to a richer plenitude of human existence rather than to morality as such); they are the first recipients of a message drawn from a divine source that they then pass on to mankind—if one considers these elements in order, then it is hardly questionable that there obtains at the very least a deep-running analogy between this description of the men of old and those conceptual determinations that Christian theology attributes to the "prophets", the "hagiographers", the divinely chosen charismatics, the inspired in the strict sense, and the authors of a holy book. The affinity, for which "analogy" is perhaps too weak a word, consists in the fact that both the "men of old" and the prophets are conceived as the first recipients[60] and transmitters of a *theios logos*, a divine saying.

At this point, we must consider a not completely unexpected objection that has been raised by certain Christian theologians and that is based only in part on a simple misunderstanding. No one, after all, can be surprised by the fact that a theology that has turned the future and hope into its more or less exclusive concern would suspect all talk of tradition—and talk involving "the men of old" even more so —of being nothing more than a kind of mythologically archaized romanticism. Can, then, the sheer fact of having been uttered "in olden times" or "since ancient times" seriously be considered a "proof of authenticity"?[61] This question is, however, truly based on a misunderstanding, which is relatively easily resolved. Of course, what is constitutive of that "wisdom" which belongs to the "men of old" is not its being "from olden times"—not even on Plato's view—but rather its descent from the divine wellspring. Moreover, the "men of old" do not stand at the very beginning of time; they are only the earliest members in a series of *tradita*, the first recipients of the revelation. And when, "under Pontius Pilate", revelation occurs anew in history, its first recipients likewise have the quality that Plato ascribes to the "men of old". Thus it cannot be considered an objection to this view that Christianity understood itself historically to be the initiator of a

---

[60] Nikolaus Monzel (*Die Überlieferung* [Bonn, 1950], p. 129) speaks in this context of the "original recipients of revelation" (*ursprüngliche Offenbarungsempfänger*).

[61] J. Moltmann, *Theologie der Hoffnung*, 2nd ed. (Munich, 1965), pp. 272f.

series of *tradita* (traditional succession) that begins with a new divine message, to be something "new".

It is admittedly more difficult to address another type of reservation, namely, the claim, offered in the form of an objection, that for traditional thinking revelation stands "at the beginning".[62] This sentence is not entirely clear: either it means that "at the beginning" a divine revelation took place, or it may mean, again, that it is part of the concept of revelation to be something primeval. The former conception is, of course, something that cannot be accepted by any Christian; the revelation of Jesus Christ did not occur "at the beginning" but rather "in the fullness of time". Plato, however, and with him countless other souls existing prior to and outside the Christian world found themselves and continue to find themselves in a fundamentally different situation. In fact, no other divine word had (or has) made its way down to them than the message embodied—and to that extent also concealed—in the traditional mythological narratives "from the olden times", like that concerning the day of judgment. I am convinced, however, in agreement with countless Christian teachers whose ranks extend from Justin and Augustine to John Henry Newman, that this message truly refers to a divine revelation that took place at the beginning, that is, to a "primordial revelation". By the same token, I am not committed to responding with a simple "yes" to the critical question of whether "the apostles [are] to be equated with the Plato's primordial men of old."[63] At the very least, I would insist that they are bound by a crucial affinity. Not only are both to be understood as the first recipients of a message descended from the divine realm and hence as the earliest members corresponding to a series of *tradita* that emanate from it; there is an even deeper affinity—visible only to Christians—with regard to the ultimate origin of that message, to which they bear witness, that origin being one and the same divine *logos* that became man in Christ.

In any event, the notion of revelation is automatically invoked anytime I inquire radically enough into the reasons behind the binding character of tradition. The notion need not be analyzed in detail here, although it should not be relegated exclusively to the realm of theological debate. In the end, revelation does not arise as a topic within

---

[62] Ibid., p. 273.
[63] Ibid.

theology but is rather a pretheological assumption, an assumption in the absence of which theology cannot legitimately exist, at least insofar as one means by theology the interpretation of revelation. If one takes philosophy in the same sense that philosophers from Plato and Aristotle to Immanuel Kant and Karl Jaspers have understood it, then the philosophical consideration of world and human existence in their full reality can hardly excuse itself from the (admittedly) extremely difficult task of at least entertaining the question of whether—given our entire critical understanding of man and reality—it is meaningful to say (and, if so, in what sense) that God spoke expressly to man in a manner comprehensible to him.

But have we not, with all this, completely deviated from our actual topic? In the beginning, we had set out to do nothing more than to identify the individual elements in the concept of tradition. Now, I believe that we are actually still in the process of responding to this question. The last point we had been discussing was the following: If someone who accepts a *traditum* as truth necessarily has to rely and depend on someone else, who, then, is this other, and what enables him for his part to provide surety for the truth of the *traditum*? It is clear that we have, in keeping with our initially declared purpose, restricted our attention to the handing down of theory and worldview to what one might call the "traditional wisdom". Now, in the attempt to give a name to the surety for those truths that have been handed down, our attention was directed, not entirely coincidentally, to Plato and his references to the "men of old". And a more precise analysis of this expression then led unexpectedly to the notion of "revelation". It is in the final analysis a divine saying on which Socrates relies when he accepts a message handed down "from the olden times" and makes it a guiding principle for his own behavior; his support is derived from the authority of revelation. With this, that fundamental affinity suddenly came into view which connects the Platonic conception of that wisdom possessed by the "men of old" with the Christian idea of a holy tradition as grounded in the prophets and the divinely inspired speakers insofar as they are the "original recipients of revelation" (*ursprüngliche Offenbarungsempfänger*).[64]

Granted, someone might here object: But there is obviously more to tradition than simply *holy* tradition. Is it not evident that there are

---

[64] N. Monzel, *Die Überlieferung*, p. 129.

also profane and even unholy traditions throughout all the realms of public life? This, of course, cannot be denied, although, as will soon emerge, the situation is more complicated than one may perhaps think. One thing, I would argue, has already become clear: a tradition of truth can be conceived only as something definitive, that is, as something that cannot, on principle, be superseded by human thought, if one is at the same time convinced that what is being handed down through it is ultimately based on divine speech, that is, revelation in the strict sense. To this extent, Scholastic theology is correct in virtually identifying tradition and revelation[65] and construing tradition as "simply the consistent development of the idea of revelation itself".[66] In another respect, however, it is incorrect, a point on which we shall soon have more to say.

Whoever, on the contrary, believes that it is impossible for something like "revelation" or "God's word" to exist at all must on pain of inconsistency not only regard any passing on of truth as provisional, contingent on its being overcome and eliminated one day though an advance in critical reasoning; more importantly, he must regard it as something that can bind no one in earnest. Authority—that is, on the one hand, authentication, reliability, surety, guarantee; at the same time, however, it also implies an unequivocal claim to being binding. A tradition, though, can be absolutely binding, that is, obligatory for everyone, only on the assumption that it is validated by a divine authority, that is, that it has its origin in revelation.

There is, however, another presupposition simultaneously being made here of which the modern consciousness, in particular, is ordinarily unaware. It is being presupposed, namely, that *not* everyone possesses immediate access to revelation; that, on the contrary, the average man—even if he were above average to the point of being a genius—could only participate in the divine communication by forming a community with its first recipients, with the "men of old", through listening. To acknowledge this is to deny the claims of "free subjectivity", which has been described as "the specifically modern form of

---

[65] "Materially, formally, and objectively, tradition and revelation . . . coincide. Everything that is the object of revelation, and only that which is its object, is also the object of . . . tradition" (Deneffe, *Traditionsbegriff*, p. 114). See also Gerhard Gloege, *Offenbarung und Überlieferung* (Hamburg, 1954), pp. 14, 27, 40.

[66] M. J. Scheeben, *Handbuch der katholischen Dogmatik*, vol. 1 (Freiburg im Breisgau, 1948), p. 44 (par. 61).

religion". If the individual consciousness has an "immediate relation to the absolute" [*unmittelbar zum Absoluten*],[67] then, of course, it does not require the intermediation of tradition. If, on the other hand, this intermediation is understood and affirmed as unavoidable, then that implies at the same time that the binding force of tradition extends as far and as deep as the binding force of the divine communication itself.

This binding force reveals its true power, however, only when the actual *content* of what is being handed down is also discussed—that content being what lays claim to our acceptance in such an absolute manner.

What, then, is the content of the message that is being offered to man in holy tradition as something to be received? It goes without saying that this unique claim to obligatoriness cannot be associated with irrelevant contents. It would be simply intolerable to man as a personal being to have to assert "it is so and not otherwise" without having the possibility to examine critically whether what was to be believed did not affect the very center of our world and the core of human existence. Precisely this possibility, however, lends to the claim its full weight. It is, in fact, just such objects that, insofar as they affect the core and the center, are the subject of that wisdom possessed by the "men of old".

Let us cast our glance again at Plato. What is the content, as indicated by the dialogues, of the "message passed down since olden times"? It says that the world came to be through the goodness of a creator free from jealousy;[68] that God holds in his hands the beginning, end, and middle of all that is;[69] that spirit rules over all things;[70] that man lost his original perfection through sin and punishment; that on the other side of death an absolutely just judgment awaits; that the soul is immortal, and so on. But even Aristotle, by a wide margin the more sober and the more critical of the two, says with patent approval in the *Metaphysics*: "Our forefathers in the most remote ages [*pampalaioí*] have handed down to us their posterity a tradition . . .

[67] H. Scholz, *Religionsphilosophie* (Berlin, 1921), p. 269.
[68] *Timaeus* 29e1–4.
[69] *Laws* 715e7–716a1.
[70] *Philebus* 30d8.

that the divine encloses the whole of nature."[71] If, now, one again examines the handing down of Christian dogma in the light of these findings, one soon sees oneself confronted with strongly voiced objections that come down to the following: surely, one does not wish to maintain in all seriousness that "the content of the Greek tradition 'from olden times' [is] the same as the content of the Christian Annunciation"?[72] On one point, I unhesitatingly agree with the critical poser of this question: Neither Plato nor any other pre-Christian or non-Christian spirit could ever have had even the vaguest notion of God's Incarnation as man or of the suffering and the Resurrection of Christ. As it is, a great Christian theologian, Thomas Aquinas, did not shrink from thinking and asserting that it was possible for someone to believe, without the explicit revelation of Christ, that God, in a manner pleasing to him, will be the "liberator of man"—which amounts to believing *fide implicita* in Christ.[73] Thus it does not appear to me to be so completely unthinkable that, even given the profound uniqueness and novelty of the Christian revelation, there could still be an affinity of content between the "holy tradition" to which Plato, for example, alludes and the Christian Annunciation. In both cases, it is maintained that God himself vouches for the purposefulness of the world and for human salvation. If, however, this by its nature extremely summary description accurately points up their affinity of content, then not only are we justified in linking the revelation and promise that have been given to us in Christ with the primeval beginning of human history and with what humanity prior to and outside Christianity believed "in olden times" to be sacred truth and preserved for millennia afterward—we are practically obliged to do so. After all, the expression *pálai légetai*, which stands for the divine speech that "since time immemorial" reverberates throughout human history, occurs not only in the Platonic dialogues but also in the opening verse of the Letter to the Hebrews in the New Testament.

Thus, if the *tradita* within the holy tradition are so constituted that their message, after having been passed down and received, can be

---

[71] *Metaphysics* 12.8.1074b1. [Quoted after the translation in Jonathan Barnes, ed., *The Complete Works of Aristotle: The Revised Oxford Translation*, vol. 2 (Princeton, 1984), p. 1698.]

[72] J. Moltmann, *Theologie der Hoffnung*, p. 273.

[73] II, II, 2, 7 ad 3.

received, in turn, then the question of why we are bound by this receiving and handing down can now be answered more adequately. From a theoretical standpoint, at any rate, such an answer is indeed possible. In reality, however, both the question and its answer tend to find their expression in a very concrete historical situation—one almost wants to say here at a certain stage in the altercation between fathers and sons—and the question, as well as its answer, can differ greatly from those explanations that are "in themselves" possible. It is completely normal and understandable that each new generation initially calls into question its obligation to the tradition. And indeed there is not yet anything particularly praiseworthy about the rather straightforward suggestion that what has been thought, said, and done "since times immemorial" should simply continue to be thought, said, and done. The glory that attaches to that which is meritorious in tradition and in the process of being handed down can only meaningfully be found in the recognition that throughout the generations *what is in truth worthy of being preserved* has been preserved and continues to be preserved. It is precisely this toward which the doubts of the young are mainly directed. How has an obligation been violated if we simply leave what has been handed down as it is in order to say, think, and do something entirely different? And one can only hope that this radical question finds an audience and an existentially credible and equally radical answer, that the new generation receives "the" answer, the one that aims at the whole: that under the many things that may have accumulated under the rubric of "tradition" and that are more or less worth preserving, there is ultimately *one* instance of tradition that it is absolutely necessary to preserve, that is, that gift which is received and passed down in the holy tradition. It is necessary because what is being handed down has its origin in the divine wellspring; because each generation of human beings needs it in order to lead a truly human existence; because no people and no individual, however brilliant, can substitute for it out of their own resources or even add anything authentic to it.

IV

Now the time has come to explore the long-postponed and steadily mounting objection to the effect that tradition amounts to more than simply *holy* tradition. As already noted, the force of this objection must first be granted. Anytime and anywhere behavioral norms, customs, ideas, opinions, or institutions are transmitted from generation to generation—if not perforce as something straightforwardly binding, then certainly as something that has been received without having been explicitly subjected to critical questioning—tradition occurs: If one wanted to bring the diverse forms of such thoroughly "mundane" traditions into an even vaguely perspicuous order, there would be no end to it.

And it is of vital importance for our shared public life that there are also such traditions as these. In particular, they assist in the indispensable emancipation and relief of both the individual consciousness and our social mechanisms. Social life runs more smoothly, and mortal energies may be devoted exclusively to their actual purposes —if only because, on the basis of the prevailing traditions, it goes without saying, for example, that we greet one another on the street; that, in the presence of a stranger, we introduce ourselves; that we say thank you for help provided; that we adhere to the conventional forms of address; that we do not discuss private and intimate thoughts with just anyone, and so on. "The reality of customs . . . is and remains for the most part something factual depending on provenance and tradition. They are assumed in freedom but are not in any way created by free insight or justified in their validity."[74] It would lead to a hardly sustainable complication of public life if the individual had first to decide on the basis of critical deliberation what "one" should do in each case.

The *Wandervogel* generation,[*] which after the First World War called into question the use of the polite second-person form, *Sie,* among many other "bourgeois" customs, might, of course, have defended this practice with many critical arguments drawn from history: Why

---

[74] Gadamer, *Wahrheit und Methode,* p. 265.

[*] [A German youth movement begun in the late nineteenth century.— TRANS.]

do we happen to address one another with the same form as the third-person plural, as if at the Spanish court? But what a disproportionate expenditure of effort and waste of energy it would be to introduce a new form of address (*Ihr*)! In my childhood no one said, on taking leave of someone else, *Auf Wiedersehen*; this now completely traditional greeting, which the rest of the world has always regarded as typically German, first replaced the French *Adieu*, which had up to that time been uncontroversial, in the years 1914 and 1915 after an act of "national" propaganda. Would it have been worthwhile to resist the change? Perhaps, one day, an expert in the psychology of perception will discover that other colors besides red and green would be better suited for use in traffic lights: Should we for this reason change the status quo?

Aquinas once raised the question with regard to human legislation generally whether a legal arrangement should in every case be adjusted as soon as a better formulation is available.[75] His response proceeds from the distinction between rational argumentation (*ratio*), on the one hand, and custom and habit (*consuetudo*), on the other; since, he goes on to argue, the obligatory force of the laws is strongly influenced by *consuetude*, an adjustment could in itself entail an impairment of the common good, which is, after all, that for the sake of which laws are enacted at all. In other words, it can be meaningful under certain circumstances to allow an existing tradition to stand in the interests of maintaining continuity, although the concrete *traditum* might perhaps be deemed problematic. This shows, incidentally, that "maintaining continuity" is not synonymous with "preserving a *traditum*". Once, in America, I was confronted directly about my opinion on what Aquinas would have said to the plight of African Americans —integration or segregation? I answered that he would undoubtedly have pleaded on behalf of integration, but I should presumably have added the caveat: Pursue it unyieldingly, but step by step! Many enlightened Americans in the North and South communicated to me their agreement.

And yet there is still a little more to be said about mundane tradition. It has already become clear that its binding force is of a different kind from that of holy tradition. Even a custom that was intended

---

[75] I, II, 97, 2.

to facilitate our living together could under different social conditions conceivably become exceedingly burdensome—so much so that it could amount to almost an obligation to abolish it. What would things come to, for example, if, on a walk, one would have to doff one's cap to every acquaintance on an overcrowded city street? Of course, one is never in the strict sense "obliged", and this was just as true, say, fifty years ago. On the other hand, a mere waving of the hand might perhaps legitimately be perceived in the individual case as "insolent". There are no general criteria for judging such things; and perhaps, from an abstract point of view, the impetus toward social critique and reform is as often justified as is the simple respect for what is just a matter of custom. In keeping with "established custom", the graduates of my old gymnasium are still in the habit of conducting a festive parade through the city in a carriage. One of these days this will become impossible, and this tradition will disappear. Should one think to oneself, "Oh, what a pity!"? In my grandparents' day, it was a fixed custom in rustic households for the father to cut the bread before meals, whereby, in slicing open a fresh loaf, he first made the sign of the cross with his knife. As witnessed by me many times as a child, this was done almost haphazardly, even clandestinely; but one never left it undone. Of course all this has changed in the meantime. Not only is it difficult to find anyone who still bakes those enormous loaves of black bread that would take a full-grown man to finish off; there is now a special bread-cutting machine as well, insofar as the bread is not already to be found presliced in the store or does not already come presliced from the bread factory. In short, even these beautiful traditions no longer exist. And not much imagination is required to picture how many potential subjects worthy of an essentially pessimistic cultural critique are hidden therein ("technologization", "citification", decline of the family, and so on). Still the question is whether such a change is simply to be regretted. Is it possible to speak in an even vaguely precise sense of a "loss of tradition"? In this case, an answer to this question is complicated by the fact that a strictly technical procedure is intimately bound up with elements of holy tradition. And it might truly be possible, it seems to me, to speak of a "loss" of or "break" with tradition if the change had extended to the family order and, above all, to what is meant by the holy sign of the cross—in other words, if *that* which had been abandoned stood in a more or less immediate relationship to the *traditum* that alone is to be preserved unconditionally. It is, however, always the case that the core of what is to be preserved is multifariously overgrown and intertwined in manifold ways with the concrete forms of historical life, and a change in externalities can very well imperil the simple preservation of the core, so that whoever casually casts off or parodies the "external" traditions is acting dangerously. A field ethnologist once recounted to me how in the case of a specific ethnic group that had been expelled from its homeland, their religious ties had evidently been loosened to the precise extent to which the people of that ethnic group had deviated from a particular method they had for baking cakes; of course, this leaves open the question of what is cause and what effect here and whether the process, considered in its entirety, is not an extremely complex one.

We are still in the process of answering the question of how unique holy tradition is and whether only it can genuinely be characterized as "tradition". On two points, I believe, we have gained clarity. The *first* is this: Only in a holy tradition, which has its origin in the divine word, does the first in the series truly pass down something "received", that is, something that is not reproducible through personal insight and is, consequently, from a strictly formal standpoint, the purest kind of tradition conceivable. *Secondly*—and this, too, is on account of the *traditum*'s divine origin—the obligatoriness and binding character of the holy tradition exceeds that of any other form of tradition. One author has even gone so far as to suggest that "a unique revelation through God's word" grounds a "traditional bond" of such strength that it has no analogy "in any other sphere".[76]

It is true that the forms of social interaction that, in the usual case, are simply accepted by subsequent generations also possess a certain binding quality so that a violation of what "one" usually does might even amount *in concreto* to an act of injustice. And even the process of collective learning, which sustains cultural progress, is based on a type of obligation. Alexander Rüstow, in alluding to our feelings of respect for, confidence in, and reverence before authority, has argued that it is these feelings that underlie "the social differences in culture from generation to generation; and whoever undermines these feel-

---

[76] Monzel, *Überlieferung*, p. 128.

ings rocks the ultimate foundations of human culture."[77] Similarly, the theologian might likewise construe the biblical injunction to "fill the earth and subdue it" (Gen 1:28) as a binding directive. Still, one hesitates to characterize this as an obligation binding the individual to cooperate in the advance of civilization. Generally speaking, it is difficult to discern in the cultural realm the kind of compelling duty that would oblige one to preserve and pass on something that has been empirically received—whether it be the "classic doctrines" of the materialists, Marx, Engels, Lenin, and Mao, or some behavior that has become institutionalized. It is "tradition" to celebrate your mother's birthday or carnival, Labor Day (the First of May), the Day of German Unity, or to participate in the fairs with their shooting competitions; but all that can be safely disregarded, as the times dictate. One might even consider whether a "national holiday", that had been introduced in a specific situation should be repealed. Not to celebrate *Easter*, though—regardless of how "un"-festive the times might be, that would be a completely different story; obviously in this case the violation of duty would be incomparably more serious. It is an obligation that can only be found in the *holy* tradition. Only if the sons would truly cease to celebrate the cultic festivals celebrated by their fathers, or if the *tradita* of the holy tradition would for some other reason fail to be received and transmitted—only in this case— could one speak of a "loss of tradition", of "traditionlessness", and "a break with tradition" in the strict and ponderous sense of these expressions.

Tradition—this is by no means a structureless fabric consisting of what has been received in a contingently historical fashion and in which everything that has been concretely handed down, insofar as it has attained a certain age, is considered to be of equal significance (or insignificance). Differentiation and order are, however, only possible if one recognizes and accepts the unique status of holy tradition. It is TRADITION in the midst of tradition;[78] Yves Congar calls it "the tradition" (in the singular), to distinguish it from "traditions" in the plural.[79] This distinction, which accurately captures the heart of the

[77] *Kulturtradition und Kulturkritik,* p. 191.

[78] This is how J. Rimaud puts it in *Thomisme et méthode* (Paris, 1925), p. XXXVII.

[79] Cf. his book *Die Tradition und die Traditionen* (Mainz, 1965).

matter, promises to open up unsuspected avenues of understanding in both historical and topical matters. Those, for example, who had become accustomed to dismissing the Middle Ages all too summarily as a completely "tradition-bound" epoch are now suddenly capable of understanding why the greatest teachers of the thirteenth century deemed the argument from tradition, the *locus ab auctoritate*, the weakest of all arguments[80]—with which they explicitly did *not* mean the appeal to "tradition" but to "the traditions". The avowed respect for the inviolability of holy tradition precedes the relativization of the traditions as such and makes them possible and defensible. This connection, which may at first perhaps appear surprising, is a recurring phenomenon that is hardly ever likely to lose its topicality.

The more determinedly the energy behind the will to preservation is committed to what is ultimately worthy of preservation, then the greater the degree of change in the exterior that can be endured and tolerated without having to fear an actual "break". A genuine consciousness of tradition frees one from, and makes one independent of, those conservative attitudes that are preoccupied to a disproportionate degree with the cultivation of "tradition". There is undoubtedly a way of "cultivating tradition" that clings to the contingent historical form of what is received and that directly hinders a genuine transmission of what is truly worthy of preservation—something that can perhaps only be transmitted amid changing historical forms. And it is conceivable that what is ultimately worthy of being handed down could be genuinely transmitted in such a way that a fundamental conservatism would not even be capable of recognizing it.

Although, as was indicated, tradition (in the singular) is naturally embodied in a plurality of traditions and interwoven with them, this should not be misunderstood as an invitation to undifferentiated experimentation and reform in the social or cultural realm. What is required here is an especially fortunate and perhaps very rare combination of prudence and courage. There is no recipe for such a combination that would hold up for all time. Conversely, it may be said with certainty that it can never be figured out—unless through heart-

---

[80] "Licet locus ab auctoritate, quae fundatur super ratione humana, sit infirmissimus, locus tamen ab auctoritate, quae fundatur super revelatione divina, est efficacissimus" (I, 1, 8 ad 2).

felt affirmation of the divine gift that is intended for us by the holy tradition.

If, however, this gift—whether it be a piece of information, a directive, or a sacrament—has really been taken up in the conduct of one's life, then it will soon become apparent that it absolutely cannot be kept, as it were, under lock and key; and that the "maintenance of its purity", which remains a strict requirement, is nothing like storing a jewel in a sealed treasure chest. The notion of a "holy" tradition does not imply that what is being handed down through it is something "specifically religious" and thus belongs to a specific, well-delimited realm but is otherwise unimportant. The Platonic Socrates very rightly and nonchalantly introduces the *traditum* concerning the last judgment into an extremely topical philosophical and political dispute, which he is in the process of conducting with a practitioner of power politics.[81] This other, Callicles, refuses to let himself be convinced that *doing* injustice is more shameful than *suffering* injustice and that there is an unconditional obligation to do justice. And as the reasoned discussion arrives at a cul-de-sac, Socrates—fully aware, however, of the fact that he is still, and now for certain, addressing deaf ears—raises his strongest argument, objectively speaking: the tale of the last judgment handed down "from olden times", whose truth, if one were only to accept and reflect on it, is aimed at fundamentally transforming man's practical life in the historical *polis*. Here no trace of the argument that it represents an outlandish esoteric teaching that is of no concern to the "practitioner" and even less so to the "politician"! One can read in the Platonic dialogue *Gorgias* how emphatically Socrates makes this myth come alive.[82] Similarly, it has tremendous consequences for one's practical behavior vis-à-vis the world whether one accepts, for example, the *traditum* concerning the created character of man and the world or not. Only someone who accepts this—who, in other words, grasps man as something essentially designed—will be able to maintain his footing [*Stand*] against Jean-Paul Sartre's thesis, which likewise derives from an article of faith, is of great portent, and is by no means purely abstract: Since there is no human nature and since man was without purpose from his inception, there exists for him

---

[81] Cf. *Gorgias* 522e5–524b1.

[82] Ibid., 525d1ff., 526c1ff.

neither the possibility of orienting himself toward certain "signs" in the world nor the possibility of any form of obligation, however constituted.

Whatever a sentence like the one from the biblical account of creation may truly mean—"the LORD God formed man of dust from the ground, and breathed into his nostrils the breath of life"—it must continually be reformulated, in consideration of everything we have learned through critical reflection in paleontology and the theory of evolution concerning the emergence of man. Otherwise the contents of the holy tradition could not be kept alive in the actual present. In other words, whoever fails to undertake this reformulation frustrates and ignores that which all tradition by definition is intended to achieve: man's genuine participation in the *tradendum*.

To tackle this infinite task is—as far as holy tradition is concerned —the business of theology; in fact, just this *is* theology: the translation of the "original text" of the *tradita*, which has to be reedited under continually changing circumstances, into the conceptual framework of the historical moment. Actually to accept the implied challenge would appear, however, to be something distinctively "Western"; one might even go so far as to say that it is a specifically *Christian* phenomenon. At any rate, no theology in this sense is evidently to be found in the non-Christian world. At certain Indian universities, for example, I have several times had the experience in discussion with professors in the Sanskrit department, which roughly corresponds to our theology faculty, that they recognize neither the possibility nor the necessity to confront in any way the religious tradition of Hinduism with the modern natural sciences being taught at the same universities. The inevitable upshot is, on the one hand, the sterility of a continuously repeated and cult-like recital of the same stock of traditions and, on the other, the abandonment of the younger generation, who in this way have lost the connection to their own spiritual origins. The only ones who are engaged in the now perhaps already hopeless attempt to make the hidden truth in the Indian doctrines of divinity accessible and present to contemporary thought through interpretation and "translation" are Christian missionaries from Europe.

Here if anywhere, it can be seen once again what a thrilling and dynamic thing the act of handing down a *traditum* is. One simply misreads the situation if one opposes "tradition", as the persistent, to "history", as the paragon of change. Not only is the preservation of the *tradita*, even when they are poorly preserved, always and at bottom a partial process within the overarching total historical process, like the rise and fall of empires or the growing exploitation of natural forces; the *tradita* cannot be experienced in their authentic presence except as the result of an imminently historical effect—"historical" to be construed here in the more rigorous sense of immediate actuality.

One would be equally well advised to avoid adopting in the first place that formulaic coupling of "tradition and progress" which has since become a habit of thought. Most of the time, it has the character of propaganda and is intended to suggest that one can "go with the times" without having to sacrifice "the tried and true". Apart from the fact that with "the tried and the true" a *traditum*, or even something that is genuinely worthy of being preserved, need not necessarily be meant, this formula too easily robs one of the insight that one could hardly do anything more appropriate for advancing into the future than to hold a divine gift communicated in olden times present to human thought through commemorative presentation and interpretation. This extremely active form of remembering is, in fact, directed, *not* toward "what has been", as a foolish formulation now in vogue would have it, but toward what is always valid and what is topical in every age but which is nonetheless continually threatened by the danger of forgetfulness and corruption.

Incidentally, there is indeed a kind of progress associated with those interpretations that have to be performed anew each generation. It can, however, hardly be doubted that a deeper understanding and interpretation of the *tradita* does not simply set in by itself or as the result of the progressive accumulation of historical knowledge; rather it is intimately bound up with the individual spirit's openness and powers of penetration. Are we, for example, "farther" along in the interpretation of revelation, or in theology generally, than Jerome, Augustine, and Thomas Aquinas simply because we have the benefit of a naturally accumulating knowledge? It presumably makes no more sense to ask this question than to ask whether Goethe came "farther" than Homer or Kant "farther" than Plato—not that there need be in this field no "coming farther", but, if so, then hardly through the sheer passage of time.

As regards holy tradition, however, its purpose has always been to allow men to represent to themselves what was originally communicated from the divine wellspring in *identical* form. As one of the later born, I am basically interested only in this—not in the reformulation and interpretation as such, but only in being able to partake beyond the representative interpretation and with its help in the same degree of salvation, knowledge, and direction that fell to the first recipients of the message. Plato uses in this context the word "save": the mythical message concerning the last judgment and otherworldly punishment was "saved" in a wondrous manner, and he adds the astonishing hope that "it will save us if we believe it."[83] If the identity of this treasure, which must be uncovered each time anew, is lost, then what is crucial to this message—that is, what was originally intended with the revelation—is also lost. The attempts to differentiate among categories of interpretation and to determine more precisely what is genuinely intended, which should not be characterized as the "development of dogma", are naturally a fascinating topic for historical reflection as well.[84] But, insofar as I am a believer, that is, someone who, as the last in the series, wishes to have a share in that "message that has come down to us", this topic hardly concerns me. What interests me is primarily the divine word and not theology.[85]

Conversely, a theology that does not understand itself primarily in terms of the task of holding the divine revelation that has come down to men identical before consciousness over time but is perhaps concerned instead with realistically reflecting and interpreting the religious impulses of our time (or what it takes them to be), perhaps even clothing them in biblical concepts and terminology—such a "theology" is not even worthy of the name.

---

[83] *Republic* 621C1. [Quoted after the translation by Paul Shorey, in *Plato: The Collected Dialogues*, p. 844.] For details, see J. Pieper, *Über die platonischen Mythos* (Munich, 1965), pp. 24f.

[84] Cf. my discussion with Joseph Ratzinger on his lecture, *Das Problem der Dogmengeschichte in der Sicht der katholischen Theologie* (Cologne and Opladen, 1966), pp. 35ff.

[85] "The religious person does not believe in dogmas but in God" (Monzel, *Überlieferung*, p. 135).

V

When we pose the question of where in the historical world "holy tradition" then really takes place, we are referred first and foremost to Christian theology, or, more specifically, to its object, the tradition that derives from Christian revelation. Now this question is not intended as a propaedeutic to a fundamental discussion of "the only true religion" but rather as an empirically decidable inquiry: Where in the world has someone actually raised the claim to be conveying a message of divine provenance that affects the whole of reality and the core of human existence—a message, let it be noted, that, insofar as one wishes to have a share of it and take part in it at all, is to be accepted simply as something to be received? The answer that most readily comes to mind is that it is the tradition of Christian doctrine that raises precisely this claim. In fact, Christianity understands itself already by virtue of its mission as being called upon to preserve a divine message that had at one time been cast into history from falling into oblivion or from admixture with alien sources and to hand down that message as a holy tradition in an orderly "succession". The actual *agens* in all holy tradition is the concern that nothing of that which had once been entrusted to man through divine revelation in "olden times" should be lost or corrupted; rather, it should be transmitted to future generations in the same form, as it is in itself. One need only reflect for a moment to recognize how nonsensical it is to judge the Church primarily in terms of the demand for "progressivity". This belongs today to the "confusion of the century", of which Pascal also spoke; it consists in a simple failure to distinguish—that is, in applying the same criteria for assessment to a foundation created for the express purpose of preservation that are applied to institutions dedicated to scientific research and technological mastery of the world and to whose nature it in fact belongs continually to transcend, rectify, and perhaps even abandon the already known in the interests of an always advancing investigation of reality. Although, as has already been explained in detail, it is true that the *tradita* likewise call for unceasing attempts at interpretation and reformulation if they are actually to reach the current generation, this type of interpretation has, by its very nature, the character of a "translation", and, as everyone

can recognize for himself, it can only be characterized as a translation
as long as the identity of the original text persists over time and remains preserved. Of course, this claim to identity cannot be plausibly
defended or maintained indefinitely if the *tradita* are not regarded as a
divinely vouchered message and if they are not really such—if at the
very least they do not stand for something more or other than, say,
the "teachings of the classic Marxist authors".

Even granting all this, it would represent an abridgment of the true
state of affairs if one were to find "holy tradition" at work only in
Christian biblical doctrines. Tradition is simply being conceived too
narrowly if, as both process and act, it is defined as being nothing
more than "the Church's message, which started with the apostles
. . . and was propagated by its followers with the same authority".[86]
And the reason is that such a restriction is already questionable on
theological grounds. Can one simply dismiss the claim of mythological traditions outside and prior to Christian revelation to have likewise preserved a communication descended from a divine source for
all time, especially if one is simultaneously convinced that there was
long before the apostles something like a "primordial revelation"? Although this notion, which has already been mentioned once, does not
occupy a particularly prominent place in contemporary discussion—
assuming it comes up at all[87]—it has since the earliest times found a
home in Christian theology, and it will always recall itself to memory
as something indispensable. The notion of a primordial revelation implies that there was an event standing at the beginning of history and
involving an act of divine speech expressly directed toward "man"—
and that means all men—and that what was communicated in this
speech has entered into the holy traditions of various peoples, that
is, into their myths, and is preserved and present there in more or
less recognizable form. In his later work the *Retractiones*,[88] Augustine
expresses this thought in an unfortunately all too misleading—and
in fact often misunderstood—way: "The thing itself which is now
called 'Christian religion' also existed at the time of the ancients; indeed, it has not been absent from the time of mankind's beginning up

---

[86] Deneffe, *Traditionsbegriff*, p. 1.

[87] As one example at least, I refer to J. H. Newman's *Grammar of Assent* (London, 1892;
German translation by T. Haecker, *Philosophie des Glaubens* [Munich, 1921], pp. 369f.).

[88] I, 12.

to the point when Christ became incarnate; from then on, the true religion, which had always existed, came to be called the 'Christian religion'." If one grants the basic validity of this notion of a "primordial revelation", together with whatever qualifications one may wish to add, and if one is at the same time convinced that "everything and only those things that are the object of revelation [are] also the objects of tradition",[89] then one can hardly refuse to recognize the primordial tradition, which is associated with this original revelation, as a fundamental form of "holy tradition".

This, however, amounts to a momentous decision! For example, one would then already have accepted as well that such holy traditions, which derive from the same divine *logos* that became man in the form of Jesus Christ, not only took place in the *pre*-Christian era but that they in some sense continue to be passed down among "pagan" people and cultures up to the present day. The meaning of "in some sense" here must, in fact, be clarified.

Before all else, however, I wish to avoid the impression of subscribing to a Gnostic or romanticizing interpretation of myth as can be found, for example, in the work of Leopold Ziegler. It is just *not* possible, it seems to me, to attribute a quasi-absolute validity to those tales that play out between the mortal and divine realms and that are, as a matter of empirical fact, encountered in European antiquity, the highly developed Asian cultures, and the "primitive" peoples— in short, to myths. What I am prepared to argue amounts to a much weaker claim: namely, that among the myriad forms of "mythological tradition", which in their totality are not easily subsumed under a common rubric, there are also *tradita* in the strict sense, along with other diversely constituted elements. It, too, is a "location", in which "holy" tradition in the full sense of that term authentically occurs. Alternately expressed, it is something to which one has not yet given a proper name, such as when one, following Hegel, speaks in this regard of the early image-making of the "playful fantasy"[90] or when one, as is customary in the scholarly literature on Plato, speaks of his poetic, allegorical language, crafted by the "myth-molding" power of

---

[89] Deneffe, *Traditionsbegriff*, p. 114.

[90] G. W. F. Hegel, *Vorlesungen über die Geschichte der Philosophie* I, vol. 15, p. 170.

a genial mind.[91] One falls even farther short of the essence of the phenomenon if myth is defined as "a religious narrative, which one knows from the start has been shaped by man and so can be continually reshaped by him"[92]—a characterization that is already definitively refuted by the Platonic Socrates' attitude toward the myths recounted to him but also by Plato's own words, according to which we "must give our unfeigned assent to the ancient and holy doctrines which warn us that our souls are immortal, that they are judged".[93] Expressed in more positive terms, there is something in mythological tradition that can only properly be grasped and characterized if one understands it as a more or less distinct echo of a primeval act of divine speech, as voiced ages ago, that is, as revelation.

Already, the word "echo" indicates that the *tradita* are, as a rule, not simply preserved in the mythological tradition. It is precisely their true physiognomy that is no longer immediately recognizable; it is hidden behind an overgrowth of fantastic accretions; the authentic is deformed and disfigured, and the Christian may be justified in feeling himself reminded of demonic distortion as well. In this case, the same is true as what was said in the *Republic* about the marble statue of the sea-god, which Plato compared to the current state of the soul: the original members of the body are crushed with accretions of shells and seaweed and rocks, so that it is more like any wild creature than what it was by nature.[94] Above all, Plato seems to have had a presentiment that even the great mythological narratives, with which he closes a few of his dialogues, are at best scraps, fragments of a tradition that is no longer intelligible as a whole—no longer and not yet. A later dialogue[95] makes explicit mention of the fact that some of the old marvelous stories have, with the passage of time, faded from man's memory; others have become widely scattered, with the individual separated from the whole; still, no one has been able to relate the historical cause that gives the setting of all of them. Now

---

[91] Cf. J. Pieper, *Über den platonischen Mythen*, pp. 25, 86f.

[92] In the words of K. Prümm (*Der christliche Glaube und die altheidnische Welt*, vol. 1 [Leipzig, 1935], p. 47).

[93] *Seventh Letter* 335a3–4. [Quoted after the translation by L. A. Post, in *Plato: The Collected Dialogues*, p. 1583.]

[94] *Republic* 611d1–7.

[95] *Statesman* 269b5–8.

it has been argued that precisely this is the remarkable achievement of Plato himself, that is, that he purified the disparate fragments and combined them into a "preexisting interpretation of the world", that of the one true "Great Myth".[96] But precisely this—the ability to distinguish between true and false on the basis of a historically transmitted stock of myths—would have far exceeded Plato's capacities as well as those of pre-Christian thought, generally. One might almost say that what makes the Platonic Socrates a tragic figure is that, on the one hand, he makes his stand on the firm foundation of a holy tradition, in opposition to the deliberately atraditional sophists, and so acquires secure footing for himself, *without*, on the other, being able to formulate the content of that tradition precisely. To the extent, however, that he refuses to regard myths as "mere tales"—to the extent, rather, that he unwaveringly accepts and reveres their meaning as true—the *tradita* pertaining to the divine guarantee of human salvation are so inescapably present to him that he is prepared to wager his existence on them.

One might ask oneself *why* Socrates actually "allows himself to be informed", as he puts it, by the "men of old", who necessarily remain nameless to him, about that mythological communication which descends from the gods. Why does he believe them? The following might be offered as a first, preliminary response: One has always regarded it as something belonging to the very nature of belief that whoever gives credence to someone realizes and desires, in so doing, "spiritual union"[97] and community with him. *We believe because we love.*[98] This identification with the witnesses and guarantors even forms the precondition for our being able to believe, that on the basis of which and by virtue of which one "believes"—whether that someone is Socrates or we ourselves. The believer is always a member of this type of body, which is present and at work imperceptibly in the history of mankind but can hardly be grasped empirically and for which *corpus mysticum* is perhaps the most appropriate term. With this term, as is well known, Christianity refers to itself; but even Karl Jaspers cannot dispense with it when referring, with the requisite vagueness,

---

[96] P. Friedländer, *Platon* 1:184.
[97] M. J. Scheeben, *Handbuch der katholischen Dogmatik* 1:291 (par. 633).
[98] J. H. Newman, *Zur Philosophie und Theologie des Glaubens* (Mainz, 1936), 1:82.

to that "ghostly realm" to which the philosophizing person is bound in belief but which is itself "nowhere objective".[99] Admittedly, this sounds like a highly assailable "speculation". And it would, in fact, be all too insubstantial if it were not able to invoke the assumption of a primordial revelation in its defense. This assumption, in fact, clears the way for a proper understanding of the *corpus mysticum*, which, spanning epochs and cultures, is grounded in the common possession of a divinely vouchered truth. And the holy tradition, "a function of a society grounded in revelation",[100] then appears, quite rightly, to be the only power, as Viacheslav Ivanov writes, that can again "unite us with the origin and with the Word, which was in the beginning".[101] As much as the mythological tradition may require purification, chastening, and interpretation in the light of the divine *logos*, as it has appeared definitively among men, in order to arrive at its own truth, it would be inappropriate for Christianity to disregard the dignity of the *tradita* embodied in it—even if it may at times prove difficult to recognize in the echo the original speech. In fact, the early Church Fathers from Justin Martyr to Origen and Augustine unanimously defended, against the sectarian narrow-mindedness of a Tertullian,[102] their belief in the seminal power of the divine word and in the grains of truth that have been operative in the folkloric wisdom of different peoples and in the teachings of the philosophers since the beginning of human history.

It is, however, not only its suprahuman origin that commands respect. Above all, it should not be forgotten that the commonality of the holy tradition creates a fundamental *solidarity* among all men, actually a unity with regard to that vital spiritual basis, which, though hidden, is for all that the more real and which first enables and, as it were, presumes communication among men. It probably belongs to one of the most ominous events that are taking place on this planet that a secularized world civilization, which appears to be in the process of once and for all forsaking and despoiling the bedrock of its great traditions, is now compelling all the remaining cultures to abandon their own *tradita* and so uproot themselves—with the result that

---

[99] *Philosophie*, p. 259.
[100] Gloege, *Offenbarung und Überlieferung*, p. 27.
[101] Iwanow, *Alte Wahre*, p. 33.
[102] Cf. *Apologeticum* 46; *De praescriptione haereticorum* 7.

even the most heroic efforts toward a deeper "understanding" have remained, almost inevitably, futile.

Our question, however, still remains "where" in the historical world of mankind holy tradition may be encountered as a fact. Of the two "locations" that were given in response to this question, the second must perforce be treated with far less specificity than the first; still, I did not want to suppress it completely. One cannot pass over the folkloric myths of different peoples in silence when inquiring into the actuality of holy tradition. The same, however, also appears to me to be true of the third location, although it does not represent more than a conjecture and despite the fact that the concept of "tradition" is perhaps applicable here at most by way of analogy.

I am referring to specific certainties corresponding to a person's core beliefs that do not manifest themselves as what they are but whose individual presence and efficacy clearly come to light under certain circumstances. It may arguably be reckoned among the certain findings of depth psychology that, *first*, there really are such normally unconscious "insights"[103] and "primordial ideas"[104] and that they center around such fundamental existential facts as salvation, sin, guilt, punishment, harmony, and happiness. *Secondly*, although these assumptions are as little subject to rational demonstration as the validity of the *tradita*, we are so thoroughly convinced of their truth that we, in practice, orient our lives with reference to them and would be at odds with ourselves if we were to attempt to live otherwise. Most contentious is the *third* point, although it is particularly relevant to our subject, that is, that convictions and ideas might have the character of *tradita*. It was, at any rate, no less a figure than C. G. Jung himself[105] who used the expression "handing down" [*Überlieferung*] in this context. Of course, the transmission must be so conceived that it does not occur by means of a personal act of communication but rather through a process of communication that is more deeply embedded and concealed in generational continuity. At any rate, the path "*on*ward" [her*wärts*] withholds itself by its very nature from the immediate experience of the receiver; the path *back*ward [rück*wärts*],

---

[103] C. G. Jung, *Psychologie und Religion* (Zurich and Leipzig, 1940), p. 76.
[104] Ibid., p. 93.
[105] Ibid.

by contrast, is traversed, under certain conditions, by memory. This is what the Platonic-Augustinian concept of *anamnesis/memoria* above all, seems to be saying. As Gilson has convincingly shown,[106] Augustine understands by "memory", not only something "transpsychological" but also something supraindividual, a power that is able to reach outside the generational sequence and to recall experiences that befell "man" in the early period of his history. How is it that we know what the blessed life is? Do we not know it by remembering? Then we must once have been blessed, perhaps in the form of that person who was the first to commit sin? Such questions wind their way hither and thither throughout the tenth book of the *Confessions*.[107] I put all this forward only conjecturally, as I have said, and with my express reservations. Nevertheless, our mention of such unconscious certainties, "assumed" in the absence of critical examination and affecting the totality of human existence, can be defended within the context of our attempting to answer our original question. Again, they, too, represent one possible "location" in which holy tradition may take place—even if it remains for our reflective capacity less a positively illuminable realm, as an area to be staked off as an empty, negative space.

From this last reflection, it is only one additional step to the question concerning the traditional character of *language*. Certainly, the latter is much more than simply a vehicle for handing down traditions; it is itself a *traditum*—and not merely in the sense that a certain stock of words, along with the corresponding grammar, is passed down from generation to generation. Attached to these words is, in fact, always an already constituted interpretation of the world and human existence that we simply adopt, without either ourselves or the "transmitter" of these traditions being able to articulate it expressly. Although here, too, what is taking place is, strictly speaking, not an act of communicative transmission, we still do not hesitate to refer to the process as one of handing down a tradition. This raises at the same time the probably irresolvable question of the *origin* of language, with which, fortunately, we need not concern ourselves here. For the time being, it may be recalled that on Plato's view it is the "men of old"

---

[106] E. Gilson, *Der heilige Augustinus* (Hellerau, 1930), pp. 497f.
[107] Cf. *Confessions* 10, 20.

who "gave things their names",[108] just as in the holy Scriptures of Christianity (Gen 2:20) the first man, Adam, is credited with having given to all the things of creation their names.

Such assumptions, as was noted quickly in passing, have nothing in common with "traditionalism". This expression, which nowadays is used extravagantly as a form of invective, should continue to be reserved for that doctrine which arose within the context of the intellectual history of the nineteenth century and which states that human reason is not by itself, that is, without recourse to the primordial revelation and tradition, able to grasp even the most fundamental facts of existence. It is clear that one can regard this thesis as fundamentally misconceived while at the same time respecting the holy tradition as something venerable and even binding. And, of course, neither the former nor the latter opinion can be equated with a conservatism that indiscriminately resists any form of innovation. Not only does such conservatism really exist, as everyone knows; it seems to number among the so-called "natural" threats and possibilities for decadence against which everyone who understands and affirms the holy tradition as the basic reality of evolving history must arm himself from the very start.

In the worldly mannerisms of such people there is always a characteristic strain of basic reverence and gratitude, an emphatic respect for what has arisen organically and for the continuity of life as a supraindividual context. The phenomenon to which I am referring here is, however, too complex and too differentiated to be correctly described and delimited in a casual first attempt. Of course, I do not mean by this that harmless, uncritical naïveté which "sees the good in everything" that happens to exist; I mean rather that selfless willingness to receive something without being able to offer recompense out of one's own resources and the humility that comes from knowing of one's indebtedness but at the same time being unable to repay the debt. It is "the power of gratitude" that I am referring to, whose loss would first leave us truly disinherited[109]—which, however, does not in itself imply that the revolutionary appeal to the purity of the origin, the primordial form of the *traditum* behind all the accumulated

---

[108] *Phaedrus* 244b6.
[109] G. Marcel, *Das große Erbe* (Münster, 1952), p. 29.

"strata of interpretation",[110] need be precluded or even that it might be. This origin, however, which continues to give and to act throughout history, is always gratefully remembered and respected. Gabriel Marcel has interpreted this "encompassing gratitude" as re-cognition and ac-knowledge-ment (*re-connaissance*), as the attempt to respond in "a mysterious act of restitution" to what is received, without being owed, through tradition.[111]

To this universal affirmation—this "yes"—there corresponds, as the reverse side of the same coin, an unequivocal "no", or, at the very least, an intensely critical mistrust: mistrust, for example, of an all too exclusive preoccupation with the future—as if mankind had only something to hope for and nothing to remember or be grateful for—and even more so, of course, the mistrust of that kind of "rock-bottom" radicalism which thinks it can begin anew as from a *tabula rasa*; but also mistrust of the tendency to portray each moment, as it happens, as a "completely new situation". Against this, one will have to insist in each case on a very precise distinction. On the one side, we have the still unreached destinations of space exploration, the still unknown methods of cancer treatment, the cultivation of the next variety of rose, progress in the construction of automobiles and photographic cameras, and so forth. I can welcome all this without reservation and even impatiently await their realization. It is a completely different matter, however, when one speaks approvingly of a "radically new" understanding of human nature, of an interpretation of the meaning of *eros* or of death that invalidates everything that had been thought true up until now, of an entirely new means of access to God's word that was first opened up in this generation, or of a completely transformed conception of the priesthood and the sacrament. At this point, a deep and unpacifiable distrust, not to be assuaged, announces itself, prior to any discussion of individual details, and rooted this time neither in some general desire for stability nor in a principled aversion to "progress" but rather in the well-founded suspicion that, in this area, "being new" might, to borrow a phrase from Jaspers, tell against "being true".[112] "In this area" means wher-

---

[110] J. Ratzinger, *Problem der Dogmengeschichte*, p. 44.

[111] Marcel, *Große Erbe*, pp. 22, 24.

[112] Jaspers, *Von der Wahrheit*, p. 192.

ever an issue concerning the totality of world and human existence is involved; wherever the message behind the holy tradition is heard; wherever the methods of the exact sciences arrive at their limits.

In fact, both aspects belong to the nature of science: it expressly refrains from inquiring into the total context of life, and tradition has no place in it. Four hundred years before Pascal, the latter had already been asserted with aggressive decisiveness by Albertus Magnus. When addressing the question of whether the dolphin is a fish or not, he does not, he writes, interrogate Aristotle or even the "ancients" as such. "In such things only experience yields certainty" (Experimentum solum certificat in talibus).[113] By the same token, though, it is inaccurate and misleading to characterize modern science as "fundamentally untraditional" or to say that its emergence presupposes a "break with tradition".[114] In this respect, incidentally, no fundamental difference exists between the experimental sciences of antiquity and today. Where there is no marriage, there is also no adultery. Of a fundamentally different nature is philosophy's relation to tradition.

VI

The act of philosophizing is absolutely distinct, in its inner structure, from the act of handing down—even in ancient philosophy. Nevertheless, some have sought to interpret Aristotle in such a way that for him "first philosophy" remains "theology" "because to it falls the task of transmitting that knowledge of the divine which has always already been given to man."[115] It can be persuasively demonstrated, I believe, that this view is based on a false interpretation. In Aristotle's *Metaphysics* it says that "first philosophy" is the most divine among the sciences for two reasons:[116] because it inquires ultimately after God and because God possesses this knowledge most perfectly. With this, a special connection to the holy tradition is at the same time

---

[113] *De vegetabilibus*, ed. C. Jessen (Berlin, 1867), p. 340. See also J. Pieper, *Scholastik* (Munich, 1960), pp. 15ff.

[114] This is Ritter's view, as expressed in Pieper, *Begriff der Tradition*, pp. 45f.

[115] J. Ritter in ibid., p. 47.

[116] 983a5–10. For more on this, see the commentary of W. D. Ross, *Aristotle's Metaphysics* (Oxford, 1924), 1:121.

being, if not directly asserted, then at least prepared and insinuated. The question, however, of the precise nature of this relationship still remains open.

Curiously, Pascal's thesis on the validity of tradition, which we cited at the beginning, does not even mention philosophy. The relationship of tradition to physics, on the one hand, and to theology, on the other, is at bottom clear and unproblematic. Physics has, in fact, nothing to do with tradition, whereas theology could practically be defined as the "science of tradition", that is, as the attempt to interpret God's word, as embodied in the *tradita*, in terms of what is genuinely meant. With regard to its actual execution, however, this act of interpretation proves to be a task of almost insuperable difficulty. The progressive investigation of man and the world by science makes it necessary continually to revise, rework, and hone each new formulation in its turn precisely for the sake of preserving the living presence of the one *traditum*; this takes place within the context of a polyphonic debate that excludes no argument or interlocutor on principle and that, when it is properly conducted and pursued with persistence, can be reckoned among the most exciting processes of intellectual history. And, incidentally, it is not as if theology were the sole beneficiary of this process. Although the *tradita*, of course, do not affect the process of knowledge acquisition either in terms of its content or from within, the sciences may possibly also receive some encouragement, as it were, from outside,[117] insofar as the resistance offered by tradition requires of science a higher degree of alertness and a focusing of one's attention in a specific direction. Still, these complications do not concern the theological act as such, which is, in essence, fully transparent, or the univocity of its relationship with the holy tradition.

And how does it stand with philosophy? Now, with this designation, we are referring not so much to a special academic discipline as to an activity that belongs inalienably to the rudiments of any type of spiritual existence and that cannot be dispensed with by anyone who aspires to lead a spiritual life. This activity—so much is already

---

[117] "Nowhere is tradition simply an inhibiting countervailing force; it is always both resistance and encouragement" (T. Litt, "Hegels Begriff des Geistes und das Problem der Tradition", *Studium Generale* 4 [1951]: 320).

clear—consists neither in simply attentively receiving and transmitting something handed down nor in interpreting it. It has never occurred to me to construe "philosophy as the enacting of tradition".[118] Rather, philosophy means reflecting on the entirety of what is encountered in experience from every conceivable standpoint and with regard to its ultimate meaning.[119] The philosophizing person is thus not so much someone who has formed a well-rounded world view as he is someone who keeps a question alive and thinks it through methodically.

And how does this questioner, then, come to be involved with tradition and, even more so, with holy tradition? First of all, it should be noted that he will not be involved with tradition at all—unless he has already stood *as a person* in a tradition and has taken part in it as a believing listener. Is this not equivalent to saying, however, that tradition does not concern me *as* a philosopher? No, it is not! Rather it suggests the following: Only after—and insofar as—I, as a person, actually take part in a tradition, insofar as I, in other words, genuinely accept the *tradita* as truth, for whatever reasons (but of course not uncritically to the point of naïveté), am I then able to philosophize earnestly, that is, to consider my object from every conceivable aspect, when I directly incorporate the expressions of tradition in the actual philosophical debate. This is just as true of the Greeks at the time of Socrates as it is of the modern Christian. The great initiators of Western philosophy, in particular, explicitly contrasted rational argumentation with mythological tradition. And if posterity continues to savor the taste of the existential in Plato's *Symposium*, then this is because Plato, in his discussion of the nature of *eros*, not only allows the sciences of biology, psychology, and sociology to speak for themselves, but also gives an interpreter of the myth concerning the original perfection and fall of man an opportunity to speak: You do not understand, he says, anything of what *eros* is and wants if you do not reflect as well on these primordial experiences of mankind, if you

---

[118] This nonsensical view is attributed to me by Odo Marquard (*Skeptische Methode im Blick auf Kant* [Freiburg and Munich, 1958], p. 77), who, in so doing, refers to one of my writings, in which he might also have read the following sentence: "Examined more closely, the philosophizing person, insofar as he philosophizes, is neither someone who hands down a tradition nor an interpreter of a tradition" (*Begriff der Tradition*, p. 54).

[119] Cf. J. Pieper, *Verteidigungsrede für die Philosophie* (Munich, 1966), pp. 14ff. (included in this volume as "A Plea for Philosophy").

fail to recognize that every erotic longing is ultimately nothing other than the pursuit of this original unity!

Of course, the expression "incorporating the *tradita*" denotes an extremely complicated procedure that cannot be examined more closely here. Suffice it to say that at the very least it involves bringing the known and the believed in a contrapuntal arrangement so that the independence of both remains clearly preserved, and, on the basis of mutual reinforcement, provocation, and even perhaps perturbation, a newer, richer harmony emerges that amounts to far more than the simple addition of their elements.

How much the existential impetus, the authenticity, the depth, and the "heartfeltness", as it were, of philosophizing depends on whether this counterpoint to the holy tradition is achieved or not—this is what I would like to demonstrate with what I have found to be an impressive foil for showing up the kind of historical experiment that can perhaps only be observed in our Western European civilization. For some time now, I have harbored a deep reverence for the historical learnedness of Japanese professors of philosophy, who discuss their Hegel, their Heidegger, or their Sartre with the sovereignty characteristic of the expert and from whom one can expect fully accurate answers to the most abstruse questions of detail. Of course, one is far from being able to philosophize simply on the basis of such knowledge. And if one attempts to discuss substantial problems with such experts—in other words, "not what others have thought but how things are in reality"[120]—then an insularity, which comes across as almost uncanny, quickly makes itself manifest despite the enormous proficiency in the use of Western terminology, somewhat like the artificial liveliness of marionettes. That is, I think, hardly surprising. The whole of European philosophy lives from the dialogue—perhaps I would be better advised to say "dispute"—with the sacred traditions of Christianity that predated it. Whoever fails to perceive this connection, which, of course, is not always evident, will necessarily find the atheism of Jean-Paul Sartre just as inaccessible as Heidegger's ontology of nothingness and death. At one of those hours-long symposia in Tokyo, I once put to my enlightened colleagues in the wee hours of the morning the following question: "What does the pre-philosophical religious tra-

---

[120] Thomas Aquinas, *De cael.* 1, 22 (no. 228).

dition look like, on the basis of which a specifically Japanese form
of philosophizing might develop contrapuntally?" This was followed
by an extensive and extremely lively debate, conducted by my table-
mates in their native language, of which the guest understood nothing. After an emphatic interruption on my part, I finally found out
that they were arguing about whether there was really something like
a "mythological tradition" of specifically Japanese provenance at all
and of what type it might be. In the event, my original conjecture
that a genuinely Japanese philosophy was more likely to be found in
the cloisters of Zen Buddhism or in the Shinto temples came closer
to being corroborated than invalidated.

If one now examines contemporary European philosophy from the
same point of view, what immediately impresses one as being its most
salient characteristic is precisely this process of an ever more consistent exclusion of the *tradita* from the ambit of philosophical discussion.
Thus one finds that diagnosis confirmed here as well—and perhaps
here more strikingly than elsewhere—which Friedrich Nietzsche had
penned around 1890: "What today is most under attack is the instinct
for, and will to, tradition; the modern spirit has lost its taste for all
institutions that owe their origin to this instinct."[121] Of course, this
sentence was intended to have a relevance far beyond the realm of
philosophy; indeed, it appears to have been intended to apply, in its
primary sense, to something else. It undoubtedly applies, for example,
to the artistic realm. In fact, the power of the fine arts to transport
and move us likewise derives from that dimension of reality which is
opened up in tradition. And "tradition" here most definitely does not
signify just any stock of formal or material conventions; rather, what
is meant is "*holy* tradition", and that in the strict sense. Whoever perceives this as being too far-fetched or even too "pious" can find the
same thought expressed in the later Goethe. In one letter to Zelter[122]
there appears an astonishing sentence: "Every genuine artist should
be viewed as someone who wants to preserve something acknowledged to be holy and to propagate it in earnest and with deliberation.
Each century, however, strives in its own way toward the secular [*ins
Saeculum streben*] and seeks to make the holy profane, the difficult easy,

---

[121] *Gesammelte Werke*, Musarion-Ausgabe, vol. 18 (Munich, 1922), p. 56.
[122] Dated March 18, 1811.

and the serious fun—against this there would be nothing to object, if only seriousness and fun did not go to ruin in the attempt."

In philosophy, at least, which forms the actual subject of our discussion, it has for some time now been the case that it has very forcefully and at a very fundamental level "striven toward the secular"; and here, too, it is true that "against this there would be nothing to object" if in this way that which was supposed to be achieved with philosophy did not "come to ruin". This, however, is true not simply of philosophy but of the spiritual life of man generally.

The exclusion of "holy tradition" from the actual act of philosophizing can, so it appears, be accomplished in either one of two ways: it can be excluded, first, by destroying its content and replacing it with a kind of anti-tradition. The paradigm example is Jean-Paul Sartre, who explicitly bases his philosophy on the tenet of God's nonexistence. The contrapuntal assignment of the known to the believed is thus, when viewed from a purely formal standpoint, preserved in its entirety. And I am convinced that this is precisely the reason for the perceived existential relevance of Sartre's philosophizing. Here that "incorporation" of ultimate positions is clearly taking place which affects human existence in its entirety and which precedes thought as that which is simply assumed uncritically—only this dogma, it is true, proclaims its opposition, in the form of sheer negation, to all holy tradition. Even more effective, however, is the other way in which the *tradita* are rendered mute in the realm of philosophy, that is, by negating, not the content, but, more generally, the formal structure of the contrapuntal arrangement itself. According to the programmatic utterances of "scientific philosophy", for example, the philosophizing person should absolutely refrain from considering the *totum* of world and human existence from every conceivable standpoint; like the physicist, he should confine himself instead to partial questions and bring them to resolution with demonstrable results. And, of course, there is then just as little incentive in such a specialized branch of science as in the exact physical sciences to appeal to tradition, be it holy or profane. In the process, however, philosophy—even if it is still so called—becomes an occupation that can be pursued only by specialists and is, in fact, of no consequence to anyone else. The role that falls to philosophy and the philosophizing person within the whole of existence remains empty.

"Empty" is also the word that two important philosophical critics of our time—despite their standing at virtual antipodes to each other and each doubtless working in isolation from the other—have used to describe the spiritual state to which such deliberately untraditional philosophizing gives rise. The one is Karl Jaspers, who, with a view to a widespread feature of contemporary philosophizing, remarked that the content of the "great tradition", without which philosophy must inevitably die off and vanish,[123] has been abandoned, and the result has been "an empty earnestness".[124] And Viacheslav Ivanov, the "Western Russian",[125] researcher of myths, humanist, and philosopher, who has already been mentioned several times, responds to the liberal historian who revels in his good fortune at being able to submerge himself in the River of Lethe, wash away all memory of religion, philosophy, and poetry, and reemerge on dry land as naked as the first man,[126] with the decisive declaration: "Freedom usurped by means of such forgetting is empty."[127]

One of the last treatises Gerhard Krüger wrote before entering on that silence which has persisted for some years now brings to expression another aspect of that calamity which, arising from the growing inability to find sacred tradition at work, threatens mankind's spiritual life altogether. It includes the frightening sentences: "We live now only from our own inconsistency, from the fact that we have not yet really silenced all tradition. . . .[128] We are moving closer toward the radical impossibility of a meaningful and shared existence, although no one can imagine what this end will be like."[129] Whoever is inclined to regard this as an all too sinister Cassandra-like warning should at least consider the possibility that it might prove to be a completely accurate statement, one that has nothing in common with

---

[123] *Philosophie*, pp. 267, 269.

[124] K. Jaspers and R. Bultmann, *Die Frage der Entmythologisierung* (Munich, 1954), p. 12.

[125] Cf. *Alte Wahre*, p. 188.

[126] W. Iwanow and M. O. Gerschenson, *Briefwechsel zwischen zwei Zimmerwinkeln* (Vienna, 1949), p. 12.

[127] Ibid., p. 72.

[128] A somewhat unexpected confirmation of this proposition may be found in Lezcek Kolakowski: "If—which, fortunately, is very unlikely—the resistance to tradition leads to its utter rejection, we may with complete justification speak of the end of the humane world" (*Vom Sinn der Tradition*, p. 1092).

[129] *Geschichte und Tradition*, p. 28.

the literary genre of unengaged contemporary social critique or with fin-de-siècle philosophies of Western decline. Krüger points, by way of contrast, to the unifying power of tradition, by which he means that the critical solidarity of the human race cannot be grounded in, or secured by, the political realization of "one world" or by any unanimity of "cultural will" or through a shared respect for art and science; not through the technical empowering of communication across the planet; not through a universally spoken world language, be it English, Chinese, or Esperanto, or even through the promotion of international athletic contests. Rather genuine solidarity among men has its origin in nothing other than the commonality of tradition in the strict sense, that is, in common participation in a sacred tradition that is grounded in the divine word.

ON THE DILEMMA POSED BY
A NON-CHRISTIAN PHILOSOPHY

I

It has become customary—as anyone can tell you—to decry the notion of a "Christian philosophy" as something problematic, not to say self-contradictory and impossible. How can one employ one's reason in the radical manner that we associate with philosophy if one has already, as a matter of faith, accepted a specific theological interpretation of the world and of human existence? Here, indeed, is a problem that cannot easily be dismissed.

But I do not propose to address it here. Rather, I would like to call your attention to the problems that follow on a non-Christian philosophy. Be advised that I am *not* referring to specific problems of substance (for example, immortality, moral obligation), which for a non-Christian philosophy would prove difficult of resolution. No, I am speaking of the problem—better said, the dilemma—that is inherent in the very conception of a non-Christian philosophy, in other words, that conception of philosophy which has predominated over the last few centuries.

At this point it behooves me to interject two explanatory remarks, or, to be more precise, two qualifications.—First, the aforesaid dilemma of a non-Christian philosophy applies exclusively within the domain of Western civilization; to the extent that India or China have not yet fallen under the influence of the West, I am not concerned with them. Secondly, what I understand by "philosophy" coincides with what the great initiators of the Western philosophical tradition— Pythagoras, Plato, and Aristotle—have meant by this term. Although this commits me to little else than to taking general usage literally, it has consequences of far-ranging significance.

Of course, no one is debarred from associating with the designation "philosophy" something fully unconventional and "original". But one will still have to contend with the fact that one is likely to be so understood as if one meant by philosophy what it *originally* signified. Still, insofar as Bertrand Russell, by including both Plato and

John Dewey in his *History of Western Philosophy*, assumes at least that much overlap between the Platonic "theory of Ideas" and Dewey's instrumentalism, I feel justified in subsuming both under the rubric "philosophy".

II

This conception of philosophy first found expression in the Western tradition with Pythagoras, Plato, and Aristotle. And this formulation continually met with unqualified acceptance at least until the onset of the Middle Ages, that is, for some two thousand years. It is of course impossible to present the ancient conception of philosophy in its full scope here. But two important elements need to be addressed.

First, one should not regard the literal meaning of the word *philo-sophia* as simply the stuff of anecdote. Plato, for his part, took the ancient account whereby Pythagoras was reputed to have said no man can be called wise (*sophos*) but at most a *philo-sophos*, a wisdom-loving seeker after truth, very much as a matter of principle. For Plato, in fact, the essence of philosophizing lies in aiming at a wisdom we nevertheless cannot "possess" as long as we find ourselves in an embodied state. This wisdom is just as little attainable for us as the chasm between divine and mortal is bridgeable. Not even Solon and Homer could be called "wise" ("the epithet is proper only to a god"). On the other hand, it is also true that "none of the gods philosophizes." Perhaps one will not find it especially surprising that Plato, whose credentials as a "religious philosopher" are somewhat suspect anyway, would say some such thing. But even Aristotle, the founder of a "scientific" philosophy, had said that the question, "What does it actually mean to be something 'real'?"—the question concerning *ousia* —is one that, "both now and of old, has always been raised and has always been the subject of doubt"—in other words, a question that man can never definitively answer. And we are also indebted to Aristotle for the following insight: This question, so he writes, aims at an answer that God alone knows—or, in any event, knows best—this being the reason, in fact, why Aristotle dubbed metaphysics, philosophy in the primary sense, "theology".

In short, the *primary* element in the original conception of philo-

sophy consists of nothing other than an uninhibited relation to theology, a methodological openness in relation to theology. Whoever entertains a philosophical question in the genuine sense (for example,
the questions: What, in the final analysis, is knowledge? What is spirit?
What is this chunk of matter—this sheet of paper—that I hold in my
hand, ultimately and "at bottom"? What does it mean to be something "real"?) is always asking at the same time about the structure
of the world as a whole; he views reality in its entirety. As a result,
whoever entertains a philosophical question is *eo ipso* compelled to
discuss everything—to speak about God and the world. This is what
distinguishes the philosophizing person from the scientist. The physician or historian need *by no means* discuss God or the world within
the context of his scientific research; indeed, raising such issues could
appear downright unscientific—whereas it would, conversely, be unphilosophical not to discuss them. Whoever investigates the question
of authorship with regard to a newly discovered medieval codex or
whoever researches the virus associated with a certain infectious dis-
ease is not automatically inquiring into the structure of the world in
its totality. On the other hand, whoever inquires after the ultimate
meaning of illness would not come very far—he would not be doing justice to his chosen topic—if he were to refrain from discussing
the structure of the world as a totality—and, hence, "God and the
world". He can hardly do otherwise than to begin, as it were, with
"Adam and Eve". It is, for example, not permissible for him to ignore the relation between illness and guilt. This should not be taken
to imply—by any means!—that there is always a positive correlation
between illness and ethical violations. But whoever inquires after the
ultimate and most underlying cause of illness in general will have at
least to take into consideration the possibility of a hidden link with
ethical violations. But what do "guilt" and "ethical violation" mean
here anyway? How could one say anything of any consequence here
if one refuses to speak of "God and the world", and of "Adam and
Eve"?

   Let us recapitulate by pointing out in what the *second* element of
philosophy, as originally conceived, consists: Since the aspect under
which philosophical questioning is conducted expressly and formally
encompasses "everything", it is impossible to delimit its field of inquiry (in contrast to the individual sciences). For example, whoever

asks in a philosophical mood "What is man?" would automatically
negate the philosophical dimension of this anthropological query if
he were to assert that the findings of genetics, medical science, or
psychology were of no interest to him. The philosophical dimension
of anthropology would be just as much compromised and violated if
one were to exclude from the very outset and on principle the data
of theology as being "uninteresting".

That Plato truly construed philosophizing in this manner is demonstrated in virtually every one of his dialogues. In the *Symposium*, the
question, "What, finally, is love?" is answered by both the sociologist
(Pausanias) and the natural scientist (the physician Eryximachus); after
them comes Aristophanes, who argues that one cannot arrive at an
adequate conception of love's essence unless one knows something
of what befell man in his primeval history—after saying which he
recounts the myth of man's fall, of original sin and its punishment.
And, finally, Socrates relates the doctrine of *eros* that Diotima, the
priestess from Mantinea, had confided to him as a kind of "mystic
theology" or wisdom deriving from the Mysteries. ("This . . . was
the doctrine of Diotima [and] I was convinced. . . .") In the *Meno*,
after the discussion has ended in a cul-de-sac, Socrates decides that it
has now become necessary to consult "those wise in divine things".
In the *Phaedo*, the question is raised whether man is the kind of being who, as completely self-determined, may justly choose to deliver
himself over to death. The answer that is given—no—is based on
an allegory told by certain mystics—that we men are put in this life
as in a sort of guard post from which we must not release ourselves
or run away—and on the received religious view of man as one of
God's possessions, one of his flock.

I strain myself to imagine how Plato would have responded if someone had tapped him on the shoulder with the admonition: "This is,
however, no longer pure philosophy; with this, you have crossed the
boundary to a foreign territory, theology." Presumably, Plato would
have answered that he is not interested in philosophy but in *sophia*,
wisdom—that is, in an answer to the question concerning the origin
of things. Still, it is precisely this kind of interest that, in his view,
is to be identified with philosophy. Plato would, conceivably, pose
the counterquestion: "If you dismiss the revelations of myth as inappropriate, how am I supposed to believe that you are in earnest with
your inquiry into the origin of things?"

And what about Aristotle? One of the most exciting findings of Werner Jaeger's classic text on Aristotle, it seems to me, is that it shows that behind the much more "scientific" ontology of the Aristotelian metaphysics there stands again the credo, "I believe so that I may come to know" (*credo ut intelligam*).

III

When Socrates is asked by his sophist interlocutor who "those wise in divine things" are and where one might chance upon them, he—and by extension Plato—does not hesitate for a moment in giving his answer. If one were to confront an educated person of India who has remained uninfluenced by Western civilization with the same question, he would presumably also answer with great certainty and matter-of-factness. Within the confines of Western civilization, however, only Christians are able to provide an answer to this question; the modern secularized American or European knows neither what "wisdom in divine things" means exactly nor where or in whose person it is to be found. With this, our actual topic has now come clearly into view: the dilemma posed by a philosophy that knows neither myth nor theology and yet continues to lay claim to being the same subject that Pythagoras, Plato, and Aristotle dubbed "philosophy".

If the original conception of philosophy by definition includes a methodological openness to theology; if philosophizing necessarily implies viewing a thing within the horizon of reality as a whole and thus relating it to God and the world; if *philo-sophia* is the loving search after wisdom such as God alone perfectly possesses—if the original conception of philosophy contains all these elements—then, as far as our Western world is concerned, "Christian philosophy" is simply *the* one and only genuine, necessary, and natural form of philosophy. (All these are elements that are clearly peculiar, not to the Christian, but rather to the Platonic/Aristotelian conception of philosophy characteristic of *classical antiquity*—otherwise how could the idea of a wisdom that is alone capable of completely satisfying man's questions ever stand in need of a fundamental correction or of an adjustment to the "progress" of the times?) From the standpoint of the Platonic/Aristotelian conception of philosophy, it is not the notion of a "Christian philosophy" that requires defense and justification. Conversely, it is extremely difficult, if not impossible, to answer the question of how something like a *non-Christian* philosophy is supposed to be possible —unless, again, one understands by philosophy something other than what has been understood by it since the name was first coined. It is an empirical finding, easily verifiable by all, that in our Western world there is simply no counterpart—apart from Christian theology—to what the myths, the "wisdom in the divine things", the Mysteries, the interpretation of the world received from the "ancients" meant for Plato. If, however, it is true that everything the mythological tradition contained by way of truth and wisdom for Pythagoras, Plato, and Aristotle has either been forgotten and lost or has been absorbed in the Christian dogmatic tradition and so neutralized, then does it not follow either that philosophy, in interpreting the world, must wholly abandon that contrapuntal polyphony which classical philosophy had possessed through its proximity to myth or that it can preserve it only through recourse to Christian theology?

At this juncture, I anticipate an interjection of the following sort: Is it not simply absurd to argue that there is no genuine non-Christian philosophy worthy of the name? To this I would reply: Granted, it is an extremely pointed formulation; but whether it is "simply absurd" cannot be resolved until it becomes clear what is meant by "philosophy" and, further, what is meant by "Christian" and "non-Christian".

As far as the first point is concerned, there are doubtless variants within contemporary philosophy that do not profess to be philosophy in the traditional sense and that, consequently, do not for themselves lay claim to the title. I think that this is true, for example, of certain systems of logic: they do not aspire to be anything other than a rigorous scientific discipline, which is of interest solely to specialists and experts, but not to human beings as such, by which I mean *every* thinking person.

Of a much greater order of difficulty is the problem of determining when a philosophy should be deemed "Christian" or "non-Christian". It is—so it appears to me—extremely difficult for someone from our Western world to prescind so completely from those presuppositions deriving from our Christian tradition that his philosophizing could appropriately be described as thoroughly "non-Christian", that is, in no way informed by its subordination to an

unacknowledged, if ultimately theological, counterpoint. This difficulty is particularly evident in the case of Descartes. Why *must* a clear
and distinct idea be necessarily true? Descartes' answer is that God is
not mendacious, and it is impossible for him to deceive me. Clearly,
this answer falls squarely within the same religious tradition on whose
methodological exclusion Descartes' philosophy was supposed to rest.
Again, when Immanuel Kant, in defending his philosophy of religion,
cites the Bible roughly seventy-five times, he hardly appears to be operating "within the limits of pure reason". Of course, no one would
for this reason characterize it as a work of "Christian philosophy". But
is it fair to characterize it as straightforwardly non-Christian? These
are the same types of inconsistencies for which Sartre famously criti-
cized the philosophy of the eighteenth century. "Atheistic existentialism, which I represent, is more consistent", he argues. Yet, for Sartre
himself, the denial of the Christian notion of creation plays such a
determinative role that a pre-Christian nihilist with the sophistic bent
of a Gorgias could never have understood him. Clearly, one must be
a Christian if one is to understand Sartre.

Philosophy will doubtless be "purged" ever more consistently of
the final traces of its one-time subordination to a theological world
view, and, inevitably, all those insights that have been built up on the
basis of *credo ut intelligam* will gradually fall victim, one by one, to
this process of attrition. Only in the final stage of this process would
there be a genuine "non-Christian philosophy", and to say of it that
it would at the same time constitute a "non-philosophy" does not
appear to me to be in any way absurd. How could it be anything but
paradoxical to characterize the deliberate "disregard" of wisdom as its
"pursuit" (*philo-sophia*)?

PHILOSOPHY AND THE SENSE FOR MYSTERY

In what follows, it is not my intent to discuss what philosophy or certain philosophers have to teach about a specific topic, "mystery". Rather, I shall be talking about the notions of philosophy and philosophizing insofar as a specific relation to mystery is peculiar to them.

I

During the high watermark of philosophical self-awareness, which, however, appears to be coming to an end, one was prone to forget that the notions of philosophy and philosophizing had from the outset been conceived as *negative* concepts—at the very least, more like negative concepts than positive ones. I need not repeat here the well-known tale of Pythagoras, already a legend in classical antiquity, whereby this great teacher of the sixth century B.C. was the first to coin the term "philosophy": God alone can be called wise; man may at best be called a wisdom-loving seeker after truth.[1] Plato, too, speaks of the difference between wisdom and philosophy, between *sophos* and *philosophos*. In the *Phaedrus*, Plato has Socrates say that neither Solon nor Homer should be described as "wise": "To call him wise, Phaedrus, would I think be going too far; the epithet is proper only to a god. A name that would fit him better, and have more seemliness, would be 'lover of wisdom,' or something similar."[2] And Diotima, who in the *Symposium* gives voice to Plato's most profound thoughts, expresses the same idea in the form of a negative: "[N]one of the gods are seekers after truth" (that is, philosophizes).[3]

---

[1] *Phaedrus* 278d 3–6.

[2] Ibid. [Quoted after the translation by R. Hackforth, in *Plato: The Collected Dialogues*, ed. Edith Hamilton and Huntington Cairns (Princeton, 1961), p. 524.]

[3] *Symposium* 204a1. [Quoted after the translation by Michael Joyce, in *Plato: The Collected Dialogues*, p. 556.]

What else can this mean if not that from the very outset philosophy
—and philosophizing—were construed as something that is *not sophia*,
not wisdom, *not* knowledge, *not* understanding, *not* the possession of
truth?

This way of thinking is, however, not peculiar to Pythagoreanism
or Platonism. Aristotle, the initiator of a critical, scientific form of
philosophizing, proceeds farther along the same path, at least as far as
metaphysics—the most philosophical discipline—is concerned. And
Thomas Aquinas, in his masterly commentary on Aristotle's *Metaphysics*, accurately presents the views of that outstanding Greek when
he writes that the metaphysical truth about Being does not, strictly
speaking, fall to man as his possession ("non competit homini ut pos-
sessio"); it is not held by man as his property but rather as a loan
("sicut aliquid mutuatum").[4] Aquinas then goes on to endow this
circumstance with a speculative significance of such extreme depth
that it can hardly be plumbed; here all that can be done is to gesture
toward it. Aquinas is arguing, namely, that wisdom cannot be man's
property precisely because it is being sought for its own sake: what
we possess fully is incapable of satisfying us to such a degree that we
would strive after it for its own sake: "That truth *alone* is sought for
its own sake which does not fall to man as his own possession."[5]

It is not that, on Aquinas' and Aristotle's view, man would be cut
off from any relation to *sophia*—this is precisely what is *not* being
said. The philosophical question does, indeed, aim at wisdom; what
in the act of philosophizing is inquired after is, in fact, an ultimate,
comprehending knowledge. *But*—and this can be affirmed with great
certainty—we not only do not possess such wisdom, but we are incapable of possessing it on principle, and this is why we will also
not possess it in the future. By contrast, we are undoubtedly capable
of possessing the answers provided by the special sciences (they, on
the other hand, cannot satisfy us to the degree that we would pursue them "for their own sake".) It belongs to the very essence of a
philosophical question that it inquire after the definitive nature, the
final meaning, the ultimate origin of the real. A genuine philosophical
question takes the form: What is man, truth, knowledge, life, or what-

---

[4] *In Met.* I, 3 (no. 64).
[5] Ibid.

ever "in the final analysis and as such"? Now that means that this type of query aims by its very nature at an answer that both includes and expresses fully and without qualification the essence of that which is being asked about. Such questioning demands an answer in which, as Aquinas says (when he is defining what it means to "comprehend"), "the thing is so far known as it is intelligible in itself."[6] Accordingly, an adequate response to a philosophical question would have to be one that exhausts its object, a statement in which the intelligibility of the real thing being questioned is drained off until nothing knowable is left and everything that remains is known. I have said that this would be an *adequate* answer to a philosophical question; "adequate" here means that the answer formally corresponds to the question; the question, however, let us recall, concerns the definitive nature, the ultimate origin of a real existing thing. The philosophical question aims, by its very nature, at a comprehending response in the strict sense. Aquinas would claim, however, that we are absolutely incapable of comprehending anything—unless it is our own work (insofar as this really is our own work: the marble as such is not part of the sculptor's work!).

All this implies that it belongs to the very essence of a philosophical question that it cannot be answered in the same sense in which it is asked. On this point, Plato, Aristotle, Augustine, and Aquinas find themselves in complete agreement with the major traditions of mankind. And it would already constitute a rationalistic aberration from the *philosophia perennis* were one to overlook this negative element in the original conception of philosophy. Let us cast another glance at the tradition of the *philosophia perennis* to see whether such an unusual and perhaps even scandalous statement can really be found there.

Aristotle, in an extremely festive and, as it were, very un-Aristotelian formulation, says that the question of what Being is, "both now and of old, has always been raised, and always been the subject of doubt."[7] Aquinas not only comments on this sentence without raising any objections, he uses such formulations himself. For example, he himself

---

[6] *Super Joh.* I, 11 (no. 213).

[7] *Metaphysics* 7.1.1028b1-2. [Quoted after the translation in Jonathan Barnes, ed., *The Complete Works of Aristotle: The Revised Oxford Translation* (Princeton, 1984) 2:1624.]

notes that the exertions of all the philosophers combined have not yet been sufficient to track down the essence of even a single mosquito.[8] And how often does the sentence recur in the *Summa theologica* and *Quaestiones disputatae de veritate*: "We do not know the essential differences between things",[9] which means that we do not know the essence of the things themselves; and this is the reason why we are also unable to give to them their essential names. Aquinas even goes so far as to speak of the *imbecillitas intellectus nostri*, of the stupidity of our minds, which are not adequate to the task of "reading off" in natural things what is naturally revealed in them about God.[10]

It would then truly appear as if Aquinas had with a very extreme formulation not only laid the foundation for a *theologia negativa* ("This is the highest form that man's knowledge of God can take: to know that we do not know God insofar as we recognize that God's essence lies beyond all that which we know of him"[11]) but also formulated the guiding principle for something like a *philosophia negativa* (although this neologism is perhaps more at risk of being misunderstood and misapplied than that of the *theologia negativa*).

This essential peculiarity of a philosophical question—aiming at an answer that cannot be given adequately—distinguishes it from the questions of the exact sciences. The sciences have a fundamentally different relation to their respective objects; it belongs to the very nature of a science that it formulate its question in such a way that it can be adequately answered—or at least in such a way that it is not in principle unanswerable. One day the medical profession will finally know what the ultimate cause of cancer is. But the question concerning the essence of knowledge, of spirit, of life—the question of the ultimate meaning of this whole world, so wonderful and awful at the same time—these questions will never be definitively answered in a philosophical manner, although they can certainly be expressed in a philosophical form. What is explicitly und unmistakably being sought in the philosophical question is knowledge of the highest cause (as Aquinas says, wisdom as such, genuine wisdom, consists in just this

[8] *Symb. Apost.*, prologue (no. 864).
[9] *Ver.* 4, 1 ad 8; see also I, 29, 1 ad 3.
[10] *Ver.* 5, 2 ad 11.
[11] *Pot.* 7, 5 ad 14.

knowledge),[12] but philosophy will persist in this search, on this path, passionately inquiring, as long as man—and mankind generally—is on this path, in *statu viatoris*. Thus any claim to have found the "cosmic formula" can be dismissed without need of further inspection as unphilosophical. It belongs to the very essence of philosophy that it cannot take the form of a "closed system"—"closed" in the sense that the essential reality of the world would be adequately reflected in it.

II

What, however, becomes of this "negative" element when philosophy becomes *Christian* philosophy? It is a commonly held opinion that Christian philosophy is superior to non-Christian philosophy *in that* it, the Christian philosophy, is in possession of more polished, final answers.

This, however, is not true. Christian philosophy really does have one advantage, though, or, at any rate, it can have this advantage at times. This notwithstanding, the superiority of Christian philosophy does not consist in its having at its disposal conclusive, exhaustive, ultimate answers to philosophical questions. Wherein does it consist, then? Garrigou-Lagrange, in his beautiful book on the sense of mystery,* writes that it is precisely the distinguishing mark of a Christian philosophy not to have at its disposal more refined solutions but rather to possess to a higher degree than any other philosophy a sense of mystery. Again, what does this distinction mean? To what extent can it legitimately be regarded as evidence of Christian philosophy's superiority—when not even Christian philosophy itself can arrive at a final resolution of these problems?

Now the superiority that is being asserted here on behalf of Christian philosophy consists in its being able to attain to a higher degree of truth. Christian philosophy really *does* contain a higher degree of truth in that it is more profoundly aware of the fact that that the world and Being itself are a mystery and for that reason inexhaustible. The more profoundly one comes to recognize positively the structure of

---

[12] II, II, 9, 2.

* [*Der Sinn für das Geheimnis und das Hell-Dunkel des Geistes* (Paderborn, 1937), pp. 112f. —ED.]

reality, the clearer it becomes that reality is a mystery. The reason for this inexhaustibility of the real is that the world is creation, a creature, that is, that it has its origin in God's incomprehensible conceptual knowledge. Now it is peculiar to all Being to be a product of God's creative knowledge, which is absolutely and infinitely superior to human knowledge; this characteristic of Being comes to the fore all the more compellingly, the more profound the insight into reality. And it may reasonably be suspected that, when reality is experienced as an inexhaustible creature, it is known and grasped in a much more profound sense than when it is simply translated into a perspicacious and seemingly closed system of theses.

But does the recourse to theological truth not make a definitive solution possible? This question may be countered with another question: whether the purpose—so to speak, the soteriological purpose —of theology is not to prevent mortal thought from arriving at "solutions" that, in their abstract transparency, may perhaps constitute a strong temptation, a powerful form of seduction, but are not consonant with the mysteriously multiform structure of reality. Such "hindrances", which are in fact a godsend, do not exactly make Christian philosophizing easy from an intellectual standpoint; one might, on the other hand, argue that the ensuing complications are, for their part, a distinguishing mark of Christian philosophy. When Aquinas appeals to theological arguments, it is not with the purpose of being able to offer more refined solutions but rather to break through the methodological confinement of "pure philosophy" and to open up the genuine impetus behind philosophical questioning—above and beyond the *aporia* of natural thought—to the realm of the revealed mystery.

Now, what is meant here by mystery is not something exclusively negative and more than simply what is obscure. In fact, when understood more precisely, mystery does not imply obscurity at all. It connotes light, but a light of such plenitude that it remains "unquenchable" for a knowing faculty or a linguistic capacity that is merely human. The notion of mystery should not suggest that the effort involved in thinking runs up against a wall but rather that this effort exhausts itself in the unforeseeable, in the space—the unlimited breadth and depth—of creation.

Thus the promise and priority of Christian philosophy lie in the fact that it is called upon to deliver a more profound insight into both the plenitude and the inexhaustibility of truth. The more profound the insight into its plenitude, the more profound is the insight into its inexhaustibility. The insight into the inadequacy of human knowledge increases in proportion with this knowledge itself.

While the sciences may properly restrict themselves to the realm of the positively knowable, philosophy, whose nature it is to inquire into the origins of what is real and so penetrate various strata of its createdness, is formally concerned with the incomprehensible, with the creature as mystery.

A POSSIBLE FUTURE FOR PHILOSOPHY

Nowadays it has become evident that when we talk about "the future" —something to which we have, in fact, become exceedingly prone— the word is not always being used in the same sense. If nothing else, it may fail to carry the same resonances, to convey the same overtones: that will depend on context. As anyone will readily perceive, the word "future" has a completely different ring in the locution "the future of space exploration", than it does in "the future of mankind"; the former has an element of triumphant optimism, the latter something more akin to sceptical concern. A phenomenon closely analogous to the latter may be observed whenever discussion turns to the future of philosophy, perhaps for similar reasons. After all, a case may be made that the future of philosophy is intimately bound up with the future of mankind, if, indeed, it can be distinguished from the latter at all. I fear that many, on hearing of "the future of philosophy", will be reminded of a terminally ill patient whose friends speak in terms of tomorrow or, at best, next spring.

It was T. S. Eliot[1] who in this connection went so far as to speak of "the sickness of philosophy", "an obscure recognition of which", he says, "moves those who complain of its decline". This sickness, he goes on to remark, "has been present too long to be attributable to any particular contemporary school of thought". His own diagnosis locates the "root cause" of its ailment in the "divorce" of philosophy from theology. If T. S. Eliot is correct in supposing that at least some elements of the contemporary crisis in philosophy are no more than the direct consequence of this "divorce" (and I am convinced he is)— if all this is true—then the future of philosophy will rest on whether its isolation from theology can be overcome in a nontendentious manner. For its part, this question cannot be answered, or even so much as elaborated, until one is in possession of a sufficiently clear conception of what constitutes a workable or desirable "marriage" between

---

[1] Cf. the introduction by T. S. Eliot, in J. Pieper, *Leisure: The Basis of Culture* (New York, 1952), pp. 12ff.

philosophy and theology. Certainly, it need no longer be argued that specific means of effecting this union now belong irrevocably to the past; thus it seems highly unlikely that the theological problem of the simultaneous unity and trinity of the Godhead will ever again incite logical controversy, as it did in the time of Abelard. Besides, what sort of "theology" is meant here? And what should one understand by "theology" anyway? It is probably true that an authoritative definition of theology can be expected only from theology itself. By the same token, I would argue that the philosophizing person can simply not afford to ignore or neglect the question of theology's nature. And to this point I would like to address a couple of remarks.

The philosopher—or, as I would prefer to call him, the philosophizing person—is not in the first instance someone who has successfully worked out for himself a multivalent view of the world but rather someone who is concerned with keeping a certain question alive, that is, the question of the ultimate meaning of the totality of what is— a question to which doubtless a series of provisional answers may certainly be found, but never *the* answer. His efforts to grasp "the complete fact"[2] remain perforce an endless enterprise. What happens when a man ceases to exist—not merely physiologically or biographically, but in every conceivable way? What really takes place in the act of knowing? What is it to be real? No one will ever be in a position to answer even a single one of these questions adequately. And yet this is the task specific to philosophy: to preserve man's openness to this incomprehensible "complete fact"; to sow distrust for any claim to have discovered the universal cosmic formula, to resist any attempt to suppress or otherwise obscure a single element of the unvarnished truth, say, in the interests of a premature systematization or harmonization.

Separate from the philosophizing person but always by his side, there is someone who likewise speaks of the totality of the world and of what is, albeit not in the same tone of uneasy questioning, but more along the lines of someone offering an unquestionably "positive" answer. This "someone" else is the theologian, and what he has to say may be paraphrased as follows: Man and world are created beings, that is, all existing things, including man himself, have the in-

---

2 A. N. Whitehead, *Adventures of Ideas* (New York, 1956), p. 203.

ner constitution of something designed and originating in the creative knowledge of an absolute intellect. Man is, moreover, not simply *creature*, but he is, in fact, created in the very likeness of his Creator. One point should be immediately obvious: Propositions of this type are concerned with exactly the same topic with which the philosopher is, by definition, concerned, that is, with the ultimate meaning of the world and existence, considered as a whole.

And for the philosophizing person, it is, in fact, a rather decisive moment when he notices the presence and proximity of this "someone" who has evidently been there all along. From that moment on, the philosophizing person is obliged to define his own activity more precisely in order to differentiate it from that of the theologian. Just this, incidentally, has been taking place from time immemorial up to the present day, spurred on solely by philosophy's compulsion to reflect on its relation to theology, to understand its own nature and its own task more clearly. But with this, of course, the circumstances of their confrontation have been all too summarily described.

Thus, it is already misleading to have presented the theologian as "someone *else*", that is, as some "other". At any rate, this need not necessarily be the case and is certainly not always so; especially at the beginning, the theologian is not "someone else". At the beginning of human history, as well as at the beginning of each individual biography, philosophy and theology are undivided, one. Every person who inquires after the meaning of the totality of world and existence begins as a believer. With, however, the first philosophical act of critical reflection, the process of differentiation, of *self*-differentiation, begins—even if that act of differentiation consists only in distinguishing between two different acts of the same person. This process is as unavoidable as it is highly portentous. For they are really two very different ways of thinking and speaking about one and the same world that lies before our eyes. And this corresponds, in turn, to a duality in the kind of legitimation to which each appeals in identifying and justifying itself. In reflecting on that question which is most properly his own, the philosophizing person directs his gaze toward the empirically encountered world; no less than the scientist, he has to use his own eyes. And whatever the philosophical assertion may happen to be, it must prove itself in the crucible of experience. By comparison, the work of the theologian is, in its logical structure, something much

more complicated and difficult, but also something much more derivative. It presupposes much more than simply that reality is there before
our eyes. When, for example, the theologian refers to man as having
been created in God's likeness or to the world as creature, then he
is not, of course, appealing to something he himself sees and knows;
he invokes divine revelation, which can in no way be inferred or derived from the empirical reality of man and world. In other words,
there can be no theology if revelation (in the strict sense) does not
exist. Theology is nothing more than the attempt to interpret those
documents in the holy tradition that relate to divine revelation. Here
"interpretation" means, not primarily textual criticism, but rather the
endeavor to determine as clearly as circumstances allow what the *sen-
sus divinus* of a text is that has, of course, been historically conditioned
in many ways. Theology, so construed, is thus at bottom a human
endeavor. It is, however, possible to conceive of one highly significant
exception to this rule, and perhaps the word "exception" here is also
not entirely correct: I am thinking of a situation in which the Author
of the revelation himself inspires its interpretation. This alone would
constitute—or rather *is* in fact—theology in the sense of the *doctrina
sacra*. This is not what we are referring to here; rather, we will be
treating theology here as a thoroughly human enterprise.

To the extent, however, that he is unprepared to cooperate with
science and philosophy, the theologian relying on exclusively human
devices will be simply incapable of pursuing his own distinctive occupation. It is absolutely forbidden for him to restrict himself to a
purely Bible-based preoccupation with the documents relating to divine revelation. How, for example, could a contemporary theologian
who undertakes to interpret the biblical account of creation be permitted to spare himself the most serious consideration of the findings
of, say, paleontology and modern evolutionary theory? The reason
for this is *not* that a modern theologian should also be scientifically
up-to-date. On the contrary, the reason is that the theologian would
otherwise not be in a position to fulfill his specifically theological
charge, which consists in making plausible to his contemporaries that
it is still meaningful to believe—and in what sense it remains so—that
"the LORD God formed man of dust from the ground, and breathed
into his nostrils the breath of life" (Gen 2:7).

Interpretation always means something akin to translation—"carrying over" [*Hinübertragung*] from one language into another. Thus, it is part of the formal structure of a theological proposition that it be expressed in the "material", as it were, of two different languages. One of these corresponds to the mind-set of that generation of mankind to whom the revelation and the holy tradition are to be made comprehensible as a meaningful and truth-disclosing communication concerning the world and human existence.

Incidentally, there is much that speaks in favor of the thesis that this way of construing the nature of theology is something distinctly "Western" or "Occidental"; there is evidently nothing similar in Hinduism or Islam. Wherever, though, this risky wager is accepted—the risk involved in a contrapuntal collaboration with the ever-expanding scientific investigation of reality—theology takes upon itself a virtually unsatisfiable requirement that would certainly tax the fortitude of any individual, regardless of how ingenious. A restriction of the "material", in keeping with the criterion of theological relevance, is, for example, impracticable, unrealistic. Thomas Aquinas would say that no one is responsible for determining in advance what facts it is unimportant for theology to know. A much greater obstacle lies in the fact, however, that such "collaboration" rarely takes the form of a more or less academic conversation between theology, on the one side, and professional philosophy, on the other. What, for the most part, actually occurs more closely resembles a wild and no-holds-barred feud for which, often enough, no common basis would appear to exist. And, once again, the theologian, in the interest of his own task, is not entitled to withdraw from this debate. From a historical standpoint, a deeper understanding of God's word is very rarely the simple result of a quiet intratheological development; rather progress has much more frequently been the fruit of a sharp confrontation.

Still, one should not argue that theological progress is merely the result of externally applied pressure; it is rather to be attributed to the fact that theology subjects itself to such painful and confusing confrontation. One falls short of grasping what really takes place here when one uses categories drawn from the realm of vegetative life (for example, those expressions denoting "growth", a "blossoming", or an "opening up"). What actually takes place is surely something distinctly human, in which freedom, decision, vulnerability to seduction, guilt, and the possibility of corruption have their place just as much as all the other challenges that normally accompany the maturing of the ethical person and, as it were, force it.

Openness to conflicts of this kind is simply a prerequisite that the theologian must bring with him to his line of work. Without the willingness to endure the pain of disagreement and contradiction, theology must remain sterile. John Henry Newman has, with great forthrightness, given a name to some of the typical aberrations: love of system, theorizing, fancifulness, dogmatism, and bigotry, and, as a result, sectarianism, sophistry, and denunciation.[3] The most important "service" that science and philosophy render to theology is to prevent it from withdrawing from the field of disputation on the basis of a presumed autarchy. Even the notorious expression *ancilla theologiae*, which has been misinterpreted a thousand times—and that in both directions —points to nothing more than the need for collaboration. Theology *needs* the association with philosophy and science, and that means, of course, a free-thinking philosophy and an independent science.

But now the other side of the medallion has to be considered; finally the time has come to discuss philosophy itself. It is certainly not as if theology were the only one that profited from their collaboration. The philosophizing person also gains something from theology that he cannot secure in any other way or from any other source. And this benefit has two aspects to it, in turn: enrichment and enervation.

To take one example: The philosophizing person, who, as a believer, understands the world in terms of creation, that is, as originating with the divine *logos*, and thus as simultaneously lucid and limpid to its very depths *and* as embodying a plan that is in principle inaccessible to all human understanding—a person who philosophizes in this way will be able to gain some idea for the first time of how the intelligibility of the world and its incomprehensibility (both more or less empirically verifiable features) could have one and the same root. This patently philosophical insight, acquired in the encounter with experienceable reality, can only become the property of one who is prepared to allow himself to be instructed by theology about something that he, by his own devices, could never know. The greatest

---

[3] *Oxford University Sermons* 4 (June 1, 1841). [John Henry Newman, "Sermon XIV: Wisdom, as Contrasted with Faith and with Bigotry", in *Fifteen Sermons Preached before the University of Oxford* (London, 1918), p. 282.]

form of enrichment that, however, the philosophizing person derives from his collaboration with theology consists in his being prevented from doing something, namely, from falling victim to the most primordial of philosophical dangers; among these the most prominent is the natural longing for the clarity and transparency that go along with a self-contained world view. For example, the idea of God's becoming man, in which the last work of creation connects up with its primeval beginning to form a complete circle, might be congenial to a "Gnostic" philosophy as the unexpected confirmation of a world view conceived in conformity with a single principle. But that historical mankind hated and killed the God-become-man "for no reason"[4] and that, with this self-same killing, the salvation of mankind is supposed to have become reality—these theological data transcend any conceivable rationale for the world. Or: A philosophy of history that reckons with the possibility of a final intratemporal cataclysm but that nevertheless, on the basis of the same apocalyptic theology, resists the despair characteristic of all philosophies of the absurd—such a philosophy *must* inevitably be much more difficult, more complex, and, as it were, "more unsatisfying" than any philosophy of progress (whether defended on idealistic, Marxist, or evolutionary grounds) or any metaphysics of decline. The enrichment that the philosophizing person experiences from the apparent "handicap" of collaborating with theology may be summed up in a single notion: higher truth. What is critical is neither the avoidance of intellectual difficulties nor the bewitching of the mind with considerations of plausibility and evidence; it is critical that not a single element of reality—that incomprehensible reality whose coming into view is commensurate with the concept of "truth"—is suppressed or concealed.

In the interests of fairness, something should be also said about the characteristically aberrant forms of a philosophy that disavows any partnership with theology. Of course—it should be kept in mind—what is meant is not a philosophizing that never had any inkling of the possibility of such a partnership; rather, I am speaking solely of a philosophizing that explicitly rejects and denies this kind of collaboration. An entire collection of such aberrant symptoms might be

---

[4] Jn 15:25.

adduced. To them might be reckoned purely formalistic game-playing —sometimes at the very highest level—which, like all other forms of entertainment, is grounded in a widespread intellectual ennui and which derives its thrill from the element of surprise. It is what Hegel has termed the "vanity of opinion". Even more baleful is the prospect that a philosophy that denies any connection with a genuine theology will almost inevitably come to understand itself as a "theory of salvation"—with all the well-known consequences: mystic-demagogic jargon, the emergence of secret societies, intolerance, and so forth. Karl Jaspers[5] has described the secret infirmity of a philosophy that has abandoned the substance of a great tradition in the most unforgiving and unsparing terms; its hallmark, he says, is "an empty earnestness".

All these things will not be unfamiliar to a contemporary observer of the philosophical scene, and it might well occur to him to ask how philosophy will continue from here. Of course, no one really knows anything about what philosophy will be like in the foreseeable future. It might be that philosophical activity will one day rejuvenate itself, drawing on unsuspected reserves, if only because philosophy, being by its very nature nonpublic, is not the prerogative of specialists but is, by implication, something that quite possibly remains unrecorded in the research literature. If, on the other hand, one allows oneself, as a believer, to be swayed by the information contained in the apocalyptic prophecy, then one "knows" possibly more about the final era of history than about the near future—about the end of time, about that undatable epoch to which the arrow of each present is directed and which, for precisely that reason, is not entirely unknown. Although the apocalyptic prophecy tells of political power, of business and trade, of propaganda, it wastes no words on worldly wisdom or philosophy. And it might, in fact, not be so astonishing that, during this final period of history, when sophistic movements and false and corrupt philosophies predominate, that the genuine philosophy returns to its primordial unity with theology and, as result, simply disappears as a distinct, independent quantity. Alternately, it might well turn out that, at the end of history, the origin of all things and the ultimate meaning of existence—in other words, those objects peculiar to philosophizing as such—will be perceived and reflected on only by those who *believe*.

---

[5] Karl Jaspers and R. Bultmann, *Die Frage der Entmythologisierung*, p. 12.

EDITORIAL POSTSCRIPT

Truth and Sense

For some time now, it has become possible to discern in philosophers' discussion of their subject two distinct points of emphasis that, at first glance, would appear to have nothing in common. The one, indicative of both a long-standing crisis and a therapeutic attempt at relief, is summed up in the question, "To what end philosophy?" (*Wozu Philosophie?*).[1] The other appears to be of lesser significance and reflects a disagreement between analytic and hermeneutic philosophers about the primacy of reference over interpretation, with the univocity of fact—determined to be either true or false—being opposed to the multivocity of sense, which varies with the mode of "givenness". There are signs, however, that, increasingly, the foundational dispute concerning our relation to the external world is being viewed as specious and as having led philosophy into that cul-de-sac from which it is currently seeking to extricate itself.[2]

What, then, does the crisis in philosophy's understanding of itself —"why do philosophy at all?"—have to do with a quarrel among philosophical schools? And if, as it appears, Josef Pieper was uninfluenced by the epistemological debate between the hermeneutic and analytic philosophies, what justifies us in linking him to this discussion

---

[1] This is the title of a collection of position papers written by the members of a philosophical study group and published in 1978 in New York and Berlin.

[2] A similar problematic may be observed in academic theology. It consists in the assertion of the priority of sense (the historicity of understanding) over truth (with respect to the event of revelation). Cf. F. Inciarte, "Wahrheit oder Sinn? Ein Konvergenzpunkt zwischen analytischer Philosophie und hermeneutischer Theologie", in *Transcendenz und Immanenz: Philosophie und Theologie in der veränderten Welt*, ed. D. Papenfuß and J. Söring (Stuttgart, Berlin, Cologne, and Mainz, 1977), pp. 67–71. In philosophy, by contrast, the priority has run the other way. Now, however, analytic philosophy, which has hitherto set the tone, appears to be abandoning its dogmatic fixation on the univocity of truth-functionality and to be growing increasingly open to the idea of assumed interpretational perspectives. Cf. R. Bubner, "Wohin tendiert die analytische Philosophie?" *Philosophische Rundschau* 34 (1987): 257–81.

(although he doubtless contributed to its central problematic, that of the sense and legitimation of "philosophizing today", very early on and with very basic arguments)? While it is true that his writings do not lack for critical remarks on scientism and historicism, they are not directly concerned with related developments in contemporary philosophy, nor is it possible to subsume the conception of philosophy expressly articulated by Pieper under any particular movement.

That an implicit and substantial connection does exist despite the apparently disparate and—as far as Pieper is concerned—marginal nature of these questions may be recognized by recalling how the differences in the philosophical schools of the present century arose. For both the analytic and hermeneutic philosophies may be regarded as attempts to come to terms with an ongoing crisis in philosophy that, beginning in the mid-1920s, was exacerbated by the achievements of the natural sciences. Far from helping overcome the crisis, though, the mutual exclusivity of their respective notions of philosophy—that is, the very opposition between truth and sense—further aggravated it: the one drew on natural science to assert the unconditional primacy of referential univocity, and the other, construing itself as a social science, asserted the unconditional priority of its postulated interpretational perspectives in an effort to secure for philosophy a proper field of study with its own methodology. From that time onward, philosophy has come—not entirely unjustly—to be viewed by many as a specialized discipline devoted to the answering of questions that hardly anyone would think to ask (except, of course, philosophers) or as a supermarket in which everyone may pick and choose, according to his own personal preference and with no obligation, among a host of competing intellectual wares, all under limited warranty.[3]

Pieper's conception of philosophy was likewise defined from the outset by its response to the crisis in philosophy, albeit a crisis he viewed as affecting not so much the discipline itself as the few still

---

[3] This last view is not only enjoying growing support but is actually being defended against other conceptions of philosophy, for example, by Richard Rorty in his book *Eine Kultur ohne Zentrum* (Stuttgart, 1993). Thus, at the end of the twentieth century, the pendulum is swinging back from the ascetic frugality of the "scientific philosophy" represented by the Vienna Circle to the other extreme: the free—because referenceless—"play of sense" (Jacques Derrida), which, while aesthetically satisfying, is indifferent to truth and thus irrelevant for the serious demands of life. From the initial attempted reduction of speech to what can be said, we have moved in the end to a speech that no longer says anything.

remaining opportunities for its living pursuit under contemporary conditions. Pieper's starting point—the everyday thought and speech of human beings insofar as the former aspire toward knowledge—dissuaded him, however, from attempting to mount a front against scientific positivism by severing truth from sense and from defending a (necessarily artificial) opposition between that to which speech refers, insofar as it has meaning, and the way in which what is meant manifests itself to the different participants in a dialogue. Truth in the untruncated sense does not exist apart from a pregiven horizon of meaning, that is, it does not lie on the other side of tradition, beyond all language and interpretation, just as, conversely, the historically transmitted sense is, by virtue of its relation to the external world, subject to certain truth conditions—a rudimentary, if still uninterpreted, form of knowledge. With this, Pieper's conception of philosophy situates itself outside the debate over truth *or* sense but within a line of argumentation that, lying beyond the philosophical dichotomy "analytic *or* hermeneutic", originates in the Plato of the later dialogues and that was sharpened by Aristotle in his struggles against the physical reductionism of his own era and the axiom-denying pluralism of the philosophically well-versed sophists.

In Plato's case this is easily inferred from the aporetic structure of his dialogues. No matter how well grounded the opinions are that are presented and examined, they remain provisional and incomplete, standing in a fundamental tension with the claim to knowledge implicit in the philosophical question insofar as the latter aims at the whole and is purposely oriented toward achieving genuine insight into justice, love, death, the origin of the cosmos, the provenance and fate of the human soul, and so on. This tension can for Plato be mitigated but not eliminated by adopting an interpretative stance toward a traditionally transmitted understanding of sense, but the taking of this stance occurs, not within philosophy, but in the philosophizing person who interprets the only imperfectly known and knowable in the light of what is assumed and believed to be true and vice versa. This insight into the fundamental inability of philosophy to keep pace with the act of philosophizing shows, already in Plato, how our knowledge of reality refers back to an interpretational perspective, that is, the mutual relatedness of truth and sense—the assumption being that it is not philosophy but the real in its incomprehensibility and relation to the inquirer that is and remains the impetus to his philosophizing.

This, incidentally, is just as true for Aristotle as it is for Plato, disregarding for the moment the not so obvious—and hence debatable—place that the mythological tradition is accorded within the Aristotelian philosophy.[4] Aristotle's understanding of how the philosophical act is structured is, in principle, the same as Plato's: To philosophize means to pose a question that cannot be answered conclusively, "What is Being?" And for precisely this reason philosophy and philosophizing are two different activities and incapable of being brought to a final reconciliation or substituted one for the other. Philosophizing does not exhaust itself in hermeneutic philosophy; philosophical questioning always extends farther than devotees of the current state of philosophy are prepared to follow.

A similar phenomenon may also be observed with regard to Aristotle's *Metaphysics*. It is a fact, all too rarely commented upon, that the effusiveness with which Aristotle extols the happiness associated with knowing and the consequent superiority of the contemplative form of life is not reflected in his matter-of-fact discussion of the speculative results of his *Metaphysics*, *once* they have been attained. The conceptually and functionally articulated recognition of that thought which comprehends itself as the highest ontological principle—metaphysics as a philosophical theory, in other words—can itself be, not an object of, or a cause for, lasting wonder, but rather the immediate relatedness to reality in the act of *theorein*: the continuing astonishment at the sight of the real, which cannot be completely expressed in language and interpretation but which nevertheless underpins it. Thus for Aristotle as well there is a difference between what can be known and said and that to which we refer in thinking and speaking—a difference that cannot be eliminated without remainder—which is why the relation to reality established in philosophizing cannot be transcended in philosophy or replaced by its pursuit.

Thus, Pieper's understanding of philosophy is informed by the juxtaposition of that philosophy with a philosophical tradition that has not yet concealed the presuppositions of its philosophizing from itself and that, in the act of the philosophizing person, quite deliberately refers what is known to what is believed. The overriding concern of Pieper's *For the Love of Wisdom: Essays on the Nature of Philosophy* is,

---

[4] Pieper refers in this context to Werner Jaeger, who also sees the maxim *credo ut intelligam* at work subterraneously in the philosophy of Aristotle.

not philosophy, but rather the act of philosophizing. This distinction is neither trivial nor arbitrary: whoever subscribes to it must be able to offer grounds for it in the contemporary philosophical discussion. And still it is Pieper's considered opinion that philosophy has never owed its existence either predominantly or exclusively to the interest shown it.[5] He finds the primary justification for this thesis—to all appearances, almost casually introduced in his writings—in Plato: "The philosophizing person is not characterized by the fact that he is interested in philosophy as a 'subject'; he is interested in the world as a totality and in wisdom in its entirety. Such is Plato's conception of philosophy!"[6] But clearly Pieper is at the same time expressing his own opinion, just as later in *A Plea for Philosophy*, when he is examining the positions of Jaspers and Heidegger, he once again leans on Plato to defend the act of philosophizing against scientist and historicist trends in philosophy.[7]

Pieper's purpose, however, in appealing to Plato's conception of philosophy is not to withdraw behind what has subsequently been thought, as a propaedeutic to being able to think the beginning anew. He does not share Heidegger's radical—and at bottom essentially romantic—conception of a still unoccluded beginning of thought in Heraclitus and Parmenides, to whom the real could still show itself, independently of its conceptual representation in philosophy.[8] For, quite apart from the question of whether this characterization in any way applies to the Platonic and Aristotelian philosophies and their perpetuation in the form of medieval Christian theology, Heidegger's

---

[5] As is well known, Wittgenstein wanted to put an end to philosophy's preoccupation with itself by applying a therapy of linguistic usage in philosophy. "Philosophy [in Wittgenstein] . . . reveals itself in the final analysis to be a *self-terminating* activity that is intended, in a meditative fashion, to give room to "man as a whole in his relation to self and world" (R. Bubner, "Wittgenstein als meditativer Denker", in *Antike Themen und ihre moderne Verwandlung* [Frankfurt am Main, 1992], p. 215).

[6] Pieper defended this thesis for the first time in unequivocal form in his essay "On the Platonic Idea of Philosophy" (included in this volume).

[7] See section 9 of "A Plea for Philosophy".

[8] Cf. the third section, "Sein und Denken" (Thought and being) of M. Heidegger, *Einführung in die Metaphysik* (Tübingen, 1953), pp. 88ff. (this was originally a lecture delivered in the summer of 1935); see also *Von Wesen der Wahrheit* (Frankfurt am Main, 1933), and *Was ist Metaphysik?* (Frankfurt am Main, 1943). In the process of historicization that the phenomenological method undergoes as a result of Heidegger's retreat behind the untranscendable givenness of phenomena, the traditional question of truth is reinterpreted and the principle behind philosophical hermeneutics is anticipated.

retreat behind the momentous and still ongoing forgetfulness of Being characteristic of our epoch disguises the real difficulties and dangers inherent in the philosophizing act. They do not lie in the disappearance of a self-manifesting reality behind the initially conceptual—and later technical—objectifications of human reason, nor, consequently, does their resolution lie in a return to a "Greek relationship to the world", as it existed in the times before Socrates. Rather, Pieper's appeal to Plato has, as its purpose, to understand once again the act of philosophizing in terms of those conditions that ensured its possibility for *all* times but that are equally capable of thwarting its execution. The major theme of Heidegger's philosophizing—loss and restoration of the original proximity to Being—projects the act of philosophizing into an unattainable mythical past beyond concrete historical reality. For Pieper, by contrast, the purpose of the return, not to the Greeks but to Plato exclusively, is to reclaim an intuitive paradigm for philosophizing, which Plato had already described as a kind of "state of emergency" that can occur at any time and that must, for that very reason, be defended from easily anticipated dangers, arising from standpoints both internal and external to philosophy.

Whether apathetically or aggressively posed, the question, "Why do philosophy at all?"—from the beginning, an essential concomitant of a philosophizing whose benefit to society is questionable—is directed at the philosophizing subject from an external standpoint. Philosophy does not make one industrious, and because that is the case, the philosophizing person cannot in times marked by a pronounced interest in efficiency shy away from questions about its point and legitimacy or ignore the deeply—because culturally—rooted sense of estrangement awakened by an activity that is so obviously without function. The strategy of evasion that has most readily suggested itself here is reflected in the phenomenon of "philosophy's assimilation to the arts"[9]—a piece of academically sanctioned arbitrariness in the express service of philosophy's hermeneutic interest in itself, which "makes the living pursuit of philosophy seem like something irremediably passé".[10]

---

[9] These were the words used by Herbert Schnädelbach to address the Fifteenth Congress of the General Society for Philosophy in Germany. A selection of the papers presented there has been edited by him and G. Keil under the title of the conference, *Philosophie der Gegenwart —Gegenwart der Philosophie* (Hamburg, 1993). the passage cited is on p. 16.

[10] Ibid. Schnädelbach sees the problem in contemporary philosophy in the attempt to se-

This is not to lobby in favor of a radical immediacy, oblivious to all tradition, but rather to insist that the role played by hermeneutic philosophy be reconsidered, insofar as it has come to displace a living relation to reality. In any event, the question of the purpose and legitimacy of philosophizing cannot be answered by pointing to philosophy's need for philosophers—that is, academically trained specialists —to preserve its own traditions. The question has the effect—where it is not dismissed straight off—of instilling a healthy disquiet in the philosophizing person, who is reminded of the claim to knowledge entailed by his activity and that the non-philosopher ascribes to him as a matter of course. It is this same claim to knowledge that must also guide us in the interpretation of historically closed systems of philosophy, using its meaning, as interpreted, to come closer to the truth, at least to the extent that truth can be ascribed to a "one-man philosophy",[11] no matter how brilliant.

Josef Pieper's willingness to accept this challenge explains the interest the general public has shown in his philosophy, just as, conversely, it seems reasonable to assume that it was the rejection of that philosophy that paved the way for the ascendancy of the "what for?" question in the mid-1970s—a period that reflected the unmistakable signs of a subject that had belatedly acknowledged non-academic realities.[12] Given the twentieth century's experience with totalitarian dictatorships and the danger of a new totalitarianism, inspired by a moral consciousness motivated primarily by considerations of palpable

---

cure its scientific character through "historicization and philologization" (ibid., p. 15), a scientific character that—given the irrevocable transformation of philosophy into one of the humanities—must necessarily signify the historical end of philosophy. For a philosophy that is oriented purely toward the humanistic sciences, regardless of the level at which it is pursued, dispenses for the sake of a historical and hermeneutical "pseudo-objectivity" with precisely that aspect which makes it philosophy: the attempt to provide "a conceptual orientation with regard to the principles of our thought, knowledge, and action" (ibid., p. 14). That is why Schnädelbach insists, with unmistakable clarity, that "philosophy is not a humanistic science, . . . to the extent that we ignore that, we are ruining our subject" (ibid., p. 19). As Pieper writes, "Philosophy betrays itself at the very moment it begins to construe itself as an academic subject" ("On the Platonic Idea of Philosophy" in this volume).

[11] Cf. T. S. Eliot's postscript to J. Pieper, *Was heißt Philosophieren?* (Munich, 1962), pp. 116f.

[12] Several study groups are now occupied with the problem of the status of philosophy. (Cf. H. M. Baumgartner and H.-M. Sass, *Philosophie in Deutschland 1945–1975* [Meisenheim, 1980], pp. 18f.). The results from one such work group were published under the title *Wozu Philosophie?* (see n. 1) in 1978, with a bibliography that includes 692 entries!

utility, the "question in question"[13] is not simply answered "with re-course to Hegel or Dilthey",[14] as if one "could be assured of being dragged along by the teleology of cultural history".[15] For Pieper, by contrast, the same might be said of the possibilities for philosophizing that Karl Jaspers once observed with regard to the spiritual climate af-ter 1945: "Now that we are once again free to speak openly with one another, our first obligation is to make sure that we *really* speak with one another. That is by no means easy."[16] Really speaking with one another cannot be limited to simply noting what others think or have thought; it involves adopting a stance that takes the other's claim to truth seriously by relating it to one's own position and discussing it.

This raises several questions, which cannot be separated from one another, but most prominently among them are the following: Who are those others, the ones worth hearing out? And how can their claims to truth be redeemed so that they are relevant to the condi-tions of the present? Depending on how these questions are answered, the philosophical act presents itself as once again endangered, this time from within, in the form of the self-endangerment of the philosoph-ical act through philosophy. One cannot come closer to the other—one's contemporaries as well as past witnesses to a philosophical and religious tradition—without really listening to him, that is, without also allowing the truth-claim associated with the received interpreta-tion of reality as a whole to enter into one's own philosophizing.

The refusal to do so takes primarily one of two forms, which have their foundation (at least at first glance) in two mutually opposed attitudes: The one adheres to the ideal of theoretical physics; it is still concerned with the question of truth, but only insofar as it is restricted to what is methodologically controllable and verifiable. The other attitude remains faithful to the ideal of the humanistic sciences; it is in its sense of history attuned to the historicity of life forms, to the evolution of different worlds of meaning, and is thus for method-ological reasons indifferent to matters of truth and error. If the two

---

[13] H. Lübbe, "Wozu philosophie? Über einen Grund des Interesses der Wissenschaften an ihr", in *Philosophie und Wissenschaft*, ed. W. Oelmüller (Paderborn, 1988), p. 250.

[14] Ibid., p. 249.

[15] Ibid., p. 250. In closing, Lübbe writes, "Either way: Whatever seemed questionable to us then in terms of its meaning, . . . philosophy as such was not part of it" (ibid., p. 254).

[16] Quoted from: *Die Wandlung*, Deutsches Literaturarchiv, Verzeichnisse, Berichte, Infor-mationen 13, ed. M. Waldmüller (Marbach am Neckar, 1988), p. 54 [my italics—ED.].

are viewed as ideal types, the first attitude corresponds to that of analytic philosophy, the other to that of philosophical hermeneutics. Both agree despite their opposition to one another in deliberately consigning the philosophical question about the all-encompassing meaning of reality, insofar as this relates to the basic facts of human existence, to the realm of meaningless questions or to that unattainable horizon which renders all philosophical questions undecidable on principle.

The thoroughgoing critique of the sense behind philosophical questioning—now that this critique has put an end to the large-scale theoretical constructs of the idealistic and transcendental philosophies—can no longer be met with foundational and factually comprehensive answers that the philosophizing person would be in a position to give on his own. Still, the impossibility of a final, philosophically satisfactory answer—despite the reservations expressed by philosophers of language—does not argue against the sense and legitimacy of the philosophical question concerning the totality of that which is. It does not tell against this type of questioning because philosophizing that arises from an existentially motivated interest is governed less by its belief in the possibility of final answers to so-called "ultimate" questions than by the intent to get to the bottom of things—and that in a way that corresponds to the earnestness of the questioning, to the genuine wanting-to-know behind the posing of this question, and that distinguishes it from a purely theoretical problematic and the explanation of its results. For genuine questioning always brings with it a relation to self in which the questioner also experiences himself, inquiringly, as disturbed by his not-knowing, as an informed ignorance, overwhelmed by an astonishment that cannot so easily be laid to rest.

Whoever poses a question in this way will scarcely be predisposed to place his faith uncritically in reason. After all, he is interested in knowing what state of affairs in reality obtains, not in self-reassurance or in truth as a life-affirming fiction in Nietzsche's sense or in the sense of philosophical pragmatism. For the same reason, the seeker of genuine existential insight will not want to confine himself to the experiential possibilities of his own reason but will want to examine and interpret each assertion, including those of religious tradition, in terms of the truth-claim being raised.

The reason why the question of truth, when philosophically posed, presupposes a pregiven horizon of sense lies in the difference between what can be known and said and that to which we refer in thinking and speaking—a difference that cannot be eliminated without remainder—which is why the relation to reality established in philosophizing cannot be transcended in philosophy or replaced by its pursuit. Plato and with him the leading figures of the philosophical tradition from classical antiquity to the heyday of German idealism—from Kant to Hegel but also including Schelling and Kierkegaard—have drawn the consequences from this and have not allowed the philosophical question to become separated from other sources of possible knowledge and to turn fallow. The relationship between what is believed and what is known, which, in formal garb, was the principle behind medieval Scholasticism, continues to mold modern philosophy's understanding of itself.[17]

Whoever believes he can give an account of all the presuppositions of his thought in the same unconditional manner as he can of that which follows from them, that is, that he can through inference and demonstration secure for himself his starting point, will—if he is sincere—be unable to advance a single step or will have to keep himself and others in the dark about the unproved and unprovable suppositions of his thought. *Every* philosophy, even empiricism and positivism, must rely on prephilosophical assumptions.[18] In keeping with this, Pieper's manner of explicitly appealing to philosophical predecessors and to the religious tradition—in addition to offering the greatest possible clarity as to the starting points of his thought—provides the necessary conditions for assessing his philosophical findings. Absolute verifiability and provability of his results cannot be expected from the philosophizing person: this is the difference between him and a scientist. The greatest possible verifiability may be expected, however, from the means that he uses to arrive at his results. This requires, in turn, a circumspect attitude toward language, both in the avoidance of linguistic ambiguity (as a cloak for putative presuppositionlessness) and in the rejection of the artificial precision of a terminology that is

---

[17] Cf. R. Spaemann, "Christentum und Philosophie der Neuzeit", in *Aufklärung durch Tradition*, Schriften der Josef-Pieper-Stiftung, vol. 1, ed. H. Fechtrup, F. Schulze, and T. Sternberg (Münster, 1995).

[18] Cf. F. Rapp, "Über die Berechtigung metaphysischer Systeme", in Oelmüller, *Philosophie und Wissenschaft*, p. 25: "On closer examination, all the presumably simple and unequivocal observations prove to be structured, ambiguous, and theory-laden. Our experimental sciences do not rest on isolated, non-theoretical elementary experiences but on theoretically prestructured perceptions, which always stand in a more comprehensive context."

able to achieve greater precision only through a reductionist approach to facts.

The analytic insistence on the transparency and verifiability of reference and the hermeneutic emphasis on the superabundance of interpretations need not be at odds with one another; the interest in philosophizing need not be sacrificed to the interest in philosophy, any more than truth need be subordinated to sense, or sense to truth. In the event, it is no longer as difficult to maintain that such a position is not inherently contradictory for the simple reason that a demonstration has already been given—in the writings of Josef Pieper. In the wide-ranging thematic of his work may be found the actual proof of a philosophizing that does not have its eye on philosophy first but on reality and precisely therein remains faithful to the idea and promise of philosophy.

ABBREVIATION KEY TO
THE WORKS OF THOMAS AQUINAS

The works of Thomas Aquinas are cited on the basis of the Marietti edition published in Turin and Rome in the following manner: Passages from the *Summa theologiae* are designated only with numerals, for example, II, II, 123, 2 ad 4 (the second part of the second section, *quaestio* 123, *articulus* 2, answer to the fourth objection). The same applies to passages from the *Commentary on the Book of Sentences of Peter Lombard*, for example, 3, d. 31, 2, 5 (the third book, *distinctio* 31, *quaestio* 2, *articulus* 5). The other works are abbreviated as follows:

C.G.	*Summa contra gentiles*
Comp. theol.	*Compendium theologiae*
Ver.	*Quaestiones disputatae de veritate*
Pot.	*Quaestiones disputatae de potentia*
An.	*De anima*
Virt. card.	*De virtutibus cardinalibus*
Virt. com.	*De virtutibus in communi*
Car.	*De caritate*
Spir. creat.	*De spiritualibus creaturis*
Subst. separ.	*De substantiis separatis*
Un. int.	*De unitate intellectus contra Averroistas*
Quodl.	*Quaestiones quodlibetales*
Reg. princ.	*De regimine principum*
In Met.	Commentary on Aristotle's *Metaphysics*
In Phys.	Commentary on Aristotle's *Physics*
De an.	Commentary on Aristotle's *On the Soul* (*De anima*)
De cael.	Commentary on Aristotle's *On the Heavens* (*De caelo*)

331

De part. Commentary on Aristotle's *On the Parts of Animals* (*De partibus animalium*)

De div. nom. Commentary on Dionysius the Areopagite's *On the Divine Names*

De causis Commentary on the *Book of Causes* (*Liber de causis*)

In Trin. Commentary on Boethius' *On the Trinity*

In Hebd. Commentary on Boethius' *On the Axioms*

Symb. Apost. Exposition of the *Apostles' Creed*

Super Joh. Commentary on the Gospel of John

Those additional numerals and letters in parentheses, inserted for ease of reference—for example, no. 59—are based the pagination of the Marietti edition.

INDEX OF PERSONS

Abelard, 312
Adorno, Theodor W., 255
Albertus Magnus (St. Albert the
    Great), 287
Anaxagoras, 114–15
Anders, Günther, 204, 205
Antiphon, 17
Apelt, Otto, 215, 229, 257
Aristotle, 13, 14, 20–21, 44–45, 60,
    65–69, 95, 106, 110–12, 117, 119,
    122, 134–35, 141, 153–54, 159,
    172, 197, 207, 221, 224, 250, 257,
    262, 264, 287, 295–96, 299, 304–5
Arius, 61
Ast, Friedrich, 179, 224
Augustine, St., 47, 78, 93, 111, 117,
    125, 141, 164, 188, 217, 246, 252,
    261, 275, 278, 282, 284, 305
Averroes, 237

Babilas, Wolfgang, 211
Bacher, Wilhelm, 253
Bacon, Francis, 40, 107, 212
Benn, Gottfried, 226–27
Bernanos, Georges, 227
Bernhart, Josef, 216
Betti, Emilio, 211
Blanche, François A., 201–2
Bocheński, Josef Maria
Boethius, 22
Bollnow, Otto Friedrich, 224
Boveri, Margret, 137
Brecht, Bertolt, 100, 226
Brémond, Henri, 91–92
Brentano, Franz, 97
Brugger, Walter, 239
Bultmann, Rudolf, 180, 220, 293, 318

Caesar, 243
Carlyle, Thomas, 17, 25
Carnap, Rudolf, 88–89, 131, 142, 144
Cassirer, Ernst, 154
Chenu, Maurice-Dominique, 139, 202
Chesterton, Gilbert Keith, 59
Choron, Jacques, 95

Christ, 61, 157, 199, 216, 261, 277,
    279
Cicero, 243, 259
Clement of Alexandria, St., 115
Congar, Yves, 271

Dante Alighieri, 223
Deneffe, Auguste, 243, 245, 263,
    278–79
Descartes, René, 96, 195, 236–37,
    301
Dewey, John, 96, 296
Dilthey, Wilhelm, 63, 90, 98, 146,
    211, 225, 326
Diogenes Laertius, 115
Dionysius Areopagite, 80
Dudinzew, Wladimir, 95

Einstein, Albert, 140, 166
Eisler, Rudolf, 239
Eliot, Thomas Stearns, 134, 150, 311
Empedocles, 69
Engels, Friedrich, 88, 126–27, 271
Ersch-Gruber, 58, 236

Fechner, Gustav Theodor, 128
Fetscher, Iring, 126
Fichte, Johann Gottlieb, 79, 86
Ficino, Marsilio, 215
Friedländer, Paul, 160, 281

Gadamer, Hans-Georg, 254–55, 267
Galilei, Galileo, 212, 236
Garaudy, Roger, 180
Garrigou-Lagrange, Reginald, 75, 181,
    307
Gehlen, Arnold, 46–47
Gerschenson, Michael O., 293
Gilson, Étienne, 284
Ginsberg, Ernst, 225–26
Gloege, Gerhard, 263, 282
Goethe, Johann Wolfgang von, 16, 25,
    57, 66, 100–1, 109, 136, 194, 196,
    208, 217, 220, 226, 254, 275, 291

Görres, Albert, 213
Gredt, Joseph, 199
Gregory the Great, Pope St., 41, 117
Guardini, Romano, 125, 212

Haecker, Theodor, 278
Hager, Kurt, 100–1
Hahn, Hans, 88
Hegel, Georg Wilhelm Friedrich, 59,
 65–66, 86, 102, 140, 166–67, 183,
 257, 279, 290, 318
Heidegger, Martin, 21, 32, 74, 95,
 151–53, 153, 185–96, 200, 205,
 225, 290
Heraclitus, 14, 323
Herder, Johann Gottfried, 194
Jerome, St., 275
Hilary of Poitiers, 188
Hoffmeister, Johannes, 198, 211, 239
Hölderlin, Friedrich, 77, 208
Homer, 64, 69, 136, 158, 275, 296,
 303
Husserl, Edmund, 97
Huxley, Aldous, 182

Ivanov, Viacheslav, 253, 282, 293

Jaeger, Werner, 154, 220, 299
Jansen, Bernhard, 14
Jaspers, Karl, 89, 129–30, 152–53,
 155, 174, 230, 248, 254, 255, 262,
 281, 286, 292, 318
Duns Scotus, 189, 194
Jung, Carl Gustav, 283
Justin Martyr, St., 261, 282

Kafka, Franz, 227
Kant, Immanuel, 13, 14, 16–18, 122,
 145, 154, 262, 275, 301
Kerényi, Karl, 24
Kittel, Gerhard, 240
Köhler, Wolfgang, 251
Kolakowski, Lezcek, 247, 293
Krüger, Gerhard, 76, 241, 248, 293,
 294

Lasker-Schuler, Else, 225–27
Lawrence, Nathaniel, 133
Leibniz, Gottfried W., 32, 95
Lenin, Vladimir Ilyich, 126, 271

Lewis, Clive Staples, 223, 253
Litt, Theodor, 288
Loeper, Gustav von, 217
Lonergan, Bernard J. F., 209
Luther, Martin, 109
Luyten, Norbert, 147

Mao TseTung, 271
Marcel, Gabriel, 174, 286
Marias, Julian, 212
Marquard, Odo, 289
Marx, Karl, 40, 110, 271
Meister Eckhart, 179
Moltmann, Jurgen, 260, 265
Monzel, Nikolaus, 260, 262, 270, 276
Morgenstern, Christian, 218
Müller, Gustav Emil, 16, 96
Müller, Max, 175

Neurath, Otto, 88
Newman, John Henry, 19, 37, 38,
 113, 261, 278, 281, 316
Nietzsche, Friedrich, 112, 140, 291
Nicholas of Cusa, 165–66
Nink, Caspar, 136
Novalis, 208

Oppenheimer, Robert J., 137
Origen, 282
Osann, Christiane, 227
Otto, Walter Friedrich, 73

Parmenides, 29, 135, 323
Pascal, Blaise, 52, 61, 170, 236–39,
 256, 277, 287, 288
Paschasius Radbertus, 199
Pauly-Wissowa, 240
Paul, St., 243, 246, 265
Pieper, Josef, 48, 95, 101, 104, 108,
 110–11, 125, 134, 149–50, 193,
 205, 215, 222, 227, 229 31, 244,
 248, 250, 259, 276, 280, 287, 289,
 311
Plato (Socrates), 13, 23, 54–56, 62,
 64, 66, 68, 70, 72, 76, 93–94,
 122–23, 128, 154, 157–64, 166–
 72, 195, 215, 220, 227, 229, 231,
 237, 249, 256, 262, 264–65, 276,
 280, 284–85, 289, 298, 303
Poseidonius, 258

Prantl, Carl, 214
Prümm, Karl, 280
Pythagoras, 64, 66, 123, 159, 218,
    296, 300, 303

Ratzinger, Joseph, (Pope Benedict
    XVI), 276, 286
Reichenbach, Hans, 88, 140, 170
Reinhardt, Karl, 258
Richter, Liselotte, 177
Ricoeur, Paul, 212
Riemer, Friedrich W., 100, 226
Riessler-Storr, 217
Rilke, Rainer Maria, 227
Rimaud, Jean, 271
Ritter, Joachim, 248, 253, 257, 287
Ross, William David, 222, 287
Rousselot, Pierre, 116
Rumphorst, Heinrich, 257
Russell, Bertrand, 132, 295
Rüstow, Alexander, 251, 270–71

Sartre, Jean Paul, 74, 121, 125, 127,
    150, 163, 173–84, 273, 290, 292,
    301
Scheeben, Matthias, 75, 152, 263, 281
Schelling, Friedrich Wilhelm, 86, 95
Scherer, Georg, 181
Schieder, Theodor, 223, 248
Schleiermacher, Friedrich, 211, 214,
    225
Schlick, Moritz, 131
Schneider, Reinhold, 226
Scholz, Heinrich, 126, 168, 214, 264
Seel, Otto, 108
Sohm, Rudolf, 240
Solon, 64, 158, 296, 303

Solowjew, Wladimir, 253
Stalin, Josef, 126
Stein, Edith, 199
Szilasi, Walter, 117

Teilhard de Chardin, Pierre, 116–17,
    181
Tertullian, 282
Thales of Milet, 35, 69, 94, 171
Thomas Aquinas, St., 15, 16, 27, 30,
    33, 37, 46, 50–51, 60, 63–65, 76,
    111, 114, 122, 134, 138, 158, 175,
    179, 181, 191, 194–208, 211, 214,
    216, 224, 265, 275, 290, 306
Thompson, Samuel, 203
Torricelli, Emilio, 237–38
Trübner, Kurt, 22

Von Uexküll, Jakob, 43–44, 46

Vulliaud, Paul, 247

Weber, Max, 20
Weiß, Konrad, 32
Whitehead, Alfred North, 84–85,
    121, 132–33, 139, 145, 312
Wild, John, 101
Windelband, Wilhelm, 16, 59, 78
Wittgenstein, Ludwig, 95, 134–35,
    139
Wittmann, Michael, 221
Wolstenholme, Gordon E., 182
Wulf, Maurice de, 78

Ziegler, Leopold, 247, 279
Zinzendorf, Nikolaus Ludwig, 20–21